Monetary economics

Modern economics
Series editor: David W. Pearce

Monetary economics

Geoffrey E J Dennis

Longman
London and New York

Longman Group Limited
Longman House
Burnt Mill, Harlow, Essex, UK

Published in the United States of America
by Longman Inc., New York

First published **1981**

British Library Cataloguing in Publication Data
Dennis, Geoffrey Edwin Janes
    Monetary economics. – (Modern economics).
    1. Money
    I. Title   II. Series
    332.4   HG221   80–40095
ISBN 0–582–45573–1

Printed in Great Britain by William Clowes (Beccles) Ltd.
Beccles and London.

Contents

Preface

Monetary theory and policy is a rapidly developing subject area of economics. The conventional wisdom concerning the central issues of monetary economics has moved through a variety of basic theoretical stances in the post-war period. The importance of the money supply and monetary targets to the application of policy in the 1970s, apart from any theoretical refinements that may occur, should ensure that many more developments will occur in the near future, some no doubt before this volume actually appears on the bookshelves. Therefore, any textbook on monetary economics is essentially marking time and this volume is no exception.

The book provides a simple introduction to the essential issues of monetary economics as they stand at the end of the 1970s. The objective is for the book to be used by second year undergraduates who are studying a general macroeconomics course or those doing a specialist course on monetary economics in the second or third years of a degree course. In addition, any student embarking on postgraduate study that includes monetary economics should consider this book as being introductory reading.

The theoretical content of the book is presented in a familiar form, although in Chapters 1 and 9 in particular, considerable reference is made to current practice on the use of money supply definitions in the UK and to recent empirical UK evidence on inflation. The emphasis of any empirical evidence and institutional detail is on the UK economy for two reasons. Firstly, many excellent textbooks written in the environment of the US monetary system already exist while the second reason is simply one of space. It is intended that the major source of product differentiation in this volume will therefore be the combination of monetary theory and practice, including empirical evidence, contained in Chapters 2, 6, 7, 8 and 10. These chapters include an analysis of the targets and indicators of monetary policy, the determination of the money supply, the influence of external money flows on the domestic monetary situation, a survey of empirical evidence on money and an analysis of post-war monetary policy, all in the context of the British economy.

I would like to express my gratitude to Tim Congdon, Peter Dawkins, Nigel Duck, Chris Gill, John Presley, Graham Smith, Brian Tew, Tony Westaway, Tom Weyman-Jones and Geoff Wood who made valuable comments which have improved this book or sharpened up my understanding of the subject through discussion. I would like to thank Max Hall, for access to some material on monetary policy since 1971, and in particular David Llewellyn who has improved my knowledge and grasp of this subject area by his useful insights into the operation of monetary policy in the UK and by encouraging justifiable scepticism in some of the conventional theory of the subject. My gratitude goes to David Pearce, the editor of the series, for his initial encouragement and for his advice during the completion of the manuscript. In addition, I am grateful to an anonymous reviewer who pointed out a number of inaccuracies and confusions. The responsibility for any remaining errors and omissions lies solely with the author. Particular thanks go to Gloria Brentnall for her speedy and efficient preparation of the final typescript and also to Linda Brewin, Brenda Moore, and Su Spencer for their typing services.

Geoffrey E. J. Dennis

University of Loughborough

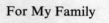

For My Family

Chapter 1

An introduction to money

1 Introduction

The basic starting point for a study of monetary economics should always be an analysis of the concept of money itself. Money is, by definition, the basis of the branch of macroeconomics called monetary economics that is the subject of this volume. Perhaps surprisingly, considerable debate has ensued over the functions of money, the advantages of a monetary economy over one where money is absent – a barter economy – and the appropriate definition of money in theory and practice. These issues, although not central to the study of monetary economics, are a vital element in the subject and are therefore treated in this initial chapter. A viable study of the role of money in an economy is meaningless unless the arguments surrounding the concept itself are set out in detail and appreciated.

2 The functions of money

In general money is often defined in one of two ways. Firstly, it is anything acceptable in payment for goods and services or in settlement of a debt. Secondly, money is regularly defined in terms of the functions that it performs i.e., money is a commodity that functions as a medium of exchange, store of value, etc. Clearly neither of these definitions is very satisfactory. In the first case how is acceptability to be defined? For example, it is true that certain forms of money (even a cheque drawn on a current account at a clearing bank) may not be acceptable to all people in all circumstances. There may therefore be a lack of uniformity in this acceptability criterion. The second definition suffers from the problem that it may not be easy to identify which assets actually perform these functions. In this case, in fact, this is not a true definition but simply a listing of the functions that this elusive concept performs. More rigorous methods of defining money will be introduced later in this chapter.

There are three major functions of money which will be analysed in turn. Firstly, money acts as a medium of exchange. It is an intermediary that can be used in exchange for goods and services in an exchange transaction. A barter economy requires the need for a person wishing to sell, for example, 1 sheep for 100 bushels of corn to find someone who both wants to buy the sheep and sell the corn at the same time and at the same exchange rate. This 'double coincidence of wants' is avoided in a monetary economy. The seller would exchange his sheep for money in a market place and then move around with his money until he found the corn required. This role of money as a medium of exchange divides the double coincidence of wants into two separate transactions (which will be far less costly than the one barter exchange). To ensure that money performs this function it is essential that the medium of exchange is widely acceptable and has the confidence of all traders. If this does not exist, money will not be used and barter will be restored.

Shackle (1971) has noted that the unified analysis of money as a means of payment and a medium of exchange confuses a basic issue. A transaction may be facilitated by the presentation of a medium of exchange but not accompanied by an actual transfer of wealth (e.g., through the use of a credit card, or the signing of a hire-purchase agreement). Credit is acting as a medium of exchange but not a means of payment. Payment will actually occur later when the credit balance is settled or the hire-purchase agreement expires. Strictly, therefore, in a sophisticated modern economy the two functions of a medium of exchange and a means of payment should be distinguished.

A second major function of money is as a store of value. This function is an essential counterpart to the role of money as a medium of exchange. The division of one barter transaction into individual acts of sale and purchase implies that it should be possible to complete the two transactions at different points in time. For this to be possible, the money held in the interim period between sale and purchase should store well. This involves convenient storage at no cost to the holder so in general ruling out perishable goods and very bulky commodities. Clearly many assets act as a store of wealth in a modern economy (e.g., houses, cars, government bonds). The distinguishing feature of money as a store of value, however, is its liquidity. In fact, it is the ultimate liquid asset (where the degree of liquidity is defined as the ease of switching without cost from an asset into money). Money can be used immediately for a transaction when the need arises.

Clearly without its store of value attribute one of the benefits of money acting as a medium of exchange (that of separating in time the sale and purchase transactions) would be lost. The two functions combined can be termed the action of *money concrete* i.e., money acting as a tangible asset that facilitates exchange.

Alternatively, *money abstract* involves the action of money in a less tangible sense and represents the final major function of money. This is money as a 'unit of account' or 'numeraire'. It acts as a standard or common denominator against which the value of all goods is measured. We will return to the exchange of sheep for corn. In a monetary economy, the exchange value of 1 sheep may be set by trade at 200 units of money. If the value of 1 bushel of corn was agreed to be 2 units of money, the function of money as a unit of account enables the exchange rate of 1 sheep for 100 bushels of corn to be finalised.

Money acting in this way is inbred into individuals in a society. For example in the UK, we grow up to value items in terms of the pound sterling and may face preliminary difficulties when travelling abroad where a different unit of account is operating. The value of this function was clearly demonstrated by the initial problems experienced in the UK when decimalisation occurred in February 1971. The pound ceased to have 240 equal units (pennies) and began to have 100 equal units (new pennies) instead. All that was happening was the alteration of the unit of account so that 1 new penny equalled 2.4 old pennies, with the value of each commodity adjusted accordingly. As a unit of account, therefore, money transmits information about the relative values of different commodities and by doing so facilitates the operation of the price mechanism. A unit of account need not, however, be a means of payment or medium of exchange. At present this applies to the various accounting devices used in the European Economic Community (EEC), e.g., the European unit of account (EUA).

A fourth function of money sometimes defined is as a standard for deferred payments. This involves the use of money to bridge the gap between the time of an exchange being struck and when payment is made. Money provides a standard in which future payments can be measured. However, it is sensible and more convenient to assimilate this function into the three major ones described earlier in this section.

3 The monetary economy

The major advantage of introducing money into a barter economy is the reduction of transactions costs that will follow from the replacement of the need for the double coincidence of wants by two individual transactions. This gain has been very lucidly rationalised in the well-known model of Clower (1969). The costs of barter are in two forms. Transactions costs are the costs of actually undertaking and completing trade. The transactions cost per unit exchanged will decline as the transactions period (the length of time between each expedition to trade) increases. This assumes that a few large transactions are less costly than numerous small ones. The second type of costs are waiting costs. These are partly subjective in form as the purchase of a desired commodity may be postponed. However, they will also have the objective form of storage costs (particularly of perishable goods) and the interest foregone on an asset the purchase of which is postponed. These waiting costs will rise as the transactions period increases.

The total costs of barter can therefore be represented as a U-shaped function (C_0) in Fig. 1 being the sum of the transactions and waiting costs. According to this model, the individual can either not trade at all or engage in one individual double coincidence transaction. What is omitted is the possibility that an individual may give up time and therefore output to accumulate information on trading possibilities and so maximise welfare in the long run. He may also, which is not made explicit in this model, engage in a series of transactions to gain the commodity he requires in the right quantities. Having accumulated information, it may be to the transactor's advantage to exchange sheep for

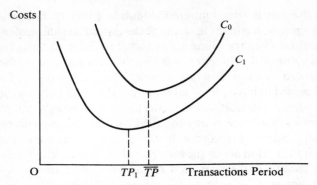

Fig. 1. Exchange costs in barter and in a monetary economy.

fish, fish for chickens, and then chickens for the corn he actually requires. This is called a transactions chain (Brunner and Meltzer, 1971).

Such a transactions chain may reduce costs and therefore increase welfare, but significant cost reductions will only occur when more convenient trading relationships are instituted. These developments may involve a 'fairground' (where transactors are brought together), a situation where a small number of dominant commodities act as exchange media and eventually a monetary economy where one commodity is defined and accepted as a medium of exchange. The major gains from introducing money can be summarised as a decline in transactions costs (but not waiting costs) which lead to a downward and leftward shift of the cost curve (C_1) in Fig. 1. The optimal length of the transactions period will fall from $\overline{TP}$ to TP_1 giving the result that, with money, an individual will trade more regularly than in the more costly barter situation.

The decline in transactions costs as a society develops from a barter system to a monetary economy, takes many forms. In a world of uncertainty (where information is not perfect), the use of money permits a reduction in this uncertainty by reducing the costs of obtaining full information. This is most easily seen in the action of money as a unit of account. If there were 50 commodities being produced and traded in an economy each would have an exchange value against the other. This situation can be demonstrated in a 50×50 matrix as in Fig. 2. There are n^2 exchange rates in the matrix (where in this case $n = 50$) although n diagonal elements are unity by definition (the exchange rate of 1 sheep against another is 1, assuming they are of the same standard). Therefore, there are $n(n-1)$ other exchange rates in the matrix. However, half of these provide no new information as the exchange rate of 1 sheep for 1 cow is the same as the inverse of the exchange rate of 1 cow for 1 sheep, that is:

$$E_{ij} = \frac{1}{E_{ji}} \tag{1}$$

where E is the exchange ratio between goods i and j. Therefore, there are $\frac{1}{2}n\,(n-1)$ independent exchange rates in the matrix. For $n = 50$ goods, this

Library Services
University of Birmingham

Title: Current issues in monetary economics
ID: 551862684X
Due: 09/04/2008 23:59

Title: Monetary economics
ID: 5512328219
Due: 09/04/2008 23:59

Total items: 2
03/12/2008 18:30

You can renew your books using 'My Account' on
the library catalogue or by phoning Library
Services Direct on 0121 414 5828.

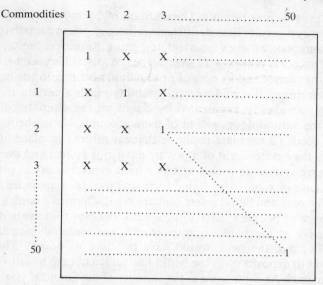

Fig. 2. An exchange rate matrix.

totals, 1,225 exchange rates. The utilisation of one of the commodities as money reduces the information required for trade to only $n-1$ or 49 separate exchange rates. The 50×50 matrix in Fig. 2 becomes a 50×1 vector, where the first good is money. Therefore, money reduces the costs of acquiring full information on trading possibilities and thereby reduces uncertainty. The increased access to information also permits the quicker location of transactors with the necessary goods to sell for money or willing to accept money for goods possessed by the individual. Finally, knowledge of the properties of the goods being sold can be obtained more readily as the general store of information is enhanced (Brunner and Meltzer, 1971).

A second facet of gains from the use of money follows from this reduced uncertainty. The smaller effort needed to complete a given volume of transactions increases the time available for either production or leisure. If production and therefore employment and living standards are increased this is a direct gain from the use of money. On the other hand, if the increased time is devoted to leisure, the welfare of the individual will increase. This is an advantage accruing from money as a medium of exchange.

Other gains have been less prominently argued but are also important. The use of money enables the separation in time of the acts of sale and purchase, while if the money type is sufficiently divisible certain previously impossible transactions may now take place. For example if a trader will not accept 1 sheep for the 1 cow he has for sale, he cannot divide the cow to facilitate the exchange. The use of money will, however, enable this deal to be struck. Finally, money holding may yield non-pecuniary returns which should be considered.

It is important to note that further developments of a monetary economy can provide new benefits. The addition of *fiat* money (where the face value of the money is greater than its intrinsic value, e.g., token coins, bank notes) to a stock of commodity money can yield new gains. Resources are saved in the production of such fiat money with seignorage (i.e., the difference between the face value of the money and its cost of production) accruing to the issuing authorities. When financial confidence and stability reach a certain level, commodity money can also be augmented by claims on the ultimate commodity itself. This is the natural development of bank accounts where cheques drawn against these accounts circulate in the settlement of debt in place of money. This facilitates the development of a private payments system and eventually a fractional reserve system. In such a system a bank retains a certain proportion of deposits in cash or some other liquid form and uses the remainder for long-term assets. The cash and liquid assets held are usually termed a bank's *reserves*. From experience of people's behaviour, a bank believes that every depositor would not arrive at the bank simultaneously, and demand encashment of deposits. If they did, the bank would have to 'close its doors'. The chosen ratio of reserves to deposits gives the banks just sufficient cash to satisfy normal daily cash demands. As confidence in the stability of the financial system grows this prudential reserve ratio will decline. The development of a fractional reserve system enables a given stock of cash to pyramid into a much larger stock of bank deposits. These institutional developments increase the benefits of a monetary economy where more sophisticated money types are introduced.

The gains to society from introducing money are therefore immense. However, a monetary economy does also have certain disadvantages which in rare circumstances are sufficiently powerful to cause money to be abandoned. These costs mainly revolve around Say's Law (1803). This law states that supply creates its own demand. In a barter economy, this is clearly true as the act of supply (sale) corresponds to the act of demand (purchase). Temporary disequilibria may occur with the producer being unable to sell all his output or alternatively unable to satisfy the whole market. In these cases an output adjustment would occur with long-run equilibrium, ensuring the satisfaction of Say's Law.

However, when money is introduced into a barter economy, the need for a 'double coincidence of wants' is removed by dividing the exchange into two separate transactions. The commodity to be sold is exchanged for money which is then exchanged for the good demanded by the individual. However, a leakage of money from the system will occur if the supplier does not use the money received to purchase other goods. Supply and demand are not equal. When this occurs equilibrium will only be attained where such leakages are matched by other injections of money (e.g., investment). In an open economy with a government sector, the leakages and withdrawals concerned are greater in number than set out in the previous sentence and the equilibrium condition becomes:

$$S + T + M = I + G + X \qquad\qquad [2]$$
$$\text{\textit{withdrawals}} \qquad \text{\textit{injections}}$$

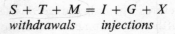

where S, T, M, I, G, X represent savings, taxation, imports, investment, government spending and exports respectively.

The introduction of money threatens the attainment of full employment equilibrium. If withdrawals exceed injections (i.e., supply exceeds demand) there will be disequilibrium, with prices and perhaps output falling as a result. On the other hand, if demand exceeds supply, there is an excess demand situation and inflation will ensue. In addition, it is strictly correct to supplement Say's Law with Walras' Law (1954) in a monetary economy. This states that if money (the nth good) is introduced into a $n-1$ good economy and if all $n-1$ goods markets are in equilibrium, equilibrium in the money market is ensured. The *relative* prices of the $n-1$ goods are therefore determined through the operation of Say's Law with the role of money being limited to the determination of the *absolute* price level (i.e., the price of the nth good, money). In disequilibrium, an excess demand for goods, for example, will be matched by an excess supply of money which drives up absolute prices until equilibrium is reached. The theoretical doubts over the interpretations of both Say's and Walras' Law and the role of money led to a vigorous debate which will be summarised in Chapter 3. However, even with the complications introduced by money, price flexibility should ensure the satisfaction of Say's Law in the $n-1$ goods markets and therefore ensure monetary equilibrium also.

While the introduction of money may therefore cause the economy to move away from full employment equilibrium, these costs will be small in nearly all circumstances relative to the benefits of having money. For while the marginal cost of holding money rises with inflation, as a given quantity of money has less and less real purchasing power, the marginal productivity of money holding rises too. This is accounted for by the fluctuations in economic activity that accompany inflation, which will increase uncertainty and the costs of acquiring information. Therefore, the value in terms of reducing this uncertainty from money holding rises. Only if inflation reaches very high or hyper-inflationary levels will the costs of money holding begin to outweigh the gains from holding the medium of exchange. This occurred in 1923, for example, in Germany when prices rose so rapidly that money ceased to function properly. As an alternative, barter was restored or different transaction chains utilised. However, it does not follow that the collapse of money will cause the restoration of pure barter. A more likely response is for longer and more complex transactions chains to be set up. Eventually in the event of the collapse of a particular monetary commodity, a new money will be established, as in Germany in that particular period. The net benefits from establishing a new currency exceed those from stabilising the worthless, existing currency, even if the latter were possible.

One further cost of a monetary economy is its effects on income distribution. The absolute price changes that can only occur in a monetary economy may affect commodities in different degrees and be unexpected. Such unanticipated changes will alter the relative position of creditors and debtors with effects on investment and growth in an economy. A cogent example of such effects has been the influence of the high inflation in the UK and other Western economies in the mid-1970s on the real value of savings and of the purchasing power of those on relatively fixed money incomes (e.g., pensioners). Such arbitrary effects on real purchasing power and the distribution of income, will alter consumption patterns and represent a considerable cost to the whole economy.

A sober comparison of the costs and benefits of a monetary economy over a barter economy may be drawn by analogy. Only in the severest hyper-inflations is money actually abandoned and some form of barter re-established. In the majority of situations the benefits of money comfortably outweigh the costs particularly when one notes that in some severe Latin American inflationary episodes in recent years (e.g., in Argentina and Brazil), money was not abandoned. The only other situation where money may be abandoned is in the theoretical world of total certainty. A world of perfect information could function equally well on barter or money terms but, given the existence of uncertainty, a monetary economy is preferable to a barter economy under nearly all circumstances.

4 The monetary commodity — theoretical

Once the rationale for introducing money into an economy is established it is necessary to investigate the different forms of money that have been used and outline the arguments concerning the constituents of the money supply in a modern economy. In earliest societies, commodities (e.g., cowrie shells, cows) were used as money as they were acceptable media of exchange.[†] However, they also had to exhibit several other characteristics. These included durability, to ensure money acted as a store of value, divisibility, to maximise the commodity's role as a medium of exchange, and portability. In addition, homogeneity required that each unit of money had to be of equivalent standard, while the money commodity had to be scarce in order to retain its value. These characteristics were most obviously satisfied by precious metals which eventually became the primary type of money.

As confidence in money grew, the need to have a monetary commodity with an intrinsic value equal to its face value declined. Fiat money, initially token coins and then bank notes, was introduced. To ensure the acceptability of this fiat money, convertibility into the ultimate precious metal of the system (usually by this time, gold) was maintained. Eventually, even this link with gold was broken, while bank accounts and a variety of credit lines were also developed. Such innovations were a sign of considerable financial stability.

In the UK today, certain assets are clearly part of the money supply. However, much theoretical debate has occurred in recent years over where to draw the line between money and near-money assets. In the remainder of this section, the 'moneyness' of asset types will be discussed in the light of traditional arguments and some of the theoretical definitions postulated in recent years. A

[†] In one of the most famous examples of the collapse of normal monetary arrangements, cigarettes circulated as a medium of exchange in prisoner of war camps in Germany during the Second World War (Radford, 1945).

full survey of these definitions cannot be included in the space available and the reader is referred to other sources for this (e.g., Pierce and Shaw, 1974). In this issue of the definition of money, four major schools of thought can be distinguished (Johnson, 1962). Firstly, some, preferring to limit money to its medium of exchange role, would define money as currency and current accounts (demand deposits). Secondly, Milton Friedman has argued that money is 'a temporary abode of purchasing power' which implies currency plus all bank deposits including deposit accounts (time deposits) (e.g., Friedman, 1964). Thirdly, the growth of non-bank financial intermediaries (n.b.f.i's) has been considerable in recent years and the addition of deposits at such n.b.f.i's to currency and bank deposits could be justified (e.g., Gurley and Shaw, 1956). Finally, a very broad concept is that of liquidity introduced by the Radcliffe Committee. In their view:

> A decision to spend depends not simply on whether a would-be spender has cash or 'money in the bank' although that maximum liquidity is obviously the most favourable springboard. There is the alternative of raising funds by selling an asset or by borrowing; and the prospect of a cash flow from future sales of a product both encourages commitment beyond immediately available cash and makes borrowing easier. (Radcliffe Committee, 1959, p.132).

Under this definition, the money supply should include various credit lines as well as all the components of the third definition. As liquidity is wider in scope, by definition, than is the money supply it could be argued that the latter should be defined narrowly but being irrelevant anyway (as it ignores credit lines) liquidity should be used as a basis for policy.

Clearly a wide choice exists and the most satisfactory way to portray the issues may be to look at each suggested element of the money supply in turn and suggest reasons for its inclusion in the money supply. To assist in this, Table 1 tabulates the results of this brief survey.

Currency is obviously part of the money supply. Notes and coins are legal tender although very large quantities of coin can be refused as payment for a large debt. Secondly, current accounts at banks are usually considered to be money, due to the ability to transfer money from such accounts by cheque in the settlement of debt. This is not universal, however, as some people do not have bank accounts and so would not accept a cheque drawn on a bank account in debt settlement. Money can therefore be restricted to currency and demand deposits at banks, on the basis that these alone can be transferred in the settlement of a debt, while in virtually all cases money in this form is acceptable to all transactors. In a controversial volume, Pesek and Saving (1967) agreed with this division between money and near-money but for a very different reason. They argued that currency and demand deposits represent net wealth to the community and so no interest inducement is needed for them to be demanded. It is the interest-payingness of an asset that disqualifies it as money, hence excluding deposit accounts which pay an interest return. However, this analysis has been criticised (Friedman and Schwartz, 1969; Johnson, 1969) on many grounds. Firstly, Pesek and Saving's analysis of a joint product (part money and

Table 1 Theoretical definitions of money

	Currency	Demand deposits	Time deposits	Non-clearing bank deposits	N.b.f.i. deposits	Credit lines
Medium of exchange	+	+				
Pesek and Saving	+	+				
Morgan	+	+	+			
Temporary abode of purchasing power	+	+	+	+		
Newlyn	+	+	+	+		
Yeager	+	+	+	+		
Gurley and Shaw	+	+	+	+	+	
Radcliffe Committee	+	+	+	+	+	+

part non-money) is faulty. An asset is a joint product when the interest rate on it is below the market rate so that if the market rate is 5 per cent and the actual rate $2\frac{1}{2}$ per cent, the asset is only half money. But, how is the market rate determined? In addition, a particular asset may receive the market rate of interest and yet not lose its moneyness (e.g., a 'sight' deposit in the UK – see Section 5 below). Secondly, in equilibrium if a money asset earned the market rate of interest, the non-pecuniary returns from holding it must (according to Pesek and Saving) fall to zero. But this is only true at the margin, and any intra marginal units will provide positive non-pecuniary services. Therefore, to assume that the non-pecuniary services of *all* units of money held is zero represents a basic confusion between marginal and average concepts. Thirdly, the underlying premise of money as net wealth forces Pesek and Saving to concentrate on the wealth transmission mechanism of money to the exclusion of the more favoured substitution effects (Laidler, 1969).

The issue of whether deposit accounts should be included in the money supply is nevertheless more controversial than the inclusion of demand deposits. Exclusion of them is argued on the grounds that they cannot be drawn on by cheque, while seven days' notice is nominally required before the funds can be utilised. However, in practice, the seven day rule is often waived by banks (with an interest loss to the depositor) while a cheque drawn on a current account may be settled with funds from a deposit account if insufficient funds are held in the former.

Morgan (1969) argues that currency and all clearing bank deposits should be included in the money supply. He defines money as any asset an excess supply/demand for which will manifest itself as an excess demand/supply for other assets, i.e., the effects of the disequilibrium are generalised. In contrast, disequilibrium in the market for a non-money asset will lead to a change in the asset's price or quantity. To ensure the generalised effect of a disequilibrium a particular asset's price must be fixed and its supply exogenous. These conditions simply mean that the price and quantity of money itself *cannot* alter endogenously and so the disequilibrium must be manifest in other markets.

Strict application of this criterion leads the money supply to consist of currency alone (as the exogeneity of supply condition is not satisfied by bank deposits). To extricate the theory from this unacceptable conclusion, an extra condition is added which is the existence of a mechanism (via the central bank) to offset the effects of endogenous action by depositors on the volume of bank deposits. This only applies, however, to banks that hold their reserves with the central bank; in the UK, clearing banks alone are required to hold reserves in this form, with non-clearing banks holding reserves at the clearing banks so forming a second tier of banking. Therefore, Morgan's definition of money would exclude all non-clearing bank deposits. There are, however, two major problems with this analysis. The Bank of England may not actually choose to offset the endogenous effects on reserve levels, and as will be made clear in Chapter 7, the Bank of England may not have the power to fix the level of bank deposits exogenously even though part of clearing bank reserves is held at the Bank of England.

Other contributions to the theoretical debate have included time deposits at clearing banks but, in addition, all deposits at non-clearing banks. Newlyn (1964) and Newlyn and Bootle (1978) define money as any asset satisfying their neutrality criterion which means:

> a payment that will not involve any change in the asset/liability complex of the public other than that between the payer and payee (Newlyn, 1964, p.336).

The transfer of currency to settle a debt will have no further repercussions on the economy, while the same is true of all bank deposits as the total level of deposits will be unchanged by the settlement of a debt, although the distribution of deposits between payer and payee will be altered. The only qualifications are in situations where banks maintain different reserve ratios for time and demand deposits or where different banks have different overall reserve ratios. In these cases a transfer of money may alter the distribution between the two types of deposit or between the different types of bank and therefore affect their credit creating ability (Chapter 7). By this criterion, money in the UK, includes currency and all bank deposits (including those at non-clearing banks now that they operate on the same reserve ratio as do clearing banks). The transfer of a non-money asset, in debt settlement, however, may affect the supply and demand for loans, e.g., a building society may have to liquidate some assets (e.g., government debt) if withdrawals of cash are made to settle debts. Therefore, such accounts at non-bank financial intermediaries are not money.

The weakness of this criterion is the assumption that the transfer of money has no secondary effects. If the payee on receipt of money is in a disequilibrium position, he will spend part or all of the newly acquired funds on consumption goods or other non-money assets. In such a case, neutrality will not hold and as this is a very likely occurrence, the concept is of limited operational relevance.

Yeager (1968) introduces another argument for limiting the money supply to currency and bank deposits. He contrasts the procedure of debt settlement using money and non-money assets. If money is used, one payment will suffice to settle a debt with an individual's cash balances or bank deposits being drawn down. In the case of a non-money transfer, two transactions are needed with the asset being encashed and then cash transferred. Therefore, disequilibrium in the money market will cause a general movement in the prices of all goods and services (as the accounting price of money itself is unity and cannot be altered). However, disequilibrium in other asset markets can lead to a change in the price or quantity of the asset concerned or to a non-market clearing solution. These safety valves for a non-market asset are sufficient to limit the effect of the disequilibrium to the asset market itself. Oddly, this criterion for defining money does not enable a clear-cut analysis of which assets actually satisfy the criterion. However, it can be argued that the general effects postulated by Yeager will flow from an excess supply/demand for currency and bank deposits alone.

The very broad definitions of money mentioned at the beginning of this section could also be considered. Following the pioneering work of Gurley and Shaw, the role of n.b.f.i's has been closely scrutinised in recent years (Ch. 7). In addition, a rapid growth of deposits held at n.b.f.i's has increased their practical importance as sources of credit. Their role is now considerable in the whole monetary sector in the UK economy. However, the exclusion of n.b.f.i. deposits from the definition of money can be justified as such deposits cannot be transferred by cheque and so do not circulate as a medium of exchange. In addition, there are a wide variety of n.b.f.i's which offer deposit terms of varying liquidity so that a new problem of defining where the division comes between money and near-money assets would be introduced. The final concept (liquidity) which broadens the money supply definition to include various credit lines also reflects the growing financial sophistication of the UK economy. However, liquidity suffers from the decisive drawback that it is unquantifiable and so is of little practical use to the monetary authorities in the UK.

In general, therefore, disagreement on the appropriate definition of the money supply has been limited to the breadth of bank deposits to be included, with opinions ranging from just clearing bank current accounts to all bank accounts (plus currency in all cases), although in the late 1970s increasing calls have been made to include n.b.f.i. deposits in a broad definition of the money supply (e.g., Kern, 1975; Pepper and Thomas, 1978). However, two other pragmatic means exist to define the money supply. Firstly, it is frequently argued that the definition utilised should depend on the particular problem being studied. For example, if a demand for money study or an analysis of the effect of the money supply on economic activity is being undertaken, the view could be taken that the appropriate definition of the money supply is the one that provides the best statistical results. This may seem like 'putting the cart before the horse', but the value of this procedure is shown by the following example. If the demand for a narrow definition of money is statistically more predictable than is the case for a broad definition, monetary policy should be couched in terms of that narrow definition.

Secondly, a method of identifying a break in the spectrum of assets to separate money from near-money could be used to define money. If the substitutability between demand deposits and time deposits is lower than that between time deposits and other liquid assets then the definition of money should be limited to currency and demand deposits. This follows as a clear break in the asset spectrum is implied. Alternatively if the substitutability between demand and time deposits is found to be high, this is at least a necessary condition for the inclusion of time deposits in the definition of the money supply (Laidler, 1969). However, whether such a substitutability criterion is sufficient to define money conclusively depends on the view taken of other definitional approaches and other possible inclusions in the definition. There is no direct evidence on this issue in the UK but in a survey of US studies, Feige (1974) argues that the evidence of close substitutability between demand and time deposits is weak and so recommends that a narrow definition of money is appropriate. Indirect evidence from a demand for money study in the UK by Artis and Lewis (1976) suggests that a narrow definition of money may be more appropriate. Also, Mills and Wood (1977) find that there is no evidence that money and the liabilities of n.b.f.i's are close substitutes in the UK. This clear evidence in favour of a break in the asset spectrum at this point weakens the case for including n.b.f.i. liabilities in a definition of money. – *whole view should now be looked at as somewhat outdated.*

5 Money supply definitions in the UK

This last section sets out the money supply definitions in the UK. Two major definitions are in use at present. M1 is a narrow concept and includes notes and coins held by the non-bank public and private sector sterling 'sight' deposits. Sight deposits are defined as those available on demand. They replaced the concept of demand deposits in June 1975 as the distinction between the latter and time deposits was becoming increasingly blurred. In particular, some time deposits were payable on demand and this total was transferred to the 'sight' deposits figure. Therefore some sight deposits are interest bearing.

This change introduces some extra complications for the theoretical definitions discussed in the previous section. For example, money as defined by Pesek and Saving would not include all sight deposits but only those not bearing interest. Certainly the blurring of the 'interest payingness' of deposits and their availability on demand, presents an extra problem for their analysis. Two minor adjustments are made to arrive at the final figure for M1. Sixty per cent of transit items (which appear as both credits and debits in bank balance sheets) are deducted (Table 2) and inter-bank transactions are netted out.

Table 2 Money supply statistics in the UK (financial years 1971/2–1978/9) (£ m.)

Financial year (end)	Notes and coin in circulation with public (1)	UK private sector sterling sight deposits^a		M1^b (4)	UK private sector sterling time deposits (5)	UK public sector sterling deposits (6)	Sterling M3^c (7)	UK Residents deposits in other currencies (8)	M3^d (9)
		Non-interest bearing (2)	Interest bearing (3)						
1971/2	3,755	7,413		11,168	8,747	557	20,472	529	21,001
1972/3	4,170	8,163		12,333	13,079	635	26,047	1,099	27,146
1973/4	4,574	8,198		12,772	18,660	733	32,165	1,773	33,938
1974/5	5,448	9,287		14,735	19,482	686	34,903	2,519	37,422
1975/6^e	5,915	9,815	2,071	17,802	18,585	933	37,320	3,150	40,470
1976/7	6,801	10,281	2,484	19,566	19,582	1,001	40,150	4,279	44,429
1977/8	7,966	12,946	3,358	24,271	20,925	1,186	46,382	4,531	50,913
1978/9	9,140	14,442	3,913	27,495	23,031	1,141	51,668	4,698	56,366

Source: *Bank of England Quarterly Bulletin*, June 1978, September 1979; the data are not seasonally adjusted.
 ^a After deducting 60 per cent of transit items
 ^b M1 = Columns 1 + 2 + 3
 ^c Sterling M3 = Columns 4 + 5 + 6
 ^d M3 = Columns 7 + 8
 ^e A break in the series occurred in May 1975 which affected the total for M1, and to a much smaller degree, sterling M3 and M3.

As an alternative to M1, the broad definition used most frequently in the UK today is sterling M3.[†] This equals M1 plus private sector sterling time deposits and all public sector sterling deposits. This concept has recently predominated over M3 which includes UK residents' deposits in foreign currency, as a large proportion of these are working balances of multinational companies and insurance companies' overseas premiums which have little connection with the monetary situation within the UK economy. Table 2 sets out the money supply statistics for the financial years 1971/2 to 1978/9 with each component separately identified.

The authorities, particularly since the introduction of monetary targets in 1976, have given more weight to sterling M3 than the narrower M1. There are a number of reasons for this. Firstly, the growth of M1 will be affected by the shifting of funds into and out of current accounts as interest rates change. As bank deposit rates increase, depositors will economise on current account deposits which will tend to reduce the growth rate of M1 although not affecting M3 which includes both current and deposit accounts. Alternatively as bank deposit rates fall the growth of M1 should pick up as funds are moved back into current accounts. Therefore, *ceteris paribus*, the growth rate of M1 will be more erratic than that of M3.

Figure 3 charts the annual growth rates of M1, sterling M3 and M3 based on quarterly data since 1970. A less erratic pattern for sterling M3 may not be apparent from Fig. 3, but the switching into and out of current accounts will have increased the volatility of M1 over what it would otherwise have been. In addition, sterling M3 being a broader aggregate will by definition fluctuate more in absolute terms than will M1. Two other points are important in this period. Firstly, the Bank of England introduced the Supplementary Special Deposits scheme (the 'Corset') in December 1973 which sought to control the growth of interest-bearing deposits. Since then this control has been imposed, and then abandoned at frequent intervals, increasing the erratic pattern of the sterling M3 series. Secondly, one of the particularly erratic episodes in the sterling M3 series in 1972–3 can be accounted for by some special factors. In that period clearing bank overdraft rates were lower than some rates in the domestic money markets. As a result companies, in particular, were borrowing to the limit of their overdrafts and depositing the funds to gain a profit in the money markets. As bank overdrafts increased this arbitrage or 'round-tripping' inflated the sterling M3 growth rate. Once interest rates altered to remove this arbitrage incentive, sterling M3 resumed a normal growth path (Stone, 1974). Both these factors increased the volatility of the M3 series in this period.

A second reason for the concentration of the authorities on sterling M3 is that this definition of money fits in well with the statistics of government borrowing and Domestic Credit Expansion (DCE) (below). This point will become clear in Chapter 8.

Aside from the theoretical arguments over the appropriate money

---

[†] M2 which equalled M1 plus time deposits was discontinued at the end of 1971.

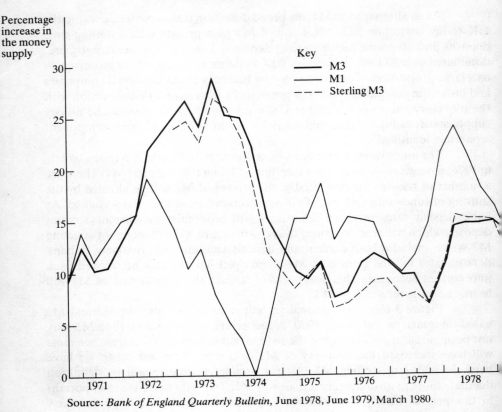

Source: *Bank of England Quarterly Bulletin*, June 1978, June 1979, March 1980.

Fig. 3. Money supply growth in the UK (1971–9). (Annual growth rates calculated each quarter – seasonally adjusted data.)

supply definition, two criticisms can be made of the treatment of the UK authorities one of which is answered by the use of yet another concept. Firstly, all money supply definitions in the UK exclude sterling deposits held by non-residents on the grounds that they do not affect the monetary situation in the UK. However, many of these deposits may affect export totals from the UK and for this and other reasons their exclusion from the money supply is rather arbitrary.

A second omission is more serious and led to the introduction of the concept of DCE in May 1969. The criticism is that a balance of payments disequilibrium will affect the money supply in any economy. For example, let a balance of payments deficit be represented as an excess of imports over exports. If the UK importer pays the excess import bill in foreign currency, use will be made of the Exchange Equalisation Account (EEA). The EEA is the official medium for exchanging foreign currency in the UK and holds the country's foreign exchange reserves. The assets held by the EEA comprise foreign exchange reserves and Treasury Bills. The UK importer will sell sterling to the EEA in return for foreign currency which will be paid to the exporting country. The EEA meanwhile will convert the new sterling holdings into Treasury Bills. Therefore, for a given Public Sector Borrowing Requirement (PSBR)[†] and non-bank demand for government debt, this payments deficit will reduce the government's recourse to the banking system for residual financing of its deficit. Fewer Treasury Bills will be sold to the banks and the money supply will fall. A more comprehensive account of the effects of various external transactions on the money supply is left until Chapters 7 and 8.

    Ideally, and this is true in most countries apart from the UK, the effect of the external position on the money supply will therefore be measured by the change in foreign exchange reserves. A payments deficit (surplus) of £200 m. will lead to a £200 m. decline (increase) in reserves and a £200 m. fall(rise) in the money supply. As will be clarified in Chapter 8, the particular institutional features of the UK economy make the effect of the external position on the money supply much more complex. However, the rationale for the DCE concept is unaltered. Domestic Credit Expansion corrects the actual (ex-post) money supply for the effect of external transactions (Bank of England, 1969a; Kern, 1970). This leaves an ex-ante total which measures the changes in the money supply of domestic origin or the monetary impulse in the economy before external events altered the actual money supply figures. Another point to note is that DCE is a flow concept whereas the money supply is a stock. Therefore it is necessary to compare DCE with a change in the money supply. The simple link between them in theory is defined as:

$$\text{DCE} = \Delta\text{Money supply} + \text{Fall in reserves : Balance of payments deficit}\ (-\text{Rise in reserves : Balance of payments surplus}) \qquad [3]$$

or

$$\Delta\text{Money supply} = \text{Ex-ante money supply of domestic origin (DCE)} - \text{Fall in reserves}\ (+\text{Rise in reserves}) \qquad [4]$$

    The arguments for the use of DCE as an extra guide for the authorities are numerous. Firstly, as is clear from the definition, DCE measures the ex-ante monetary impulse on the economy. By doing so, a clearer analysis of the stance of domestic monetary policy is possible, particularly where the balance of payments is in substantial disequilibrium. Secondly, the use of a DCE target is more logical than a money supply target. For example, a tight money supply target could be achieved not simply by restrictive monetary policy but also by an easy policy matched by a large payments deficit. Domestic Credit Expansion would not be influenced by the external position and a target in terms of DCE would be missed. A DCE target may also be self-correcting. Take the case where a DCE target of £1,000 m. is attained by a combination of money supply growth of £500 m. and a payments deficit of the same amount. An exogenous rise in the deficit would cause the money supply to be reduced (through the action of the EEA) and leave DCE near its target range again. However, if in these circum-

---

[†] The PSBR may be defined as the excess of public sector expenditure of all types over revenue.

stances a money supply target were being pursued, action would be taken to raise the money supply towards the target level which (if a simple link between money and expenditure exists) would worsen the balance of payments deficit. This in turn reduces the money supply again and so on. Therefore, in certain circumstances the discipline imposed by a DCE target may be greater than that imposed by a money supply target.

There are, however, a number of problems with the concept of DCE both in theory and in operation in the UK. Firstly, it has been criticised for being a lending total (measured on the assets side of the banks' balance sheets) which makes its linkage with the money supply (measured on the liabilities side of the balance sheets) very complex. It is necessary to complete a number of extra adjustments to the money supply figures, apart from the external situation, to move to the DCE figure. These adjustments (Ch. 8) which are needed simply because of the use of different sides of the balance sheet seem, on the face of it, to be arbitrary. Secondly, the DCE model, as established by the IMF, envisaged one of its advantages to be its exogeneity (Artis and Nobay, 1969). This has simply not been the case in the UK economy with the authorities until recently much more concerned with stable interest rates than in controlling the ex-ante money supply. Thirdly, a DCE target may be very difficult to police even if the authorities wish to control it. Despite the assumed exogeneity of DCE, it, like the money supply, is dependent on the size of the PSBR, the non-bank demand for government securities and bank lending to the non-bank private sector. The size of the PSBR is particularly prone to seasonal, short-term influences while market confidence can soon alter to affect the sales of government securities.

Therefore, although the gains to society from having money are proven, the definition of the monetary commodity is not straightforward. Each particular version has problems with the UK authorities publishing data on a number of aggregates as alternatives although sterling M3 is the most favoured one at present. While the study of the monetary commodity itself is both interesting and useful, it is only a preliminary to the analysis of the role of money in theory and in practice, which is made in the following chapters.

Chapter 2

The targets and instruments of monetary policy

1 Introduction

Monetary policy represents one of a number of policies available to the authorities in the pursuit of macroeconomic objectives. These objectives are usually limited to four well established ones; namely low inflation, high or full employment, balance of payments equilibrium and a satisfactory rate of growth of real income. These objectives can be extended to include others and considerable debate has ensued over the wisdom and costs of pursuing some of these objectives. However, such arguments will not concern us in this chapter. These macroeconomic objectives will be referred to, in this chapter, as the **goals** of economic policy (e.g., Fisher, 1973, 1976; OECD, 1977).

To assist in the attainment of these goals, the government has available to it a series of policies; each policy in fact consists of a range of different instruments. These policies include fiscal, monetary, prices and incomes and finally exchange rate policies. Again, the list is not necessarily exhaustive. In the course of this chapter monetary policy will be considered exclusively. The elements of monetary policy will be termed **policy instruments.**

2 The target/indicator problem

The structure of the monetary policy problem has been summarised by Saving (1967). The authorities have a goal function (G) which may include one or more arguments (e.g., low inflation, high employment):

$$G = G(Y_i) \qquad [1]$$

where Y_i are the endogenous variables in the economic system. These endogenous variables themselves are not influenced solely by the policy actions of the authorities. If they were the policy problem would be solved. A certain monetary policy action would be taken which would automatically lead to the particular Y_i that maximised the goal function in [1]. Unfortunately, the determination of the endogenous variables in a particular period (Y_{it}) is more complex than this:

$$Y_{it} = f(Y_{it-i}, X_{jt}, X_{jt-i}, Z_{kt}, Z_{kt-i}) \qquad [2]$$

where X_{jt}, X_{jt-i} are current and past values of j policy variables, Z_{kt}, Z_{kt-i} current and past values of k exogenous variables and Y_{it-i} past values of the i endogenous variables themselves. With the existence of Y_{it-i}, Z_{kt}, Z_{kt-i} the making of policy to 'hit the goal' is more difficult. In particular the extent of exogenous influences (Z_{kt}, Z_{kt-i}) will be uncertain.

The problem can be represented more practically by looking at the links between the instruments of monetary policy and the goals. The instruments of monetary policy are numerous. A brief summary of each of them is needed at this stage to explore fully the targets and indicators debate. Fuller explanations of many of the links and the policies themselves will unfold as the book proceeds. Monetary policy instruments can be grouped in a number of ways. Bain (1976), for example, uses a distinction between general and specific control weapons. The following is a list of the main instruments, the first two of which are general control weapons:

1. Open-market operations
2. Discount rate (Bank Rate or Minimum Lending Rate in the UK)
3. Reserve requirements
4. Special Deposits
5. Lending ceilings
6. Interest rate ceilings
7. Moral suasion
8. Hire-purchase controls

Open-market operations are the sale and purchase of government securities to finance the Public Sector Borrowing Requirement (PSBR). The discount rate is the rate at which the authorities will rediscount short-term bills presented to them by financial institutions. This was called Bank Rate in the UK until October 1972, when it was replaced by the market-determined Minimum Lending Rate (MLR). In May 1978, the MLR formula was abandoned and a discretionary MLR established which is similar to the former Bank Rate. Reserve requirements represent a request to banks that a certain proportion of the value of either assets or deposits be held in specified assets. This control is placed both for prudential and monetary control purposes (see Ch. 7). At present in the UK, $12\frac{1}{2}$ per cent of a bank's eligible liabilities must be held in certain specified reserve assets. These requirements are in effect altered by Special Deposits. This is the technique whereby a certain percentage of liabilities is 'frozen' at the Bank of England and so cannot be used for credit creation. Other policies include ceiling controls on bank advances to limit credit expansion and controls on interest rates although the latter have only been used once in the UK between September 1973 and February 1975 to protect building societies from bank competition. At times moral suasion may be used instead of, in particular, lending ceilings. They usually have similar effects. Finally hire-purchase controls involve the specification of the minimum down-payment (deposit), the maximum length of the repayment period and implicitly the minimum interest rate charged, on commodities bought with the aid of hire-purchase credit.

These are the **instruments** of monetary policy. They are directly controllable by the authorities. However, the links between these and the goal variables are very complex. These instruments affect another set of variables which may be called **indicators**. These include bank assets and liabilities, high-powered money (or the monetary base) and short-term interest rates. They are termed indicators as they 'indicate' the direction and strength of monetary policy in a particular period being closely related to the instruments themselves. For example, open-market operations will affect the size of high-powered money which consists of bank reserves plus reserve assets held outside the banking system. In a cash base situation this reduces to:

$$B = R + C_p \qquad [3]$$

where B is the monetary base, R the level of bank reserves and C_p the currency holdings of the public. The transactions of the authorities in government debt will affect the number of securities sold to the banks and also the size of bank deposits (as the public purchase or sell government securities). Perhaps the best example of an indicator in use in the UK is the monthly data on the liabilities and assets of the banking system. Appearing two weeks before full money supply figures, these data are used as an early indicator of the level of the money supply and therefore of the stance of monetary policy. In addition, figures on eligible liabilities are contained within these statistics; the level of these could be related to the Supplementary Special Deposits ('Corset') instrument and will also act as an indicator of the money supply in the future.

The full links between the instruments of policy and indicators are set out in Fig. 1. The indicators are not directly controllable by the authorities for two reasons. Firstly, there may be uncertainty over the exact links between instruments and indicators. Secondly, and more importantly, exogenous factors may influence the indicator variables. Indicator variables in turn affect a further set of variables called **targets**. These include the various monetary aggregates, bank credit and long-run rates of interest. Particular values for these variables are not desirable in their own right. However, they are the targets of monetary policy which the authorities believe will facilitate the attainment of the ultimate macroeconomic objectives **(goals)**. The distinction between the **targets** of monetary policy and the **goals** of overall economic policy is therefore crucial.

Figure 1 summarises the four types of variables involved in the operation of policy from the autonomously controlled policy instruments at one end to the goal variables at the other. In addition, examples of some of the concepts concerned are given for the UK with suggested links between them (neither the links nor the variables are necessarily exhaustive).[†] The elaborate framework of Fig. 1 is necessary as the authorities cannot be certain of the ultimate effects of a particular policy action on the goal variables and also as these

---

[†] It may be assumed that the goals are not independent of each other. Attainment of one will influence the ability of the economy to attain some or all of the others.

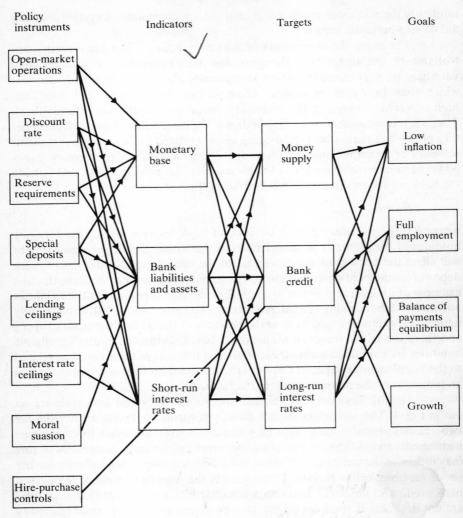

Fig. 1.

actions may have lagged effects on the goals. The first problem of uncertainty over the links in Fig. 1 is potentially the more serious. Such uncertainty usually takes one of two forms. Firstly, the actual structure of the economy may be unknown so that the authorities have no clear idea how a call for Special Deposits, for example, affects the goal variables. Secondly, within a well-established structure, stochastic variations will occur in the basic functions. For example, the demand for money function may shift due to an exogenous disturbance and this may affect the result of any change in a particular policy instrument. It is the existence of large potential exogenous influences that introduces major uncertainty into monetary policy. The aim of an indicator variable is to give a clear independent (of exogenous factors) signal of the strength and direction of policy. If it does so any divergence of the money supply, for example, from its target level can be assumed to be due to exogenous factors. In general, the further is a variable away from the policy change itself the more likely is it to be affected by exogenous influences. Figure 2 is an abbreviated form of Fig. 1 including the impact of exogenous variables:

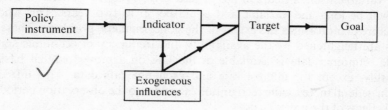

Fig. 2.

An example may help to illustrate the operation of the scheme in Fig. 2. Let the authorities undertake a selling operation in the market of government securities. Assume that despite this (which should lead to a decline in the money supply), the money supply increases. The unexpected reaction of the money supply could be due to a number of exogenous factors. Two only will be identi- fied. The banking system as a whole may decide to reduce its reserve ratio (as long as it did not fall below the minimum level) in response perhaps to an in- crease in the demand for credit. Therefore, bank credit and the money supply will rise. In this case a change in the relevant indicator, of monetary policy (high- powered money) is not the cause of the rise in the money supply. An exogenous impact on the *target* variable is the cause. Alternatively, an inflow of capital from abroad may inflate high-powered money (the indicator) more than the open-market operation has reduced it. Therefore, in this case, the money supply has risen due to an exogenous influence on the *indicator*. It should be repeated that as the indicators of policy are closer to the policy actions themselves they will be less susceptible to exogenous factors than are the target variables.

The second major reason for the complex framework in Fig. 1 is the existence of lags in the implementation and effect of monetary policy. It is, in fact, the lagged response of certain variables to a policy change that is one of the key reasons for the use of intermediate (indicator and target) variables at all (Saving, 1967). The lags involved in the effect of any policy can be divided into inside and outside lags. (This is equally true for any other economic policy as it is for monetary policy.) The inside or implementation lag is the delay that ensues between the need for a policy change occurring and the policy adjustment actually being made. In terms of Fig. 2 there is a delay even before the policy instrument is altered. This inside lag can itself be subdivided into a recognition lag, between the need arising and it being recognised, and an administrative lag, between recognition and the policy change being made. The latter will be fairly short for monetary policy, as action can soon be taken to alter the scale of open- market operations, change the discount rate or amend any other monetary policy instruments. The outside lag is the time elapsing between the policy instrument being adjusted and the effect being felt on the goal variables. It is the time lag involved in the framework in Fig. 2. The outside lag can also be subdivided. It consists of the intermediate lag, between the adjustment of the policy instrument and its effect on the major target variable (e.g., the money supply) and the reaction lag between the change in the target variable and the effect on the goal variable itself. Friedman has argued (e.g., 1968, 1970b) that the reaction lag will be long and variable and could be up to two years. This whole lag structure demonstrates the extent of the policy-makers' problems. These problems are heightened by the availability and frequency of economic statistics. Little economic data is available in the UK on a more frequent basis than monthly, except for interest rate and exchange rate data. This infrequency will in general increase the recognition lag and also the observation period of the total effects of the policy.

The existence of these lags leads monetarists to advocate a policy of steady growth of the money supply (Ch. 5). Another solution would be to persevere with counter-cyclical policy in the hope that with experience, the outside lags, at least, will become more predictable and such policy will become more successful. A theoretical solution is to cut out part of the outside lag by the use of indicator variables, as described in this chapter. However, this is difficult in practice due to the exogenous influences on such indicators, described above.

Before an analysis is made of the criteria for successful indicators and targets, the definitional problems in this area should be noted. The general framework in Fig. 2 used a four-variable distinction. However, there is no agreement amongst monetary economists on either the number of concepts to be distinguished or the labels to be attached to each variable type. For example, many studies combine the intermediate variables (indicators and targets) into one, while the use of the term indicator, in particular, is not universally consistent.

The scheme used in Fig. 2 is consistent with the use of the word 'target' for the money supply in the UK in the late 1970s. The practice of certain authors of describing the money supply as an indicator of policy is rejected here. Again, an example should help. For reasons outlined in detail in Chapter 5 and briefly referred to later in this chapter, the monetarists argue that if a certain rate of growth of the money supply is achieved a given combination of goal variables will be attained. The money supply is therefore the target of monetary policy. However, much of the theoretical debate has wrongly centred on the choice between the money supply, the rate of interest and other variables as policy *indicators*. The choice is a crucial one but the choice is as a policy *target*.

In June 1977, the Bank of England noted that:

> The conjunction this year of rapidly falling interest rates and of unexpectedly slow growth in the monetary aggregates may appear paradoxical. On one measure, monetary policy could appear easy; on the other hand restrictive. (Bank of England, 1977b).

The authorities seem to be using the money supply and the level of interest rates to indicate the stance of monetary policy. However, such indications are provided by other variables such as high-powered money, the level of bank assets and liabilities and certain short-term rates of interest. What should be concerning the authorities are the relationships between the observed variables and their target values. The fact that a paradoxical indication of the stance of monetary policy is being received is due to the differing impact of exogenous factors on the variables concerned. If these variables are moving away from their target levels, corrective action is needed. However, if these exogenous factors are affecting the targets but not the indicators of policy, this shows the relative inefficiency of the indicators themselves.

3 The choice of indicator and target variables of monetary policy

Having established the framework of section 2 above, criteria for successful indicators and targets may be established. In the case of an indicator four separate criteria are identified. Firstly, the value of an indicator should be observable. If it is not then the indicator is a subjective reference point of policy and open to ambiguous interpretation. This should rule out a familiar indicator used in the USA – 'the tone and feel' of the market. Secondly, there should be close and statistically stable links between the policy instruments and the indicator. This implies a third criterion which is that policy-induced and exogenous effects on the indicators should be separate and identifiable. Finally, the indicators should have similar close and statistically stable links with the targets of monetary policy. Clearly, indicators will satisfy these criteria in differing degrees. Given this, the exogeneity criterion which establishes an unambiguous link between instruments and indicators is the most crucial.

The criteria for a successful monetary policy target are similar in style. Firstly, the target should be stably related to the goals of policy. This is the major criterion and explains why much of the debate in this area has centred on the transmission mechanisms between target variables (e.g., the money supply, rates of interest) and goal variables (e.g., the rate of inflation). This will be returned to below. Secondly, the target variable should have a close and statistically stable relationship to the indicator variable. As in the previous paragraph, this implies a third criterion. This is that the exogenous influences on the target variable can be separated from the policy-induced influences and easily identified. Finally, although less important than in the case of indicators, a target variable should ideally be observable.

These criteria are similar to those for a good indicator variable. The difference lies in the relative importance of particular criteria for the two types of variable. For example, when a school of thought advocates the use of a particular variable as a policy target, the first criterion has usually dominated with the others sometimes ignored. For example, the monetarist view is that the money supply is a good target of monetary policy on the basis that it has a guaranteed effect on certain goal variables even if the transmission mechanism itself may not be clear; in addition the rate of interest is too capricious to be a good target variable. A Keynesian would not necessarily argue against the money supply as a target, but relative to a monetarist he would favour an interest rate target. On the other hand, Radcliffe economists would favour the use of bank credit as the target, and the Yale School, headed by James Tobin, the equity yield (Brainard and Tobin, 1968). Therefore, the choice of the authorities of the best target of monetary policy would be affected by their views of the appropriate economic 'model'.

The most popular target of monetary policy in the UK at least until the mid-1970s was a group of interest rate variables. The authorities usually aimed for stability in the rates of interest on long-term government securities (sect. 5 below). While such long-term rates were the target of policy, other short-run ones such as the rate on overnight money, the three-month inter-bank rate and the Treasury Bill rate were used as indicators of policy. Therefore, the following arguments for and against an interest rate target refer in this period to the long-term rate of interest. The major argument in favour of an interest rate target is that it is observable while information on the level of interest rates is available very promptly, and the administrative lag will, in general, be short. Therefore, the lag between the need for policy action being recognised and any interest rate being affected is fairly short. In addition, Keynesians recommend an interest rate target due to their belief in the instability of the demand for money, an argument demonstrated below.

However, interest rates do have many drawbacks as targets. The major one is that even within the group of long-term rates of interest many alternative rates are available. It is not clear which is the best interest rate to act as the target. Secondly, measured interest rates are 'nominal' rates while a true target of policy should be a particular 'real' rate. This real rate is difficult to observe as it is not easy to measure price expectations accurately. Thirdly, interest rates are very sensitive to exogenous influences. For example, an open-market sale of government securities may be accompanied by a fall in the demand for bonds such that bond prices actually fall and the rate of interest rises. Such influences which may dominate the effects of policy action will make the attainment of a particular interest rate target difficult. Fourthly, Friedman argues that the rate of interest is a 'will-o-the-wisp'. An expansionary monetary policy will initially cause interest rates to fall, but as demand in general in the economy, including the demand for credit, picks up and price expectations increase, interest rates will turn up and eventually move in the same direction as the money supply (Ch. 5). Fifthly, stable nominal rates of interest will not in general reflect a passive, steady monetary policy. This will only be the case if the real rate of interest is constant and price expectations are also unchanged. For a given real rate of interest, the maintenance of stable nominal interest rates will have a destabilising effect on the economy if price expectations change. If prices are rising and these are reflected in an expectation of higher future prices, a stable nominal rate will be expansionary and so will feed the growth in demand. On the other hand if, in a deflationary situation, price expectations are falling, stable nominal rates will reflect higher real rates which will accentuate the downturn. Finally, Poole (1976) argues that the containment of an interest rate within a particular range will be almost impossible unless the range is very wide.

This is because an attempt to maintain rates within a narrow band when market forces dictate otherwise will be destabilising. The abandonment of the cheap money policy of low interest rates in 1947 and the difficulties of debt-management policy in the 1960s are good examples of this argument in post-war British monetary history. The argument sometimes used that certain rates of interest in an economy are administered, and therefore non-market clearing rates, is not relevant here. The usual interest-rate target of monetary policy (i.e., a particular long-term government bond rate) is unlikely to be a disequilibrium one of this type.

The money supply is the variable usually selected as an alternative to the rate of interest as a target of monetary policy. The main argument in favour of the money supply is the existence of considerable evidence that the links between money and the ultimate goal variables of income and prices are well determined. The evidence from the UK (summarised in Chapter 6) is mainly from demand for money studies as other work linking economic activity to current and lagged money supply variables has been much less conclusive. In the context of the monetary targets debate, there is evidence that the demand for money function is stable and changes in the money supply are not offset by movements in the velocity of circulation (McClam, 1978; Pepper and Wood, 1976). However, two qualifications must be made. Firstly, the stability of these functions is less clear in the UK than it is in the USA. The arguments for a money supply target are therefore more powerful in the USA than in this country. Secondly, since 1971, there is evidence of some instability in the demand for money function in the UK (Hacche, 1974; Artis and Lewis, 1974, 1976; Hamburger, 1977a). It is not yet clear whether the demand for money function has actually shifted due, perhaps, to the introduction of the Competition and Credit Control system (Bank of England, 1971a) in 1971, or whether the observed instability is due to there being an excess supply of money for much of the early 1970s. (See Chapter 6.)

The preference for a money supply policy over an interest-rate policy, given a stable demand for money function (i.e., LM curve) is demonstrated in Fig. 3. In a situation of instability in the expenditure functions (IS curve) but not the money demand function (LM curve) a policy of maintaining stable interest rates at $\bar{r}$ would cause income to fluctuate between y_1 and y_2. A stable money supply policy would lead to smaller income fluctuations ($y_3 - y_4$). This is a familiar result (Poole, 1970) and has been extensively used to justify a money supply policy under the assumptions of Fig. 3. However, it is important to reiterate that it depends on the stability of the demand for money which is in rather more doubt now for the UK than in the 1960s. In addition, Goodhart (1975) argues that such a conclusion may be too simple. The introduction of lags into the system may cause much larger and perhaps unacceptable, interest rate fluctuations, while the use of the IS/LM model itself implies that the structure of the model is known and the only source of uncertainty is stochastic disturbances.

The money supply also has the advantage as a target of policy in that it should be broadly acceptable to people with diverse theoretical views. Pepper

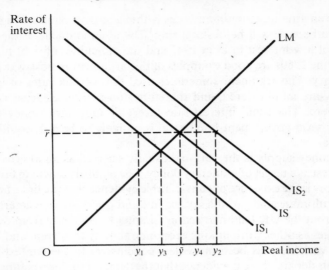

Fig. 3.

and Wood (1976) argue that with Keynesians favouring a fiscal target based on the PSBR and monetarists a money supply target, agreement should be straightforward due to the fairly close relationship between the PSBR and monetary growth (Ch. 7).

However, the money supply does have a number of drawbacks as a policy target. Firstly, which monetary aggregate should be used? In the UK, there are series for M1 and M3 and sterling M3, while calls for even broader aggregates are frequently heard. The choice should hinge on the aggregate with the greatest stability with respect to the goal variables. This will militate against M1 which will fluctuate as money is shifted between time and demand deposits, as interest rates change. Secondly, the money supply is particularly prone to exogenous influences. The most obvious example is through the total currency flow in external transactions. Thirdly, the money supply suffers by comparison with interest rates in the availability of data. Money supply data at present in the UK is only available monthly and nearly a month in arrears. Clearly, the money supply as a target does not possess desirable qualities in terms of controllability and observability.

The controllability issue concerning the money supply as a target of monetary policy has been investigated by McClam (1978). He argues that the variance of money supply growth (M3) in the UK has increased since 1975 and concludes therefore that the existence of a target for monetary policy does not ensure that the target is hit. The viability of a money supply target is naturally lessened if it is difficult to control that variable closely (Argy, 1974; Pierce and Thomson, 1973). Assuming, however, that the authorities are able to manipulate the money supply so that the target is attained, conditions may still exist where an interest rate target should replace a money supply target. In Fig. 4, if the

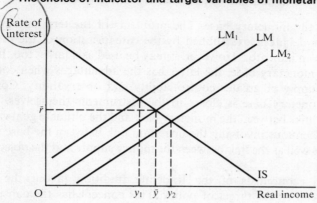

Fig. 4.

demand for money alone is unstable (with the money supply held constant at the target level) the LM curve will vary between LM_1 and LM_2 and income between y_1 and y_2. However, with an interest rate target $(\bar{r})$, the LM curve will be returned automatically to its original position leaving income unchanged $(\bar{y})$. For example, a fall in the demand for money, will drive the interest rate down and income up as the LM curve shifts to LM_2. A monetary policy aimed at keeping the rate of interest at $\bar{r}$ will lead to the money supply being reduced to compensate for the reduced demand leaving income at $\bar{y}$ in equilibrium.

Therefore, the choice between an interest rate and money supply policy in seeking to minimise the fluctuations in real income depends on the relative stability of the IS and LM curves (Laidler, 1973a). Keynesians favour an interest rate policy as they consider that although the IS curve is volatile, the instability of money demand is greater than the instability in the components of the IS curve. On the other hand, monetarists believe both functions are more stable than do the Keynesians. However, the basic premise of monetarism, that the demand for money is stable, dominates, causing them to advocate a money supply policy.

An alternative to the money supply as a target of policy is Domestic Credit Expansion (DCE). The arguments for and against DCE are similar to those relating to the money supply. One additional advantage is that a DCE target is an automatic stabiliser. If the external deficit rises so will DCE if the money supply is held constant. Adherence to a DCE target will therefore cause a deflationary adjustment to be made by the authorities which will initially reduce the domestic component of the money supply and so help to remove the payments deficit. On the other hand, a money supply target could in practice be attained by a combination of an expansionary monetary policy and a large external deficit. This is not possible with a DCE target. In general, DCE may be an appropriate indicator of policy in an open economy, where currency flows distort the money supply figures.

An alternative aggregate that the authorities may seek to use as a policy target is the monetary base. The problems of the terminology in the target/indicators debate is exemplified by the categorisation of the monetary base in Fig. 1 as an indicator. However, it may be used as a target too. If policy is aimed at the monetary base, the latter has the advantages when compared to the money supply of greater controllability and observability. Control is easier as the monetary base is closer to the instruments themselves. On the other hand, the links between the monetary base and the ultimate goal variables are particularly tenuous involving the uncertain link between the base and the money supply as well as the link between the money supply and the objectives of policy.

Certain economists of the Radcliffe tradition favour the use of 'liquidity' or credit as the target of policy. This concept has the considerable advantage of being more wide-ranging than the money supply as it includes credit extended by non-bank financial intermediaries. It is in fact an asset total and not a liability total as is the money supply. However, liquidity cannot be measured in any meaningful form, while it is clearly not under the control of the monetary authorities. These disadvantages are virtually conclusive and the concept has never been used in the UK as an explicit target of monetary policy. This is notwithstanding the aim of the authorities to control bank credit in the 1950s and 1960s. Close control of bank credit may be possible as the assets of the banking system can be measured. But in its broadest sense, liquidity cannot be measured or, therefore, controlled.

Another target of monetary policy is the equity yield on assets. It is advocated by members of the Yale School, headed by James Tobin. The arguments hinge on a transmission mechanism that involves the equity yield. As the money supply expands the real rate of return on equity falls so that new investment is encouraged as the value of existing capital equipment increases. It is therefore the real cost of acquiring new capital relative to the price of existing capital that influences investment and is the appropriate transmission mechanism of monetary policy (Brainard and Tobin, 1968). Such an indicator is easily observed, except that indices are not available for all types of assets. However, a major disadvantage is that any movement in equity yields may reflect purely financial transactions and have little to do with the investment intentions of manufacturing industry.

These are the major targets of monetary policy available in the UK. The list is not exhaustive as other theoretical concepts have been suggested for use in the USA (see Tanner, 1972). However, the actual choice is effectively limited to those discussed above. *A priori* choice between the available concepts is difficult and empirical evidence on their appropriateness has been used to discriminate between them.

4 Empirical evidence on policy targets

In this section, the schema in Fig. 1 is implicitly used although this may conflict with the choice of words of the respective authors, in particular with respect to the 'indicator' and 'target' concepts. Empirical evidence in this debate has taken three major forms. Firstly, a number of studies have looked at the stability of links between the instruments of policy and the intermediate variables (indicators and targets) and also between these intermediate variables and the goal variables. Secondly, a study has been made on the general concurrence of available targets. Thirdly, use has been made of what are termed 'reaction functions'. Each of these types of evidence will be reported from studies using UK data.

Studies of the first type seek to 'rank' different variables in terms of the stability of the links set out in the previous paragraph. The only study that endeavours to do this that includes the UK is one by Keran (1970b). He uses the one-equation approach that has become associated with work done at the Federal Reserve Bank of St. Louis. The typical form is set out in eq. [4] with Y representing nominal income:

$$\Delta Y = \alpha_0 + \alpha_1 \, \Delta M + \alpha_2 \, \Delta F + e \qquad [4]$$

Equation [4] will include various monetary (M) and fiscal (F) variables. The test involves the significance of α_1 for each alternative concept of monetary policy. For the UK he found that money stock changes were positively and significantly related to changes in nominal income while for interest rates the results were either insignificant or of the wrong sign. Thus he concludes that for the UK (and in fact in general) the money supply is a better target of monetary policy than are interest rates.

However, this conclusion can be criticised heavily. Firstly, it only tests the link between target and goal and ignores the link between the policy variable and the target. This makes the study no more an investigation of targets and indicators than are any of the studies of the links between monetary variables and economic activity set out in Chapter 6. Secondly, the list of tested monetary targets is too short. For instance, credit is ignored while use was only made of one interest rate variable (the rate on long-term government bonds). DCE would also presumably be a candidate in such a test today. Thirdly, the basis for the preference for the money supply over other targets may also be criticised. Money multipliers have been notably less stable and predictable in the UK than in the USA (see Ch. 6). Indeed, Artis (1974) argues that the approach 'fails to yield evidence that could convince even the converted'. The conclusion of Keran in favour of a money supply policy is therefore distinctly dubious for the UK. Other tests for the USA have not fallen foul of all these criticisms to the same extent. Hamburger (1970) and Tanner (1972) in particular use a wide range of policy variables and investigate their exogeneity too. Work along these lines is needed for UK data.

A second method of tackling this problem was utilised by Artis (1972, 1974). He sought to discover whether the debate over alternative policy variables was empirically relevant. Do the targets of policy give different signals on the direction and scale of monetary policy? He concluded that the variables studied (a short-run interest rate, the equivalent expected real rate, the growth of M3, normalised real M3 growth calculated by adjusting for growth potential and price expectations, and bank advances narrowly and broadly defined) gave similar pictures of the direction of short-run policy changes but not the scale of these movements. The series therefore had similar turning points. Very short-run (quarterly) movements of the indicators did yield significantly different signals. A correlation matrix showed that the concurrence of money supply and advances changes was rather low, while real and nominal interest rates also moved independently to a considerable extent. The conclusion of the study was that the target choice was a crucial one for very short-run policy analysis and for investigations over a period of years when the cumulated scale differences became important.

A third form of evidence comes from the 'reaction function' literature. This approach inverts the chain of causation between instruments and goals and therefore assumes that the authorities 'react' to changes in the size of goal variables by altering the policy instruments available. This technique was pioneered by Reuber (1964) and Dewald and Johnson (1963). Studies of this type for the UK have been made by Fisher (1970), Pissarides (1972), Nobay (1974) and Coghlan (1975).

In these studies it is expected that a decline in foreign exchange reserves and the level of unemployment, and a rise in the rate of inflation would lead to deflationary adjustments in policy instruments. The instruments used included Bank Rate, Special Deposits, hire-purchase controls and bank lending requests. In all cases, Bank Rate responded significantly and in the expected direction to changes in the goal variables while the results for Special Deposits were also good apart from an insignificant response of this instrument to a change in the level of reserves. Hire-purchase controls were used in response to changes in the level of unemployment and the rate of inflation, and bank lending requests to changes in the level of unemployment and foreign exchange reserves. These results using data from 1955 to 1970 simply confirm the importance of these monetary policy instruments in this period. The study by Nobay (1974) merits particular attention as it is different in a number of ways. Firstly, the idea that instruments are set simultaneously so that they become endogenously determined is utilised. Secondly, the objectives of policy are respecified in terms of certain money market variables such as debt-management considerations. He believes that the authorities react more noticeably to such variables than to the usually specified objectives. In addition, the author includes a surrogate variable, to reflect fiscal actions, which is used as an implicit preference function. For example, an increase in the surrogate (defined as the cumulative impact of first round effects on GDP of defined taxation changes) will reflect the authorities' preference for an expansion of the economy. The task is then to analyse how monetary variables react to the movements in this surrogate. The preliminary and tentative nature of the work is noted by the author, but the general approach is interesting in the way in which instruments are seen to respond to the degree of success in attaining the stipulated policy objectives.

5 UK policy and the target choice

This section looks at the choice of monetary policy target made by the UK authorities since 1945. This analysis is unfortunately not clear-cut. Two well-defined periods exist (before 1968 and after 1976) but a considerable 'grey' area exists between them when changes of emphasis were made and confusion abounded as to which variable was the target of policy.

Before 1968, policy was clearly conducted in a fashion very sympathetic to the views of the Radcliffe Report. The targets of policy were interest rates on government securities and secondly bank credit. The two obviously conflicted at times. The authorities were mesmerised by the need to maximise the demand for government debt due to the size of the National Debt itself and therefore the need for refinancing, and due to the fact that in general the Debt was being added to by a positive PSBR each year. To achieve this aim, the authorities followed two principles of policy. Firstly, they aimed to keep gilt-edged prices and therefore interest rates steady. Secondly, the Debt was funded when possible (i.e., short-term debt retired and long-term debt issued) in an attempt to keep the average maturity of the debt stable.

The first of these two principles needs some explanation. In microeconomics, demand for a commodity is assumed to be a negative function of its price. The same does not necessarily follow for government securities because expectations of future prices play a much greater role in this particular market. In any market, transactors will consist of 'sceptics' and 'norm believers' (Cramp, 1971a). A sceptic sees a price fall due to excess supply as being the prelude to future price falls, while a 'norm believer' expects any price change to be reversed and the norm quickly re-established. The effects of the behaviour of the two types of transactor is shown in Fig. 5.

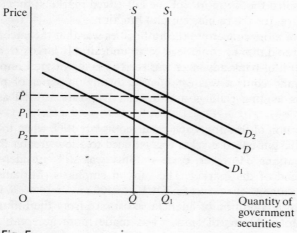

Fig. 5.

This diagram may be used to represent the market for government securities. The supply function is vertical to incorporate the assumption of a fixed PSBR to be financed in a given time period. An increase in the PSBR and therefore debt sales (to S_1) will cause the price to fall to P_1 on the original demand curve (D). Sceptics will believe that prices will fall further and so will reduce their demand to D_1 so that the price falls to P_2. This group is said to have extrapolative expectations. On the other hand, norm believers view the old price as being the norm and therefore seeing the possibility of a capital gain increase their demand to D_2. Price returns to $\bar{P}$. In this case, the response to the price change exhibits regressive expectations. An important point to note is that the actions of the market operators are self-fulfilling and so there is no reason for them to alter their behaviour.

The authorities believed in this period that sceptics dominated the gilt-edged market. Therefore, they acted to iron out price fluctuations by, for example, buying on a 'falling' market. In the example in Fig. 5 the authorities themselves would artificially raise demand to D_2. This purchase of large quantities of stock by the authorities increases the amount of debt that must be sold at a later date. The authorities could alternatively have allowed prices to fluctuate until supply equalled demand. This assumes that at some price level, however low, all available stock would be purchased. However, the ensuing interest rate changes implied by this policy were seen as undesirable. This policy of 'leaning into the wind' to iron out any price fluctuations, caused the loss of money supply control by the authorities. If the market would only take a certain quantity of stock without large price fluctuations, the remainder would ultimately be taken up by the banks and, to the extent that the assets qualify as reserve assets would cause high-powered money and therefore the money supply to rise. However, in the Radcliffe tradition of that period this did not concern the authorities. The loss of control of the money supply which followed from the interest stabilisation policy was an acceptable cost during this period. The authorities fulfilled the 'support' (of the gilt-edged markets) function and eschewed the 'control' (of the money supply) function.

What was of more concern to the authorities was that the uncontrolled growth of high-powered money could lead to an undesirably large extension of bank credit. The level of bank advances was seen as being of vital importance by the authorities and control was established through a series of portfolio constraints such as lending ceilings and Special Deposits as well as moral suasion.

A modification of this approach occurred in late 1968 when the degree of intervention in the gilt-edged market was reduced to allow greater price and interest rate fluctuations. However, price stability was still considered to be vital at the short end of the market. The shift in emphasis (Midland Bank, 1969) was closely related to the target for DCE of £400 m. for 1969–70 imposed on the authorities as a condition of financial assistance from the International Monetary Fund. In addition, the move was made more acceptable by an increasing belief that the dominance of the gilt-edged market by sceptics was simply untrue. The prevalence of sceptics in the gilt-edged market was an untested hypothesis that began to be questioned in the late 1960s.

This was a long way, however, from a conversion to money supply targets, let alone monetarism. Even the advent of Competition and Credit Control (CCC) in 1971 did not seem to clarify which was the approximate monetary target of the authorities. Various statements by the authorities did suggest a greater sympathy with money supply control:

> We have increasingly shifted our emphasis towards the broader monetary aggregates. (Bank of England, 1971c).

However other statements suggested that little had changed:

> In future, the authorities would seek to influence the structure of interest rates through a general control over the liquidity of the whole banking system. (Bank of England, 1971c).

In fact, it seems that the main aim of CCC was to seek control of various aggregates (including the money supply and liquidity) by the movement of interest rates. It was the free competition in money and credit markets which permitted the interest rate to establish equilibrium, that was the novelty of CCC. What is clear from this (the new system is discussed more fully in Ch. 10, Sect. 5) is that a money supply target was not a definite feature of monetary policy in 1971. The DCE target of 1969–70 was succeeded by one of £900 m. for 1970–1, but then not replaced. It can therefore be assumed that in the early years of the 1970s, the authorities still regarded bank credit and interest rates as much as the money supply as the targets of monetary policy.

The clear move towards money supply targets did not, therefore, occur until 1976. The first hints of the new policy appeared in the budget of that year when a 15 per cent growth rate of M3 for 1976–7 was established as a tentative target. The crucial, unambiguous birth of such targets was, however, in December 1976 when a series of planned growth rates for various concepts including the PSBR was accepted as part of another IMF loan package. Since that date, the announcement of successive targets and the strictures necessary to attain them have become an important part of policy making.

Clearly, the UK has not acted in isolation. Since 1974, the USA, Germany, France, Switzerland, Canada and the Netherlands are among those countries which have announced growth rates for the money supply (McClam, 1978). Indeed, it has been suggested that the correlation between successful economies and the adoption of monetary targets may be more than a mere coincidence (Bank for International Settlements, 1975). Clearly the shift of emphasis is broadly based and can be traced to both international factors and those peculiar to the UK.

Firstly, the adoption of monetary targets is seen as a response to the failings of economic policy in the early 1970s. The collapse of the fixed exchange rate system of Bretton Woods, the worsening of the inflation-unemployment trade-off and the failure of interventionist, fine-tuning policies all called for a new approach. That fixed money supply targets could provide the answer was encouraged by the growth of monetarism and the evidence that at least in the long run, the link between the money supply and prices was a close one. A second set of factors followed from the existence of high rates of inflation in the early 1970s. The announcement of monetary targets imparts a discipline into policy such that the control of inflation is seen as the primary goal of policy (Greenwell & Co. 1976a). This discipline should affect all sections of society. The government is forced by a monetary target to adopt a consistent and prudent public expenditure programme and to link general fiscal policy to the monetary target. In the private sector, monetary targets may cause wage bargainers to moderate their claims in the knowledge that above-average wage increases will not simply be accommodated. In an environment of monetary targets such increases may lead to a rise in unemployment in the same sector of the economy as firms are unable due to the shortage and cost of money to pass on the increases to the public in higher prices. Monetary targets, therefore, introduce considerable discipline into the economic behaviour of all sectors. In addition, they will encourage countries that have successfully resisted inflationary trends in the past to continue to do so and encourage the less-successful nations, to improve their inflation performance.

Thirdly, a vital argument for money supply targets is their effect on expectations. Irrespective of any effect such targets have on *actual* inflation, a reduction in inflationary expectations will help governments in their policies, particularly in the gilt-edged market. Linked to this, a fixed money supply target may lead to greater short-term fluctuations in gilt-edged prices (as a given quantity of stock is sold whatever the price). However, if the greater control over the money supply causes both actual and expected inflation to decline, interest rates should fall in the long term and thus gilt-edged prices rise.

Finally, in the case of the UK, the role of the IMF should not be underestimated. The adoption of monetary targets would no doubt have occurred at some time without IMF encouragement, but their role in the watershed of December 1976 was very important. For the UK at least, the conversion to monetary targets had a pragmatic cause to line up alongside the other factors.

The argument for money supply targets must be balanced by the large number of doubts that remain. Some technical problems in the targeting procedure will also be considered in the next section. On the theoretical side, a choice has to be made of the monetary aggregate to be used as the target. The choice for the UK is between M1, sterling M3, M3 and DCE. Targets can be announced for all available aggregates but they may give contradictory signals. This point is taken up in the next section.

Secondly, the long-run link between money and economic activity may have been established (although not yet conclusively in the UK), but the short-run period which is vital for the policy maker does not exhibit such stability. This lack of stability in the short-run link between indicator and goal introduces uncertainty into the operation of monetary targets and may lead to short-term income fluctuations that are both unpredictable and undesirable. The recent instability in money demand in both the USA and UK is just one example of the general problem.

A third problem involves the stability of the link between the policy instruments and the money supply itself. It has been argued that the particular institutional and structural features of the UK economy make the exogeneity of the money supply very doubtful. The Governor of the Bank of England argued in 1976 that:

> The difficulties of adopting such an approach appear particularly great in a country like the United Kingdom, which is a much more open economy than is, for example, the United States, and where we have preferred to have much of the national debt in the form of long term liabilities.

As far as the economy's openness is concerned, the problem is that capital flows particularly of a short-term, speculative nature, by influencing the money supply, will make the attainment of a monetary target very difficult. The difficulty is enhanced by the importance of London as a financial centre. The second difficulty relates to the size of our National Debt relative to national income and the extent to which it is held in long-term assets. Both proportions are higher than is the case for most other countries which places considerable strain on the gilt-edged market. However, as emphasised earlier in this section, money supply control should still be feasible if all attempts to influence rates of interest are abandoned. What may be true is that the costs of money supply control in terms of the degree of interest rate fluctuation may be greater for the UK than for other countries. The issues of the openness and the large National Debt of the UK economy are considered in more detail in Ch. 7, sect. 2.

6 The procedures and technical problems of monetary targets

A discussion of the operation of money supply targets is not complete without an appreciation of the targetting procedures being adopted by the UK authorities and of the technical problems of monitoring such targets. The authorities have announced target ranges for sterling M3 and DCE based on the information available to them at the time, in particular the PSBR, and the future goals of policy. Table 1 summarises these targets in the first four years of their operation; the performance of the economy is shown in brackets below the relevant target figure. Figure 6 shows the path of sterling M3 and the specified target ranges in the first four years of the operation of explicit monetary targets (1976–80).

The following points may be made about the targeting procedures in the UK. From April 1976 to April 1978 fixed period targets were adopted. These involve each target period being completely separate from any other. In April 1978, a rolling target scheme was introduced so that the twelve-month target period from April 1978 to April 1979 was superseded in October 1978 by a new overlapping period to run for twelve months from then (Fig. 6). This is therefore a rolling target scheme where the 'roll-over' period is six months in length compared to the three-month period used, for example, in the USA. The intention is that for the six-month period after October 1978 the authorities should aim to keep the money supply within the target range ending in October 1979 and so on. The major rationale for rolling targets is to stop unexpectedly large fluctuations in monetary growth late in a target period from preventing

Table 1 UK monetary targets and performance

	PSBR (£ b.)	DCE (£ b.)	Δ£ M3%
1976/7 (Apr.)		9.0	9–13[a]
		(4.9)	(7.2)
1977/8 (Apr.)	8.7	7.7	9–13
	(5.6)	(3.8)	(14.4)
1978/9 (Apr.)	8.6	6.0	8–12
	(9.2)	(7.3)	(11.6)
1978/9 (Oct.)			8–12
			(13.4)
1979 (June)–	8.25		7–11[b]
1980 (Apr.)			
1979 (June)–			7–11[b]
1980 (Oct.)			

[a] M3. (Sterling M3 was introduced in late 1976.)
[b] Annualised rates.

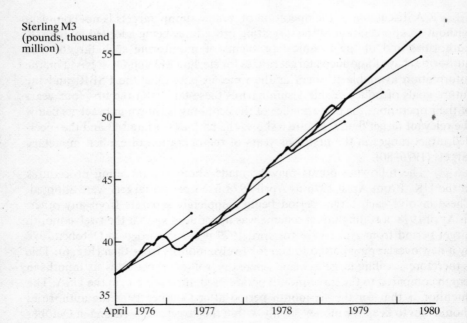

Fig. 6. Sterling M3 money supply target and performance (1976–80).

the attainment of a particular target. This may occur simply because insufficient time is available for correction to occur. The problem is crucially related to data availability and the interpretation of short-term data fluctuations. As argued above, data on monetary aggregates is available in the UK on a monthly basis with a delay of almost a month. In addition, the authorities are unlikely to act immediately if one month's figures are inconsistent with the monetary target. The authorities will wish to wait for two to three months to judge whether any unusual movement in the series is a minor statistical fluctuation or a fundamental change in the growth rate. The delay before action is taken may therefore be as long as four months. Then time will elapse before action on the policy instruments will affect the money supply itself. After all this time, the end of the target period may have been reached and the target missed.

A good example of this occurred in the 1977–8 target period (Fig. 6). Up to the end of 1977, the growth of sterling M3 was consistent with the target range. However, in the final months of the financial year, monetary growth increased rapidly partly caused by funding difficulties as inflation increased and confidence declined. Had the authorities been using rolling targets their aim would have been to iron out these fluctuations and put the money supply on course for the target period ending in October 1978. The main danger of rolling targets is that, in a sense, the end of the target period is never reached. However, the authorities must hope that the introduction of the scheme does not reduce confidence in their resolve to monitor the growth of the money supply.

A point of issue is whether a monetary target should be expressed as a range which is used in the USA and Canada or as a single point as in Germany for example or Switzerland (see Pringle, 1977; McClam, 1978). The UK uses a growth range for the major target variable (sterling M3) although a point is used for the secondary target of DCE. A single figure has the advantage of maximising certainty over the intentions of policy makers. However, it is, by definition, almost impossible to hit a target point. Therefore, the costs of missing it in terms of declining confidence are more likely to be suffered than with a target range. A useful compromise is to establish a target growth figure with permitted deviations around this trend (Poole, 1976). For the UK in 1978–9, for example, the target could be expressed as 10 ± 2 per cent. This may be a sensible compromise which combines the merits of the target point and target range ideas.

Three major technical problems of monetary targets should be discussed. Firstly, a more formal method of linking target periods than is implicit in a rolling targets scheme may be needed. Should the target range be missed, the use of the actual money supply at the end of the previous target period as the base for the new period, effectively builds the error (in the sense that the monetary target is missed) into the new target range. A good example of this was the overshoot of the money supply in 1977–8 that inflated the base for the target period commencing in April 1978 (Fig. 6). For consistency over a series of target periods the base for each successive target should be either the mid-point or at some other suitable point within the previous target range. Such consistency would aid confidence in the resolve of the authorities to fight inflation although it does remove even more flexibility from monetary policy. This may be viewed as an extra cost. It moves the economy further towards the fixed monetary growth rule of the monetarists where discretionary monetary policy is virtually impossible. In addition, discretion to alter the base for a target period may be needed under certain circumstances (e.g., a fall in the demand for money). The authorities in November 1979 in effect adopted a procedure of this type when they extended the 7–11 per cent target range for sterling M3 for another six months (to October 1980) with the base sterling M3 level (June 1979) still applicable.

A second problem is the need for consistency in the announcement of multiple targets. Two cases may be isolated. Firstly, interest rate movements will affect the levels of M1 and M3. As the rate of interest on bank deposits rises, people tend to switch deposits from current to deposit accounts thus reducing M1 relative to M3. If erratic interest rate movements are anticipated, these must be taken into account in the announcement of targets for M1 and M3 to prevent a confusing pattern from emerging (Stone, 1974; Davis, 1977). More relevant to the UK is the possibility that the targets for DCE and sterling M3 may be inconsistent. If the target growth rates of sterling M3 in Table 1 are translated into absolute values for comparison with DCE, they imply a growth in sterling M3 of between £4 and £5 billion per annum. This was considerably below the target growth of DCE in these periods. Therefore, the implicit assumption being made was that the balance of payments would be in deficit causing an outflow of reserves and a decline in sterling M3.[†] However, in 1977–8 due to large inflows of funds into the UK particularly in the early part of the financial year, the balance of payments was, in fact, in surplus. Therefore, while the growth of sterling M3 exceeded the target range (14.4 per cent) DCE at £3.8 b. was well below its target level. Difficulties such as these have virtually forced the authorities to concentrate on sterling M3 alone.[‡]

Finally, a clear procedure is needed on the adjustment time allowed should the monetary aggregate exceed its target in a particular period. Very rapid adjustment may cause severe fluctuations of interest rates which may be undesirable. On the other hand, adjustment should not be delayed for too long to prevent the actual behaviour of the money supply having undesirable effects on the rest of the economy. Davis (1973) has estimated for the USA that substantial deviations from trend must exist for at least six months for there to be a

[†] The exact definition of the external deficit used to move from DCE to sterling M3 is given in Chapter 7. Other minor adjustments are also necessary to move between the two aggregates.

[‡] Atkinson (1977) argues that following the IMF agreement in December 1976, the DCE target combined with an assumption of 5 per cent growth in real income per annum plus the expectation of a balance of payments surplus in 1977–8 forces the conclusion that money supply growth in excess of real growth could be 27 per cent between April 1977 and April 1979. Therefore a double-digit rate of inflation was implicitly being expected. However, a more important point is that the announced DCE and sterling M3 targets were simply inconsistent with an expected external surplus as implied in the text. This episode demonstrates how imperative it is that monetary targets are established in the light of the current forecasts of other relevant macroeconomic variables.

significant impact on national income. The policy of the authorities seems to be that if monetary growth exceeds the target then adjustment should occur quickly; however, if it is below the target, this is considered to be favourable and so a slower adjustment is justified. While such a behaviour pattern is understandable given the concentration in the 1970s on the control of inflation, it is, strictly, an inappropriate procedure. The undershoot of a monetary target should be as important as an overshoot.

7 Monetary targets and monetarism

The conversion of the monetary authorities in the UK and in many other Western countries to monetary targets does not imply that monetarism in its full sense is accepted by these governments. To use the now familiar term, governments are, if anything, 'practical monetarists' in that they have tempered the extreme premises and proposals of monetarism (Volcker, 1977). Certain crucial aspects of monetarist doctrine (see Ch. 5), such as the constant rate of growth of the money supply that is in line with the growth potential of the economy, are far from being implemented. In addition, much fine-tuning of monetary policy, rejected by the monetarists, is still occurring. It may indeed be impracticable for there to be full conversion to monetarism in the real world. The controllability of the money supply may be sufficiently limited in the short run that to observe announced monetary targets without fine-tuning may be impossible.

Chapter 3

Money in the Classical model

1 Introduction

The next three chapters set out the three major models that have dominated the study of modern macroeconomics. The analysis of real factors such as employment, output and real wages is deliberately brief in order to emphasise the role of money. Indeed, the determination of such real variables is discussed only when this is essential to present a full picture of the role of money. Before the Keynesian revolution of the 1930s that altered the whole fabric of macroeconomics, the Classical approach to economic theory and policy represented the orthodox view. Although no Classical model, as such, existed at that time, the ideas of these economists have typically been set out as a model in modern textbooks. This approach will also be followed here. According to the Classical school, the role of money in a macroeconomic model was clear. It was seen as 'a veil behind which the action of real forces is concealed' (Pigou, 1949, p. 18). Real magnitudes in an economic system were determined by real factors such as expenditure, income and the relative demands and supplies of commodities and assets. Money determined the absolute level of final goods prices in the economy alone, and had no role in the determination of relative prices. Despite this apparently subordinate role for money, the control of the amount of money in an economy was seen to be important due to its influence on the rate of change of the price level. In its extreme form, a proportional relationship between the money supply and absolute prices was postulated and in any version of the Classical model, the role of money in determining the price level was paramount. Economic policy was therefore dictated by the need to control the money supply in order to achieve the desired rate of price change. This hypothesis has become known as the Quantity Theory of Money.

These basic premises of the Classical theory had had a long history; in a variety of forms by the 1930s. Jean Bodin, the French economist is credited with an early form of the quantity theory of money, dating as far back as 1568, while David Hume in a still relevant early contribution to the development of this idea stated:

If we consider any one kingdom by itself, 'tis evident, that the greater or less plenty of money is of no consequence: since the prices of commodities are always proportion'd to the plenty of money. (Hume, 1741, p.33).

In addition, Hume argued that money is 'the oil which renders the motion of the wheels more smooth and easy' (Hume, 1741, p.33) and by doing so accepted the psychological impact of monetary growth on industry, commerce and the general expectations held by all economic agents. In addition, he observed the difference between a long-run increase in the money supply which would lead to a proportionate rise in prices and the short-run effects over the time period during which the adjustment to the increased money supply occurs:

> There is always an interval before matters be adjusted to the new position: and this interval is as pernicious to industry, when gold and silver are diminishing, as it is advantageous, when these metals are increasing. (Hume, 1741, p.40).

In the short-run disequilibrium situation, an increase in the money supply acts as a lubricant to industry and commerce and only in the long run, as will be seen in more detail later, does the proportionality result follow.

Other statements of the quantity theory were made by among others Ricardo, Jevons and Wicksell until its structure became formalised in the early twentieth century primarily in the work of Fisher, Marshall and Pigou. This chapter in setting out the monetary sector of the Classical model draws on the historical contributions of many of the precursors of the quantity theory as we know it today.

2 The real sector in the Classical model

Only a brief summary of the real sector is given here. (For a full model, see Shapiro (1978) Ch. 14; Westaway and Weyman-Jones (1977) Ch. 10.) To attain full employment in a monetary economy, expenditure must equal income for all units, or, alternatively, withdrawals equal injections. In the closed economy model with no government sector used by the Classical economists, this condition reduces to an equilibrium between the income not spent by households (savings) and the new investment by firms:

$$S = I \qquad\qquad [1]$$

where S, I represent savings and investment respectively.

The assumption introduced in the previous paragraph that all income not spent is saved implies that money is not held in the form of idle balances – there is no hoarding. The idea that money is demanded for transactions purposes alone is a famous assumption of the Classical model. However, even if some money were hoarded such that expenditure fell short of income, and excess commodity and asset supplies built up, price flexibility would ensure that, in the long run, supply equalled demand.

The Classical model can be segmented into individual markets for labour, goods and money. Each involves a built-in equilibrating mechanism to ensure that full employment is the natural equilibrium position of the whole economy.

The labour market is based on the neo-classical theory of factor pricing. This assumes that firms are profit maximisers and are buying labour in a perfectly competitive factor market, with each factor paid the value of its marginal product,

$$W = MP_N \cdot P \tag{2}$$

and therefore

$$W/P = MP_N \tag{3}$$

where W, P and MP_N represent the wage rate, the price level and the marginal product of labour respectively.

Therefore, assuming all other factors are fixed, the demand for labour (N_D) function is given by:

$$N_D = N_D(W/P) \tag{4}$$

with

$$N_D'(\ ) < 0 \tag{5}$$

reflecting the diminishing marginal product of labour as the amount of labour employed increases.[†] On the supply side, it is assumed that:

$$N_S = N_S(W/P) \tag{6}$$

with

$$N_S'(\ ) > 0 \tag{7}$$

which abstracts from the possibility that at higher levels of the real wage, the supply of labour falls with the function becoming backward-bending. The equilibrium condition is:

$$N_D = N_S \tag{8}$$

and the whole market situation is shown in Fig. 1.

The equilibrium is a stable one and with flexibility of real wages assumed, full employment is the long-run equilibrium state.

The transformation of equilibrium labour supply $(\bar{N})$ into output (y) is made by a neo-classical production function:

$$y = y(N, \bar{K}) \tag{9}$$

with

$$y'(\ ) > 0 \tag{10}$$

and

$$y''(\ ) < 0 \tag{11}$$

[†] Note that an area of increasing marginal product of labour is included in Figs. 1 and 2 but not, for simplicity, in eqs. [5] and [11]. Strictly, $N_D'(\ ) > 0$ and $y''(\ ) > 0$ for all labour employed up to N_1 in the two Figures.

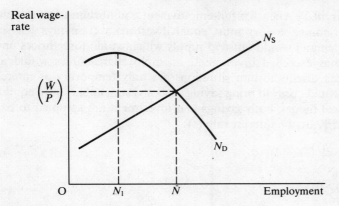

Fig. 1. The Classical labour market.

This assumes that for a given level of the fixed factor $\bar{K}$, output increases as the employment of labour rises, but after N_1 output rises at a decreasing rate, i.e., there are diminishing returns to labour. Combining the production function and the labour market in Fig. 2 output or real income is determined corresponding to full employment of labour.

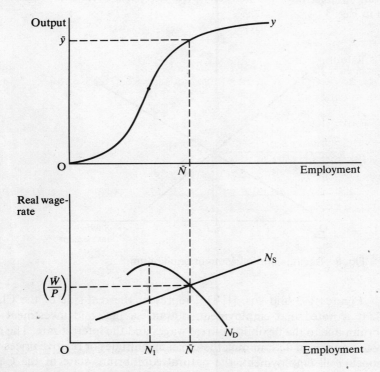

Fig. 2. The Classical output sector.

As argued earlier, for full-employment equilibrium to be attained in a monetary economy, savings must equal investment. If savings fell short of investment, demand would outstrip supply which would force prices upwards, while if savings exceeded investment, unemployed resources would appear. However, such disequilibrium situations are only temporary as interest rate movements would occur to bring savings and investment back into equilibrium. In the Classical model, both savings and investment are assumed to be determined primarily by the interest rate (r):

$$S = S(r) \qquad\qquad [12]$$

with

$$S'(r) > 0 \qquad\qquad [13]$$

and

$$I = I(r) \qquad\qquad [14]$$

with

$$I'(r) < 0 \qquad\qquad [15]$$

Combining [13] and [15] the equilibrium condition is

$$S(r) = I(r) \qquad\qquad [1]$$

Assuming interest rates are perfectly flexible [1] will hold. This equilibrium is shown in Fig. 3.

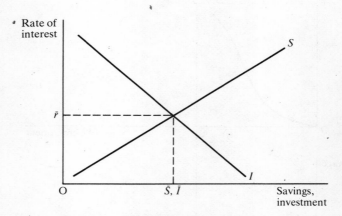

Fig. 3. Savings and investment equilibrium.

Figures 1–3 and eqs. [1]–[15] represent the real side of the Classical model. It is noted that employment, output, savings and investment are in equilibrium due to the flexibility of real wages and the interest rate. The money supply has no role in determining these real magnitudes or relative prices within the model. Full employment, the natural equilibrium state of the Classical model, is ensured by the flexibility of W/P and r.

3 The monetary sector in the Classical model

The role of money in the Classical model is not then to determine relative prices or real magnitudes. Money is a 'veil' (Pigou, 1949), although, as suggested earlier, it also helps to oil the economic machine and by doing so fulfils another useful function. It would, however, be contradictory to leave the role of money in these vague terms and in this section it is explored in depth within the framework of the Classical model.

The monetary sector revolves around the famous quantity theory equation,

$$MV_T = PT \tag{16}$$

with M, V_T, P, T representing the money supply, transactions velocity of circulation, the price level and the level of real transactions respectively. This equation is credited to Irving Fisher (1911) and represents the transactions version of the quantity theory equation. (The alternative Cambridge version is set out later in this chapter.) It is in fact an identity. In other words, the amount of money in an economy (M) multiplied by the average number of times that money rotates around the system in a given time period (V_T) must by definition equal the money value of transactions (PT). These are, in fact, two ways of saying the same thing. Clearly, whether one accepts the validity of the Classical model or not, [16] is incontrovertible. Some definitional points arise from [16]. The money supply is usually defined in narrow terms in the Classical model as the amount of currency (notes and coins) in the economy plus the value of demand deposits (or current accounts) at certain specified banks. The choice of M will clearly affect the size of the velocity of circulation. For a given value of transactions (PT), the broader the definition of M used, the slower on average will that money revolve around the economy and the lower will be the velocity of circulation. On the other hand, the narrower the definition of M, the larger will be the value of V_T. The price level definition (P) in use must also be appropriate to the definition of transactions (T).

In order to convert the quantity theory identity into an economically meaningful hypothesis, the Classical economists made certain assumptions concerning the variables in the equation.

Money is only demanded for transactions purposes

The Classical economists, accepting money as a veil with no particular value except its command over real goods and services, assumed that money was only held for transactions purposes or in effect as a medium of exchange. The idea of money being hoarded or held in idle balances was introduced with the Keynesian revolution. The hypothesis on the demand for money in the quantity theory was therefore solely based on transactions demand. Money was held because the timepaths of income and expenditure were not synchronous with the typical situation being one with income received only once at the start of the payment period and expenditure fairly evenly spread over the same period. For example, let the payment period be one week with an income of £70 received at the beginning of the week. Clearly the average size of cash balances held by the individual will depend on a variety of factors. To analyse these factors, let us assume for convenience that the expenditure pattern of the individual is regular with £10 being spent on each day of the week. Figure 4a, b depicts the cash (stock) and expenditure (flow) pattern over a typical week. Average money holding $\bar{C}_W$ is equal to $M/2$ or, in this case, £35. This is shown as a horizontal line in Fig. 5 (strictly this assumes that expenditure is equally spread

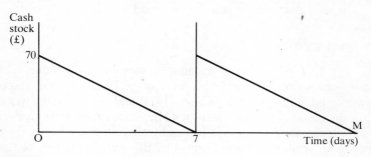

Fig. 4a.

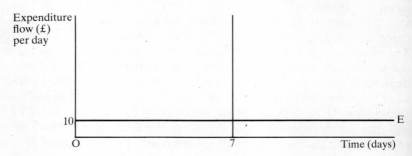

Fig. 4b.

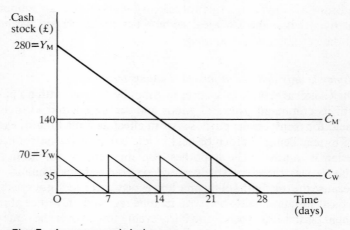

Fig. 5. Average cash balances.

across each day as well as across the week as a whole).
In this simple model, money holding depends on:

(i) *The level of transactions*. This is to be completed in the week which in
the absence of saving or hoarding will be equal to the level of income. If the
level of income is doubled, average money balances will double. This is the
central Classical result that all money is held for transactions purposes and that
the level of transactions or income is the prime determinant of the demand
(or need) to hold money.

(ii) *The length of the payment period*. If the individual – while continuing
to be paid the equivalent of £70 per week – is now paid monthly (or four weekly
for convenience), his income received at the start of the payment period is now
£280 (Y_M) and assuming his expenditure is regular, his average cash balance
($\bar{C}_M$) rises to £140. Note that this is easily calculated from the size of the cash
balance held halfway through the payment period.

(iii) *Expenditure pattern*. The regular expenditure pattern assumed so far
(C_1E_1 in Fig. 6a, b) may be too extreme an assumption. Any other pattern can
be introduced and will have an effect on the average cash balance according to
how the expenditure is distributed over the week. The more bunching there is
towards the beginning of the week (C_2E_2) the lower will be the average cash

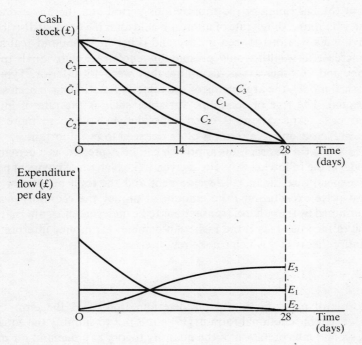

Fig. 6.

balance and the more towards the end (C_3E_3) the higher will be the cash balance. C_2E_2 seems the most likely case in the real world.

(iv) *Other factors.* Numerous other factors will affect the need to hold money to finance a given volume of transactions. For example, the more sophisticated is an economy in a financial sense (the use of credit cards, the ability to transfer money by telegraph, the scale of hire-purchase credit), the smaller the amount of conventional money needed to complete a certain volume of business. Such institutional determinants of money holding have tended to dominate Classical theory (to say that such factors determine the demand of money is equivalent to stating that the same arguments are included in the determination of transactions velocity). However, certain behavioural determinants of money demand or velocity were included both in the traditional transactions velocity version of the quantity theory (eq. [16]) and the Cambridge cash-balance approach, considered later in eq. [20]. These economic factors are usually associated with the cash-balance approach, but were also explicit in Fisher's transactions version. He suggested that:

the rate of interest on money and alternative assets, the expected rates of inflation, the wealth of society and asset preferences between liquid and non-liquid assets

would all be important determinants of velocity. For example, the expectation of a higher rate of inflation would cause a rational individual to concentrate his purchases at the beginning of the transactions period and thereby economise on his money holding. A high rate of interest would alter the optimal distribution of an individual's wealth between money and other financial and real assets, while an increase in wealth would presumably encourage individuals to hold more money and all other assets, assuming they were not inferior. Typically, in the Classical model, the arguments of the velocity function have been said to be institutional. The role of economic variables such as the rate of interest, wealth and price expectations is often concealed behind these more static technological factors and as a result is often not seen to be important.

The Classical transactions approach can be expressed as a demand for money model in the following way. For a given V (i.e., length of payment period, pattern of expenditure, financial development and the level of interest rates, wealth, and price expectations) the amount of money the economy *needs* to hold is determined by the value of transactions to be undertaken, or alternatively, by the level of income. This is the Fisherian demand for money interpretation of the quantity theory [16] which can be rewritten as:

$$M = \frac{1}{V_T} PT \qquad\qquad [17]$$

Given the role of many factors in the determination of V, the term should strictly be written in functional form in [17] but is not to simplify the equation.

A second interpretation of the quantity theory as a demand for money model is the Cambridge cash-balance approach. While the Fisher version concentrated on the determinants of transactions velocity (V_T) and so on the *need* to hold money, the Cambridge view of, in particular, Pigou (1917) and Marshall (1924), posed a different question. On a micro level they asked what determines the amount of money people wish to hold? In this approach the quantity theory equation is modified to:

$$MV_y = Py \qquad [18]$$

and

$$M = K_y Py \qquad [19]$$

with

$$K_y = \frac{1}{V_y} \qquad [20]$$

Equation [19] therefore states that the demand for money is a proportion (K_y) of the nominal level of income. Clearly transactions velocity (V_T) is only equal to the income velocity of money (V_y) to the extent that $T = y$. But V_T and V_y will be functionally related even if $T \neq y$. From [17]

$$M = \frac{PT}{V_T} \qquad [21]$$

equating [19] and [21] and solving gives:

$$V_T = \frac{1}{K_y}\left(\frac{T}{y}\right) \qquad [22]$$

Making the assumption that T and y are stably related, the transactions velocity (V_T) is proportional to the inverse of the income velocity ($1/K_y$).

The major feature of the Cambridge cash-balance approach is that it introduces the concept of money being desired. It asks the question 'how much money do people wish to hold?' not 'have to hold' as does the transactions approach. As a result, this version places more emphasis on the behavioural economic variables than does the transactions approach, although, as stated earlier, the latter also includes these variables. In the Cambridge version, an individual's wealth, the attractiveness of other assets as measured by the rate of interest on bonds, and the expectation of a capital gain or loss as measured by one's view of future price movements dominate the demand for money function to the exclusion of the technological and institutional factors of the earlier approach. By introducing an opportunity-cost element into money demand theory, the approach moves decisively towards the *general* theory of the allocation of wealth among competing assets, of which money is one. In doing so, the cash-balance approach is centred at the microeconomic level of the individual while the transactions version employing the broader institutional arguments is a theory at the macroeconomic level.

Strictly, therefore [19] can be rewritten with K in functional form:

$$M = K_y(WE, r_i, \dot{P}^e)Py \qquad [23]$$

with WE, r_i and $\dot{P}^e$ representing wealth, the rate of interest on alternative assets, and the expected rate of price inflation, respectively.

Stable velocity function

Traditionally, quantity theorists are criticised for making the simplistic assumption that velocity (either V_T or $1/K_y$) is a constant. The discussion in (a) suggests that while this variable should not be highly unstable, it will not be rigidly constant either. The true Classical assumption is that the velocity function, however defined and whatever its arguments, will be stable such that a change in the money supply, for example, will not be significantly reduced or augmented in force by a rapid change in velocity. The explanation of this is in the type of arguments in the velocity function. Many of the variables are institutional and so will only change slowly over a long time period. While the economic determinants of velocity may change in the short run, the stability of velocity is justified by the dominant role played by institutional arguments. In disequilibrium, however, velocity may change. For example, a rise in the money balances of an individual may not be immediately used for transactions. Short-term hoarding will lead to a fall in velocity but once expenditure is undertaken and macroeconomic equilibrium regained, velocity will return to its former level. Therefore, in equilibrium, velocity is stable.

Full employment

The flexibility of relative prices and interest rates in the Classical model ensures that the natural equilibrium state is one of full employment (Fig. 2). From this result, the assumption is therefore made that the volume of transactions (T) in [16] (or alternatively y in [19]) will be fixed. Constancy of T or y reflects the full-employment level of real income or output. As with velocity, short-term variations in T or y, as the economy moves to a new equilibrium position, are not ruled out but in equilibrium T and y regain their former levels. Long-run growth of the economy (an increase in T or y) is possible but the static Classical model abstracts from this and assumes constant T or y in equilibrium.

The money supply as the independent variable

A final assumption in the monetary sector of the Classical model is that the price level (P) will not change without a prior change in the money supply (M). The money supply, which is assumed to be exogenously determined, is seen as the independent variable which, in the long term, determines the movement of prices in the model. This is not to suggest that prices will never change independently of a change in the money supply but it is argued that in the long term the price level adjusts to the value of the money supply.

Combining all these assumptions, eqs [16] and [19] can be written as

$$M\bar{V}_T = P\bar{T} \qquad\qquad [16a]$$
$$M = \bar{K}_y P\bar{y} \qquad\qquad [19a]$$

with a bar over the top of a variable depicting that variable as having a constant value. Clearly with V_T, T and K_y, y fixed any change in the money supply will lead to an equal proportionate change in the absolute price level

$$M = P\left(\frac{\bar{T}}{\bar{V}_T}\right) \qquad\qquad\qquad\qquad [16b]$$

$$M = P(\bar{K}_y \cdot \bar{y}) \qquad\qquad\qquad\qquad [19b]$$

This is the role of money in the Classical model, then. It determines the absolute level of prices without influencing the level of output or income. The monetary sector can be summarised in the following diagram:

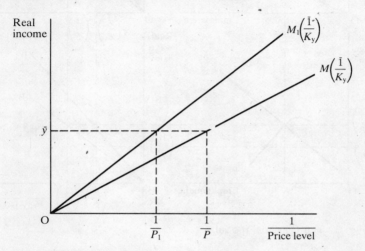

Fig. 7. The monetary sector.

Real output (y) is measured on the vertical axis and the inverse of the price level ($1/P$) on the horizontal axis with the slope of the function representing $M \cdot (1/K_y)$. Therefore, for given $\bar{y}$ the product $M.(\bar{1}/K_y)$ determines the price level ($\bar{1}/P$). It can be seen that a rise in the money supply is represented by a steepening of the function and therefore for given y, causes the price level to increase ($1/P_1$).

The full Classical model can now be presented combining Figs 2 and 7 and introducing a fourth quadrant which determines the money wage rate (W).

The role of money in this model is confirmed by a simple example. Let the money supply rise to $M_1(\bar{1}/K_y)$. Nothing has happened within the labour market to cause any movement from equilibrium there and the effect of the higher money supply is to reduce the inverse of the price level to $1/P_1$ (at $\bar{y}$) and therefore increase the price level. This has, however, reduced real wages W/P, and as this would lead to excess demand for labour, the money wage rises to W_1 to bring real wages back to equilibrium at $\bar{W}/P$. This example confirms that, in the new long-run equilibrium, only the absolute price level and the money wage rate have risen in response to the monetary expansion. More specifically, the real variables in the model – including the real wage – are unaffected. Monetary forces therefore determine absolute prices or nominal magnitudes

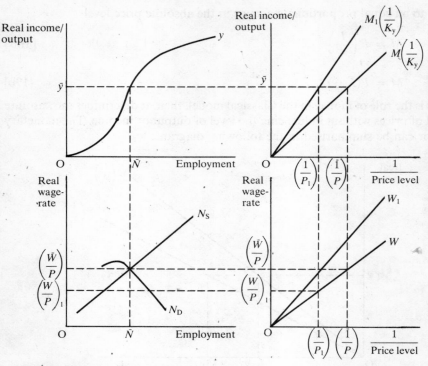

Fig. 8. The Classical model.

(e.g., money output – Py) alone and do not affect real variables (e.g., real output – y).

4 The transmission mechanism of money and the Classical dichotomy

If V_T and T or K_y and y are constant as the extreme version of the Classical model [16b, 19b] states, the proportionality result will follow whereby a 10 per cent rise in the money supply, for example, will lead to a 10 per cent rise in absolute prices. Even without the strict constancy of V_T and T their presumed stability ensures a close link between the level of monetary growth and price inflation. The more interesting discussion which this section considers is *how* or *through what channels* increased monetary growth affects prices. The debate, within any type of economic model, over how a change in the money supply affects other variables of the model involves a discussion of the transmission mechanism of money. Therefore, in what follows the transmission mechanism will refer to how a change in the money supply is channelled through a particular model to influence real and nominal variables.

Traditionally, and unfortunately in error, 'the usual caricature of the quantity theory . . . is that the theory is based on a direct and mechanical link between money and prices. If the money supply rises by ten per cent, then prices must rise by ten per cent, no more and no less; and the process by which an increased money supply leads to higher prices is presented as if it were an engineering relationship . .' (Griffiths, 1976, p. 36). Quite apart from the earlier argument that such an 'engineering relationship' must rely on the strict constancy of V_T and T which is far too simple an interpretation of Classical theory, this direct link between money and prices masks the actual mechanism through which the monetary impulse operates. This direct link is usually justified in the following way. From a position of long-run equilibrium with the supply of money equalling the demand for money, let the money supply rise. In the new situation, actual real balances M/P held by individuals exceed their desired level – the position maintained before equilibrium was disturbed. Individuals react to this excess holding of money balances by attempting to run them down by purchasing goods, consumer durables and financial assets. However, someone must hold the increased money balances and so it is not possible for everyone, simultaneously, to spend their excess holdings. In addition, output is fixed in the short run and the attempt to purchase more goods, durables and assets in aggregate cannot succeed. As a result, prices rise until the new higher level of nominal balances is equivalent to the equilibrium level of real balances again. Once prices have risen sufficiently so that desired and actual real balances are equal, the process is ended and equilibrium restored. Prices have risen by the same proportion as the money supply.

This direct mechanism is a crucial part of Classical theory, having been postulated by Hume and Cantillon, amongst others. However, an 'indirect' mechanism whereby money affects the price level through interest rates was suggested by Henry Thornton (1802) and later used by Wicksell (1935). Thornton argues that while the direct mechanism is appropriate for a simple commodity money, a more sophisticated system in which commercial banks exist introduces the rate of interest as a key part of the transmission mechanism.

The 'indirect' mechanism to be described is dependent on the divergence between the natural and the market (or actual) rate of interest (Makinen, 1977). The natural rate of interest is defined in terms of our model as the rate at which savings equal investment (i.e., full-employment equilibrium). Figure 9 explains this mechanism. The demand and supply for bank loans are expressed in real terms.

Assume that the banking system represented in Fig. 9 is in equilibrium $(D_0 S_0)$ at r_N. This equilibrium is then disturbed by an open market purchase of government debt by the authorities leading to an increase in the reserves of the banks. Bond prices will rise and the interest rate on them fall. Assuming there exists excess demand for credit, these surplus reserves will be lent out (S_1) so that bank loan rates fall. The divergence between the market and the natural rates of interest encourages firms to invest in new capital assets and, because their price has fallen relative to government debt, in consumer durables too. With output unresponsive to this increased demand, the rise in MV_T forces the price level upwards. This rise in prices leads to a reduction in the supply of loans in real terms causing the interest rate to return to its natural level and

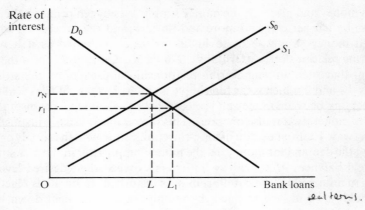

Fig. 9.

the money supply to stop growing. The proportionality result between money and prices is ensured in the long run.

Therefore, a divergence between the natural and market rates of interest is symptomatic of an excess supply of money which is eventually removed by a proportionate rise in the price level, increasing the demand for money and restoring full equilibrium. An area of concern with this transmission mechanism is not its logical validity, but its relation to the remainder of the Classical model. The model as set out in this and the previous section assumes that the rate of interest is uniquely determined by the levels of savings and investment with the money supply playing no role at all. However, in this mechanism, the money supply has a role in the determination of the market rate of interest and thus the divergence between it and the natural rate. There is no real conflict though as money's role is a disequilibrium one in the determination of the rate of interest, as the rise in the money supply, by causing a decline in the interest rate, calls forth new investment to return the rate to its equilibrium level. However, these alternative transmission mechanisms do present problems for the IS/LM model in section 5 below.

A crucial issue in the role of money is the time lag between the disturbance of equilibrium and the full adjustment of the price level such that equilibrium is restored. The assumption that the constancy of k_y and y is accepted is only made for long-run equilibrium. Nowhere in Classical writings is it postulated that K_y and y will in fact be invariant in the short run. Clearly, if an increased money supply does not lead instantaneously to a proportionate rise in prices some short-run variability in either or both of velocity and output must occur while the natural and market rates of interest will diverge. It is, in fact, only in this intermediate period before full adjustment that 'the increasing quantity of gold and silver is favourable to industry' (Hume, 1741, p.38). The demand for labour and therefore output may be expected to rise in the short run and as money wages adjust so the supply of labour will rise and as argued earlier the larger money balances held by individuals may not be fully reflected in higher transactions immediately they are received. However, prices eventually catch up, real wages fall back to their equilibrium level and output resumes its path dependent on the long-run growth rate of the economy. All excess money balances are worked off and the stability of K_y restored. In the short run before prices adjust in the proportion that the money supply has risen, money is said to be non-neutral. It affects real variables such as output, employment and relative prices, while only in the long run, when equilibrium has been restored is money said to be neutral. The neutrality of money – a central result of the Classical model – relies on the long-run constancy of K_y and y and states that monetary growth is neutral in its effects on real magnitudes and only influences nominal magnitudes.

This result has become known as the Classical dichotomy. The economy is dichotomised into two sectors – a real sector in which output, employment and all real magnitudes are determined and in which money has only a temporary role and a monetary sector which determines all nominal magnitudes and absolute prices. The two sectors are completely separable in the long run. It was this result that led money to be termed a veil, or to be neutral in its real impact. But it is instructive to ask on what the Classical dichotomy or, in other words, the neutrality of money depends.

As already stated, neutrality is ensured in the long run if V_T and T are constant. But what does this involve? Firstly, wages and prices must be completely flexible. This ensures that a monetary change results in a change in absolute prices and not real variables, so that W/P resumes its equilibrium value after the monetary disturbance has been worked off. Clearly this assumption is unlikely to be valid in practice with downward rigidities of W and P a typical Keynesian criticism of this Classical condition. Secondly, there must be no money illusion. This involves individuals in the economic system responding to real and not monetary variables so that if money income (Py) rises but real income (y) does not, due to a rise in prices (P), real spending will be unchanged even though money income has risen. If money illusion exists, a monetary expansion could lead the recipients of higher income to raise their spending in real terms even though real income has not risen. If this occurred, neutrality would not follow as prices would rise by a greater proportion than the money supply has increased. Thirdly, there must be no 'distribution effects' in the economy. Any price-level movement following a monetary change will alter the relative wealth positions of debtors and creditors. (The real value of debts and therefore credits is assumed to be fixed during the adjustment period.) The absence of distribution effects implies that the result of these shifts in wealth distribution is not an overall change in expenditure. Finally, expectations must be held about the future level of prices that do not lead individuals to convert money into real assets (in the expectation of future price rises) to a larger extent that the rise in the money supply warrants, or increase their money holdings (if prices are expected to fall) to a lesser extent than is warranted by the rate of monetary growth. More simply this means that a monetary expansion which causes prices to rise must not establish expectations of new price changes which will cause individuals to either cumulate or decumulate money balances and therefore induce further price changes and by doing so, destroy the neutrality of money.

These assumptions are highly restrictive. They are implicit in the Classical model, but are unlikely to hold in practice. To the extent that the conditions for neutrality did not hold, a monetary change would cause changes in either or both of K_y and y as well as P. If all the above conditions held and the proportionality result was achieved the link between money and prices can be expressed as a rectangular hyperbola as in Fig. 10.

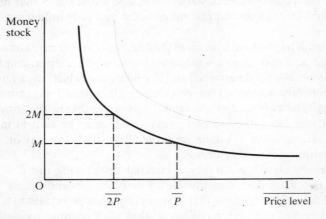

Fig. 10. The neutrality of money.

Such a hyperbola ensures that the area under the curve is the same at any of the infinite number of points on the curve, i.e.,

$$M \cdot \frac{1}{P} = \frac{y}{K_y} \qquad [24]$$

at any point on the curve. If the money supply is doubled, neutrality ensures that the price level also doubles:

$$2M \cdot \frac{1}{2P} = \frac{y}{K_y}$$

A long-run increase in real income (y) and decrease in velocity ($\downarrow V_y; \uparrow K_y$) would shift the function to the right with a leftward shift following a fall in real income and a rise in velocity.

While the conditions for the Classical dichotomy are unlikely to hold in practice, the dichotomy itself has been the subject of vigorous theoretical debate. (For a fuller summary than can be given here, see Rousseas (1972) Chs. 4 and 5, and Johnson (1971a) Chs. 14 and 15.) The starting point of the debate was the discovery in the late 1940s and early 1950s by Lange (1942) of a basic inconsistency in Classical monetary theory. As argued in Chapter 1, with money as the nth good, equilibrium in the $n-1$ goods markets will ensure equilibrium in the money market also. Therefore, for full equilibrium, the relative prices determining the supply and demand for commodities alone need be known. The money market may be ignored.)

As a result, if the demand and supply functions of commodities depend only on relative prices, how can an increase in the supply of money (a nominal and not a real change) lead to an increase in the demand for commodities and therefore the rise in prices necessary to achieve the neutrality of money? The dichotomy of the real and monetary sectors, it is argued, leads to an inconsistency in Classical theory, such that monetary and value theory need to be integrated. An attempt to resolve this problem was made by Patinkin (1956) by the inclusion of the value of real balances as an argument in the demand function for each good i

$$D_i = f\left(\frac{P_1}{P_1} \cdots \cdots \frac{P_i}{P_1} \cdots \cdots \frac{P_n}{P_1}, \frac{M}{P_1}\right) \qquad [25]$$

where P_1 represents the price of commodity 1, the numeraire. If the money supply rises therefore, even though relative prices are unchanged, all nominal commodity demands will rise which forces up prices until the level of real balances returns to equilibrium and commodity demands return to their previous real levels. The Classical dichotomy is disposed of, and the proportionality result preserved, by introducing the real balance effect.

This reconciliation of the Classical dichotomy was criticised on two main grounds. Firstly, what is the true role of the real-balance effect? Archibald and Lipsey (1958) argued that the real-balance effect is merely a transient phenomenon which is irrelevant in long-run equilibrium. Only in the adjustment period between the disturbance of the old equilibrium and the establishment of the new one do real balances affect the demand for goods and services. In long-run equilibrium, the effect is irrelevant, and as the Classical model is essentially an equilibrium system which is conventionally analysed in comparative static terms, it is argued by Archibald and Lipsey, that the real-balance effects adds little to the model. Alone it ensures the stability of the price level without playing any role in the determination of a new equilibrium position.

Secondly, the empirical significance of the real-balance effect has also come under challenge. To state that the demand for goods depends on the real balances held by an individual, such that an equi-proportionate rise in the money stock and prices leaves real demand unchanged, implies the absence of money illusion. As argued in the last section this is unlikely in practice.

However, of more importance is whether an increase in the money supply will actually increase net wealth and therefore generate a real balance effect. The traditional distinction drawn in this debate is between inside and outside money. Inside money is money created against private debt such that the stock of inside money is an asset to those who hold it and a debt to those who issue it. On the other hand, outside money is either not a debt to those who issue it or alternatively causes any debt that is incurred to be ignored. Therefore, for net wealth to rise, the stock of outside money must increase; should all the money supply increase be of the 'inside' money variety, the increase in wealth of those who hold the money will be cancelled out by the increase in debt of those who issue it, leaving net wealth unchanged such that the real-balance effect does not operate. However, recent work has blurred the distinction between inside and outside money such that non interest-bearing inside money may be part of net wealth and interest-bearing outside money may not be. A full analysis of the conditions under which all wealth effects operate is left until Ch. 4, sect. 6.

However, this issue of the validity of the real-balance effect and the overall consistency of Classical monetary theory is crucially dependent on the type of transmission mechanism of money postulated. If the direct and real-balance effect alone exists all the above arguments are valid. However, if an indirect mechanism is accepted, then the real and monetary sectors of the Classical model are linked by the role of money in influencing the market rate of interest. This role, although only a disequilibrium one, reduces the importance of the debate on the real-balance effect. The proportionality result may follow from the indirect mechanism even if the theoretical and empirical problems prevent the real-balance effect from achieving it. The fact that Classical theory can embrace both transmission mechanisms does not infringe the Classical dichotomy (in long-run equilibrium) but does diminish the role of the pure real-balance effect.

5 Monetary and fiscal policy in the Classical model

In this section, an analysis of the effects of monetary and fiscal policy in the Classical model will be made. In order to isolate the effects of fiscal policy from those of monetary policy, it is assumed that any increase in government spending (ΔG) if not matched by tax receipts (ΔT) will be financed by sales of government debt. The results of the shift in the IS curve due to the expansionary fiscal policy will therefore not be confused by a shift in the LM curve as would happen if the fiscal policy were financed by a rise in the money supply. (See Chick (1973) pp.55–7, for a short analysis of some of the links between monetary and fiscal policy.)[†]

The analysis is to be made in the framework of the static IS/LM model (see, for example, Westaway and Weyman-Jones (1977) Ch. 11). All variables are defined in real terms. In the Classical model, the IS curve is represented by the following equations:

$$S = a_0 + a_1 r \qquad [26]$$
$$I = b_0 + b_1 r \qquad [27]$$

with

$$a_0, a_1, b_0 > 0, \ b_1 < 0$$

[†] The possibility that an increase in the volume of bonds may lead to a change in the demand for money (which would cause a shift in the LM curve) is ignored. The same assumption is implicitly made in Chapters 4 and 5.

and

$$S = I \qquad\qquad [1]$$

Equations [26], [27] are more explicit forms of [12] and [14] respectively. Substituting into [1] and simplifying:

$$r = \frac{b_0 - a_0}{a_1 - b_1} \qquad\qquad [28]$$

This extreme form of the Classical model, therefore, involves a fixed value for r as given by the parameters in [28] and a horizontal IS curve in Fig. 11. This implies that at the equilibrium rate of interest, savings and investment will be equal for any level of real income.

The LM curve is represented by the following equations:

$$M_S = \bar{M} \qquad\qquad [29]$$

$$M_D = K_y Py \qquad\qquad [19]$$

$$M_S = M_D \qquad\qquad [30]$$

using the Cambridge cash-balance version with M_D representing the demand for money. Substituting into [30]:

$$\bar{M} = K_y Py \qquad\qquad [31]$$

in equilibrium. This formulation, with interest rates having no role in the monetary sector equations, is consistent with the idea of money only being held for transactions purposes and results in a vertical LM curve. Any increase in the money supply therefore leads to an increase in Py – or in full-employment equilibrium P. This is consistent with the direct transmission mechanism of M on P mentioned earlier in this chapter.

In this extreme version of the Classical model, the interest rate ($\bar{r}$) is determined in the real sector and the level of income ($\bar{y}$) is determined by the

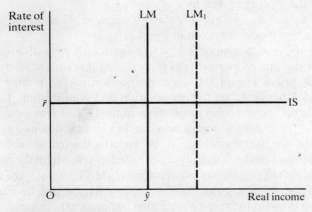

Fig. 11. The extreme Classical model.

full-employment assumption. Tracing the effects of a disturbance to this equilibrium in Fig. 11 presents a severe problem as the IS and LM functions are equilibrium relationships. Therefore, as real income is fixed in equilibrium, it may be more appropriate to depict the IS relationship as one point at $(\bar{r}, \bar{y})$ and not a horizontal line. An increase in the money supply is usually represented as an outward shift in the LM function (e.g., LM_1). However, this is not an equilibrium state as money supply exceeds money demand. The rise in prices that results will reduce the real value of the money supply and return the LM function to its original position and equilibrium will be restored. To represent the IS relationship as a point is strictly correct and will prevent the possible error of assuming that any income level other than $\bar{y}$ is equilibrium.

With the interest rate unchanged throughout the transmission mechanism, Fig. 11 depicts the direct mechanism. The indirect mechanism can be included in this model in one of two ways. Firstly, by treating IS and LM as strictly equilibrium relationships, the disturbance that causes the interest rate to move need not be included on the diagram as the equilibrium interest rate does not change. Secondly, a more general model can be postulated which makes use of a downward sloping IS function. (Chick (1973) calls this the 'money only' model as opposed to the 'extreme Classical' model with a horizontal IS curve.) Let the savings function be modified to include an income variable:

$$S = a_0 + a_1 r + a_2 y \qquad [32]$$

$$I = b_0 + b_1 r \qquad [27]$$

$$S = I \qquad [1]$$

with $a_2 > 0$.

Substituting into [1]:

$$r = \frac{b_0 - a_0}{a_1 - b_1} - \frac{a_2}{a_1 - b_1} y \qquad [33]$$

with the slope of the IS curve given by $-a_2/(a_1 - b_1)$.

As both a_2 and $a_1 - b_1 > 0$, this slope is negative. Combining with the vertical LM curve this model is set out in Fig. 12:

A rise in the money supply (LM_1) will again only be a disequilibrium state. In this case the rate of interest falls (r_1) causing investment to rise. With real output fixed, prices rise in the same proportion as the money supply, returning the LM function to its former position and equilibrium. Therefore to include the indirect transmission mechanism in the IS/LM framework either the assumptions of the IS function must be altered to make it downward sloping or analysis within the framework must be strictly limited to equilibrium positions. The Classical model is usually represented as one where the monetary sector plays no role in the determination of interest rates. Therefore, the extreme Classical model (Fig. 11) is a more familiar representation of Classical views concentrating as it does on the real-balance effect of monetary policy.

Fiscal policy is represented by a movement of the IS curve. It is strictly

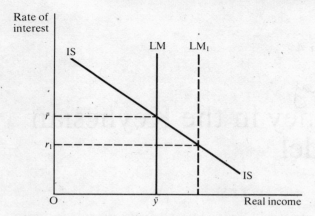

Fig. 12. The indirect transmission mechanism of money.

necessary in order to analyse fiscal policy to redefine the IS curve and its under-lying relationships as an equilibrium function of withdrawals and injections. (See Westaway and Weyman-Jones (1977) Ch. 11.) To focus on monetary policy and to simplify the analysis this is not done here. Such policy can be analysed in either of the two versions of the Classical model with the result being essentially similar. Using the downward sloping IS curve, for example, a rise in government spending will cause the IS curve to shift to the right (IS_1).

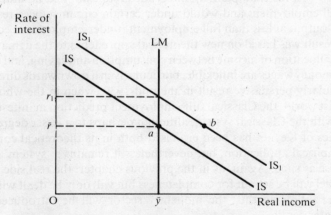

Fig. 13. Fiscal policy in the Classical model.

The full multiplier effect of this is the distance ab. However, the bond financing of this expenditure causes the interest rate to rise (r_1) which chokes off private investment. Room is therefore left for the increased government expenditure at the constant level of output ($\bar{y}$) (Carlson and Spencer, 1975, pp.4–5). This is the simplest example of the 'crowding-out' concept. Therefore, in the Classical model, fiscal policy has no long-run effect on the level of real income.

Chapter 4

Money in the Keynesian model

1 Introduction

The Classical view of the role of money in an economy – outlined in the previous chapter – dominated macroeconomic theory and policy until the inter-war years. Then Keynes while formulating a completely different approach to macroeconomics as a whole, addressed himself simultaneously to the role of money in the economy (Keynes, 1923, 1936). By altering certain assumptions of the Classical model, the Keynesian system (as it came to be known, although whether the 'Keynesian' system is a strict account of Keynes' views is an issue of some debate – see, for example Leijonhufvud, 1968) exhibited no automatic tendency to full employment and would under certain circumstances result in an equilibrium output at less than full employment (under-employment equilibrium). Such a result was based on new theoretical approaches to the demand for money and the allocation of income between consumption and saving, and on the postulate that money wages are inflexible, particularly in a downwards direction. It was a particularly persuasive result in the mid-1930s when in the whole advanced capitalist world, the Classical full-employment prediction manifestly did not apply. As with the Classical system, although perhaps to a lesser degree, the macroeconomics of Keynes has been criticised both in its theoretical constituents and its empirical application, but nevertheless it remains a 'system' and is useful to analyse as such. Again, as in the previous chapter, the real side of the Keynesian model will be set out for completeness but will only be dealt with as a basic structure; following this, the monetary sector will be introduced and analysed in greater depth.

2 The real sector in the Keynesian model

Keynes rejected the crucial Classical assumption that wages and prices are perfectly flexible. The Classical solution to unemployment – a cut in money wages – would be resisted and a sharp reduction in the supply of labour would occur. Even if money wage rates were successfully reduced, the decline in effective demand that follows would reduce the demand for labour; therefore, the level of unemployment would rise. Due to the existence of money illusion, labour is assumed to bargain for money wages so that a reduction in real wages through a rise in the price level is a more successful way of dealing with unemployment than is a cut in money wages.

In what is to follow, it is important to notice the small, but crucial, amendments made by Keynes to the Classical model which are sufficient to remove the automatic tendency for full employment and radically alter the potency of monetary policy. The analysis of the Keynesian model will be made in a sequence reminiscent of the previous chapter. In the labour market, all other factors of production are again assumed to be constant. The demand for labour (N_D), based on the profit-maximising marginal productivity doctrine of factor pricing, is dependent on the real wage W/P (Fig. 1).

$$N_D = N_D(W/P) \qquad [1]$$

$$\text{with } N_D'(\ ) < 0 \qquad [2]^\dagger$$

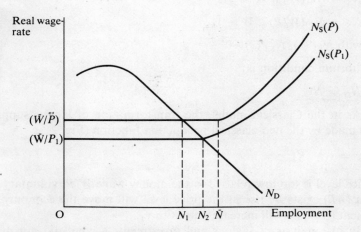

Fig. 1. The Keynesian labour market.

Turning to the supply of labour, Keynes replaced the Classical hypothesis that labour bargain individually for real wages. He suggested that either in a group or as individuals, labour would resist any cut in money wages as there is no certainty that others will experience the same cut. However, a rise in prices which will lead to a cut in real wages would not be resisted in the same way, as this is a general loss of purchasing power; also, as argued above, labour is assumed to suffer from money illusion. In Fig. 1, the supply of labour function $N_S(\bar{P})$ is a horizontal line up to employment level ($\bar{N}$). This reflects the fact that the labour supply will be withdrawn in the event of a cut in the money wage

---

† As in Ch. 3, sect. 2, an area of increasing marginal product of labour is included in Figs. 1 and 2 but not in eq. [2].

rate below $\bar{W}$. To raise employment beyond $\bar{N}$, an increase in real wages is required to attract the extra labour supply. With the demand for labour function (N_D), the difference between labour supply and labour demand at $\bar{W}/\bar{P}$ is voluntary unemployment $(N_1 - \bar{N})$. Indeed, N_1 is an under-employment equilibrium position.

With labour bargaining for a money wage rate, the only way to remove this unemployment is to cause the price level to increase (P_1). This shifts the labour supply function to $N_\text{S}(P_1)$ and increases the demand for labour to N_2 where it is equal to labour supply. The difference between N_2 and $\bar{N}$ is the amount of labour withdrawn due to the rise in the price level. This partial withdrawal reflects the fact that money illusion is not perfect. There is now full employment in the sense that labour supply will only increase further if the real and money wage rates increase; alternatively, all labour offered at $\bar{W}$ is employed. (For a fuller derivation of the Keynesian labour supply function, see Westaway and Weyman-Jones (1977) Ch. 12.)

The labour supply function is therefore in two parts:

$$N_\text{S} = N_\text{S1}(W) \text{ if } W = \bar{W} \tag{3}$$

$$N_\text{S} = N_\text{S2}(W/P) \text{ if } W > \bar{W} \tag{4}$$

$$\text{with } N_\text{S1}'(\ ),\ N_\text{S2}'(\ ) > 0 \tag{5}$$

The equilibrium condition is:

$$N_\text{D} = N_\text{S} \tag{6}$$

As in the Classical model, the transformation of labour supply into output is made by the neo-classical production function (Fig. 2).

$$y = y(N, \bar{K}) \tag{7}$$

If the price level is too low relative to the money wage $\bar{W}/P$, voluntary unemployment (AB) exists. A rise in the price level will move the economy to full employment (N_1) and will increase output to y_1.

In his analysis of savings and investment, Keynes did not deny the existence of a flexible interest rate but did question its ability to equate savings and investment at all times as it does in the Classical model. Keynes particularly dwelt on the clear separation of the activities of savings and investment in a modern economy. As a result, there is no guarantee that they will be equated notwithstanding a flexible interest rate. Keynes supported this view by postulating that the division of a household's income between consumption and saving would be primarily dependent on the level of income through the consumption and therefore savings functions. As a result, real savings are primarily dependent on real income (y) with the interest rate afforded a more minor role.

$$S = a_0 + a_1 y + a_2 r \tag{8}$$

with

$$a_0 < 0,\ 0 \leqslant a_1 \leqslant 1,\ a_2 > 0 \tag{9}$$

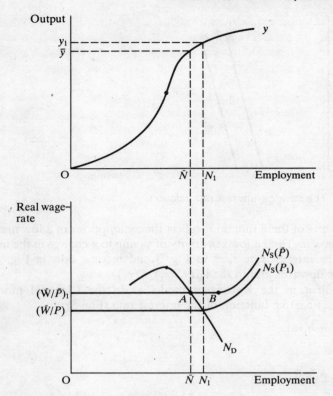

Fig. 2. The Keynesian output sector.

Equation [8] was used as a less extreme version of the Classical model in Chapter 3. However, the emphasis here is different with the role of income dominating that of the rate of interest. Equation [8] can be represented with either income or the interest rate as the independent variable (Figs. 3 and 4):

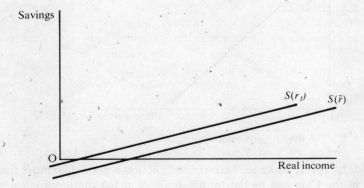

Fig. 3. The savings/income relation.

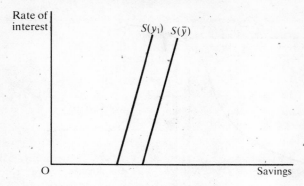

Fig. 4. The savings/interest rate relation.

The slopes of these functions reflect the assumptions of a low marginal propensity to save (a_1) and a low sensitivity of saving to a change in the interest rate (a_2). As the interest rate rises in Fig. 3 and income falls in Fig. 4, the functions move upwards and to the left ($S(r_1)$, $S(y_1)$).

Investment in the Keynesian model as in the Classical model, is assumed to be a negative function of the interest rate (Fig. 5):

$$I = b_0 + b_1 r \qquad [10]$$

with

$$b_0 > 0, \, b_1 < 0$$

Other factors were put forward by Keynes as possible determinants of investment, along with the interest rate. These other arguments, which included expectations of the future demand for a firm's output, would be shift factors influencing b_0 (the position of the investment function).

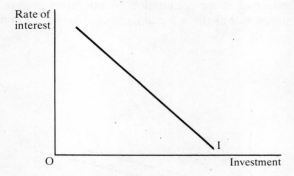

Fig. 5. The investment relation.

Keynes did, however, make the investment function a good deal more rigorous than that in the Classical model by his analysis of the marginal efficiency of capital (Keynes, 1936, Chs. 11, 12). However, the function in Fig. 5 is a simple interpretation of Keynes' views which assumes that the shift factors are stable. The equilibrium condition is given by:

$$S = I$$ [11]

This equilibrium can be depicted in two ways. Firstly, in Fig. 6a, savings and investment are plotted against the interest-rate. The role of income in the determination of savings is included in Fig. 6b with investment measured from the right. From a position of equality between savings and investment $(\bar{S}, \bar{I})$, a rise in income leading to an increase in saving must be associated with a fall in the interest rate to bring forth the necessary extra investment. Thus, for equilibrium between savings and investment, income and interest rates must move in opposite directions as shown in the traditional IS curve, Fig. 6c.

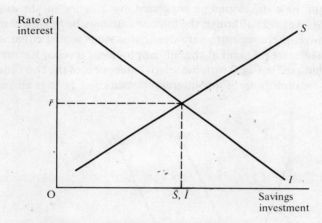

Fig. 6a. Savings/investment equilibrium.

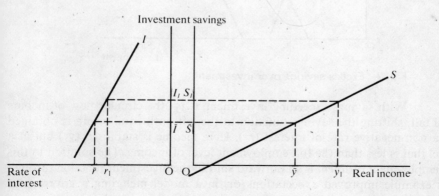

Fig. 6b. Savings/investment relationships.

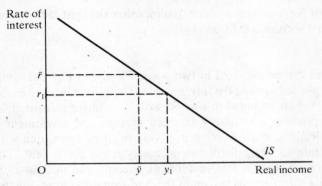

Fig. 6c. The IS curve.

The major new development suggested by Keynes in the savings/ investment analysis was that although the interest rate may be flexible throughout most of its range, there was no guarantee that savings would equal investment at a **positive** interest rate and at the full-employment level of income (y_F). This situation is depicted in Fig. 7 with the relative steepness of the two functions reflecting Keynes' assumptions of low interest elasticities of savings and investment.

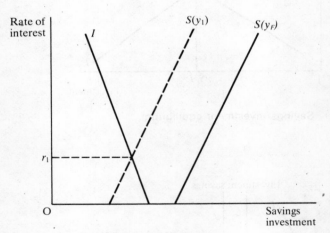

Fig. 7. Excess savings over investment.

With savings exceeding investment at y_F, the circular flow of income will fall, shifting the savings function to the left until equilibrium is obtained at a non-negative rate of interest (r_1). Here income is stabilised (y_1) but at a level that is less than the full employment level of income. The solution to this unemployment problem is an outward shift in the investment function through for example improved expectations or, in a model including a government sector an increase in government expenditure (G) that will shift the injections function ($I+G$).

3 The monetary sector in the Keynesian model

The major new idea introduced by Keynes into the analysis of the monetary sector was liquidity-preference theory. This theory divided the demand for money into three distinct motives:

Transactions motive

The transactions motive for money holding is identical to the Classical idea that as expenditure and income are not perfectly synchronised, money has to be held as a medium of exchange to carry out transactions on a day-to-day basis. (If expenditure and income were perfectly synchronised this motive would not exist.) The size of transactions balances held will 'chiefly depend on the amount of income and the normal length of the interval between its receipt and its disbursement' (Keynes, 1936, p.195). Given that this interval of time is assumed to be constant, it is clear that the Keynesian transactions motive (M_T) is equivalent to the complete Classical demand for money approach:

$$M_T = M_1(Py) = k_1 Y \qquad [12]$$

The equivalence of the two approaches is demonstrated by the use of k_1 to depict the proportional relationship between money income and the transactions demand. It is interesting to note that Keynes did state that the transactions motive 'is not very sensitive to changes in the rate of interest' (Keynes, 1936, p.171). Although the rate of interest is a minor argument in the transactions motive, its inclusion does justify later work (Baumol, 1952; Tobin, 1956) which aimed for a more general approach by combining all three motives (below). The transactions motive for money holding on behalf of firms was termed by Keynes the business motive. This would depend in principle on the value of current output – analogous to income for the corporate money holder.

Precautionary motive

The precautionary motive for money holding embraces any argument that leads an individual to seek security (provided by cash as a riskless asset that earns no interest) over the real value of one's resources. More specifically, Keynes said that precautionary balances would be held 'to provide for contingencies requiring sudden expenditure, and for unforeseen opportunities of advantageous purchases, and also to hold an asset of which the value is fixed in terms of money to meet a subsequent liability fixed in terms of money' (Keynes, 1936, p.196). These three elements may be summarised by stating that precautionary balances are held due to uncertainty over the exact size or pattern of expected receipts and disbursements.

Modern work on the precautionary motive has enabled a more rigorous approach to be developed (Whalen, 1966; Laidler, 1977a) which, however, by emphasising the opportunity cost of money holding and the cost of obtaining cash at short notice, is consistent with Keynes' original approach. The analysis assumes that an individual will hold transactions balances that on average (over a number of payment periods) are just equal to total expenditure. However, in

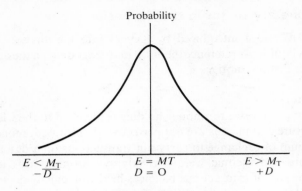

Fig. 8. Probability distribution of expenditure transactions balances.

any particular period, expenditure may differ from the volume of transactions balances held. Figure 8 depicts a probability distribution of the deficit between transactions balances and expenditure where E, M_T and D represent expenditure, transactions balances and the deficit $(E - M_T)$ respectively. It can be inferred from the diagram that the probability of the deficit being positive $(E > M_T)$ or negative $(E < M_T)$ is equal, while the probability of a given deficit occurring falls as the size of that deficit increases. The likelihood that an individual will hold a certain quantity of precautionary balances to cover a deficit in a particular period will depend on the cost and benefits of holding such balances. The cost of holding precautionary balances is the interest income that is foregone and the benefit is the avoidance of illiquidity. Should illiquidity occur, both real and subjective costs are suffered. If an individual has to convert an asset into cash to cover excessive expenditure he will be liable to pay a conversion cost or brokerage fee. In addition, there may be a subjective cost in terms of the time spent and nuisance incurred in encashing the asset. While the marginal cost (MC) of holding precautionary balances is constant, the marginal benefit (MB) (in terms of avoiding illiquidity) will fall as the deficit rises, i.e., the marginal benefit is high when the deficit is low as a small deficit of this size is more likely to occur.

Figure 9 depicts these MC and MB schedules. The marginal benefit curve is the righthand section of the probability distribution in Fig. 8. Equilibrium is at E with precautionary balances of $\bar{M}_P$. From this it may be seen that the marginal benefit curve is also the demand curve for precautionary balances.

Using this model, the major determinants of the demand for precautionary balances may be specified. Firstly, as the level of income rises, the variability of expected receipts and expenditures will increase so that the primary determinant is the level of income. Secondly, a rise in the interest rate (r_1) will increase the cost of holding money balances and so will reduce precautionary demand (M_{P1}). Thirdly, as the benefits from holding precautionary balances rise (i.e., the cost of illiquidity rises through, for example, an increase in the brokerage fee), the demand for such balances will rise. In Fig. 9, with marginal

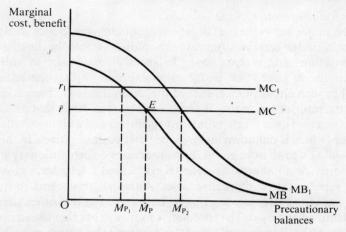

Fig. 9. Marginal cost and marginal benefit of precautionary balances.

benefit increasing to MB_1, the demand for precautionary balances rises to M_{P2} on the original MC curve. The demand for precautionary balances may be summarised as:

$$M_P = M_P(Py,r,C) = k_2 Y \qquad [13]$$

where C is the cost of illiquidity. The importance of the income variable is emphasised by the absorption of C and r into the constant k_2. It is usual to combine the transactions and precautionary motives:

$$M_1 = M_T + M_P = M_1(Py) = \ell_1 Y \qquad [14]$$

The relationship in [14] is usually assumed to be a proportional one. However, if an argument in the constant term, such as an increase in relative cost of cash holding through a rise in the rate of interest on alternative assets, changes, this causes the M_1 function to pivot at the origin to M_1^* with lower demand for active balances $(M_T + M_P)$ at all income levels.

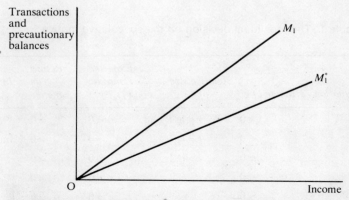

Fig. 10. Transactions and precautionary demand for money.

Speculative motive

The major innovation of Keynesian liquidity-preference analysis was the idea that under certain circumstances money would be held over and above transactions and precautionary balances in preference to an interest-yielding alternative asset. This is due to an expectation that the return from money will in such circumstances exceed that from the asset. The rationale for this is that the return from money is assumed to be zero, while that on any other financial asset consists of a rate of interest (positive) and a change in the asset's capital value (which is unknown and may be positive or negative). In this choice between holding wealth not needed for transactions or precautionary purposes in either money or an alternative asset, Keynes used a long-term government bond as a representative alternative asset. Although this seems to make the analysis of liquidity preference too simple, he pointed out that other alternatives could be identified and used. The speculative motive exists because an investor is uncertain over the future level of interest rates. The investor is, however, assumed to form an opinion of the 'normal' or expected interest-rate for the future and to hold this opinion *with certainty*. The only uncertainty is over what the future level of the rate of interest will actually be.

The existence of the speculative motive (or the holding of idle balances as this motive is often paraphrased) is crucial in the rejection of the Classical neutrality of money. Once all extra money is not used for transactions purposes, irrespective of whether there is full employment or not, real variables in the economy will be affected and the increase in the money supply will not result in an equi-proportionate rise in the price level.

The expected return from bond holding is $r + g^e$ where r is the rate of interest and g^e the expected capital gain defined as:

$$g^e = \frac{P^e_b - P_b}{P_b} \qquad [15]$$

with P_b representing the price of a bond and superscript e referring to expectations. Remembering that r is always positive, the alternative choice situations are summed up in Table 1:

Table 1 The individual decision on the speculative motive

Situation	Range of g^e	Relative size of $r + g^e$	Expected return on bond $(r + g^e)$	Return on money	Investment decision
1	<0	$r < \lg^e 1$	<0	$=0$	Money
2	<0	$r = \lg^e 1$	$=0$	$=0$	Indifferent
3	<0	$r > \lg^e 1$	>0	$=0$	Bonds
4	$=0$		≥ 0	$=0$	Bonds
5	>0		>0	$=0$	Bonds

In Table 1, r is expressed as an interest return in absolute terms and not as a 'rate' of interest to enable comparison with the expected capital gain.

Before looking at the alternative choice situations in Table 1, the relationship between the expected capital gain and the price of a bond should be set out. (Note that the price of a bond is inversely related to its rate of interest. See, for example, Westaway and Weyman-Jones (1977) Ch. 8.)

$$P_b = \frac{1}{r_b} \text{ and } P_b{}^e = \frac{1}{r_b{}^e} \qquad [16]$$

As

$$g^e = \frac{P_b{}^e - P_b}{P_b} \qquad [15]$$

Then

$$g^e = \frac{r_b}{r_b{}^e - r_b} = \frac{r_b}{r_b{}^e} - 1 \qquad [17]$$

Therefore, for a capital gain to be expected ($g^e > 0$), $P_b{}^e > P_b$ (i.e., $r_b > r_b{}^e$), so that the interest rate must be expected to fall and the bond price rise. For a capital loss, the interest rate is expected to rise and conversely the bond price fall. If the current interest rate is low, the individual is more likely to believe that the future or 'normal' interest rate will be above it. In that situation, a capital loss is expected. In this situation of an expected capital loss, an individual will hold money if the interest return from bond holding is more than wiped out by the capital loss as the bond price falls. On the other hand, at a high current rate of interest, a fall will be expected so that the expectation of a capital gain will lead the individual to hold bonds. This argument (and the point that at a high interest rate to hold money implies considerable sacrifice of interest return) causes the demand for speculative balances to be inversely related to the interest rate.

It should be clear now that the relationship between the demand for speculative balances and the rate of interest is not a smooth one for the individual. A study of Table 1 will clarify this issue. If the expected capital loss is large enough to offset completely the interest return and lead to an overall loss on bond holding (Situation 1), the individual will hold money and no bonds. If the capital gain is positive (or negative but smaller than the interest return), he will hold bonds only (Situations 3–5). Only at one crucial interest rate ($\bar{r}$) in relation to his normal rate of interest ($r_b{}^e$) will the expected capital loss exactly equal the interest gain so that the individual is indifferent between holding bonds and money (Situation 2). In this situation, the investor may diversify his portfolio to hold both bonds and money although the fact that the zero return on money is certain, while that on bonds is not, will not guarantee this result. Therefore, even at $\bar{r}$, diversification may not occur. This is the switchover or critical rate above which ($r > \bar{r}$) bonds alone are held and below which ($r < \bar{r}$) money alone is held. Figure 11 depicts the individual speculative demand for money function with M_{sp} the total resources available for investment in bonds or money.

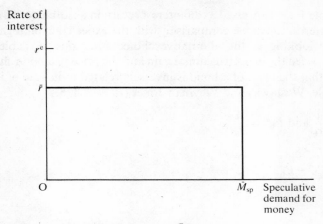

Fig. 11. Individual speculative demand.

The level of the critical interest rate ($\bar{r}$) can be derived. This rate is defined as the level at which

$$r_b + g^e = 0 \qquad [18]$$

From [17]

$$r_b + g^e = r_b + \frac{r_b}{r_b^e} = 1 \qquad [19]$$

Simplifying

$$r_b = \frac{r_b^e}{r_b^e + 1} \qquad [20]$$

From [20] it is confirmed that the critical interest rate or switchover point is below the normal rate ($\bar{r}_b < r_b^e$) so that a small interest rate rise will lead to just sufficient capital loss to wipe out the interest return. One crucial result of this analysis is that there is no portfolio diversification between money and bonds except at the critical interest rate ($\bar{r}$). This can be traced back to the assumption that the normal interest rate is held with certainty. The lack of portfolio diversification except at $\bar{r}$ is a clear weakness of this model. By using a risk analysis of liquidity preference, Tobin (1958) derived the more acceptable result that diversification would in the majority of circumstances be the optimal policy (see Appendix below).

While Fig. 11 represents the speculative demand function for an individual in a given state of expectations, the aggregate function is rather different. Keynes assumed that individuals hold differing opinions over the level of future interest rates and that no one investor dominates the market with his view of the future so that all other investors are influenced by this opinion. Given these assumptions, the higher is the current interest rate, the more people will expect it to fall and bond prices to rise, so that the more speculative balances will be converted into bonds. At the opposite extreme, the lower is the current rate of interest, the more people will hold idle balances. As a result, the rectangular individual function of Fig. 11 becomes a smooth downward sloping curve at the aggregate level:

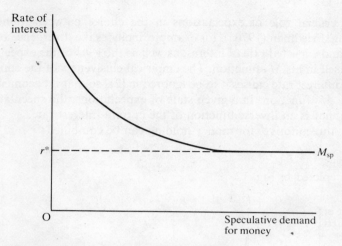

Fig. 12. Aggregate speculative demand.

The most discussed feature of Fig. 12 has been the horizontal section at a particular low rate of interest (r^*). At r^*, all investors are expecting the interest rate to rise. In fact, it is assumed by all to have fallen to its minimum level and so no investor will hold bonds; all idle balances are held in money. This region is known as the liquidity trap. Here, the demand for money with respect to the interest rate becomes infinitely elastic, with bonds and money becoming perfect substitutes. Any increase in the money supply requires only a minute (or in the limit, a zero) change in the rate of interest to encourage investors to take up the extra cash. Monetary equilibrium is restored with no change in the rate of interest and therefore no effect on the real variables in the economy. The existence or not of a liquidity trap has been the subject of considerable theoretical and empirical debate. Keynes in a famous quote states that 'whilst this limiting case might become practically important in future, I know no example of it hitherto' (Keynes, 1936, p. 207). In fact, due to institutional limits on the ability of the interest rate to decline below 2–2½ per cent and because of the unlikelihood that the monetary authorities would, by open-market operations, force interest rates low enough, he thought the liquidity trap unlikely to exist as a practical possibility. In fact, Patinkin (1974) sees Keynes' true interpretation of this phenomenon as causing unemployment because the rate of interest falls too slowly, not that it has a lower limit. Empirical attempts to capture a liquidity trap have also been notably unsuccessful (see Ch. 6).

Following the arguments of this section, the role of the rate of interest in the speculative motive is clear. However, the traditional algebraic formulation of the motive:

$$M_S = M_2 = \ell_2(r) \tag{21}$$

with $\ell_2'(\ ) < 0$

ignores the crucial role of expectations in the choice between money and bond holding. Friedman (1970a), for example, includes the divergence between the current and expected rate of interest as well as the level of the expected rate of interest itself in his M_2 function. The empirical elusiveness of the concept of an expected interest rate causes it to be ignored in [21] so that it becomes a shift factor in the M_2 function. In a given state of expectations, the speculative demand for money is an inverse function of the current interest rate.

The three motives for money holding can be combined:

$$M_D = \ell_1 Y + \ell_2(r) \tag{22}$$

and this is depicted in Fig. 13.

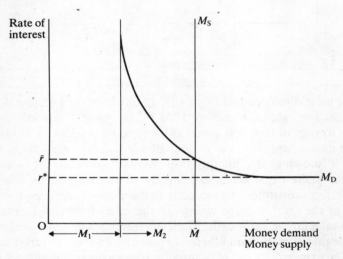

Fig. 13. The Keynesian money market.

This formulation of the demand for money has been criticised for the way it compartmentalises the motives into at least two distinct elements. Johnson (1962) states that apart from being 'mathematically inelegant' such an approach involves a mechanical treatment of the transactions demand for money which Keynes was very critical of in the Classical model and which he has failed to answer in eq. [22]. The idea that individuals separate money balances into three distinct 'pools' is clearly unrealistic and later work begun by Baumol (1952) and Tobin (1956) was primarily inspired by the unsatisfactory nature of these divisions. (See Appendix below.)

As in the Classical model, the money supply is assumed to be exogenous to the model being determined by the actions of the monetary authorities:

$$M_s = \bar{M} \tag{23}$$

Combined with eq. [22], monetary equilibrium is given by

$$\bar{M} = \ell_1 Y + \ell_2(r) \tag{24}$$

A vertical money supply function is superimposed on Fig. 13 to show this equilibrium position. It can also be depicted in the familiar LM curve. For a given money supply which must be divided up between the transactions and precautionary motives (dependent on income) and the speculative motive (dependent on the rate of interest), a series of combinations of income and the rate of interest will yield monetary equilibrium. Clearly the lower is the level of income and therefore transactions and precautionary demand, the higher will be speculative demand (to exhaust the money supply) and so the lower will be the interest rate. Any rise in income is thus associated with a rise in the interest rate for monetary equilibrium. (No causation is implied in this discussion, merely the necessary movement of income and the interest rate to maintain equilibrium in the money market.) Therefore, the LM curve is upward-sloping apart from a horizontal section at low interest rates to allow for the theoretical possibility of a liquidity trap and a vertical section which constitutes the range where the demand for money is inelastic with respect to the rate of interest. This corresponds to the 'Classical range' (Ch. 3) where all money is demanded for transactions purposes and so is unaffected by a change in the rate of interest (Fig. 14). Any change in the price level will cause the LM curve to shift as the horizontal axis is labelled as real income (y) and the demand for M_1 is a demand for real money balances. Therefore a rise (fall) in the price level causes a fall (rise) in the real money supply. Monetary equilibrium is restored by a reduction (rise) in the demand for real balances generated by a fall (rise) in real income.

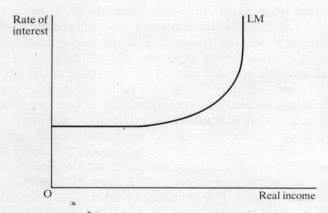

Fig. 14. The LM curve.

Combining the forces which determine the IS and LM curves, permits a unique level of income ($\bar{y}$) and the rate of interest ($\bar{r}$) to be determined:

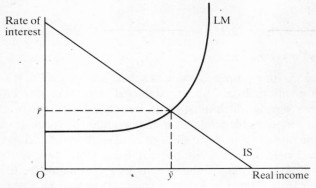

Fig. 15. IS/LM equilibrium.

The summary of the Keynesian system in Fig. 15 ignores the labour market. However, the linkages between the two can be found in Westaway and Weyman-Jones (1977), Ch. 12.

4 The transmission mechanism of money in the Keynesian model

The analysis of the role of monetary policy in the Keynesian system should begin with the quantity theory equation itself. Keynes stressed the argument that it is a tautology with little economic meaning unless extra assumptions are made. The Keynesian attack on the assumptions made in Classical theory was severe. Firstly, real world experience (particularly in the 1930s) showed that full employment was not the natural equilibrium state of an economic system; T was not fixed. In addition, Keynes noted the relative inflexibility of prices (P) particularly in a downwards direction. Any monetary impulse from the lefthand side of the equation (MV_T) will change T primarily and will only affect P should the 'special case' of full employment exist. This analysis rejects the Classical results of the neutrality of money and the proportionality of changes in money and prices. Later Keynesians have embellished this position with a non-monetary 'cost-push' determination of the price level and the rate of inflation. Secondly, Keynes argued that far from being constant, V_T was likely to be highly unstable and volatile. The introduction into demand for money analysis of the speculative motive implies that not all new money balances will be used for transactions. In fact, he assumed that, as a rule, they will be absorbed at first into speculative demand so that any increase in M is, partly or wholly, nullified by a reduction in V_T. The instability of V_T is heightened by the assumed volatility of the demand for idle balances dependent on expectations concerning the future rate of interest.

Given these two assumptions, any monetary impulse will be weakened by an opposite movement in V_T, and if MV_T is on balance affected, the impact will, in normal circumstances, be on T and not P. Note Keynes did not dispute the quantity theory equation, for it is tautologous. He amended its assumptions and thereby radically altered the potency of monetary policy.

Thirdly, the Keynesian critique argued that to treat the money supply as exogenous is too simple (notwithstanding eq. [23]). The unidirectional movement from M to PT was disputed. At the other extreme, it has been argued by Keynesians that under certain circumstances the money supply is completely demand-determined. Any increase in PT causes an increase in the demand for money which may be automatically matched by a rise in money supply. This is a particularly valid argument in a fractional reserve system where the government is concerned with interest rate stability and not monetary control (Ch. 7).

Keynesians reduced, therefore, the power of monetary policy (making it non-neutral in effect on the economy) and cast doubt on the independence of monetary control. The justification for these views revolved, in addition, around the Keynesian view of the transmission mechanism of money on the economy. Rejecting the naive direct mechanism of the Classical school and even doubting the simplicity and potency of the Classical link through interest rates, the role of money was investigated in a new direction.

The basic assumption of Keynesian analysis is the close substitutability between money and other financial assets, such as Treasury Bills or other short-term paper. A small rise in the rate of interest on such assets, would cause investors to move out of them and into money. The elasticity of the demand for money with respect to interest rates on such liquid assets was therefore high. This viewpoint is justified on three grounds. Firstly, Keynes noted the ambiguity of any definition of the money supply. 'We can draw the line between "money" and "debts" at whatever point is convenient for handling a particular problem' (Keynes, 1936, p. 167). The reason for this ambiguity is the absence of a clear dividing line between money and 'near-money' in an advanced economy. One would expect a high degree of substitutability between money and these other financial assets, as a result. Secondly, and related to the first point, it is easy and cheap to move between money and financial assets. Thirdly, the existence of a spectrum of assets from money (earning no interest and perfectly liquid) to long-term government debt for example (earning high interest and relatively illiquid) facilitates movement between assets throughout the range. These three arguments revolve around the inability to distinguish – at least in some of their characteristics – between money and a variety of liquid, financial debt instruments (Goodhart and Crockett, 1970). In addition, Keynesians assume low substitutability between money and real, physical assets such as houses, cars and other consumer goods. The Keynesian view is that a large change in the (implicit) rate of interest on real assets is needed to encourage shifts between them and money.

With the background of these substitutability assumptions, the Keynesian transmission mechanism can now be analysed. It completely rejects any direct effects on income or wealth implicit in certain versions of the quantity theory. Without such effects, money only affects the economy through substitution among financial and/or real assets dependent on the interest rate movements generated by the monetary change (Davis, 1969). As in the Keynesian scenario, these substitution effects are limited, by assumption, to financial assets, the reduced potency of monetary policy can be foreshadowed.

As in Ch. 3, the money supply is assumed to increase due to an open-market purchase of government debt by the authorities. The excess demand for bonds generated by the actions of the authorities in the market will push up the price of government securities until just enough bond holders are persuaded to replace the bonds in their portfolios with the new money. Due to the high substitutability between money and bonds, the necessary rise in bond prices (or fall in interest rates) to re-establish equilibrium in the money and bonds markets will be small. However, the new money holders will in general be in portfolio disequilibrium and so will substitute financial assets for this money. The prices of these financial assets will rise in turn. 'The effect of a change in the money supply is seen to be like a ripple passing along the range of financial assets, diminishing in amplitude and predictability as it proceeds farther away from the initial disturbance' (Goodhart and Crockett, 1970, p. 161). However, not everyone can divest themselves of this surplus cash and adjustments will occur until such a time that the fall of the rate of interest on financial assets causes the extra money to be willingly held. The speculative demand for money is increased (Fig. 16).

The second stage of the transmission mechanism postulates that the fall in the interest rate will cause an increase in the demand for investment goods. Referring to [10] and Fig. 5, a fall in the rate of interest, *ceteris paribus* will cause a movement down the investment schedule. More projects exist with a higher rate of return than the interest cost of borrowing money. In addition, the opportunity-cost argument applies, with it being more profitable for a large number of firms to purchase new investment goods rather than merely deposit any surplus cash in the money market. The return from the latter activity having fallen, firms will increase the amount of new investment.

The impact of monetary policy on the level of income occurs in the third stage of the transmission mechanism. The increase in investment being an injection into the circular flow of income causes that flow to increase through the multiplier process. However, the transmission mechanism does not end there. The rise in income by generating an increase in the demand for transactions and precautionary balances exerts a feedback effect on the economy. Money is withdrawn from speculative balances leading to a rise in the interest rate, a new fall in investment and income leading to a further feedback effect. Equilibrium in the economy is reached in a cyclical fashion.

The three-stage transmission mechanism is usually termed the 'cost of capital' channel. Ignoring the feedback for a moment, it can be summarised as

↑ money supply ⇒ ↓ rate of interest ⇒
↑ investment ⇒ ↑ income

It is represented in this form in Fig. 16. The indirect transmission mechanism of money is clearly seen in the above schema and in the figure. The rise in the money supply to M_{s1} generates a decline in the rate of interest (r_1), a rise in investment (I_1) and a rise in income (y_1). Equilibrium in the circular flow is restored by the increase in savings (S_1) generated by the rise in income.

The feedback effects are difficult to capture in a schematic or diagrammatic form due to their cyclical nature. However, the first stage of the feedback can be represented as:

$$\uparrow M_s \Rightarrow \downarrow r \Rightarrow \uparrow I \Rightarrow \uparrow y \Rightarrow \uparrow M_1 \Rightarrow$$
$$\downarrow M_2 \Rightarrow \uparrow r \Rightarrow \downarrow I \Rightarrow \downarrow y \Rightarrow \ldots\ldots$$

Diagrammatically the increase in transactions demand (M_1^*) is reflected by a rightward shift of the liquidity-preference schedule to M_{D1} in Fig. 16. The impact of only one round of feedback effects is set out in the diagram, with all the relevant variables bearing the subscript 2.

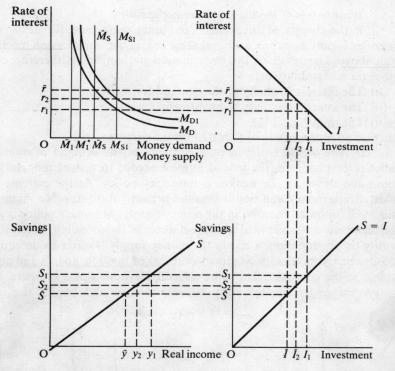

Fig. 16. The cost of capital transmission mechanism of money.

Monetary equilibrium is restored by this combination of interest rate and income changes (Keynes, 1936, pp. 200–1) with the demand for money rising to equality with the increased money supply.

Two conclusions emerge from this analysis. Firstly, a monetary expansion only affects the level of income and economic activity indirectly. The money held for transactions and precautionary purposes is altered only through the effects of portfolio re-adjustment on the real variables in the economy. It is by playing on the speculative motive that monetary management . . . is brought to bear on the economic system' (Keynes, 1936, p. 196). The fact that real assets are not substituted for money, and economic activity is merely influenced indirectly, is due entirely to the view that the elasticity of the demand for money with respect to the interest rates on such assets is zero. Money and real assets are not substitutes. Secondly, although the feedback effects on money demand due to rise in income are both complex and difficult to represent diagrammatically, they are essential parts of the transmission mechanism. Although final equilibrium is approached in stages, it is clear that, for a rise in the money supply, income will be lower and interest rates higher following the working out of the feedback effects compared to the position after the first round of the transmission process.

Weaknesses of the transmission mechanism

In the absence of direct effects of money on income, Keynesian monetary policy is only as strong as the weakest link in the transmission mechanism set out above. The debate on this transmission mechanism has therefore centred on the size and stability of:

(i) The interest elasticity of the demand for money.
(ii) The interest elasticity of investment.
(iii) The multiplier.

Particular attention has been focussed on the first two.

(i) The higher is the interest elasticity of the demand of money, the smaller is the change in the rate of interest needed to restore monetary equilibrium and therefore the weaker is monetary policy. At the extreme of the liquidity trap, money and bonds become perfect substitutes. No interest rate change will follow an increase in the money supply. Monetary policy is powerless with no effects transmitted to the real sector of the economy. In terms of the quantity theory equation, a rise in the money supply is offset by an equal and opposite change in velocity, as money is absorbed into idle hoards and does not circulate in the economy. The more general Keynesian case is where, due to the assumed high substitutability between money and bonds, the interest

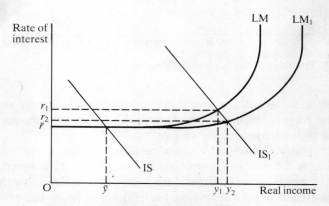

Fig. 17. Monetary policy and the slope of the LM curve.

elasticity of money demand is high but not infinite. The liquidity-preference schedule is relatively flat so that a given increase in the money supply will generate only a small fall in the rate of interest.

Fig. 17 demonstrates these two cases. The increase in the money supply is represented by an outward shift of the LM curve (to LM_1). In the liquidity trap (IS) the interest rate is unchanged, while when the money demand elasticity is high but not infinite (IS_1) the interest rate change is small.

In addition, the first link of the transmission mechanism is threatened by the possible instability of the whole liquidity-preference schedule. A primary argument of this function is the expectations of money holders over future rates of interest. If these are highly volatile the liquidity-preference schedule will be unstable as it shifts about with changes in expectations. This is most clearly seen in Fig. 18.

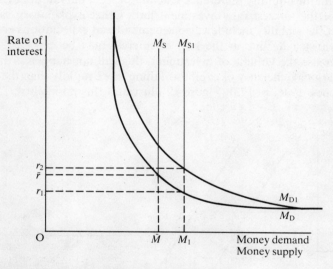

Fig. 18. Instability of liquidity preference.

The increase in the money supply (M_{S1}) should cause the rate of interest to fall from $\bar{r}$ to r_1. However, the accompanying rise in liquidity preference (wholly due to speculative demand) causes the rate of interest to *rise* to r_2. The increase in money supply has been completely offset by the rise in money demand. The interest rate will still, however, move in the expected direction if liquidity preference increases less than the money supply (Keynes, 1936, p. 173). It can be argued therefore that a money supply change will cause a small and unpredictable change in the rate of interest. This is the origin of the Keynesian view that this first link should be by-passed and direct control of the rate of interest sought.

(ii) The lower the interest elasticity of investment, the smaller will be the change in investment spending for a given change in the rate of interest. Keynes argued that while the rate of interest is a key variable in the investment decision, the degree of responsiveness to an interest rate change may be small. It has been a typical conclusion for many years based on Keynes' views and some highly influential empirical studies (Meade and Andrews, 1938; White, 1956; Eisner and Strotz, 1963) that a low interest elasticity of investment may be expected. However, theoretical developments (e.g., Jorgenson, 1963) suggest that a more systematic approach to the determination of investment should be used where the rate of interest is but one of a number of explanatory variables. This systematic framework has altered the direction of empirical studies of investment although increasingly now the role of the rate of interest is seen to be significant. (See Junankar, 1972; Levacic, 1976; Laidler, 1978; and Savage, 1978, for summaries of this evidence.) The lower is this elasticity, the steeper will be the investment demand (and therefore IS) schedule and the more impotent, *ceteris paribus*, will monetary policy be.

As with the liquidity preference schedule, a secondary doubt exists over the stability of the interest rate/investment link. Other explanatory variables that will affect the stability include various demand and expectations concepts. Therefore, 'whilst a decline in the rate of interest may be expected, *ceteris paribus* to increase the volume of investment, this will not happen if the schedule of the marginal efficiency of capital is falling more rapidly than the rate of interest' (Keynes, 1936, p. 173). Figure 19 illustrates this possibility:

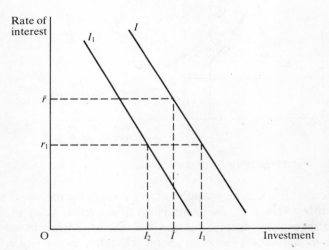

Fig. 19. Instability of investment.

The fall in the rate of interest to r_1 combined with the downward shift in the investment schedule causes investment to fall to I_2.

(iii) Assuming monetary policy has some impetus remaining after the initial links in the transmission mechanism, the stability of the investment/income relation via the multiplier is less controversial. However, 'whilst an increase in the volume of investment may be expected *ceteris paribus* to increase employment this may not happen if the propensity to consume is falling off

(Keynes, 1936, p. 173). Keynes clearly saw as not beyond the realms of possibility the result of a decline in income (and employment) when investment rises due to an offsetting decline in consumption expenditure. In general, however, this link is accepted to be more stable than the previous two.

To summarise, the Keynesian transmission mechanism of money is complex and indirect. Its strength is derived from the size and stability of a set of elasticities. A caricature of the weak Keynesian transmission mechanism is depicted in Fig. 20. Although any feedback effects from income to money demand and the possible instability of the elasticities are ignored, the weakness of monetary policy is clear when the typical Keynesian assumptions of a high interest elasticity of money demand and low interest sensitivity of investment are used. The effect of the money supply increases on income is very small as its effects have been dissipated earlier in the transmission mechanism.

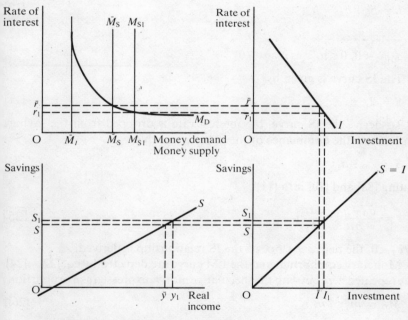

Fig. 20. Weak cost of capital effect.

In the Keynesian model, then, monetary policy is seen to derive its potency from the stability and strength of a series of behavioural relations. This is not, however, the complete analysis of the impact of monetary policy on an economy even within a Keynesian framework. Debate in recent years has centred on the existence of alternative channels of monetary influence which either augment the power of monetary policy (if they are accepted as theoretically and empirically valid) or do not reduce it (if they are rejected). These additional channels which have introduced new elements into the Keynes v. the Classics debate on monetary policy will be analysed later in this chapter.

5 Monetary and fiscal policy in the Keynesian model

Before a discussion of further channels of monetary influence is made, the analysis of monetary and fiscal policy within the static IS/LM model is undertaken. The material is ordered in this way as the cost of capital channel of monetary influence is implicit in the IS/LM model. As in the previous chapter, the independence of monetary and fiscal policy is ensured by the assumption that any fiscal change is 'bond-financed'. The basic general Keynesian model will be set out and the impact of monetary and fiscal policy analysed. Then the special cases of the liquidity trap and zero interest elasticity of investment will be analysed. As in Chapter 3, all variables are defined in real terms.

Recalling [8] and [10], the savings and investment functions are given by the following:

$$S = a_0 + a_1 y + a_2 r \tag{8}$$

$$I = b_0 + b_1 r \tag{10}$$

with

$$a_0, b_1 < 0, \; 0 \leqslant a_1 \leqslant 1, \; a_2, b_0 > 0$$

The IS curve is given by

$$S = I \tag{11}$$

To derive the IS curve, the interest rate is dropped from the savings function to show the dominance of the income variable:

$$S = a_0 + a_1 y \tag{8a}$$

Substituting [8a] and [10] into [11]:

$$r = \frac{a_0 - b_0}{b_1} + \frac{a_1}{b_1} y \tag{25}$$

with $a_1/b_1 < 0$, the negative slope of the IS relationship is derived.[†]

Monetary equilibrium and the LM curve are depicted by eq. [22] – [24]. These are repeated here but with the speculative motive expressed as a proportion:

$$M_D = m_1 y + m_2 r \tag{26]‡}$$

$$M_s = \bar{M} \tag{27}$$

$$\bar{M} = m_1 y + m_2 r \tag{28}$$

[†] Had the interest rate term been left in the savings function, the equation for the interest rate would have been:

$$r = \frac{a_0 - b_0}{b_1 - a_2} + \frac{a_1}{b_1 - a_2} y$$

This would have affected the slope and position of the IS curve without influencing the basic arguments concerning fiscal and monetary policy.

[‡] In Fig. 21 and all other IS/LM curve diagrams in this chapter, the LM curve is non-linear. The linear form in eq. [26] is therefore a convenient simplification.

with

$$m_1 > 0, m_2 < 0$$

substituting [26] and [27] into [28]:

$$r = \frac{\bar{M}}{m_2} - \frac{m_1}{m_2} y \qquad [29]$$

The slope of the LM curve is positive as $-m_1/m_2 > 0$. Equations [25] and [29] are shown in conventional IS/LM form in Fig. 21.

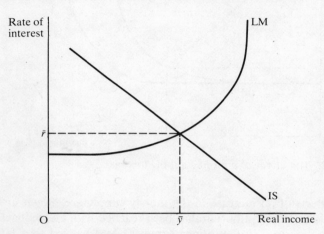

Fig. 21. The general IS/LM model.

Equilibrium in both markets is given by the intersection of the two functions $(\bar{r}, \bar{y})$. Solving [25] and [29]:

$$\frac{a_0 - b_0}{b_1} + \frac{a_1}{b_1} y = \frac{\bar{M}}{m_2} - \frac{m_1}{m_2} y \qquad [30]$$

$$y = \frac{m_2(b_0 - a_0)}{a_1 m_2 + b_1 m_1} + \frac{b_1}{a_1 m_2 + b_1 m_1} \bar{M} \qquad [31]$$

From [31] it is clear that a change in the money supply affects the level of income with a strength dependent on the parameters, a_1, b_1, m_1 and m_2, which are all slope parameters of the IS/LM model.

$$\Delta y = \frac{b_1}{a_1 m_2 + b_1 m_1} \Delta M = \frac{1}{a_1 m_2/b_1 + m_1} \Delta M \qquad [32]$$

The sign of the coefficient on ΔM (which can be termed a money multiplier) is unambiguously positive unless $b_1 = 0$ (due to the interest inelasticity of investment) or $m_2 = \infty$ (due to the existence of the liquidity trap), when the multiplier is zero. The cost of capital channel of monetary policy in the Keynesian model is seen to operate through $m_2(\Delta M \to \Delta r)$, $b_1(\Delta r \to \Delta I)$ and $a_1(\Delta I \to \Delta y)$, with $m_1(\Delta y \to \Delta M_D)$ acting as the feedback effect. (There is no suggestion in the Keynesian model that m_1 represents a real-balance effect reminiscent of the Classical model.) The larger is b_1 and the smaller are a_1, m_2, m_1, the greater is the power of monetary policy. In particular, the smaller is m_1 the smaller will be the feedback effect from income to the demand for M_1 (active balances) and the greater will be the power of monetary policy.

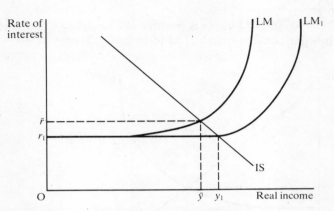

Fig. 22. The effect of a money supply increase.

The effects of an increase in the money supply are shown in Fig. 22. It is assumed that a new equilibrium has been reached with all feedback effects worked off. The increase in the money supply (LM_1) has led to a fall in the rate of interest (r_1) and therefore increases in investment and income (y_1). Monetary equilibrium has been restored by an increase in both transactions and precautionary demand and also speculative demand for money.

The potential weakness and instability of the cost-of-capital channel has led to the domination of an autonomous expenditure theory of income determination in Keynesian economics. As a result, fiscal policy is seen to be

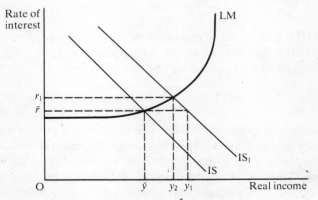

Fig. 23. The effect of an expansionary fiscal policy.

more powerful than monetary policy. The effect of an expansionary fiscal policy is shown in Fig. 23.

The rise in government spending (and/or reduction in taxation) has shifted the IS curve to IS_1. The rise in autonomous spending has increased income (y_1). However, a rise in the rate of interest (due to bond sales to finance $\uparrow G$ and to a switching of money from speculative balances to transactions demand) has caused some investment to be choked off. The damped multiplier effect (y_2) shows that partial crowding-out has occurred (compared to the complete crowding-out in the Classical model). Fiscal policy in its pure form is assumed to be devoid of the problems of the cost-of-capital channel of monetary policy. It has a more predictable and stable impact on income.

Special case 1. The liquidity trap

In this special case, the IS curve is again given by eqs. [8a], [10], [11] and equilibrium by [25]:

$$r = \frac{a_0 - b_0}{b_1} + \frac{a_1}{b_1}y \qquad [25]$$

The LM curve, however, differs in construction from the general model. As argued earlier, the liquidity trap signifies a situation where the rate of interest is so low that every money holder believes it will rise. No one is prepared to hold bonds and so risk the expected capital loss. All new money goes into idle balances and is not utilised for bond purchases. Money demand can therefore be represented by:

$$M_D = m_1 y + m_2(r_{MIN}) \qquad [33]$$

Using [27] monetary equilibrium is given by:

$$\bar{M} = m_1 y + m_2(r_{MIN}) \qquad [34]$$

As bonds and money are perfect substitutes, and the demand for money is perfectly elastic with respect to the rate of interest, the effect of the rise in the money supply is an immediate rise in money demand at the existing interest rate (r_{MIN}). Monetary policy is powerless, affecting neither income nor the rate of interest. This situation is shown in Fig. 24 with the money supply increase leaving equilibrium income $(\bar{y})$ unchanged.

In a liquidity trap, a shift in the IS curve is required (IS_1) to increase the level of income. An increase in government spending, for example, will cause income to rise to y_1 (on LM). This has moved the economy out of the liquidity-trap position so that monetary policy can now make a contribution. (Note that a smaller rise in government spending – IS_2 – by leaving the economy in the liquidity-trap position has an undamped effect on income as the interest rate remains at its minimum level. The flatter the LM curve, therefore, the more powerful is fiscal policy, and the less powerful monetary policy.)

This case is the direct opposite of the pure Classical position with a vertical LM curve where all new money was used for transactions. In that situation, the direct effect of monetary policy on income was all powerful.

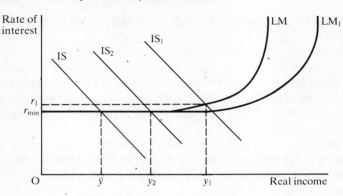

Fig. 24. Monetary and fiscal policy in the liquidity trap.

Here, the cost of capital channel fails at its first hurdle and the direct effect does not exist.

Special case 2. The interest inelasticity of investment

The empirical doubt raised earlier over the role of the rate of interest in investment is seen in its extreme form to have a considerable effect on the potency of monetary policy. In this situation eq. [10] becomes:

$$I = b_0 \qquad\qquad\qquad\qquad\qquad\qquad\qquad\qquad\text{[10a]}$$

with all arguments in investment determination subsumed in b_0. Combining with [8a] and [11]:

$$y = \frac{b_0 - a_0}{a_1} \qquad\qquad\qquad\qquad\qquad\qquad\text{[35]}$$

Income is uniquely determined by the parameters of the real sector. A vertical IS curve at this fixed income level ($\bar{y}$) is the result (Fig. 25).

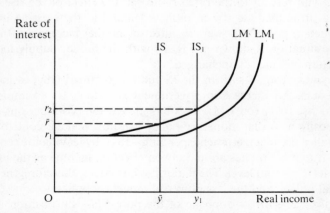

Fig. 25 Monetary and fiscal policy and the interest inelasticity investment function.

Money market equilibrium is given by [26] – [28] and yields:

$$r = \frac{\bar{M}}{m_2} - \frac{m_1}{m_2} y. \qquad [29]$$

The effect of the monetary expansion on the rate of interest is, as in the general model, determined by the size of m_2:

$$\Delta r = \frac{1}{m_2} \Delta \bar{M} \qquad [36]$$

This is however, the end of the effect of this monetary policy action as the fall in the rate of interest leaves investment and therefore income unaltered. Expressed in another form,

$$\Delta y = \frac{b_1}{a_1 m_2 + b_1 m_1} \Delta M \qquad [32]$$

With b_1 equal to zero there is no effect on income of an increase in the money supply.

This special case involving a vertical IS curve is depicted in Fig. 25 above. The rise in the money supply (LM_1) causes the rate of interest to fall (r_1) with income, determined in the real sector, unchanged at $\bar{y}$. Fiscal policy by shifting the IS curve (IS_1) is needed to increase the level of income (y_1). At the same time, the rate of interest rises (r_2) but this does not choke off any investment spending as the latter is interest-inelastic in this case.

Special case 3. The liquidity trap and the interest inelasticity of investment

The combination of the liquidity trap (horizontal LM curve) and the interest inelasticity of investment (vertical IS curve) has logically the same outcome for monetary policy as the simple liquidity trap case does. A monetary

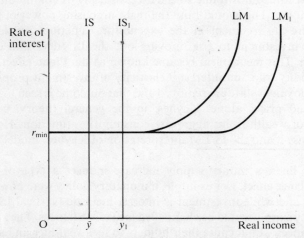

Fig. 26. The liquidity trap and the interest inelasticity investment function.

expansion leaves the rate of interest unchanged and so, in fact, the response of investment to an imaginary fall in the rate of interest is irrelevant. The situation is depicted in Fig. 26.

In this extreme Keynesian model, both income and the interest rate are independent of any increase in the money supply. As in the previous special cases, fiscal policy to shift the IS curve (IS$_1$) is needed to increase the level of income. Whether there is a simultaneous rise in the rate of interest depends on whether the IS curve is moved out of the liquidity-trap range.

6 Alternative transmission mechanisms of money

Keynesian monetary policy couched in terms of the IS/LM model operates through the cost of capital channel and rejects the Classical direct effect of money on income. The role of money in such a system is limited by the complexity of this chain of influence and its potential weaknesses. Part of the Classics riposte to Keynesian analysis was to argue that the real balance or direct effect of money on income should be included in any analysis of monetary policy. In addition, many argued that an extra escape valve from a situation of under-employment equilibrium – the Pigou effect (Pigou, 1943) – existed. These and other possible channels of influence of monetary policy have been vigorously debated in recent years. Some of these will be investigated in this section.

Wealth effects

The under-employment equilibrium result of the Keynesian model has been seen to depend on three factors – the rigidity of money wages and prices, the liquidity trap and the interest inelasticity of investment. This view was eventually challenged formally by Pigou (1943) who postulated the following situation. If an economy were in a Keynesian type unemployment state, the price level could be forced down due to the excess supply of commodities and factors in the economy. This would raise the real purchasing power of wealth, and, if wealth were an argument in the expenditure function, would cause consumption and investment to rise, moving out the IS curve and causing income to increase. This mechanism became known as the **Pigou effect**. If this occurred, the liquidity trap and interest inelasticity of investment props to the Keynesian unemployment state are removed and that outcome is seen to depend on rigid wages and prices alone. Keynes, in the general theory, certainly included the role of wealth in his aggregate consumption function. However, he did not emphasise it and the IS/LM interpretation of Keynes' model ignores it completely.

On similar lines, a money supply increase induces a type of wealth effect – the **real-balance effect**. For example, if monetary policy were powerless – in a liquidity trap and while investment is interest-inelastic (vertical IS curve) – a rise in the money supply would be channelled into idle balances. The accumulation of such balances would cause their holders to feel wealthier and some of this increased money would spill over into consumption expenditure. Again,

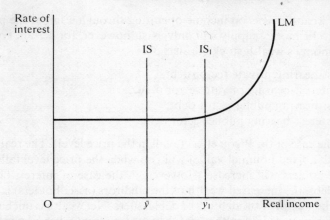

Fig. 27. The Pigou and real-balance effects.

the IS curve is moved to the right (IS$_1$) and income increases (y_1). (Fig. 27).

The real-balance effect by moving the IS curve following a money supply change avoids any problems of the interest sensitivity of money demand or investment. So even if the cost-of-capital channel fails to operate, monetary policy will have a role through this effect. It is, indeed, akin to the direct effect of the Classical model.

A third type of wealth effect is termed the **Keynes windfall effect**. It operates through a fall in the rate of interest following an increase in the money supply, which will raise the value of financial and real assets. This increase in the market value of such assets will cause consumption and investment to rise. The main difference in the sphere of operation between the Keynes windfall effect and the real-balance effect is that the former will only work when an interest rate change occurs. Therefore it will fail in a liquidity trap situation.

Table 2 summarises these three types of wealth effect and when they operate in relation to monetary policy and to two of the 'props' to Keynesian underemployment equilibrium:

Table 2 Wealth effects

	Operational condition			
	Without Δ money supply	With Δ money supply	Liquidity trap	Vertical IS curve
Pigou effect[a]	✓	?	✓	✓
Real-balance effect[a]		✓	✓	✓
Keynes windfall effect		✓		✓

[a] The definitions of the Pigou and real-balance effects are not universally accepted. Some sources treat the Pigou effect as being due to an increase in the money supply causing a rise in real balances and not a fall in prices causing a rise in real balances. However, those used here are the most widely accepted.

Direct wealth effects on income operating through a fall in the price – level or a rise in the money supply will only exist, however, for certain types of wealth. An economy's wealth stock consists of:

(a) Interest-bearing private sector debt,
(b) Non interest-bearing private sector debt,
(c) Interest-bearing public sector debt,
(d) Non interest-bearing public sector debt.

Consider first the case of the Pigou effect (a fall in the price level). The real value of an asset (with a fixed nominal value) will rise when the price level falls. The wealth of asset holders will increase. However, in the case of interest-bearing private sector debt, the increased wealth of the creditors (asset holders) is offset by a decline in the wealth of the debtors or debt issuers. Net wealth is unchanged. This offset to the increase in wealth is not, however, present when non interest-bearing debt is considered. The best example of this phenomenon is the balance sheet of a private bank. In general, the majority of its assets are interest bearing, while interest is paid on only 50 per cent approximately of its liabilities. Assume in this example that all assets are interest bearing and all liabilities non interest bearing. The decline in the price level will increase the real value of the banks' assets and also its liabilities leaving net wealth unchanged. In addition, however, the real value of the bank interest income will rise without any corresponding increase in the bank's interest liabilities (which remain at zero). Therefore, although the assets held by the bank are all inside wealth (i.e., backed by a corresponding liability), a positive net wealth effect will occur dependent on the proportion of non interest-bearing liabilities in total liabilities. For private sector debt, therefore, the key distinction which determines the applicability of wealth effects is that between interest-bearing and non interest-bearing debt.

The same statement is true for public sector debt, but with a different line of argument. As argued in Chapter 3, all outside money or wealth was traditionally assumed to be part of net wealth. All government debt including notes and coin falls into this category. Although an increase in the sales of public sector debt does increase the National Debt, the government is unconcerned about the rise of the National Debt. Therefore, there is no relevant offsetting liability and all government debt is outside wealth. However, it is now argued that the full value of interest-bearing government debt is not net wealth as the interest payments on such debt must be financed by taxes levied on the private sector. To the extent, however, that the sector that receives the interest payable on government debt is different from that which pays the taxes, the wealth effect may not be completely cancelled out. To summarise, apart from the above proviso, all interest-bearing government debt should not be included in a definition of net wealth and therefore the operation of the Pigou effect in this example is limited.

Wealth effects may also occur when the money supply increases. In this case, an additional factor determining the effect on net wealth is the method of issue. A simple increase in notes and coin (non interest-bearing government debt) will lead to an increase in net wealth as the National Debt is unchanged, there being no corresponding liability. A second case is where the excess of government expenditure over receipts that would lead automatically to an increase in the money supply is financed by bond sales to the non-bank private sector. The money supply is constant but the stock of interest-bearing public sector debt has risen. In the framework of the earlier analysis, net wealth will only increase to the extent that tax liabilities are not considered to offset wholly the increase in assets held by the public. Should the government sell debt to the banking system, a similar analysis is valid. However, this case will generate an increase in the money supply through the extension of bank credit as bank reserves will rise when short-term public sector debt is sold to the banks. Although bank deposits are inside money, net wealth will increase assuming that part of the increase in bank deposits is non interest bearing.

Clearly the validity of wealth effects on expenditure is dependent on a variety of factors. If there is no change in net wealth following a fall in the price level or an increase in the money supply, any increase in expenditure following these changes depends on distribution effects between creditors and debtors. However, to rely on a substantial impact on expenditure from such effects is optimistic. This is particularly true as wealth holders who benefit when net wealth increases are likely to be in a higher income bracket and therefore have a low marginal propensity to consume (MPC) *vis-à-vis* debtors whose income may be lower and MPC higher.

Availability effects

A second set of alternative transmission mechanisms are the 'availability' effects following an increase in the money supply. These effects are based on the rationing of credit due to the absence of a market clearing price (Radcliffe Committee, 1959). Interest rates may be slow to adjust to changing market conditions or they may be administered (such as the building society deposit and mortgage rates in the UK) and so will be at equilibrium only by chance. Rates may even be pegged as was broadly the situation in the gilt-edged market in the UK in the 1950s and 1960s.

Figure 28 represents a typical market for credit with a non-equilibrium interest rate forcing the rationing of credit (Q_1Q_2). To continue the example of the last paragraph, this diagram may represent the market for building society funds where the mortgage rate is usually at a level below the market-clearing rate.

Such availability effects will occur whether the money supply is being changed or not; however, a money supply change can alter the size of the availability effects by causing a shift of the supply curve of credit. For example, let an increase in bank reserves lead to an increase in bank credit and the money supply. If Fig. 28 refers to a bank, this development will lead to an outward shift of the supply function (S_1) causing a reduction of credit-rationing to Q_3Q_2. If the diagram refers to a non-bank financial intermediary such as a building society, part of the increased money supply may be deposited with the intermediary leading to the same outcome. The decline in rationing can be assumed to have a quick, predictable effect on expenditure. The effect on total

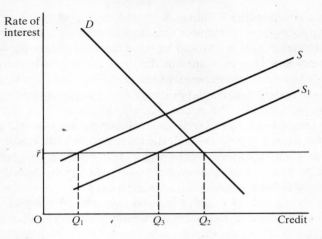

Fig. 28. Credit rationing at an administered interest rate.

credit in the economy is more uncertain as the response of all financial institutions must be analysed. But, as argued above, the overall effect is likely to be a rise in credit, particularly as rationing existed before the rise in the money supply.

Another effect relates to the interest rate on government bonds. Should the authorities decide to engineer a once-and-for-all rise in the rate of interest on such bonds, then banks which hold such securities are 'locked in' to potential losses on them. (They don't want to sell and so suffer capital losses, or wish to wait and see if the price moves up again (Silber, 1969).) This 'locking in' effect is postulated to lead to a reduction in the supply of bank loans to take account of potential losses on what have become highly illiquid bonds. Bank credit is therefore rationed – at a given loan rate – and this will lead to a reduction in investment and other expenditure financed by such credit.

In Fig. 29, the 'locking in' effect by reducing the supply of bank loans at all rates of interest (S_1) causes credit rationing ($Q_1\bar{Q}$) at a constant interest-rate

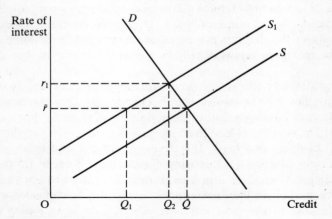

Fig. 29. The 'locking in' effect.

$(\bar{r})$. Even if this rate adjusted instantaneously (r_1), the amount of credit made available would still decline (Q_2). Only if the demand for loans were completely inelastic and the rate of interest on them adjusted immediately, would the volume of credit advanced remain at $\bar{Q}$. Clearly this effect is unrelated to the movement of an exogenous money supply. However, by influencing the flow of credit such actions are monetary in nature and so should be considered as a monetary transmission mechanism.

Expectations effects

A final set of effects of a money supply change occurs due to its impact on expectational variables. Firstly, expectations of the future rate of inflation may increase when a money supply increase occurs. This may have two conflicting results. A liquidity effect may lead certain individuals to reduce expenditure and hold more money balances to maintain living standards when prices rise in the future. Alternatively, others may spend more now to 'beat the price increase'. It is impossible to say which of these will dominate. However, both of them assume that price expectations are determined by the stance of monetary policy. Again, if the money supply increase is followed by a price increase and expectations are formed on the basis of actual price changes, these expectations effects will follow. But whether in this latter case they are due to the money supply increase is more debatable. Secondly, a money supply increase may encourage investment by generating expectations of cheaper and more accessible finance, and of demand increases. In this case too, such an effect may however be offset. In a period of money supply targets, for example, a particular increase in the money supply may generate expectations of restrictive policy action. This may lead to a negative effect on expectations and investment. Any net impact on expenditure occurring as a result of such changes in expectation will also shift the IS curve. However, the direction of any shift is ambiguous due to the number of conflicting effects.

When these three alternative types of transmission mechanism are considered together, they will either augment or conceivably reduce the power of monetary policy by shifting the IS curve. If they have on balance a positive effect on expenditure, as would be expected, a further increase in income in addition to that caused by the cost of capital channel will follow the money supply increase. Figure 30 represents the combination of the cost of capital channel and the alternative transmission mechanisms of monetary policy.

From an equilibrium position $(\bar{r},\bar{y})$, an increase in the money supply (LM_1) will cause the rate of interest to fall (r_1) and income to rise (y_1) due to the cost of capital effect. The additional effects on expenditure by shifting the IS curve to IS_1 cause income to rise further (y_2) and the rate of interest to reverse its downward movement (r_2). It is important to reiterate that the Keynesian transmission mechanism of money concentrates on the cost of capital channel alone and rejects the alternative mechanisms. However, the latter have become major elements in the debate on the role of money, and in particular they are part of the Classical reply to Keynesian analysis and are essential to the monetarist theory which is considered in the next chapter.

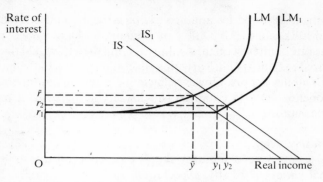

Fig. 30. The total transmission mechanism of money.

7 Appendix

This appendix sets out subsequent attempts to rectify some of the major weaknesses of the Keynesian demand for money analysis. These weaknesses include:

  (i) The separability of the demand for money function due to the independence of the three motives.

  (ii) The non-diversified portfolio result of the speculative motive.

 (iii) The existence of long-term bonds as the only alternative to holding money.

A brief analysis of the solutions to each of these problems is looked at in turn.

The separable demand for money function

'Keynes' theory of demand for money is therefore a rather awkward hybrid of two theoretically inconsistent approaches, with the transactions demand being regarded as technologically determined and the asset demand being treated as a matter of choice' (Johnson, 1967a, p.92). This quote is typical of the unease over the amalgamation of three distinct motives for money holding. A number of ways exist for reconciling the diverse motives into a consistent single theory with the most common one being an attempt to rationalise a non-zero interest elasticity of transactions balances. (Hansen had by 1949 postulated that at high interest rates money holders would economise on transactions balances.)

The Baumol Model
The first rigorous attempt to link the three motives came from Baumol (1952). Although concentrating on the demand for transactions balances, he postulated a link between this demand and the demand for money as an asset. He did this by arguing that if the size and timing of transactions were known with certainty, it would benefit the transactor to hold a minimum inventory in cash and invest income needed for transactions later in the transactions period, in bonds until that need arose. Therefore, in this model

and the Tobin model to follow, the route taken to establish a non-separable demand for money function is to derive the result that the demand for transactions balances is interest-sensitive. In Baumol's analysis of the demand for cash as an inventory, he distinguished two separate cases:

Expenditures precede receipts. In this case, bonds are encashed or money borrowed to provide cash balances to make the necessary transactions. Transactions (T) are perfectly foreseen and evenly spread throughout the transactions period (say, a year). The transactor has to complete all his transactions, but wishes to minimise the cost of doing so. As money holding yields no positive return, its costs are the interest foregone on not holding bonds to be set against the cost of encashing bonds (involving 'administrative and psychic costs' as well as any brokers' fee – for convenience all these costs will be termed a brokerage fee). Assuming withdrawals of cash (M) of equal size are made (this can be shown to be optimal if the interest foregone is minimised with respect to any fraction of the transactions period) the total cost of money holding is:

$$C = r\frac{M}{2} + b\frac{T}{M} \tag{A1}$$

where $M/2$ is the average money holding (as money balances are assumed to decline linearly from M to zero for each withdrawal), r the interest foregone by holding money, and b the brokerage fee per withdrawal. Minimising this cost function with respect to the cash withdrawal (M):

$$M = \sqrt{\frac{2bT}{r}} \tag{A2}$$

This is the famous square-root rule for transactions demand.

Receipts precede expenditure. This case is more complex and has been the subject of much controversy (Brunner and Meltzer, 1967; Morris, 1971; Grace, 1975; Ahmad, 1977). Its complexity arises as the firm holds money in hand before it is required for expenditures and so must decide whether to invest in bonds only to encash them later, or to hold money throughout. In fact, some compromise of these two extremes is recommended. In this case, therefore, there are brokerage fees for cash deposit as well as withdrawal. The transactions period is split into two parts:

(i) The initial time period (A) when expenditure is financed by money withheld from bonds (R).
(ii) The secondary time period (B) during which the amount invested in bonds at the start of the period (I) is encashed where:

$$T = R + I \tag{A3}$$

The cost of money holding in time period A is therefore

$$\frac{T-I}{2} \cdot r \cdot \frac{T-I}{T} \tag{A4}$$

where $(T-I)/2 = R/2$ represents the average cash balance held, on which interest r is foregone for a fraction $(T-I)/T = R/T$ of the period.

The cost of money holding in time period B has two elements. Firstly, the interest loss (analogous to [A4]):

$$\frac{M}{2} \cdot r \cdot \frac{I}{T} \qquad \text{[A5]}$$

where M is the size of each withdrawal.

Secondly, there are two elements of the brokerage fee:

$$b_d + b_w \cdot \frac{I}{M} \qquad \text{[A6]}$$

where b_d, b_w represent the fixed costs of depositing and withdrawing money. The cost of depositing money (b_d) is paid in one lump sum at the start of the period, while the costs of withdrawing money (b_w) is a fixed cost per withdrawal (I/M).

(The introduction of the variable cost element by Baumol is considered below.)

The total cost (TC) of money holding [A4–A6] is therefore:

$$TC = \frac{T-I}{2} \cdot r \cdot \frac{T-I}{T} + \frac{M}{2} \cdot r \cdot \frac{I}{T} + b_d + b_w \cdot \frac{I}{M} \qquad \text{[A7]}$$

Differentiating [A7] with respect to M and setting to zero yields

$$M = \sqrt{\frac{2b_w T}{r}} \qquad \text{[A8]}$$

equivalent to [A2] with $b_w = b$.

Therefore, in this case, the square-root formula is applicable too.

The size of the cash withheld from bonds (R) at the start of the period is determined by differentiating [A7] with respect to I and setting to zero:

$$\frac{\partial TC}{\partial I} = -\frac{(T-I)}{T} r + \frac{M}{2} \frac{r}{T} + \frac{b_w}{M} = 0 \qquad \text{[A9]}$$

Solving for R:

$$R = T - I = \frac{b_w T}{rM} + \frac{M}{2} \qquad \text{[A10]}$$

From [A8]

$$\frac{b_w T}{rM} = \frac{M}{2}$$

therefore

$$R = M \qquad \text{[A11]}$$

The conclusion from [A11] is that the optimal investment strategy for the individual is for each encashment (M) to equal the size of the balances withheld from investment at the start of the period (R), i.e., only one encashment (M) is required.

The main interest of this analysis lies not with the novel approach itself, but the results of it, in particular [A8]. The familiar direct relationship between income and transactions demand, and the novel inverse relationship between money and the rate of interest are obtained while the magnitudes of the relevant elasticities are also important. From [A8], the elasticity of transactions demand with respect to the rate of interest is $-\frac{1}{2}$, and with respect to the level of transactions $+\frac{1}{2}$. This latter result implies that as the level of transactions rises, the demand to hold transactions balances rises at half the rate, so that there are economies of scale in cash holding. In microeconomic terms, money is a necessity such that the demand for it rises at a slower rate than the level of transactions. Another interesting result follows from this. Any given increase in the stock of money (with an unchanging rate of interest) leads to a more than proportionate rise in transactions or income, i.e., in order for the public to take up the extra cash, income must rise by a larger proportion than does the money supply. The role of monetary policy is thereby enhanced. Finally, the role of the brokerage fee (b_w) is crucial. If this were zero, the demand to hold cash balances would be zero with bonds being encashed at the exact moment when each transaction had to be completed. It is only the balancing of the brokerage fee against the interest return on bonds that persuades people to hold an inventory of money.

The most interesting result of the Baumol model has been challenged by Brunner and Meltzer (1967). They dismiss the first case of expenditures preceding receipts as being unrealistic for an aggregate of firms and only possible for a single firm over a very short time period. In the case where receipts precede expenditure, the square-root formula [A8] only follows if there are no variable costs of investment and withdrawal (i.e., $k_d, k_w = 0$). If the brokerage fee consists of fixed and variable cost elements, total brokerage fees (F) are:

$$F = b_d + k_d I + (b_w + k_w M)\frac{I}{M} \qquad [A12]$$

The inclusion of these variable costs will modify the total cost expression [A7] to:

$$TC_1 = \frac{T-I}{2} r\frac{T-I}{T} + \frac{M}{2} r\frac{I}{T} + b_d + k_d I + b_w\frac{I}{M} + k_w I \qquad [A7a]$$

Following the same procedure as before, this is differentiated with respect to I:

$$\frac{\partial TC_1}{\partial I} = -\left(\frac{T-I}{2}\right)r + \frac{M}{2}\frac{r}{T} + \frac{b_w}{M} + k_d + k_w \qquad [A9a]$$

By setting to zero, solving for R and assuming [A8] holds:

$$R = M + T\frac{(k_w + k_d)}{r} \qquad [A13]$$

Average money balances throughout the period are given by:

$$M = \frac{R}{2}\left(\frac{T-I}{T}\right) + \frac{M}{2}\left(\frac{I}{T}\right) \qquad\qquad\qquad \text{[A14]}$$

Substituting for R from [A13] and re-arranging, Brunner and Meltzer derive the expression:

$$M = \sqrt{\frac{b_w T}{2r}\left(1+(k_w+k_d)/i\right)+T/2[(k_w+k_d)i]^2} \qquad\qquad \text{[A15]}$$

which reverts to the square-root formula [A8] if $k_d, k_w = 0$. Therefore, Brunner and Meltzer argue that the Baumol result that the simple square-root formula determines the demand for money depends on the absence of any variable brokerage fees. From [A15], the elasticity results also change. Brunner and Meltzer argue that the elasticity of the demand for money with respect to the level of transactions approaches unity unless b_w is large or the level of transactions (T) small. Only in these unlikely special cases, argue Brunner and Meltzer, will the economies of scale result of Baumol follow.

The above dispute centred around the likelihood of non-zero variable brokerage fees and the empirical issue of the relative sizes of b_w and T. But this in no way invalidates the whole approach as a more general Keynesian one. The crucial result for this generality is that the elasticity of transactions demand with respect to the rate of interest be non-zero. Therefore, the Keynesian demand for money can now be written in a non-separable form:

$$M = L(Y,r) \qquad\qquad\qquad\qquad\qquad\qquad\qquad \text{[A16]}$$

Ahmad (1977) has questioned the value of this interest elasticity as $-\frac{1}{2}$. If the Brunner and Meltzer revision of the appropriate money demand function is correct, this elasticity has a limit of -2.0, when b_w tends to zero or T to infinity. This does not invalidate [A16] and, in fact, strengthens it as it enables Ahmad to suggest that while the new money demand function [A15] in one sense moves the model towards the quantity theory (which requires that the elasticity of money demand with respect to transactions is unity) it moves it away in another sense (in that the elasticity of part of money demand with respect to the rate of interest is further from zero). Therefore, the non-separable money demand function [A16] gains credence as a Keynesian construction from the result for the interest elasticity of transactions demand.

The Tobin model   A more direct attempt to justify a non-zero interest elasticity of transactions balances was the objective of the work by Tobin (1956) in this field. He utilises the second Baumol case with receipts preceding expenditure. As with the Baumol model, Tobin asks why should transactions balances not be held in bonds; the advantage of doing so is the yield on such bonds with the drawback being the transactions costs of the money-bond-money exchange. He first considers the case where the cost (a) of a transaction is independent of its size. Therefore, if there are n transactions, the total cost of undertaking them is na. As transactions balances – defined to include bonds as well as money – decline linearly from the initial income level (Y) to zero, average transactions balances are:

$$\frac{Y}{2} = \bar{T} = \bar{C} + \bar{B} \tag{A17}$$

where $\bar{T}$, $\bar{C}$ and $\bar{B}$ represent average transactions balances, money balances and bond holdings respectively. From this base Tobin seeks to establish a relationship between $\bar{B}$ (and thus $\bar{C}$) and r.

He states explicitly that the number of transactions (n) must be a positive integer or zero such that if

$$n \neq 0, n \geqslant 2$$

In other words, $n = 1$ is impossible as a money-bonds exchange must be followed by at least one bonds-money exchange in the transactions period. To maximise the interest return from bond holding, all cash to be invested in bonds must be converted at the start of the period and any given transaction from bonds to money should only occur when existing money balances are completely exhausted.

The general rule is established that the optimal schedule is to buy $(n-1/n) \cdot Y$ bonds at the start of the period and encash them in $n-1$ instalments of size Y/n at times

$$\frac{i}{n} \text{ for all } i \text{ from } i = 1 \ldots n-1 \tag{A19}$$

through the period. Average bond holdings are therefore

$$\bar{B} = \frac{(n-1)}{2n} \cdot Y \tag{A20}$$

with the net return including the rate of interest and transactions costs being:

$$NR_B = r \frac{(n-1)}{2n} Y - na \tag{A21}$$

The general problem of defining the optimal number of transactions dependent on the relationship between r and the transactions costs is solved in the model. This, however, is of less importance than the implication of [A20] and [A21] for Keynesian theory. From [A20], average cash holding is:

$$\bar{C} = \frac{(n-(n-1))}{2n} \cdot Y = \frac{1}{2n} \cdot Y \tag{A22}$$

with the net return from [A22] being zero. Average transactions balances ($Y/2$) are therefore made up of:

$$\frac{Y}{2} = \frac{(n-1)}{2n} Y + \frac{1}{2n} Y \tag{A23}$$

with the net return on them:

$$NR_T = r \frac{(n-1)}{2n} Y - na \tag{A24}$$

From [A23] the direct relationship between the level of transactions and money holding is clear. In addition, as the return from bond holding increases with r [A24] (for constant na), optimal bond holding will be directly related and money holding inversely related to the rate of interest. The negative interest elasticity of transactions money balances is demonstrated and the non-separable demand for money function [A16] seen as a valid implication of this approach. (The inclusion by Tobin of a transactions cost factor, dependent on the size of any given transaction, establishes a number of other conditions for the model without affecting the essential results.)

The non-diversification of speculative demand

The most unsatisfactory and unrealistic result of Keynesian money demand theory is that all speculative balances are either held as money or converted into bonds. This is clearly not true in the real world. The result is due to the certainty with which a money holder holds his view of the future normal rate of interest. Tobin (1958) established a new approach based on uncertainty over the future rate of interest which permits portfolio diversification between money and bonds. The model contains the following assumptions. Firstly, the return from holding money is zero (this implies constant prices). Secondly, the interest return from holding the alternative to money, namely bonds, is counterbalanced by the risk attached to such bond holding. The risk involves, of course, a capital loss if bond prices fall. Thirdly, the interest income from bond holding is known with certainty. It is the change of the capital value alone that is uncertain. Fourthly, equal probability is attached to a fall in the price of a bond as a rise in its price. This leads to the expected return from holding bonds being equal to the rate of interest.

An individual will therefore divide his initial wealth between cash (A_1) and bonds (A_2 – Tobin uses consols as an example) such that the return on his wealth is:

$$R = A_1(0) + A_2(r+g)   0 \leqslant A_1, A_2 \leqslant 1 \tag{A25}$$

where $A_1(0)$ reflects the zero return on money and $A_2(r+g)$ the interest rate and capital gain/loss elements of the return on bonds. By assumption the expected value of g is zero so that the expected return on the portfolio is:

$$E(R) = A_2 r = \mu R \tag{A26}$$

In other words, the mean μ of the probability distribution of returns (R) is the expected return on the portfolio. Tobin also assumes that the risk element (through the variability of g) is captured by the standard deviation of the distribution (σR). Clearly, the standard deviation of the distribution of returns is the product of the standard deviation of σg and the proportion of the portfolio held in bonds:

$$\sigma R = A_2 \sigma g \tag{A27}$$

By substitution from [A26]

$$\sigma R = \frac{\mu R}{r} \sigma g$$

and

$$\mu R = \frac{r}{\sigma g} \sigma R \qquad\qquad\qquad [A28]$$

The return and risk from the portfolio are related by the expression $(r/\sigma g)$, and as r, $\sigma g > 0$, a larger mean of the distribution of returns must be associated with greater risk.

Tobin utilised the following diagram to express these possibilities:

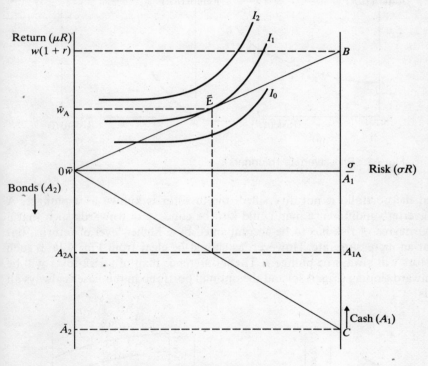

Fig. A1. Liquidity preference and risk.

In Fig. A1, the locus $\bar{w}B$ represents all attainable combinations of expected return and risk given initial wealth of $\bar{w}$. The slope of this line is $r/\sigma g$. In the lower half of the diagram, the locus $0C$ shows the distribution of the portfolio between bonds and money. At C for example, all wealth is in bonds $A_1 = 0$, $A_2 = \bar{A}_2$ while at 0, all wealth is held in money $A_2 = 0$ and $A_1 = \bar{A}_1$. To find the optimal position for any individual on the locus $0B$, an indifference map has to be superimposed. However, before this is done, two different types of investor must be described. A risk-averter is one who will only accept more risk if there is a higher expected return. On the other hand, a risk-lover is one who will accept lower returns to have the opportunity of experiencing greater risks. The indifference curves of a typical risk-averter that needs ever increasing increments to expected returns to accept equal extra elements of risk, are concave upwards, as shown in Fig. A1. The highest attainable indifference curve given wB is I_1 with equilibrium at $\bar{E}$ with the risk-averter diversifying his portfolio between bonds (A_{2A}) and money (A_{1A}) such that its expected return is $\bar{w}A$ where $\bar{w} < \bar{w}A < \bar{w}(1+r)$. There is, however, nothing to prevent a risk-averter choosing to hold all bonds (Fig. A2a) or all money (A2b) this being dependent on the indifference map:

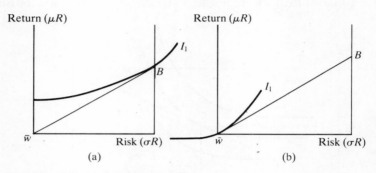

Fig. A2. Risk-averters (plungers).

When the portfolio is not diversified, the investor is known as a plunger. A risk-averter's indifference map could also be concave downwards such that a higher degree of risk has to be accompanied by a higher level of returns, but not at an increasing rate. However, as should be clear from Fig. A3a, b such investors will always be plungers. The indifference map of a risk-lover will be downward sloping (Fig. A3c) and the optimal portfolio in this case is always all bonds:

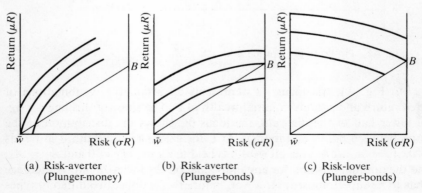

(a) Risk-averter   (b) Risk-averter   (c) Risk-lover
(Plunger-money)   (Plunger-bonds)   (Plunger-bonds)

Fig. A3. Alternative indifference maps.

Clearly a diversified portfolio is not an automatic result of this theory – the major criticism of Keynes' theory that this approach was designed to sweep away. However, for risk-averters who have to be compensated for higher risk by ever increasing returns, it is the likely result.

Likewise, it is not obvious that the inverse relationship between idle money balances and the rate of interest will follow from this approach. This result is however, proved in Fig. A4. A rise in the rate of interest increases the mean of the probability distribution of returns such that the locus $\bar{w}B$ pivots upwards to $\bar{w}B_1$. The effect on the optimal portfolio is determined in a way analogous to the effect of a price change on consumer equilibrium in elementary demand theory.

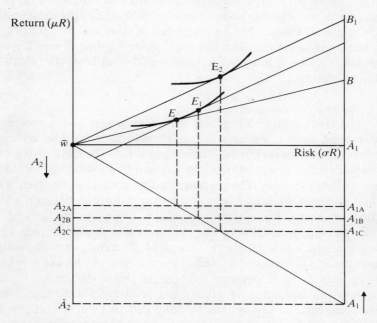

Fig. A4. The effect of a rise in the interest rate on the optimal portfolio.

The rise in the rate of interest will induce both a substitution and an income effect. The substitution effect will cause bonds (now yielding a relatively higher return) to be substituted for money in the portfolio. This is represented by the move to E_1, with bond holdings rising to A_{2B} and cash holdings falling to A_{1B}. However, the income effect could induce a switch either way. If it is positive so that it reinforces the substitution effect and causes more bonds to be held, final equilibrium would be at a point such as E_2 with bond holdings rising to A_{2C} while the holding of cash balances is reduced further to A_{1C}. However, the investor may choose to have the same expected return with less risk and so the income effect will be negative and exactly counteract the substitution effect. As long as this negative income effect is not sufficiently powerful to swamp completely the substitution effect final equilibrium will be to the right of $\bar{E}$ and bond holdings will rise. As a result, money holdings and the rate of interest will be inversely related; it is clear, however, that a direct relationship between the demand for idle balances and the rate of interest is not ruled out by this model. The student should verify the effect of the rise in the rate of interest on the other indifference maps. The plungers will remain so although the risk-averter plunger may switch all his resources from money to bonds (or vice-versa when the rate of interest falls). The diversifiers will either remain with a diversified portfolio or be induced to plunge all their resources into bonds.

This model is successful in introducing portfolio diversification into Keynesian theory. It replaces a simple naive bootstrap theory ('the interest rate is what it is because it is expected to be something else' – Johnson 1971a, p. 81) with one that ironically may be too complex to be at all applicable to the real world. The model also has the weakness that it relies on constant prices with money being a riskless asset. This is inappropriate – although very Keynesian – and the addition of risk in money holding would complicate the calculation of portfolio equilibrium.

The money v bonds choice

The restriction of Keynesian theory to money and a representative long-term bond alone is a source of considerable criticism. This criticism can be answered in two ways. Firstly, Tobin's analysis of the relationship between the expected return on a portfolio and risk can be modified to include other alternative assets to money. The alternative asset (bonds) can represent a bundle of various real and financial assets of differing maturities between which the individual establishes his optimum portfolio, subject to the interest return available. The only restriction of the analysis is that it must include a riskless asset against which this bundle is compared. If money is not riskless this extension of the Tobin model, as well as the model itself, breaks down.

A second, more popular response to this criticism is to return to Keynes himself. Leijonhufvud (1968) has reinterpreted Keynes' views of liquidity preference by saying that liquidity can be held not only in money form but in a variety of short-term assets such as building society accounts and Treasury Bills. The choice is then between holding short-term or long-term assets. This is a neat solution but it does suggest that short-term assets are perfect substitutes for money and if so money will only be held for transactions and precautionary purposes. Idle money balances are zero by definition, and any interest rate movements will induce shifts between long- and short-term assets alone. The natural outcome of thoughts of this kind is a comprehensive theory of portfolio choice which is the approach that has been developed by the Yale school led by the same Professor Tobin (e.g. Tobin, 1965). In this approach, portfolio balance is seen to depend on the rates of return on numerous liquid and non-liquid assets and the elasticities of substitution between them.

Chapter 5

Money in the monetarist model

1 Introduction

In the post-war period, particularly since the mid-1960s, a considerable challenge to Keynesian macroeconomic thinking has appeared from the 'modern quantity theorists' or 'monetarists'. As is suggested by these two labels, this group is mainly concerned with a re-emphasis of the role of monetary forces in a modern economy. Their views represent a return to some of the principles of the Classical school although as with all counter-revolutions (Friedman, 1970b) the initial position that was brought back into favour has been modified to a considerable extent.

Keynesian economics, with its complex and potentially limited role for monetary actions in the determination of economic variables, held the 'orthodox' position certainly until the mid-1960s. In the UK, the zenith of Keynesianism is often said to be the report of the Radcliffe Committee (1959). However, soon after, the tide began to turn most noticeably at first in certain academic, public and commercial institutions in the USA while more recently, there has been a marked shift towards the views of the monetarists in the UK. It is the plan of this chapter to analyse in depth the theoretical structure of the monetarist case in order to derive the radically different policy prescriptions from those of Keynesian economics. In the next chapter, empirical evidence on the rival theories will be reported.

The very gradual decline of Keynesian orthodoxy – which itself only held total sway for a generation from 1936 – and its replacement in many economists' minds by the monetarist viewpoint can be traced to a number of factors. (An interesting common feature about these reasons for change is that they are all empirically based, which is symptomatic of the fact that many have considered monetarism to have gained much of its credence from empirical evidence and little from theoretical novelty.) Firstly, the immediate post-1945 period in both the USA and the UK saw the major concern of governments being a return to the high unemployment of the Great Depression. To prevent this, fiscal policy was expansionary with a vast increase in public spending – which in the UK corresponded conveniently with the expansion of the public sector desired by the new Labour government (e.g., the National Health Service) – while interest rates were cut to very low levels to facilitate borrowing. In orthodox Keynesian fashion, this was seen as the sole contribution of monetary policy. 'Cheap money' would encourage investment. The result of such policies was, in fact, inflation, partly caused by the expansionary monetary policy, and not unemployment. 'Cheap money' was abandoned in the UK at the end of 1947 when it became clear that long-term rates of interest would not remain at the level of 2½ per cent which was the yield on undated government securities in this period (Dow, 1970). Most other countries eventually followed the abandonment of 'cheap money' and the policy was seen as being notably unsuccessful (in that it contributed to inflation) throughout the Western world, although it had helped to prevent a rise in unemployment. One consequence was a new enquiry into the power of monetary policy. 'Had Keynesianism underestimated its role?'

Secondly, and rather later in the post-war period, a number of studies began to appear which linked cyclical relationships between various definitions of the money supply and certain variables such as economic activity, incomes and prices. The major such study was the famous volume by Milton Friedman and Anna Schwartz (1963a). Closer review of this and other important evidence (Friedman and Meiselmann, 1963; Friedman and Schwartz, 1963b; Anderson and Jordan, 1968) must be left until the next chapter, but a simplified general conclusion was that cycles of monetary variables have coincided with, and in some cases, led cycles in economic activity, incomes and prices, while monetary forces have played a considerable role in the statistical determination of these variables, especially in the USA. Despite the criticism which such tests received (e.g., Hester, 1964; Ando and Modigliani, 1965; De Leeuw and Kalchenbrenner, 1969), the broad pattern of results obtained did lead to a shift in favour of greater reliance on monetary policy. The studies symbolised a new change of emphasis away from Keynesian orthodoxy, although as will be clear from the next chapter, much of the empirical evidence is subject to doubt and often inconsistency.

Thirdly, the usual view of the role played by monetary forces in the Great Depression in the USA has been questioned by monetarists. Traditionally, it was believed that monetary policy had failed to pull the economy out of the slump as there were no willing borrowers of the available funds. 'You could lead a horse to water but you could not make him drink' (Friedman, 1968). However, this period from 1929 to 1933 was littered with bank failures in the USA which were not prevented by the authorities acting as lender of last resort. The major cause of the bank failures was a cumulative crisis of confidence which led to a withdrawal of cash by many depositors. High-powered money – or the monetary base – did not fall in this period (in fact it rose by over 10 per cent between October 1929 and 1933) but the money supply fell steeply, by 35 per cent, in the same period. More active support for the banking system by the authorities and a greater increase in the monetary base would have perhaps prevented the bank failures and also offset the rise in the public's currency/deposit ratio to enable the money supply to rise. The decline in the money supply is seen as 'tragic testimony to the power of monetary policy' (Friedman, 1968). Kaldor (1970) in a famous critique prefers to explain the decline of the money supply in terms of a lack of willing borrowers which led to an increase in bank reserve ratios. Whatever the true interpretation of the Great Depression, these episodes have, nevertheless, played a crucial role in the advancement of monetarist ideas.

Now that monetarism is becoming more acceptable, new evidence on the role of monetary forces encourages further analysis of the doctrine. As seen in the next chapter, such evidence is considerable, but the initial enthusiasm for the monetarist position is still ultimately traceable to the three factors above. An excellent survey of the political and economic context of monetarism, with particular reference to the UK, is contained in Congdon (1978).

Monetarist theory and policy prescription can be analysed within the framework of the IS/LM model more familiarly associated with Keynesianism. However, as is demonstrated later in this chapter, a comparison of the Keynesian and monetarist views is not purely limited to the slopes of the IS and LM curves, but also their stability. In the field of monetary policy certainly, the wider transmission mechanism postulated by the monetarists makes its representation in the IS/LM model less valid than is the case with the narrower Keynesian mechanism. The use of the framework to analyse monetarism, however, implies a basic structural similarity when comparing the monetarist and Keynesian models.

Despite these similarities the monetarists – in particular Professor Milton Friedman – introduced some modifications to the basic Keynesian market structure. Firstly, Friedman has criticised the narrowness of the concept of absolute income used in Keynesian consumption and demand for money analysis. He postulated that wealth is the appropriate budget constraint in such analyses. Therefore, comparing two individuals receiving the same current disposable income, the individual commanding the larger store of wealth – whether in human or non-human form – will consume more and, in addition, demand larger money balances for transactions purposes. This point is very difficult to test empirically, due to a total absence of data on wealth in the UK, while such US data as there is, is of limited coverage and relevance. To overcome this problem, Friedman uses permanent income as the appropriate budget constraint. This concept can be defined in a number of ways (for a full definition of the concept, see Friedman, 1957), such as the 'present value of the future stream of labour income' or 'that income which if consumed will leave wealth intact'. To measure such an elusive concept, Friedman suggested using a weighted sum of present and past values of income with geometrically declining weights attached to past income levels. It is this proxy for expected income which, it is argued, is the relevant budget constraint in both the consumption and demand for money functions. A second major source of differentiation is in the wider choice of variables in the demand for money analysis of the monetarist model.

2 The demand for money in the monetarist model

The revival of the quantity theory tradition and the true birth of monetarism, can be traced to Friedman's analysis of the quantity theory as a demand for money theory (Friedman, 1956). Rather unusually, he argues that 'the quantity theory is in the first instance a theory of the *demand* for money. It is not a theory of output, or of money income, or of the price level' (Friedman, 1956, p.4). The quantity theory is seen by economists as a model which determines prices in the traditional form and nominal income in the neo-quantity theory version. Friedman's determination to call it a demand for money theory establishes the importance of the arguments of the demand for money function in the transmission mechanism of money and also the role of the stability of the function in monetarist analysis. The relevance of the previous sentence should become clear as the chapter unfolds.

Friedman argued that money is an asset – a rather unique one perhaps – but one the demand for which should be analysed in exactly the same way as the demand for apples, butter, cars or any other commodity. The demand for money will depend, given a budget constraint, on its price, the price of closely related assets and on tastes:

$$M_{Dt} = f(W_t, P_{Mt}, P_{it}, U)$$ [1]

where W is wealth to represent a broad budget constraint, P_M, P_i are the price of money (M) and the price of other assets i in time period t, respectively, while U is a taste variable. Such a wide ranging function is a considerable departure from the simple Keynesian demand for money function. In addition, Friedman separates out the demand for money by 'ultimate wealth holders' and by 'business enterprises'. This is similar to Keynes' distinction between the transactions and finance motives. The theory for 'ultimate wealth holders' is considered initially.

As suggested above the budget constraint used in the monetarist demand for money analysis is wealth. Friedman defines this as:

$$W = \frac{Y}{r}$$ [2]

where Y/r represents the flow of income divided by the interest rate (r). This formulation is used as income and consumption services are the flow which is provided by wealth, with the interest rate (r) providing the link between wealth and such income services. This use of wealth in demand for money analysis 'is probably the most important development in monetary theory since Keynes' General Theory' (Johnson, 1962). However, despite this, the application of monetarist demand for money analysis to empirical evidence usually calls for the use of a proxy for wealth through some estimate of permanent income (see Laidler, 1977a). A further complication is posed by the fact that wealth can be held in many different forms some of which will be highly liquid and others less so. Friedman in particular distinguishes non-human wealth, which can be held in assets of varying liquidity, and human wealth. An individual's human wealth represents his skill and expertise gained through a period of education and the experience gained in performing a particular job over a certain time period. Such human wealth is as important an element in an individual's wealth stock as any other asset, with the major difference being that it will be highly illiquid. Human wealth is basically non-marketable. Non-human wealth can be sold and the proceeds used for the acquisition of new human wealth, but this apart, substitution possibilities are limited, particularly from human to non-human wealth. To overcome this problem, Friedman argues that the ratio of non-human wealth to human wealth (h) should be included as an argument in the demand for money function. As h falls, so that the proportion of human wealth in the total stock rises, the demand for money increases. This increased demand for a liquid asset balances the movement towards greater illiquidity in the wealth stock. Such a principle is generalisable to all forms of wealth – not merely human wealth – so that an index of the liquidity of an individual's wealth stock could influence the demand for money.

A second set of arguments in the demand for money are the rates of return on money and various substitute assets. Wealth can be held in a number of forms apart from money and the rates of return on such wealth forms relative to that on money are important in the analysis of the demand for money. These alternative wealth forms are bonds, equities, physical goods and non-human wealth.

The nominal return on money holding is typically assumed to be zero. Two factors may make this assumption invalid. Firstly, certain bank deposits (e.g., some sight deposits and all time deposits) may be classed as money and yet yield an interest return. Secondly, when the price level is changing the real return on money holding will be non-zero. The first of these is ignored in the monetarist demand for money analysis and the price level (P) alone used to represent the rate of return on money holding. The true return on money is provided by the services that money performs. The rate of return on bonds is in two parts. A bond – for convenience, a long-term security issued by governments – is a fixed term loan to the government which yields an interest rate (r_b), which is determined when the bond is purchased, and a change in its capital value, which may be positive or negative. The capital gain on a bond is denoted by $-((1/r_b)\cdot(dr_b/dt))$ where $1/r_b$ is the price of the bond. When dr_b/dt is negative, the bond price is rising which requires the use of a negative sign for the whole expression in order that it yields a positive capital gain. The total return from bond holding is therefore:

$$r_b - \frac{1}{r_b} \cdot \frac{dr_b}{dt} \tag{3}$$

A third form of wealth holding distinguished by Friedman is an equity. An equity, under this definition, provides the wealth holder with a stream of income of constant 'real' amount. The return on an equity includes a purchasing power clause to maintain the real value of the income stream $(1/P)(dP/dt)$:

$$r_e - \frac{1}{r_e} \cdot \frac{dr_e}{dt} + \frac{1}{P} \cdot \frac{dP}{dt} \tag{4}$$

where the subscript e refers to an equity. Wealth held in the form of physical assets yields a return which is in the form of services from the ownership of the assets – a return in kind – while in addition the real value of the assets will change as the price level changes. It is this latter element $(1/P)(dP/dt)$ which is used by Friedman to represent the return from holding such assets. Finally, the return from holding wealth in human form is virtually impossible to define given that such wealth is basically non-marketable. It is therefore ignored and the role of human wealth in money demand is limited to the ratio h defined earlier.

The third set of arguments in any demand function is usually the catch-all element, tastes and preferences. These are included in the monetarist scheme as the term U. They are assumed to be constant when the role of other variables in money demand is investigated empirically.

For 'business enterprises', money is like any other productive resource. According to Friedman, the demand for it can be looked at in a very similar way to that for 'ultimate wealth holders'. However, the wealth term is less meaningful for business enterprises and is replaced by a term for the volume of transactions, while the 'catch-all' term U must be broadened. It must, for example, include the technological production conditions. Aside from these minor amendments, the demand for money can be aggregated across all wealth holders and business enterprises.

The full demand for money function is therefore:

$$M_D = f\left(\frac{Y}{r}, h, P, r_b - \frac{1}{r_b} \cdot \frac{dr_b}{dt}, r_e - \frac{1}{r_e} \cdot \frac{dr_e}{dt} + \frac{1}{P} \cdot \frac{dP}{dt},\right.$$
$$\left.\frac{1}{P} \cdot \frac{dP}{dt}, U\right) \tag{5}$$

This is simplified (Friedman, 1956, pp. 9–10) to:

$$M_D = f\left(Y, h, P, r_b, r_e, \frac{1}{P}\frac{dP}{dt}, U\right) \tag{6}$$

The crucial monetarist flavour is given to this general demand for money analysis in the assumptions firstly that the function is homogeneous of degree one in prices and incomes and secondly that the function is stable. To develop, Friedman argues that all demand functions are typically specified in real magnitudes, hence:

$$f\left(\lambda Y, h, \lambda P, r_b, r_e, \frac{1}{P}\frac{dP}{dt}, U\right) =$$
$$\lambda f\left(Y, h, P, r_b, r_e, \frac{1}{P}\frac{dP}{dt}, U\right) \tag{7}$$

Let $\lambda = 1/P$

then [6] can be rewritten as

$$\frac{M}{P} = f\left(\frac{Y}{P}, h, r_b, r_e, \frac{1}{P}\frac{dP}{dt}, U\right)$$ [8]

The validity of the assumption that the elasticity of the demand for money with respect to the price level is unity, so that a demand for money function expressed in real terms is acceptable, can be tested empirically. As demonstrated in the next chapter, not all studies which test this assumption find it borne out in the results.

In addition, let $\lambda = 1/Y$ then [6] becomes,

$$\frac{M}{Y} = f\left(h, \frac{P}{Y}, r_b, r_e, \frac{1}{P}\frac{dP}{dt}, U\right)$$ [9]

Re-arranging [9] and letting

$$V( ) = \frac{1}{f( )}$$ [10]

$$Y = M \cdot V\left(h, \frac{P}{Y}, r_b, r_e, \frac{1}{P}\frac{dP}{dt}, U\right)$$ [11]

where $V( )$ is the velocity function.

As Friedman argues (1956, p.15) 'almost every economist will accept the general lines of the preceding analysis on a purely formal and abstract level'. However, the modern monetarist assumes, most crucially, that the demand function for money (i.e., the velocity function) is stable – although the velocity of circulation need not be constant. In addition, factors affect the money supply which do not influence the demand for money and the liquidity trap special case of the Keynesian model is rejected.

The primacy given to the stability of money demand by monetarists is traceable, therefore, to Friedman's 1956 essay. However, as a re-statement of quantity theorists' views on the role of money, the model has been challenged by Patinkin. He argues that 'Milton Friedman provided us in 1956 with a most elegant and sophisticated statement of modern Keynesian Theory' (Patinkin, 1969, p. 108). The reasons for this view are critical. Patinkin argues that the oral tradition of Chicago, referred to by Friedman, is very different from the approach of Friedman's model. The oral tradition of Simons, Mints, Viner, Knight and others argues that the quantity theory is a theory of output and prices and not of the demand for money, and one that assumes that the velocity of circulation is subject to 'sharp changes'. This dispute of interpretation is, however, only one aspect of Patinkin's critique. He also argues that the traditional quantity theory and the Chicago view of the 1930s and 1940s dealt with the relationship between the stock of money and the flow of expenditure with no explicit transmission mechanism linking the two, i.e., an increase in M caused an increase in PT in a purely mechanical way. On the other hand, the Keynesian view of money and (Patinkin argues) that enshrined in Friedman's 1956 model deals with the relationship between the stock of money and the stock of other assets. As a result, the modern quantity theory involves a complex transmission mechanism with portfolio adjustment amongst a range of assets.

These views of Patinkin may be valid but do not present a fair picture. As will be shown in the next section, the monetarist theory does involve a complicated transmission mechanism but one that is as different from the narrow money/bond Keynesian one as it is from the mechanical $M \rightarrow PT$ quantity theory link. The closeness of monetarist theory to traditional quantity theory views lies not in the type of transmission mechanism but in the stability of the demand for money function and therefore the importance of the money supply as a major determinant of nominal income.

3 The transmission mechanism of money in the monetarist model and monetary policy

The previous section makes clear that a stable velocity of circulation term is a crucial part of monetarist theory. This differentiates monetarism from the pre-Keynesian quantity theory and its constant velocity assumption, in that the traditional quantity theory sees V as being determined primarily by institutional factors and so being fixed in equilibrium. However, given that the velocity function in the monetarist model is a more complex one, based on certain behavioural variables, this theory is limited to an assumption of stable velocity. The monetarist view is therefore very different from the Keynesian one in this respect too. In addition to stable velocity, monetarists do not assume that either the level of transactions (T) or the price level (P) is fixed, so that any impulse from the lefthand side of the equation is reflected in movements in both prices and transactions (i.e., nominal income PT). (Attempts by Friedman (1970a, 1971) to rationalise a division of effect between P and T have been a source of controversy in this area in recent years.)

As a result, money is non-neutral. It does influence output (transactions) as well as prices although output may have a tendency to move around its natural level and so be stable in long-run equilibrium (see Ch. 9). The final element of the monetarist view of the quantity theory formula is that the money supply is exogenous and that it dominates any other impulse on nominal income (PT). These assumptions combine to yield a monetary theory of nominal income. It does not preclude the influence of non-monetary factors on income, but merely relegates them in importance to below that of monetary variables.

With this background and that of Friedman's demand for money model, the channels by which a change in the money supply affects economic variables can be set out. Much of what follows relies heavily on an assumption concerning the uniqueness of money as an asset. 'Money is to be regarded as an asset in a generalised portfolio, in sharp contrast to the Keynesian tradition of considering money to be a substitute for financial assets' (Nobay and Johnson, 1977, p.478). In other words, the Keynesian money/bonds choice is replaced by one where portfolio adjustment involves a wider array of assets, both financial and real. These include goods and services. Money is a unique asset, which is a substitute – but not necessarily a close one – for assets of all sorts. 'The crucial issue . . . is not whether changes in the stock of money operate through interest rates, but rather the range of interest rates concerned' (Friedman and Meiselmann, 1963, p.217). From this analysis comes the assumption that the elasticity of the demand for money with respect to the rate of interest on bonds is low.

In monetarist theory, disturbance to equilibrium which will cause portfolio adjustment is often assumed from the following situation. The monetary authorities can only determine the nominal supply of money. However, the demand for money by individuals and firms is couched in real terms. This presented no dilemma to 'Keynesian' theory where prices were assumed to be inflexible and so the distinction between real and nominal variables ruled out. However, this distinction is crucial in monetarist theory, with its assumption of price flexibility. From a position of equilibrium (M_{Se}) should there be an increase in the nominal money supply (ΔM_s) there will be excess money holdings in the economy:

$$\frac{M_{Se} + \Delta M_s}{P} > \frac{M_{De}}{P} \qquad [12]$$

Equilibrium can be restored either by nominal money holdings of individuals falling so that the left hand side term reduces to M_{Se}/P again, or by the price level rising so that the extra nominal balances ($M_{Se} + \Delta M_s = M_{S1}$) are demanded. The first adjustment will not occur unless the authorities reduce the money supply again, as not everyone can divest themselves of the excess balances. Therefore, the price level must rise (P_1) so that:

$$\frac{M_{S1}}{P_1} = \frac{M_{D1}}{P_1} \qquad [13]$$

So far the adjustment appears to imply the cash balance mechanics which is part of Classical theory. However, this 'direct' effect is only a minor element (and this is a source of dispute), in the monetarist transmission mechanism. Adjustment is assumed to occur through the purchase of a wide range of assets (including goods and services) until yields are reduced and asset prices driven up so that the extra nominal money supply is willingly held. The 'cost of capital' channel of Keynesian economics is not rejected and initially 'close' financial assets such as bonds may be purchased affecting investment and output in familiar fashion. But in monetarist theory, the adjustment is wider and a 'ripple' effect will be set in motion across all asset markets. The range of assets included in this transmission mechanism is set out in eq. [6] in the form of rates of return.

So far, then, the monetarist transmission mechanism of money can be represented in the usual IS/LM diagram. Figure 1 has three major changes from the typical Keynesian diagram (Ch. 4, Fig. 15). Firstly, the LM curve is much steeper. This reflects the low substitutability between money and bonds assumed in monetarist theory and therefore the low interest rate elasticity of money demand. Secondly, there is no liquidity trap. An increase in the money supply will always alter the rate of interest, at least initially (see below). Thirdly, the IS curve is less steep. This reflects greater faith in the size of the interest elasticity of investment held by the monetarist school. Therefore, in comparison to the Keynesian model, for a given money supply increase, the interest rate

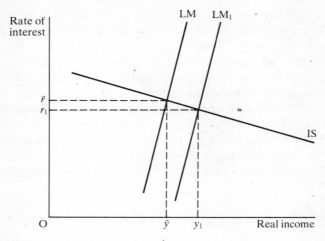

Fig. 1.

falls and income rises to a greater extent. A pure cost of capital analysis shows the money supply to be a more powerful policy weapon under monetarist than under Keynesian assumptions.

In addition, in monetarist analysis the full transmission mechanism of money is wider and more powerful than the cost of capital channel represented in Fig. 1 allows. These changes are reflected not in the slopes of the IS/LM curves but in the stability, in particular, of the IS function.

Firstly, the wider portfolio adjustment following a monetary expansion will lead to a rise in aggregate demand which will shift the IS curve to the right. This involves either a direct mechanical cash-balance argument for increased spending, or, more usually, the assumption that consumption is interest sensitive – a possibility not considered important in Keynesian economics. Secondly, a monetarist criticism of Keynesian economics – as well as an immediate post-Keynesian reaction – was the absence of wealth effects following a monetary expansion. Notwithstanding the doubt over whether wealth effects are theoretically valid (Ch. 4), the existence of them would shift the IS curve to the right also. Finally, monetarists place considerable importance on the transmission mechanisms through expectations outlined in Chapter 4. This set of effects does not lead to an unambiguous shift in the IS curve, however. The size and direction of the shift will depend on the relative importance of these conflicting effects (see Ch. 4). However, combining all the 'extra' transmission mechanisms specified in this paragraph, the IS curve, on balance, is likely to shift to the right (Fig. 2).

The increase in the money supply is now seen – assuming the IS curve shifts far enough to the right – to lead to a rise in income and a rise in the rate of interest. The actual situation is, however, rather more complex than is demonstrated in Fig. 2. Firstly, with real income defined on the horizontal axis, any increase in the price level following the monetary expansion will shift the LM curve back to the left. Secondly, many of the alternative mechanisms outlined

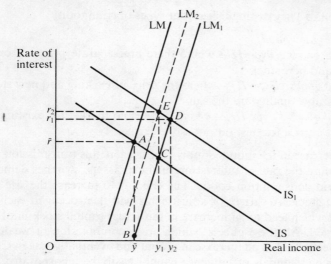

Fig. 2.

above take time to operate. To suggest that the economy moves through a series of static equilibrium situtations is far too simple; in fact, the dynamic nature of these mechanisms cannot be properly reflected in such a diagram. Basically, we do not know where the IS curve (or even the LM curve) is and certainly not whether the economy is in equilibrium or not. Finally, as demonstrated by Zwick (1971) and Teigen (1971), if the monetary sector adjusts faster than the real sector, the cost of capital channel itself may be split up into a liquidity effect ($\downarrow r$) and an income effect ($\uparrow y$). In such a case the adjustment path would be something like $ABCDE$ in Fig. 2. One must conclude that the IS/LM diagram is an unsatisfactory way of setting out the variety of channels through which the supply of money operates in monetarist theory.

The positive relationship between money supply and interest rate movements which follows from the above analysis is as crucial a part of monetarist theory as is the negative relationship of Keynesian theory. Friedman (1968) argues that interest rates are a misleading indicator of whether monetary policy is 'tight' or 'easy'. This is because their initial downward movement following a monetary expansion is very quickly reversed. He, in fact, emphasises the effects on spending through lower interest rates, and, due to the existence of higher cash balances, the effects on the demand for loans, the real quantity of money and price expectations. However, whatever the exact channels are, the increase in aggregate demand will, after a certain length of time cause the rate of interest to rise and eventually move above its previous equilibrium level.

In the 1970s, further developments took place concerning the transmission mechanism of money in the monetarist model. Brunner and Meltzer (1972a) criticised the above monetarist transmission mechanism as being essentially 'Keynesian'. They argued that the true mechanism is based on relative price adjustment across all asset markets, and they particularly included the role of real capital. They distinguished four types of commodity:

1. *Consumption goods.*
2. *Capital goods (Type I)* – where there are separate prices of existing stock and new stock.
3. *Capital goods (Type II)* – where the price of existing and new stock of comparable quality are the same.
4. *Capital goods (Type III)* – where there is no market for existing stock so, that a price for new output alone exists.

The increase in the money supply that triggers this transmission mechanism by reducing the rate of interest on financial assets, switches demand to these capital and consumption goods. The effect is to increase the size of the optimal capital stock. A variety of adjustments will then occur in each commodity market which lead to an increase in the actual capital stock until equilibrium is restored. All these effects (which are a combination of wealth and substitution effects) lead to an increase in output and eventually prices. Clearly, such wide-ranging channels of influence cannot easily be incorporated in the IS/LM model. However, it is convenient to assume that they also lead to an outward shift of the IS curve and so augment the power of monetary policy (see Brunner, 1976 and Park, 1972).

A major problem with the transmission mechanisms investigated so far is that the division of a monetary impulse $(\Delta M \cdot V_T)$ into a change in the price level (ΔP) and the level of transactions (ΔT) or output (Δy) is determined by *a priori* assertion. For Classical theory the price level alone changes, with output fixed in long-run equilibrium, while for Keynesian theory all the effect is on output with the price level fixed. Monetarists, by arguing that a money supply change will affect both output and the price level, have attempted to specify a more 'general' model. However, the task remains to determine what proportion of a given money supply increase, for example, has its effects on the price level and what proportion on output. This is an important issue as the size of the money multiplier will differ dependent on whether the price level, the level of income or neither are fixed (Laidler, 1978).[†] A convenient solution to this problem of dividing up money's role is the Phillips' curve relation between the level of excess demand and wage inflation (see Ch. 9). Modern work (to be

---

[†] Recalling eq. [32] in Chapter 4, the effect of a change in the money supply on real income is given by the money multiplier:

$$\Delta y = \frac{1}{a_1 m_2 / b_1 + m_1} \Delta M \qquad [32]$$

The real money supply can be split into its two elements M^*/P where M^* is the nominal money supply. Assuming that P and r are now the endogenous variables with real income (y) held constant at full employment, the effect of a change in the money supply on the price level is given by:

$$\Delta P = \frac{1}{y[m_1 + a_1 m_2 / b_1] - m_2 / b_1 (b_0 + a_0)} \Delta M^*$$

described more fully in Chapter 9) argues that a change in the money supply will lead to a change in output in the short run only. Output will eventually return to its 'natural' level consistent with the natural rate of unemployment. For example, an increase in the money supply will increase the demand for factors of production, particularly labour as firms anticipate the rise in prices and hence the fall in real wages. Labour supply will also rise if a money wage increase is awarded, as labour is assumed to base its expectations of prices largely on current prices which are stable. This rise in the demand for and supply of labour causes a rise in employment and output. However, when product prices actually do rise, employees become aware that real wages are unchanged and so withdraw the extra supply. Employment and output fall towards their natural level and prices rise even further as the supply of commodities falls. Therefore, output and employment, and, in fact, real variables in general, are only influenced by the money supply in the short run. In the long run, nominal variables such as nominal income, interest rates and, of course, the level of prices alone are influenced. Monetary growth has at best a transitory impact on real variables.[†]

However the various channels of influence are specified, monetary forces will always have a crucial, though complex, role in the determination of nominal income in monetarist thought. Of equal importance is that monetary forces are widely assumed by monetarists to be subject to 'long and variable lags'. In particular, Friedman has said (1970b) that a change in the rate of monetary growth will be followed by a change in the level of output about six to nine months later and the rate of inflation six to nine months after that. The length of these lags is uncertain and, of course, they vary considerably across countries and time periods, reflecting as they do the time involved for the various transmission mechanisms to operate. In this lagged process, there is an overshooting of the new equilibrium. As the money supply rises, prices remain un-

---

[†] A crucial element of the natural rate theory is the level of inflationary expectations. If such expectations are formed 'rationally', a money supply increase will not affect output even in the short run. This is because over time economic agents learn that an increase in the money supply is eventually followed by rising prices. Therefore, their immediate response is to raise prices and so by-pass the transitional effects on real variables. If agents act in this way, with the price adjustment being virtually automatic, the exact monetary transmission mechanism in operation is almost irrelevant (see Laidler, 1978).

These two expressions reduce to the same multiplier

$$\Delta y = \frac{1}{m_1} \Delta M \text{ and}$$

$$\Delta P = \frac{1}{m_1 y} \Delta M^*$$

and

$$\Delta Py = \frac{1}{m_1} \Delta M^*$$

if $m_2 = 0$ (vertical LM curve) or $b_1 = \infty$ (horizontal IS curve) *and* assuming that the real income elasticity of money demand is equal to unity.

changed initially so that the excess holding of balances is spent on the basis of the anticipated price level, which will be largely dependent on existing, stable prices. As prices begin to rise, holdings of real balances will be below those required for equilibrium so that the demand for cash balances will rise again and expenditure begin to fall. As prices drop back, real balances will now be above their desired level and so further adjustment will occur. Equilibrium will therefore be approached cyclically with the price level eventually shouldering the full burden of adjustment. When full equilibrium is reached, the output change has been reversed and the full effect of the money supply increase is on the level of prices.

The complexity of the transmission mechanism of money in monetarist theory has a consequence for the type of macroeconomic model used to test the theory. Monetarists see the channels of monetary influence, and the whole economy in general, as being too complex to capture in a large, structural model. Even the largest of models cannot capture all the complexities of the real world. So, monetarists favour the use of small, reduced form models which may only have a single equation. This is consistent with the gross association between money and nominal income which comes from monetarist theory, ignoring as it does intimate detail of how each sector reacts to a monetary change. In general, the large detailed information on individual sectors provided by structural models is considered superfluous to monetarist thought. The only sector which is important for monetarism is the money market.

On the other hand, Keynesians view the transmission mechanism of money as being clear. A definite channel through interest rates and investment is postulated and sufficient detail to capture this channel is required in a typical Keynesian model. In addition, the allocative impact of policy changes in individual sectors (e.g., consumption and investment) is considered vital for a full picture of Keynesian thought.

The preferences of each school for a particular type of economic model are firmly couched in basic doctrine. However, there may be more to these different views from a pragmatic stand point:

> The most famous of all reduced form models, the Anderson-Jordan model (1968) yields monetarist conclusions while structural models generally yield Keynesian conclusions. (Mayer, 1975, p.215).

This *ex-post* rationalisation has not, however, always been valid and the theoretical arguments should be judged to be the major ones. The reduced form and structural models used for empirical testing are compared in Ch. 6, Sect. 2.

A final reason why monetarists tend to ignore microeconomic detail in their preferred models is their belief that the private sector is inherently stable (e.g., Brunner, 1970). This is linked to the view that output and unemployment will tend towards their 'natural' levels. Any disturbances that do occur in an economy are due, according to this thesis, to the combination of a fluctu supply of money and a stable demand for money. A Keynesian, ho would include detail on individual sectors, not because the private s necessarily unstable but because stability cannot be guaranteed.

It is clear from the material presented so far in this chapter that a supply target is a vital part of monetarist doctrine. Control of the money supply will, through a stable money demand function, achieve the control of nominal income. Therefore, the stability of the money demand function is sufficient for monetarist policy prescriptions to follow. This is the case whatever the stability of the IS curve *vis-à-vis* the LM curve. However, recalling the analysis in Ch. 2, Figs. 3 and 4, the relative stability of the two curves is important for the choice of target of *monetary* policy. Monetarists believe that the demand for money, and therefore the LM curve is highly stable, while the IS curve though possessing some stability is more liable to fluctuation. Therefore, they recommend the use of the money supply rather than the rate of interest as the target of monetary policy as the former will minimise the fluctuations in income. The greater presumed stability in money demand provides another reason for the adoption of a monetary target according to the monetarists (see Laidler, 1973a, for a full derivation of these results).

However, the monetarist monetary policy recommendation is not merely for a monetary target which could be one policed month by month or even more frequently. It is in fact for a constant rate of growth of the money stock over time. This 'fixed throttle' recommendation, representing a special case of a monetary target does not follow logically from the stability arguments of this section. It is due to the fact that money supply changes operate with a long and variable lag. The time scale that will elapse before a monetary change has had its full effects is uncertain. In such a complex, difficult situation, monetary authorities are simply advised to maintain a constant rate of growth of the money supply.

The actual target rate of growth of the money supply selected has been considered less important than the stable growth principle itself. Opinions vary and indeed Friedman's own views have altered over time. Assuming that the income elasticity of money demand is unity, a rate of growth of the money supply that is equal to the rate of growth of output will guarantee zero price inflation. Therefore, growth rates of the money supply of around 3–5 per cent are typically recommended (e.g., Friedman, 1968) being in line with average growth rates of output in Western economies. However, evidence in the UK that the income elasticity of money demand is now probably less than 1 (see Ch. 6) necessitates a *lower* growth rate of the money supply than real income to obtain price stability.

4 Fiscal policy in the monetarist model

Monetarist views on the efficacy of fiscal policy in influencing nominal income are much further from Keynesian views than is the case for monetary policy. Keynes – and also Keynesians – do under certain circumstances accept a role for money supply changes. Matters are much less clear when it comes to considering monetarist views on fiscal policy. Monetarists do not dispute that an expansionary fiscal policy in the first round will increase income. But this is only part of the story. Secondary effects follow from the need to finance the resultant government deficit and it is the method of financing which may partially or totally eradicate any influence on income. If the method of financing is a rise in the money supply, then monetarists would call this monetary and no fiscal policy and as will become clear any secondary effects do not cancel ou the first round impart. If the rise in government spending is financed from highe: taxes there is a shift of the IS curve equal to the increase in government expen diture. (This is the case of the balanced-budget multiplier which is assumed to equal 1 in this example.) In the discussion that follows it is assumed that the method of financing is by the sale of government securities, unless argued otherwise.

It was originally believed that monetarists based their views on fisca policy on the fact that the elasticity of the demand for money with respect to the interest rate is near zero. In its extreme form, this reverts to the Classical case against fiscal policy.

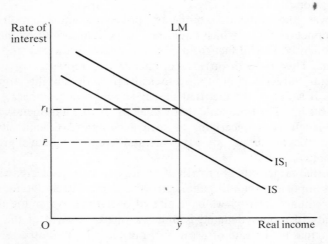

Fig. 3.

With an inelastic money demand (vertical LM), an expansionary fisca policy financed by bond sales causes the rate of interest to rise – as bond price: fall – and a switch of spending from the private to the public sector. Income is constant at $\bar{y}$. (If this expansion had been financed by monetary growth, the LM curve would have moved out and real income been raised in the short run. This extreme case is however indefensible. Money demand has rarely been show to be completely inelastic with respect to the rate of interest and Friedman in deed denies that this was ever a part of monetarist doctrine.

While a vertical LM curve may be invalid, a steep LM curve does follow from the monetarist view that money and financial assets are not close substi tutes. This case has been used to demonstrate a partial crowding-out of fisca policy with income rising to y_1 (Fig. 4). A monetary-financed fiscal expansion would have left the rate of interest at $\bar{r}$ and caused income to rise to y_2. The distance $y_1 y_2$ is then the 'fiscal crowd-out'. This case demonstrates the point that total crowding-out is not needed to demonstrate the relative inefficiency

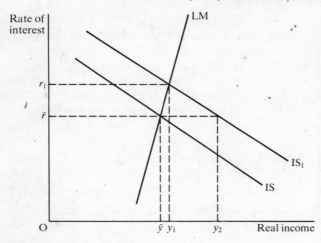

Fig. 4.

of fiscal policy. However, this case too is not the full monetarist story. James Tobin argued:

> In terms of the Hicksian language of Friedman's article, I thought (and still think) it (the issue) was the shape of the LM locus. (Tobin, 1972).

In a direct reply to this point Friedman concludes that:

> In my opinion, no 'fundamental issues' in either monetary theory or monetary policy hinge on whether the estimated elasticity can for most purposes be approximated by zero or is better approximated by -0.1, -0.5 or -2.0, provided it is seldom capable of being approximated by $-\infty$. (Friedman, 1969, quoted in Friedman, 1972).

The slope of the LM curve is therefore not the reason for the dismissal of fiscal policy.

A possible case noted by Carlson and Spencer (1975), which would qualify as a justification of the monetarist rejection of fiscal policy is that of the horizontal IS curve. However, this example is also part of Classical doctrine. Carlson and Spencer call this 'the Knight case' based on the writings of Frank Knight. An expansionary fiscal policy will not shift the IS curve at all, with saving being switched, one for one, from private investment to government securities. This is, however, tantamount to considering the interest rate as being exogenous. In this case, fiscal policy is automatically crowded-out and monetary policy alone affects income, without altering the rate of interest.

The full case against fiscal policy is more complex than these previous examples and is demonstrated in Fig. 6. The first round effect of the expansionary fiscal policy is a rise in income (y_1) and in the rate of interest (r_1). In addition, the increase in private wealth as bond holdings rise (assuming positive wealth effects exist) will lead to an increase in consumption expenditure and a further outward shift of the IS curve (IS_2). However, monetarists argue that there are a

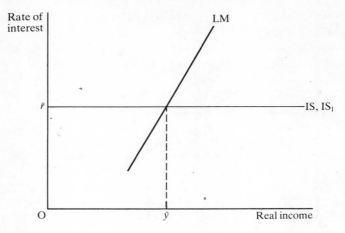

Fig. 5.

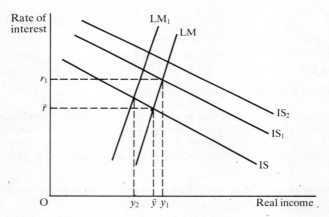

Fig. 6.

number of reasons why the long-term effects of bond financing will cause the IS
curve to shift back to the left again. A switch of resources from private to public
investment will lead to a fall in private investment and a reduced production of
physical assets. This may also be linked with a declining Marginal Efficiency of
Capital (MEC) as expectations worsen, a possibility mentioned by Keynes. In
addition, the increase in government expenditure has to be financed year by year
until the deficit is removed. Unless the deficit is a once for all occurrence, there is
a cumulative increase in public debt issues and a corresponding decumulation
of private sector assets. Finally, if the price level eventually rises following the
expansionary fiscal policy, the real value of the wealth stock will fall. Bond sales,
forcing the rate of interest upwards, may follow. Combining all these effects
the IS curve will move to the left and income may revert to its former level ($\bar{y}$

and could even fall below it. This total crowding-out has occurred despite a positively sloped LM curve.

These arguments must, however, be considered in the light of the substantial recent literature on the government's budget constraint and its influence on fiscal and monetary policy (see, for example, Christ, 1968; Blinder and Solow, 1973, 1976; Tobin and Buiter, 1976). According to this approach, long-run equilibrium will only be attained if the government's budget constraint is satisfied. This occurs when the change in the government deficit, including interest payments on bonds, is equal to the increase in the market value of the bond stock plus the increase in the money supply. Therefore, assuming the economy is stable, a bond-financed increase in the government deficit (although having a smaller impact multiplier) will lead to a *larger* long-run effect on income than a money-financed deficit. Bond issues and the consequent interest payments must be financed by higher taxes and it therefore requires a greater rise in income to induce tax receipts that are sufficient to finance the government's deficit and so satisfy its budget constraint.

Two doubts over the simplicity of this result remain, however. Firstly, the system may be unstable. If bond financing of a deficit induces wealth effects which increase the demand for money, these will shift the LM function to the left (LM_1). Should these effects outweigh the combined effects on the IS curve (which may be small following the analysis of the previous paragraph), the level of income will fall (y_2 – drawn in Fig. 6 with the effects of the fiscal policy on the IS curve completely offset). In this case, tax receipts will decline, increasing the budget deficit again and causing the process to feed on itself. The system is unstable with income spiralling downwards. Therefore, while a stable system generates a favourable result for bond-financed deficits, instability is more likely to occur than when deficits are financed by increases in the money supply. Secondly, once the price effects of bond-financed government spending are included, while nominal income may indeed increase, real income may be unchanged in the long run as the price level rises.

A final point is the conditions under which public investment is likely to displace private investment. It is considered that this is, on balance, less likely at a position of substantial unemployment than it is at full employment; the crowding-out of fiscal measures is much more feasible at a position where an economy's resources are under strain already. With a restrictive monetary policy, an economy in this situation is said to be 'financially constrained' so that fiscal expansion is less likely to lead to a rise in income, than when unemployment is low or the money supply increases simultaneously with the fiscal expansion.

There, according to the monetarists, the only unambiguously powerful fiscal policy is one financed by printing money. This case is illustrated in Fig. 7. The outward shift in the IS curve (IS_1) may be matched by the appropriate rise in the money supply (LM_1) to leave the rate of interest at $\bar{r}$. A major problem is how to determine the appropriate increase in the money supply to leave the rate of interest unchanged. The extent of the shift in the IS curve is given by:

$$y_1 - \bar{y} = \Delta y^* = m\Delta G \qquad [14]$$

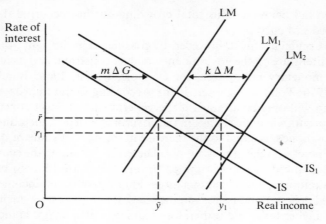

Fig. 7.

where ΔG is the change in government spending and m is the autonomous expenditure multiplier. Only in the case where this multiplier is unity (e.g., the simple balanced budget multiplier) is the resultant change in income equal to the change in government spending. In order to keep the rate of interest constant, the increase in the money supply must generate the same increase in the level of income:

$$y_1 - \bar{y} = \Delta y^* = k\Delta M \qquad [15]$$

where k is the money multiplier. Therefore, accurate estimates of these two multipliers are needed in order to achieve the necessary rise in the money supply that leaves the rate of interest unchanged. This is known as a 'validating' monetary policy in that the increase in government spending is validated by a rise in the money supply. Note also that if

$$\Delta y^* = k\Delta M = m\Delta G \qquad [16]$$

$\Delta G = \Delta M$ only if

$$k = m \qquad [17]$$

Only if [17] holds will the policy of maintaining a constant rate of interest ($\bar{r}$) also lead to an exact financing of the deficit ($\Delta G = \Delta M$). Indeed, if $k > m$, and the rate of interest has been held at r, full financing has not occurred ($\Delta G > \Delta M$). Further monetary expansion (LM_2) which will reduce the rate of interest to $\bar{r}_1$ or new sales of government debt which would leave the LM curve at LM_1 are needed to fill the remaining gap between government expenditure and revenue. If $k < m$, full monetary financing of the deficit would leave the rate of interest above $\bar{r}$.

An important debating issue between monetarists and Keynesians is (in the context of Fig. 8) which policy is the more powerful. The final level of income (y_1) is only achieved due to a combination of fiscal and monetary policy. If fiscal policy alone were used, income would rise to y_F with the increase in the

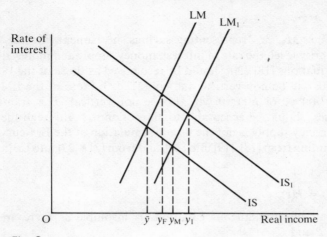

Fig. 8.

rate of interest resulting in partial crowding-out. If monetary policy alone were used, income would rise to y_M with the rate of interest falling. The combined result increases income more than either of these two individual cases.[†]

5 A theoretical framework for monetarism

The final section of this chapter follows closely the assembly of a theoretical framework for monetarism by Friedman (1970a, 1971, – reprinted in Gordon, 1974). It was presented as one way in which monetarism can be modelled and was not intended to be the final word on the issue. The aims of the framework were twofold. Firstly, the intention was to derive a theoretical model which would explain nominal income through the behaviour of the money stock. Secondly, Friedman sought to answer mounting criticism that monetarism was based solely on empirical evidence without any theoretical background. The following framework seeks to answer that criticism.

Friedman set out what he called a simple common model:

$$S = f(y,r) \qquad\qquad\qquad\qquad [18]‡$$

$$I = g(r) \qquad\qquad\qquad\qquad [19]$$

$$S = I \qquad\qquad\qquad\qquad [20]$$

$$M_D = P \cdot l(y,r) \qquad\qquad\qquad\qquad [21]$$

$$M_S = h(r) \qquad\qquad\qquad\qquad [22]$$

[†] The only exceptions to this rule are where the IS and LM curves take on extreme (either vertical or horizontal) shapes. The student should check the efficiency of the two policies in these extreme cases. In this section, long-run price increases, that will cause the LM curve to shift to the left, following a policy change have been ignored to simplify the analysis.
[‡] In fact, Friedman specified eq. [18] as a consumption function. The savings function is derived assuming $y = C + S$.

$$M_D = M_S \tag{23}$$

with S, I, y, P, r, M_S, M_D representing savings, investment, income, (all in real terms) the price level, the rate of interest, money supply and money demand respectively. Equations [18]–[20] should be recognised as those of the IS curve, which if $g(r) < 0$, will be non-vertical and eq. [21]–[23] those of the LM curve which if either $l(r) < 0$ or $h(r) > 0$ will also be non-vertical. This framework, Friedman argues, should be acceptable to all economists, although the endogeneity of the money supply is not the usual formulation of the LM curve.

Substituting from [18], [19] into [20], and from [21], [22] into [23]:

$$f(y,r) = g(r) \tag{24}$$

$$P \cdot l(y,r) = h(r) \tag{25}$$

This pair of simultaneous equations is insoluble as there are three unknowns – y, P and r.

The various schools of thought differ in the methods adopted to solve this system. An assumption of exogeneity has to be made with regard to one variable in [24], [25]. The simple quantity theory response is to assume there is full employment in equilibrium so that real income $(\bar{y})$ is uniquely determined in the labour market:

$$f(\bar{y},r) = g(r) \tag{26}$$

$$P \cdot l(\bar{y},r) = h(r) \tag{27}$$

The system can now be solved sequentially with [26] setting r and then given r, [27] solves for P. The model is exactly determined. The situation is set out in Fig. 9. The LM curve fluctuates as the price level changes $(P_3 > P_2 > P_1 > \bar{P})$, and no determinate equilibrium on IS is identifiable. However, with income fixed exogenously at $\bar{y}$, the price level (P_1) and the rate of interest $(\bar{r})$ solve the system.

The Keynesian approach is to assume that the price level is inflexible

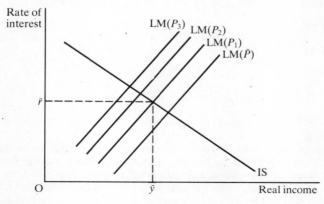

Fig. 9.

($\bar{P}$). This typical Keynesian assumption modifies equation [25]:

$$f(y,r) = g(r) \tag{24}$$

$$\bar{P} \cdot l(y,r) = h(r) \tag{28}$$

These can now be solved simultaneously for y and r. Figure 10 summarises this case:

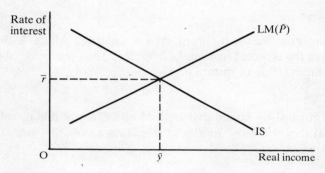

Fig. 10.

The rigid price assumption fixes the LM curve at $LM(\bar{P})$ and a unique solution for r and y is obtained.

To derive a monetarist solution to the under-identified system [18]–[23], Friedman makes a number of assumptions as the analysis proceeds, which clearly underpin the validity of the final outcome. The first of them is that money demand is homogenous of degree one with respect to real income. Then [21] becomes:

$$M_D = P \cdot y \cdot l(r) = P \cdot \frac{Y}{P} \cdot l(r)$$

$$M_D = Y \cdot l(r) \tag{29}$$

Friedman then introduces the distinction between the nominal and real rate of interest with

$$r = \ell + \dot{P} \text{ and} \tag{30}$$

$$r^e = \ell^e + \dot{P}^e$$

where ℓ is the real rate of interest, $\dot{P}$ the rate of inflation and superscript e refers to expected values. His second assumption is that

$$r = r^e \tag{31}$$

which he justifies by saying that 'we take over from Keynes the idea that the current market rate of interest (r) is largely determined by the rate that is expected to prevail over a longer period' (Friedman, in Gordon, 1974, p.35).

Substituting in [30]:

$$r = \ell^e + \dot{P}^e \tag{32}$$

As

$$Y = Py \text{ and therefore}$$
$$\dot{Y}^e = \dot{P}^e + \dot{y}^e \tag{33}$$

Then

$$r = \ell^e + \dot{Y}^e - \dot{y}^e \tag{34}$$

Friedman now makes his third vital assumption which is that the difference between the expected real rate of interest (ℓ^e) and the expected rate of growth of real output ($\dot{y}^e$) is a constant (k_0):

$$\ell^e - \dot{y}^e = k_0 \tag{35}$$

This is justified by saying that both ℓ^e and $\dot{y}^e$ are stable in value, or alternatively that they will move together. Substituting from [35] into [34]:

$$r = k_0 + \dot{Y}^e \tag{36}$$

The full model now consists of the original [22], [23], [29] and [36], i.e.

$$M_D = Y \cdot l(r) \tag{29}$$

$$M_S = h(r) \tag{22}$$

$$M_D = M_S \tag{23}$$

$$r = k_0 + \dot{Y}^e \tag{36}$$

Given that the rate of interest is now an exogenous variable, the level of nominal income will adjust to bring money supply and demand into equilibrium. The model is therefore exactly identified with, in effect, three equations [22, 23 and 29] and three unknowns (M_D, M_S, Y). However, Friedman now assumes that the money stock is exogenous after all:

$$M_S = \bar{M} \tag{37}$$

so that having just achieved an exactly identified model, this assumption makes the model over-identified. Pursuing Friedman's analysis by substituting into [23]:

$$Y \cdot \ell(r) = \bar{M} \tag{38}$$

and

$$Y = \frac{\bar{M}}{\ell(k_0 + \dot{Y}^e)} \tag{39}$$

Equation [39] gives the result that the level of nominal income (Y) is determined by the money supply (M) given the velocity function $\ell(\ )$, i.e.

$$Y = V(\ ) \cdot \bar{M} \text{ where} \tag{40}$$

$$V(\ ) = \frac{1}{\ell(\ )}$$

The final assumption made is to determine the path of expected nominal income changes ($\dot{Y}^e$). Friedman assumes that Y^e is determined by past levels of nominal income which themselves depend on the money supply in previous periods [39]. Combining these results, nominal income depends on past and present values of the money supply:

$$Y_t = F(M_{t-i}), \bar{M}_t \qquad \qquad [41]$$

where t and $t-i$ are time subscripts.

This monetarist framework was criticised heavily in the symposium (Gordon, 1974) which followed the publication of the two relevant articles. The comments on it can be studied in two parts. Firstly, the assumptions of the models are challenged and secondly, the framework is looked at as an overall attempt to represent monetarist thought.

Many of the assumptions of the model can be questioned. Firstly, before the monetarist 'approach' is even set out, the labelling of the rigid price assumption as Keynesian can be challenged. Although Friedman qualifies this price rigidity assumption by arguing that Keynes allowed for relative price changes, he still felt justified in making the rigid price assumption. Keynes in the General Theory certainly did not envisage prices to be invariant but it is a fact that textbook versions of Keynesian economics have made this simplification. Tobin accuses Friedman (Gordon, 1974, p.80) of trying 'to saddle his opponents and critics with an extreme assumption and to claim the entire middle ground for himself'. Certainly the polar extremes of fixed output and flexible prices for quantity theorists and flexible output and rigid prices for Keynesians are a dichotomy that has been heavily criticised although as demonstrated in section 3 above it is a useful caricature of these models.

More important for the approach itself are the assumptions used. Four were identified in the text and these can be looked at individually. Firstly, the assumption of homogeneity of degree one of money demand with respect to real income cannot, on Friedman's own admittance, be justified theoretically. However, more seriously perhaps, it is also a very debatable empirical result. Estimates vary widely and it is not clear that assuming a unitary elasticity is a justifiable procedure. Secondly, the assumed equality of the actual and expected rate of interest represents a specific Keynesian assumption and is not a general usage of a familiar Keynesian idea as Friedman suggests. In particular, it assumes that the actual rate of interest is in equilibrium because only then will the expected rate be equal to it. It certainly, as Friedman argues, 'carries the idea to the limit' (Friedman in Gordon, 1974, p.35). Thirdly, the constant difference between the expected interest rate and growth rate of real output is a convenient assumption which has little empirical support, although the logic of his argument, that both are stable anyway, is convincing. Finally, the assumption that the expected growth rate of nominal income depends on past levels of nominal income is a familiar one in economics. The idea that the expected value of a variable depends on its own current and past values is one used by Friedman in his permanent income hypothesis and is an acceptable simplification.

A final point on the structure of the model relates to the treatment of the money supply. If it had been assumed to be exogenous initially the LM curve would have been in familiar form. However, to assume it depended on the rate of interest is a realistic assumption. The problem occurred when Friedman arbitrarily dropped that assumption in the model, making the money supply predetermined, because this led to the model being over-identified from then on.

The symposium which discussed the framework suggested a number of criticisms, many of which have been tackled already in this chapter. These include the oral tradition of monetarism (Patinkin), the narrow transmission mechanism and down-grading of fiscal policy (Brunner and Meltzer) and the role of the slope of the LM curve (Tobin). Other criticisms have been made also. The model as it stands does not divide up the effects of a monetary impulse into changes in prices and changes in output. As argued in section 3 above, this is a difficult problem for monetarist analysis. In the context of Friedman's framework, Patinkin (1972) would have preferred a full labour market and production function specification which, assuming the capital stock is fixed, would solve for the level of employment and, hence, output. The inclusion of a real-balance effect in the model would have reflected quantity theory tradition more fully. However, Patinkin appreciates that the cost involved in making these changes is a more complex system which could not be solved sequentially. Finally, Davidson (1972) argues that the Keynes summarised by Friedman is not the true Keynes, but a Keynesian. This criticism covers the assumption of price rigidity (mentioned by Davidson) as well as other points. Davidson in particular dislikes the certainty of the Keynesian model postulated by Friedman. All expectations are assumed to be fulfilled and this is not so in Keynes' world. Keynes assumed much uncertainty existed and indeed it is argued that many institutions (including money) only exist because uncertainty is present also.

Many more points of conflict, clarification and agreement were aired in the symposium which followed Friedman's work. A full reading of the symposium is essential to come to terms with these. As an attempt to give monetarism a theoretical base, the work of Friedman's framework is very valuable. Many disputes, however, remain and empirical evidence alone can decide a large number of them.

Chapter 6

Empirical evidence

1 Introduction

Following the analysis of the theoretical role of money in the last three chapters, the task of this chapter is to review the main empirical evidence on the role of money in the determination of economic activity. There is a vast amount of evidence of this sort covering many countries, time periods and also a large variety of types of test. Most of the pioneering empirical work was completed for US data, but concentration will be limited to the 'classic' early studies from that country. A more complete survey of UK results will be undertaken.

Before embarking on such a survey, it is important to establish the main issues that the empirical work should attempt to resolve. This is particularly important as the main point of disagreement between the rival schools of thought is now different from what it was at the beginning of the empirical debate. Initially, given the Keynesian environment in which policy was conducted, the studies set out to establish whether the money supply was a significant determinant of the level of economic activity. This was attempted using single-equation money multipliers, large-scale structural models of the economy and demand for money models. Secondly, tests were carried out to observe whether the money supply or autonomous expenditure, and then monetary or fiscal policy, were more important determinants of economic activity. Thirdly, the lag involved in the operation of such policies was analysed. However, when a summary is attempted of all the work completed since the debate began in earnest in 1963, it is agreed by all sides, at least for the USA, that monetary policy does play a significant role in the determination of economic activity. The theoretical and empirical debate is therefore now concerned with establishing 'the short and medium-run impact of pure fiscal actions on aggregate money income' (Modigliani and Ando, 1976). However, it is the task of this chapter to survey the evidence on the role of money (which is much less conclusive for the UK than it is for the USA) and to refer to studies comparing the power of fiscal and monetary policy where appropriate.

2 Structural and reduced form models of the role of money

An issue that has become of major importance in this empirical debate is the type of economic model to be used. Firstly, the role of money can be examined in a full 'structural' model of the economy. In such a model, equations are specified to explain fully the endogenous variables of the model such as consumption and investment in terms of both exogenous and other endogenous variables. Ideally, all the many complex links between economic variables should be included in a model of this type. However, the result is usually a highly complex model with an enormous number of equations that may be viewed as being too cumbersome to evaluate the role of one variable like the money supply. Alternatively, therefore, the 'reduced-form' approach has become popular in this area. A reduced-form equation may be defined as a relationship derived from a full structural model between the endogenous variable to be explained (e.g., economic activity) and the exogenous variables that determine it. Use of such an approach may reduce the number of equations to be estimated to one and so minimise the complexities of obtaining the results. However, in most cases, the structural model underlying the reduced form is left unspecified so that the validity of the reduced form itself is doubtful.

Strictly speaking, this debate over the type of estimating model to use is independent of the debate between Keynesians and monetarists on the role of money. However, as argued in Chapter 5, it has become part of the debate as the reduced-form studies are favoured by monetarists and generally yield monetarist results. On the other hand, structural models are favoured by Keynesians, *a priori*, and also because of the results they yield (Mayer, 1975).

A number of arguments may be advanced in favour of the 'reduced-form' approach, most of which may be associated with the monetarist school. Firstly, it is argued by monetarists that the transmission mechanism of money is too complex and operates through too many channels for a structural model (however complicated) to capture it in full. Therefore, a reduced-form approach is more practical. Secondly, monetarists are generally interested in the gross association between money and variables such as economic activity, nominal income and the price level. As such, the numerous avenues through which money affects these variables are of limited interest to them. This is particularly apparent when combined with a third factor in favour of such models, namely that for monetarists, allocative detail concerning various sectors of the economy is of limited importance. For example, the division of a monetary impulse between consumption and investment is far less important than the net effect on national income. Fourthly, the belief that the private sector's economic behaviour is basically stable is important. This is the main reason for the lack of interest in allocative detail and can therefore be advanced as another argument in favour of the reduced-form approach.

The arguments advanced in favour of the structural model approach are partly the reverse of those outlined in the last paragraph. In particular, a large amount of potentially useful information is ignored in reduced-form models. Variables may be aggregated when it is both interesting and important to determine the separate components of the aggregates. This is especially true for Keynesians, who believe that the inherent instability of economic behaviour of the private sector makes the analysis of individual sectors very important. In addition, structural models involve *a priori* restrictions on certain coefficients and the specification of certain variables as being exogenous. Such information is ignored in the reduced-form approach so that it is unclear whether results obtained are even consistent with a particular (unspecified) structural model (Gramlich, 1969). A crucial issue, as will become clear in this chapter, is which variables are assumed to be exogenous in the reduced-form approach. An inappropriate exogeneity assumption may invalidate results obtained from a reduced-form model. A structural model has the advantage that it specifies the relevant transmission mechanisms of money. This is easily undertaken in a Keynesian model where the cost of capital effect is the major channel of effect, although other mechanisms are increasingly being used in structural models. Gramlich (1969) also notes that reduced-form models by specifying the level of economic activity as being determined by monetary and fiscal forces alone, relegate all other potential determinants to the status of random elements. The real choice is therefore between simplicity and ease of operation against realism and operational complexity.

Attention in this chapter is placed on empirical work from reduced-form studies. This reflects the large amount of evidence on the role of money available in the UK from such models relative to that from full structural models. Large structural models do exist in the UK; for example, the Treasury, London Business School and National Institute models (see Laury, Lewis and Ormerod, 1978). In general, however, such models have only recently been concerned with a detailed analysis of the monetary sector. In addition, the famous structural models of the US economy, such as the Federal Reserve Board–Massachusetts Institute of Technology (FRB–MIT) model (De Leeuw and Gramlich, 1968, 1969) and the Brookings model (Fromm and Taubman, 1968), will not be considered in detail. A recent trend has been to specify intermediate models of between three and fifteen equations that seek to combine the merits of the reduced-form and structural approaches. A general monetary model of this type is set out in Chapter 9, while other examples are the models of Moroney and Mason (1971) and Arestis, Frowen and Karakitsos (1978), the latter being estimated for the UK as well as for other countries.

3 Money and economic activity

A large amount of the evidence on the role of money has come from a variety of studies that have linked the money supply or monetary policy to economic activity. These studies have taken three forms. In the description of these tests, the first part of this section will be devoted to a brief analysis of the classic, pathbreaking contributions in this field. Then concentration will be placed on evidence gained from similar tests for the UK.

Firstly, in a number of studies in the early 1960s, Friedman and Anna Schwartz (1963a, 1963b, henceforth FS) investigated thoroughly the length and variability of the time lags involved in the influence of money. They did this by studying time series of the money supply and of business activity. By identifying cycles in these two variables, FS were able to date the turning points of the series. The results had a startling impact on monetarist views concerning the stabilisation role of monetary policy. They found that, on average, peaks in the rate of change of the money supply preceded peaks in the level of economic activity by 16 months with the equivalent figure for troughs being 12 months. Moreover, these lags were not only long but highly variable leaving FS with no option but to recommend the abandonment of fine-tuning and all counter-cyclical monetary policy. It was evidence of this type that was the major reason for the monetarist proposal for a money supply rule. In addition, the highest correlation between the money supply and business activity occurred when the latter was subject to a lag of 6 months.

This consistent evidence in favour of a lead of money over activity was subject to severe criticism. Many general worries that apply to the other types of study are taken up later in this section. However, a particular concern over this type of work was the actual measurement of the lag (Davis, 1968). Friedman (1958) and Culbertson (1960) had already exchanged views on this before the publication of the 1963 results. The problem was the comparison of turning points in the *rate of change* of the money supply and of the *level* of business activity. For any data series, the rate of change will peak before the level does so that even if, in terms of levels, both cycles were exactly contemporaneous the peak in the rate of change of the money supply would *precede* the peak in the level of business activity (Shaw, 1977). Therefore, argue the critics, the observed lags may in certain cases be due to an invalid statistical technique. Kareken and Solow (1963) re-ran the experiment using first differences of the series; they concluded that there was equal evidence of a lead of business activity over the money supply as there was of the relationship being in the opposite direction. Kareken and Solow also argue that the effect of monetary policy will be spread over a long time period building up from a small immediate impact to full effects after around 6 to 9 months. However, Mayer (1967) argues that Kareken and Solow spoil their case, as some of their other evidence suggests a longer lag for part of GNP than even Friedman and Schwartz estimate.

Another general criticism is that evidence of a lag of one variable behind another does not allow any automatic conclusion on causality. This is a general point to be taken up in the next section. However, with specific reference to this analysis, Tobin (1970b) derived an 'ultra Keynesian' model in which the money supply is demand-determined and yet the turning points of the rate of change of the money supply led those of nominal income. Likewise, in a 'Friedman' model where the demand for money was dependent on permanent income and the money supply was exogenous, the turning points in the rate of change of the money supply actually lagged the peaks and troughs in nominal income. It is clear, therefore, that evidence of money *leading* economic activity must be translated with great care into statements that changes in the money supply *cause* changes in economic activity.

The second pioneering piece of work was an attempt by Friedman and

Meiselmann (FM – 1963) to compare the stability and predictive power of the money supply and autonomous expenditure in the determination of national income. The aim was a direct comparison of quantity theory (or monetarist) and Keynesian models. The basic relationships which underlie these tests are familiar. National income is the sum of induced (consumption) and autonomous components:

$$Y = C + A \qquad [1]$$

where Y is nominal income, C consumption and A autonomous expenditure. Specifying a consumption function:

$$C = a + bY \qquad [2]$$

the reduced-form equation for nominal income may be derived:

$$Y = \frac{a}{1-b} + \frac{1}{1-b} A \qquad [3]$$

The crucial test of this Keynesian model is the stability of the investment multiplier $(1/1-b)$. Running a regression of [3] would have produced biased results as A is a component of Y. Therefore, by subtracting A from both sides, FM derived a relationship between consumption and autonomous expenditure:

$$C = a_0 + a_1 A \qquad [4]$$

where $a_0 = a/1-b$ and $a_1 = b/1-b$. Of course, a_1 is not now the national income multiplier.

The quantity theory equation itself was the origin of the rival model with M and V representing the money supply and transactions velocity respectively:

$$Y = V \cdot M \qquad [5]$$

The stability of V – the money multiplier – is the crucial test of the quantity theory relationship. As with the Keynesian model, consumption was used as the dependent variable for the quantity theory model:

$$C = b_0 + b_1 M \qquad [6]$$

Equations [4] and [6] formed the basic relationships that were tested; in addition, the following equations were fitted to the data:

$$C = c_0 + c_1 A + c_2 M \qquad [7]$$

$$C = d_0 + d_1 A + d_2 M + d_3 P \qquad [8]$$

$$C = e_0 + e_1 A + e_2 P \qquad [9]$$

$$C = f_0 + f_1 M + f_2 P \qquad [10]$$

$$Y = g_0 + g_1 M \qquad [11]$$

$$Y = h_0 + h_1 M + h_2 P \qquad [12]$$

Equation [7] simply combines the two models. Equations [8] – [10] include a price index (P) as an independent variable as all variables are expressed in nominal terms. Finally, equations [11], [12] were fitted as they are true quantity theory relationships; this was particularly important as FM believed that to test the quantity theory with consumption as the dependent variable would favour the Keynesian model.

Using the above regression equations and also by calculating correlation coefficients, FM found that for every sub-period of their data (which ran from 1897 to 1958) except for the immediate depression period of 1929–39, the correlation coefficient between C and M was greater than that between C and A. In addition, the money supply equation yielded more stable and significant effects on consumption than did the autonomous expenditure equation. The lower and less significant effects of autonomous expenditure did not mean, however, that FM doubted that the simple multiplier would be around unity as they were regressing consumption (not income) on autonomous expenditure (Gramlich, 1971).

The impact that this piece of work had on the economics profession was great. It focussed attention on the role of money and generated vehement criticism from many economists predominantly Keynesians (sect. 4 below). However, the debate was carried forward by the results of a third type of empirical test. In 1968, Anderson and Jordan (AJ – 1968), from the Federal Reserve Bank of St. Louis, published a study that looked at the influence of various measures of fiscal and monetary policy on GNP. The basic equation tested was:

$$\Delta Y_t = a + b \sum_{i=0}^{n} \Delta M_{t-i} + C \sum_{i=0}^{n} \Delta F_{t-i} \qquad [13]$$

where Y, M, F are gross national product, monetary policy and fiscal policy respectively. By using first differences (which removed any trend in the variables) and testing the hypothesis for post-war data (1952–68), AJ answered some of the criticisms advanced since the FM results had been published. To represent monetary policy, the authors used the money supply and the monetary base. Their measures of fiscal policy were the high-employment budget surplus (i.e., the surplus adjusted for economic activity), government expenditures and government receipts.

Their major result was that

> the response of economic activity to monetary actions compared with that of fiscal actions, is larger, more predictable and faster. (Anderson and Jordan, 1968, p.22).

A rise in the money supply of $100 m. had a positive effect on GNP of $160 m. in the first quarter. Depending on the definitions of the variables used the cumulated money multiplier over four quarters was around 6. However, for fiscal policy, the best result was a fiscal multiplier of 0.9 after two quarters and in that case subsequent negative effects reduced the four quarter multiplier to 0.2. In all the equations tested, over 50 per cent of the variation in GNP was explained by changes in fiscal and monetary policy. However, monetary policy was the only significant variable in each case.

The extraordinary fact concerning these results – which are in many ways more dramatic than those of FM – is the discrepancy between them and the results of alternative economic models. The fact that the fiscal policy multiplier was virtually zero cast considerable doubt on Keynesian policies as did the dominant role of monetary policy in determining GNP (Davis, 1969). These studies, whatever the criticisms that may be made of them (sect. 4 below), did play a role in the revival of faith in monetary policy in the USA.[†]

Studies of the role of monetary forces in the UK have been completed along similar lines for all the three types of test set out above. Two studies which looked at the cyclical fluctuations of money and income have been made. Walters (1971) found that for post-war data a six month lag between the money supply and GNP gave rise to the highest positive correlation between the variables. The similarity between the length of this lag and that measured by Friedman and Schwartz for the USA is probably coincidental given the great differences between the two countries. A much more comprehensive study was completed by Crockett (1970). He not only studied the lags between aggregate expenditure and the money supply but also between their components. The main relationship between the aggregate variables confirmed the lead of money over GNP, but Crockett found that it was bimodal. There appeared to be a peak correlation when money led by one quarter and a further peak when the lead was four quarters in length. However, the size of the correlation coefficient ($r = 0.34$), even though the data was in first difference form, suggested a large degree of slippage in the relationship. The other result of major interest was the low correlation between changes in the money supply and consumption. The correlation coefficient reached a maximum of 0.2 when money lagged consumption by six quarters. This allows the reader to anticipate the relatively poor results of a Friedman-Meiselmann type test for the UK since 1945.

A summary of the main UK results for the other two types of study is given in Table 1 (pp. 144–8). There is an underlying theme running through studies which look at the role of money and autonomous expenditure in the determination of GNP. For the period up to the First World War, Barrett and Walters (1966) found that both money and autonomous expenditure were significant determinants of consumption with money playing the greater role. In an income equation, Walters (1966) estimated the money multiplier to be 0.75 although within two years of the change in the money supply, the effect on GNP was negative.

For the inter-war period, Barrett and Walters found that the autonomous expenditure variable became the major determinant of consumption. However, the money stock lagged one year remained significant. The money

[†] However, as noted in Ch. 2, sect. 5 and Ch. 5, sect. 1, other factors contributed to the growth of monetarism and the introduction of monetary targets, both in the USA and world wide; the importance of such academic studies in this process should not be overemphasised.

Table 1 Summary of UK studies on money and economic activity
(a) Money and autonomous expenditure multipliers

Study		Barrett and Walters (1966)						Walters (1966)		
Dependent variable		ΔC	ΔC	ΔC	ΔC	ΔC	ΔGNP	ΔGNP	ΔGNP	ΔP
Data Period		1878–1914 1920–1938 1948–1963	1878–1914 1920–1938 1948–1963	1878–1914	1921–1938	1878–1938	1880–1913	1922–1938	1955(3)–1962(4)	1922–1938
Independent variables	Lag									
Constant		0.011 (0.002)	0.005 (0.002)	0.003 (0.002)	-0.003 (0.001)	-0.005 (0.004)	0.004 (0.005)	-0.002 (0.003)	0.017 (0.003)	-0.012 (0.009)
M_s (money supply)	0						0.431 (0.245)	0.789 (0.413)	-0.295 (0.421)	0.807 (0.406)
	1	0.456 (0.132)	0.406 (0.106)	0.576 (0.088)	0.250 (0.133)	0.838 (0.116)	0.455 (0.275)	0.587 (0.453)	0.490 (0.441)	0.555 (0.447)
	2						-0.132 (0.224)	-0.388 (0.311)	-0.881 (0.400)	-0.556 (0.337)
A (autonomous expenditure)	0		0.204 (0.033)		0.194 (0.038)	0.087 (0.041)				
	1			0.087 (0·031)						
Y/p (real income)	0									-0.512 (0.410)
R^2		0.139	0.442	0.579	0.678	0.541	0.354	0.608	0.153	0.705
$\bar{R}^2$		0.46	0.41	0.58	0.25	0.84	0.287	0.518	0.066	0.607
Money multiplier		C					0.75	0.99	-0.69	0.81
Autonomous expenditure multiplier		0.20	0.20	0.09	0.19	0.09				
Money supply variable		$I+G+X-M$	C	C	C	C	C	C	C	C
Autonomous expenditure variable			$I+G+X-M$	$I+G+X-M$	$I+G+X-M$	$I+G+X-M$				

(partial column-source headings at top, faint/cut off: "(1957)" … "(1971)" … "Goodhart and Crockett (1970)" … "Artis and Nobay (1971)")

Dependent variable	Lag	ΔC	Y	ΔGDP	ΔQ	ΔGDP	ΔQ	ΔP	ΔP
Data period		1951–1967	1954(2)–65(2)	1957(2)–69(3)	1953(2)–69(3)	1964(3)–69(3)	1964(3)–69(3)	1960/1–72/3	1960/1–74/5
Independent variables									
Constant		497.6 (116.9)	−41.8 (20.7)					0.026 (0.007)	0.009 (0.01)
M_s (money supply)	0	1.083 (0.412)		0.35 (0.17)	0.14 (0.06)			0.064 (0.09)	−0.036 (0.12)
	1	0.062 (0.402)	1.407 (0.573)	0.28 (0.18)	0.22 (0.06)		0.07 (0.05)	0.190 (0.12)	0.068 (0.14)
	2				0.18 (0.06)	0.28 (0.11)		0.032 (0.16)	0.642 (0.13)
	3			0.49 (0.15)	0.12 (0.06)	−0.31 (0.12)	0.20 (0.05)		
	4				0.15 (0.06)	0.32 (0.12)			
	5			0.63 (0.17)	0.09 (0.06)	0.20 (0.11)			
	6			−0.39 (0.20)					
	7			0.45 (0.18)					
A (autonomous expenditure)	0	−0.050 (0.218)							
	1	0.428 (0.160)							
LDV	1		0.745 (0.105)						
R^2 / $\bar{R}^2$		0.618	0.955	0.565	0.588	0.742	0.772	0.58	0.83
Money multiplier		1.14	1.41	1.81	0.90	0.49	0.27	0.29	0.67
Autonomous expenditure multiplier		0.38							
Money supply variable		B	F	A	A	C	C	G	G
Autonomous expenditure variable		$I+G+X$							

Table 1 Summary of UK studies on money and economic activity
(b) Monetary and fiscal policy

Study		Artis and Nobay (1969)					
Dependent variable		Δ GDP					
Data Period		1958(1)–1967(3)					
Independent variable	Lag						
Constant		122.0	97.0	77.6			
LDV	1	−0.7 (0.12)					
	2	−0.5 (0.13)					
GFM	0				4.67 (3.01)	2.70 (2.45)	
	1	11.6 (1.90)	9.3 (3.1)	10.8 (3.0)	2.64 (2.22)	1.06 (1.63)	
	2		−7.0 (3.0)	−8.3 (2.96)	−0.42 (1.83)	−0.75 (0.79)	
	3				−1.41 (1.88)	−0.66 (1.83)	
	4				0.17 (1.42)	1.29 (1.36)	
	5				2.21 (2.51)	2.93 (2.31)	
	Sum				7.86	6.57	
FER	0	0.8 (0.16)					
ADV	4			0.2 (0.11)			
	5	0.5 (0.11)					
Money supply (definition D)	0				−0.08 (0.11)		−0.01 (0.04)
	1				−0.02 (0.09)		0.02 (0.06)
	2				0.07 (0.09)		0.07 (0.08)
	3				0.14 (0.11)		0.07 (0.08)
	4	0.2 (0.08)			0.14 (0.13)		
	5				0.09 (0.12)		
	Sum				0.34		0.15
R^2		0.73	0.23	0.31	0.134	0.083	0.034
Monetary policy multiplier					0.34		0.15
Fiscal policy multiplier					7.86	6.57	

Study		Keran (1970a)				Matthews and Ormerod (1978)	Arestis, Frowen and Karakitsos (1978)
Dependent variables		ΔQ	ΔQ	ΔGNP	ΔGDP	ΔGDP	ΔGNP
Data period		1953(2)– 1968(4)	1962(1)– 1968(3)	1962(1)– 1968(3)	1962(1)– 1968(3)	1964(2)– 1974(4)	1965(1)– 1974(4)
Independent variable	Lag						
Constant		0.21 (0.07)	0.12 (0.16)	0.45 (0.20)	0.54 (0.22)		−0.174
LDV	1						1.949
	2						−1.307
	3						0.254
	4						0.087
	5						−0.037
FED	0					0.606 (0.22)	
	1					−0.105 (0.20)	
	2					0.066 (0.21)	
	3					0.167 (0.22)	
	4					−0.754 (0.26)	
	Sum					−0.019 (0.08)	
G	0						1.396
	1						−2.236
	2						1.055
	Sum		0.37 (0.37)	−0.62 (0.43)			−0.122
	3						
	Sum				−0.01 (1.00)		
MB	0					0.081 (0.54)	−0.110
	1					1.25 (0.50)	0.065
	2					1.14 (0.39)	−0.025
	3					0.827 (0.53)	0.228
	4					1.41 (0.58)	−0.340
	5						0.129
	Sum					4.78 (0.66)	
Money supply (definition E)	0–2		2.50 (0.82)	0.80 (0.99)			
	0–3	1.41 (0.54)					
	0–6				0.58 (1.14)		
R^2		0.35	0.21	0.05	0.02		
$\bar{R}^2$						0.64	
Monetary policy multiplier						4.70	0.67[b]
Fiscal policy multiplier						−0.02	1.70[b]

Table 1 Summary of UK studies on money and economic activity

Key to symbols

C = Consumer expenditure
GNP = Gross National Product
GDP = Gross Domestic Product
Q = Industrial production
Y = National income
P = Consumer prices
I = Investment
G = Government expenditure
X = Exports
M = Imports
GFM = Government Fiscal Measures
FER = Full-Employment Government Receipts
ADV = Bank Advances
FED = Full-Employment Public Sector Budget Deficit
MB = Monetary Base
LDV = Lagged Dependent Variable.

The definitions of the Money supply used were:

A : Cash + current account deposits at clearing banks.
B : Cash + current account deposits in the banking sector.
C : Cash + all deposits in the banking sector.
D : Definition C — Government and inter-bank deposits in the banking sector.
E : IMF definition (similar to A).
F : All deposits at clearing banks.
G : Current official M3 definition.

All studies used quarterly data except Barrett and Walters (1966), Argy (1969), Tarling and Wilkinson (1977) and the pre-1939 work of Walters (1966).
The figures in parentheses below the coefficients represent the standard deviations of the estimated coefficients.

Notes
[a] All variables not significant at the 20 per cent level in this study were omitted. The lag structure in the equations using money supply definition C was truncated after five quarters.
[b] The multipliers were calculated after sixteen quarters.

multiplier results (Walters, 1966) were fair with current money supply marginally significant while the lagged money supply variables did not play a significant role, The money multiplier was around one. The results of these studies for the post-war period are more interesting and yet less clear-cut. Using annual data, Barrett and Walters were unable to obtain any 'positive results'. Argy (1969) found a significant role for current money and lagged autonomous expenditure giving the unusual result that money operates with a shorter lag than does autonomous expenditure. Crouch (1967) found that in a study using levels of data, only a small part of the explanatory power in an equation for income came from the lagged money supply, Of greater interest are the results for money multipliers. Using quarterly data from 1955 to 1962, Walters found that the money multiplier after only two quarters was actually negative and the overall explanatory power of the equation was low. In a more recent study, Goodhart and Crockett (1970) used alternative definitions of economic activity and money and included lags of up to seven quarters. The best results were obtained for the industrial production equations with money multipliers of 0.9 for narrow money and 0.27 for broad money over different time periods. The explanatory power of the equations was in general good which restores some faith in the role of monetary forces in the UK economy since 1945.

Two studies have investigated the role of changes in the money supply over a number of time periods in the determination of the rate of price inflation. Walters (1966, 1971) completed a mysterious set of results for the inter-war period by observing that 61 per cent of the change in prices was determined by an equation that included first differences of the money supply and real income (the latter being insignificant). The paradoxical result that the money supply affected prices but not output in a period of high unemployment is difficult to explain. In a more recent study, Tarling and Wilkinson (1977) using data from 1960 to 1973 obtained rather poor results for the relationship between the change in prices and changes in the current and lagged money supply. However, when the data period was extended to 1975 the significance of the monetary variable with a two-year lag increased dramatically. While the authors prefer a non-monetary explanation of the 1973–75 inflationary episode, the long lag of the effect of money on prices is consistent with both monetarist theory and some equivalent evidence obtained by Mehra (1978) with US data. Therefore a monetary explanation of that period is plausible (Laidler, 1976a).

The most important test of the third type for UK data was undertaken by Artis and Nobay (1969). As measures of monetary policy, they used the broad money supply (BMS – with this series being constructed by the authors themselves for the period before 1963), narrow money supply and bank advances (ADV). The measures of fiscal policy were full-employment receipts (FER) and expenditures, the full-employment budget surplus and government fiscal measures (GFM). The latter variable captured the first-round effects on GDP of changes in taxation and hire-purchase terms. The results of a stepwise regression programme with the variables included according to their significance showed that for the period from 1958 to 1967(3) the narrow money supply was insignificant. Comparing the best fiscal (GFM) and monetary (BMS) variables alone, the latter was insignificant and so was excluded from the equation. A second set of equations using current and lagged values of GFM and BMS individually to explain GDP fitted rather badly. Fiscal policy had an immediate substantial impact with a multiplier of 3.8 after two quarters; the multiplier after six quarters rose to 6.6 (after falling to only 2.3 after one year). By contrast, the money supply had a negative effect on GDP in the current quarter, while the money multiplier was only 0.2 after six quarters. The reversal of the results for the UK (compared to the USA) with the impact of fiscal policy being larger, more predictable and faster than monetary policy is quite dramatic.

Keran (1970a) in a multi-country study obtained some rather erratic results for fiscal and monetary policy in the UK. Using data from 1953(2) to 1968(4), the money supply is a significant determinant of changes in economic activity. However, a relatively low R^2 of 0.35 and a more significant constant demonstrate the fact that the explanatory power of money is still rather low. When a fiscal variable (government spending) is used, the results are poor and extremely sensitive to the definition of the income variable. Only when the dependent variable is defined as economic activity (proxied by industrial production) is the role of either policy significant with monetary influences dominating fiscal policy.

The confusion bred by these different studies is increased by the study of Matthews and Ormerod (1978) using British data from 1964(2) to 1974(4). These authors seem determined to demonstrate the general problems of such single-equation studies by proving that 'St. Louis-type' results with monetary policy dominating are obtainable for the UK; these results therefore run counter to those of earlier studies for this country. In their study, they have represented monetary policy by the monetary base and fiscal policy by the full-employment budget deficit.[†] The dependent variable is the change in GDP. They find the impact multiplier of fiscal policy (0.61) to be greater than that of monetary policy (0.08) but summing the coefficients over four quarters the money multiplier is 4.71, while the fiscal policy multiplier is −0.02. The authors, however, are sceptical of the conclusion that monetary forces have become more important in the determination of GDP in the 1970s. Rather, they argue, like Artis and Nobay did, that the problems of these types of study, in particular the definition of the policy variables and the determination of the lag structure, are severe.

Finally, in a small structural model for the UK, Arestis *et al.* obtained estimates of dynamic policy multipliers. Over a period of sixteen quarters, the monetary base multiplier is 0.67 and the fiscal policy multiplier 1.70. The larger fiscal policy multiplier is mirrored for West Germany and Canada in their study but not for the USA. The general conclusion of this section therefore must be that the role of monetary forces (Matthews and Ormerod's work being excepted) in the determination of economic activity in the UK is probably subsidiary to the role of autonomous expenditure and fiscal influences. This result is in contrast to the USA and a discussion of why this discrepancy may exist is contained in section 5 below.

4 Problems of the empirical tests

Many criticisms were made of the work of Friedman, Schwartz, Meiselmann, Anderson and Jordan. The validity of this empirical work, and by implication, of the similar UK studies was questioned on five main grounds:

  (a) The definitions of the variables,
  (b) The possibility of reverse causation,
  (c) The validity of the tests from a theoretical viewpoint,
  (d) The sensitivity of the results to changes in the observation period,
  (e) The discrepancy between such results and those obtained from structural models.

[†] The authors seem to have attempted to derive results that are as dramatic as possible although the measures of fiscal and monetary policy used to obtain the results can be supported as appropriate variables to reflect such policies.

(a) Most criticism was generated by the definition of autonomous expenditure used by FM. They defined it as:

$$A = I + (G - T) + (X - M) \tag{14}$$

where I, G, T, X, M are investment, government expenditure, taxes, exports and imports respectively.

This choice was made by FM not on theoretical grounds (as they did not wish to use an established Keynesian model) but on the basis of a series of correlation tests. The particular concern of the critics was the inclusion of taxes, imports and inventory investment (Ando and Modigliani, 1965; De Prano and Mayer, 1965), while Hester (1964) wished to add capital consumption or depreciation allowances back in so that the actual investment concept was a gross one. The critics of FM disliked the rejection of an *a priori* definition of A, although FM accused Hester in particular of

> pulling definitions out of an alleged theoretical hat. (Friedman and Meiselmann, 1964, p.370).

In addition, FM argued that while the components of A may not be constant in the short run, they will be stable over time which is the crucial condition for this test. The critics then expended much energy demonstrating the sensitivity of the correlations between C and A to the different definitions of A. In particular, as the definition of A was narrowed, these correlations increased (De Prano and Mayer, 1965). For UK data, Barrett and Walters used the FM definition but without subtracting taxes.

An important related issue is the need for the income variable to be appropriate to the chosen definition of A. If

$$Y = C + A \tag{1}$$

then any discrepancy between the aggregate $C + A$ and national income (Y') must be subtracted from national income to obtain the appropriate income concept (Y). Therefore the appropriate income variable in the FM model is disposable income ($Y' - T$) minus certain adjustments including undistributed profits and net wage accruals minus transfers (W):

$$Y' - T - W = Y = C + A \tag{15}$$

In the debate on the FM study, the issue of the appropriate money supply variable was relatively underplayed compared to the debate on A. This was probably due to the ease of measuring the money supply; the more difficult problem is finding a money supply concept that is exogenous.[†] If the variables on the righthand side of a reduced-form equation are not exogenous, then biased results will be obtained. FM defined the money supply as all bank deposits plus currency. However, they were criticised for using a money supply concept that was affected by consumption (and other variables), therefore

---

[†] In the discussions over the exogeneity of fiscal and monetary policy variables to follow, it should be clear that this issue overlaps considerably with the causation issue under (b).

biasing the results in favour of the quantity theory. Ando and Modigliani (1965) suggest an alternative variable which is the maximum amount of money which can be created from reserves supplied by the authorities. However, this assumes as FM point out that the banks do not hold excess reserves at any time.

The problems for the studies of monetary and fiscal policy are even more complex. They require a variable that is both exogenous and an adequate measure of monetary policy. Mindful of these twin constraints, AJ chose the monetary base. However, De Leeuw and Kalchenbrenner (DK – 1969) took them to task as even this definition is partly endogenous. Two of the three elements of the monetary base (borrowed reserves and currency) are endogenous, leaving the appropriate monetary variable for this test as the remainder, i.e. non-borrowed reserves.[†] However, as with the Ando-Modigliani measure, this is purely a theoretical definition and is in fact irrelevant as a concept of monetary policy (Davis, 1969; Anderson and Jordan, 1969). In addition, the authorities may be able to offset endogenous movements in both the money supply and the monetary base thereby making them exogenous. An important consequence is that although the Ando-Modigliani monetary variable does not lead to significant changes in the results, adjustment of the monetary base in the way suggested by DK does so. The power of fiscal policy is enhanced (aided by a small re-definition of the fiscal policy variable, below) and that of monetary policy reduced.

Finally, the definition of the fiscal policy variable has also led to controversy. While the full-employment budget surplus (FES) used by AJ corrects for fiscal drag as economic activity rises, it is endogenous to price changes. Adjusting the FES for price changes is undertaken by DK and this new variable is included in their equation that improves the performance of fiscal policy. Corrigan (1970) confirms this improved response to fiscal policy by specifying a completely new fiscal variable. Again, however, the added sophistication of these fiscal variables may reduce their practical relevance so that the usual full-employment concepts should be adequate for these reduced-form tests.

(b) The exogeneity issue is also a vital part of the next problem of these studies, namely the possibility of reverse causation. The fact that a relationship between current income and current money fits the data well is not proof of a monetary multiplier. While influence may run from M to Y, many reasons may be deduced for reverse causation from Y to M. For example, in the UK until late 1968, the main aim of the monetary authorities was to keep interest rates on government debt stable. Any increase in the demand for money as income rises will lead to a fall in bond prices and a rise in the rate of interest. Bond purchases by the authorities to reduce the rate of interest will cause the money supply to rise. The supply of money is therefore demand determined. This effect would be even more direct if the aim of the authorities was to keep

---

[†] In the UK context, currency is also demand determined while reserve assets can be 'created' by banks. The correspondence between the two situations is therefore close.

the velocity of circulation stable. Alternatively, the relationship between income and money could be a negative one. An increase in income by causing an increase in demand for imports may lead to a reduction in the domestic money supply as the balance of payments moves into deficit. The lack of an unambiguous sign on the relationship between current income and money is therefore a further complication.

Two traditional methods of establishing causality may be set out. Firstly, as in sect. 3 above, evidence that cycles of money supply growth lead cycles of nominal income have been used to justify causality from M to Y. Secondly, the following relationships may be tested:

$$Y_t = a_0 + a_i \sum_{i=0}^{n} M_{t-i} \qquad [16]$$

$$M_t = b_0 + b_i \sum_{i=0}^{n} Y_{t-i} \qquad [17]$$

The relative significance of the coefficients a_i and b_i are then used to make a judgement on the causal relationships between M and Y. However, such evidence merely demonstrates that one variable *leads* another and does not *prove* causality, although it may be indicative of the latter. Evidence that the money supply leads nominal income may not involve causality for at least two reasons. Firstly, both money and income may be influenced by a third factor with money reacting more rapidly. Secondly, Kaldor (1970) used the now famous Christmas example to argue that the increase in the money supply that occurs before a rise in expenditure (or income) does not necessarily cause the latter. The fault with this example is the certain knowledge that expenditure will rise at this time of the year. (It would have risen without a money supply increase.) As future income movements are in general unpredictable, it is therefore unreasonable to use this argument to reject entirely the notion of causality.

A recent test was devised by Sims (1972) to test strict exogeneity by fitting the following equations:

$$Y_t = a_0 + a_i \sum_{i=-n}^{n} M_{t-i} \qquad [18]$$

$$M_t = b_0 + b_i \sum_{i=-n}^{n} Y_{t-i} \qquad [19]$$

These equations include future values of the independent variable as well as the usual current and lagged values. If M leads Y, then the regression eq. [18] should show insignificant coefficients on the future values of M and eq. [19] insignificant coefficients on the lagged values of Y. The results should be reversed if Y leads M. The first result which rejects any feedback from Y to M is

a necessary condition for it to be reasonable to interpret a distributed lag regression of Y on current and past M as a causal relation. (Sims, 1972, p.541).

Despite this statement, it has been shown that the Sims test is merely one of leads and lags (and exogeneity) but not one of causality. Using his test, Sims found strong evidence that money led income but not the reverse for post-war US data. This recently has been confirmed by Elliott (1975). However, Elliott found evidence of a two-way lead/lag relationship in the government expenditure equation. Allowance for this feedback does not, however, significantly affect the fiscal and monetary policy multipliers. A similar study for the UK by Williams, Goodhart and Gowland (1976) was much less clear-cut. Tentative evidence of a lead of income over money was found in contrast to the US results. However, there was some evidence of the money supply leading prices. Clearly, the relationship between money and nominal income in the UK is a particularly complex one. There is, however, a further consideration. As is argued in section 5 below, the validity of the Sims test is an open economy where the money supply is endogenous is limited. Therefore the difference in results between the USA and the UK should be neither surprising nor necessarily cast doubt on the role of money in the UK.

(c) Many doubts have been raised over the type of study used to test the relationship between money and economic activity. Firstly, the use of a simple reduced-form model does not do justice to the complex Keynesian theory. It may bias the results in favour of the quantity theory which is a simpler theory. Johnson has argued (1970) that the major test of a good theory is 'its ability to predict something large from something small', but if the deductions made from these results are invalid given the underlying structure of the economy, such simple models have doubtful value. This is particularly true in the FM test as not all of the regression equations can be derived from the theoretical models (Edge, 1967). In particular the appearance of a constant term in the quantity theory equation is inappropriate. Also, these models imply that the monetary and fiscal variables are the only exogenous influences on the dependent variable.[†]

Secondly, evidence of good correlations in the FM-type tests between C and M or between C and A are not necessarily valid tests of the rival theories. For example, if the quantity theory relates money and income, correlating money with consumption may discriminate against this theory (Hester, 1964). Should the role of money work through a cost of capital channel, M and A will not be independent as the money supply will affect the level of autonomous expenditure through the rate of interest. (This is part of the excellent analysis of the different types of causal nexus in Pierce and Shaw (1974).)

Thirdly, the FM results were presented in terms of levels of variables and the presence of time trends in the variables used generated some criticism. However, this doubt was answered by Anderson and Jordan by the use of first

---

[†] Despite the arguments of this paragraph, the results from small structural models (e.g., Moroney and Mason, 1971, the Arestis *et al.*, 1978) while increasing the relative power of fiscal policy in the USA do not reverse the conclusion that monetary policy is the dominant influence on GNP.

differences. It is now believed that this traditional way of avoiding the trending problem does not alter the results significantly.

Finally, many studies suggest that the results are sensitive to the lag structure employed (e.g., Matthews and Ormerod, 1978, for the UK). Since it is difficult to evaluate *a priori* the length of lags for all endogenous variables, free estimation of the lag structure (so that the appropriate length of lag is determined by the data) through the method of Almon lags (Almon, 1965) is now seen as imperative in studies of this type.

(d) The sensitivity of these tests to the time period used for the analysis has led to concern over the long-run stability of these relationships. For the UK, the very different conclusions obtained by Barrett and Walters (1966) for the three major time periods illustrate this point. Indeed, much of the weight of the FM results favouring the money multiplier comes from the period before 1929. Of more concern is the apparent variation of performance over the post-1945 period. (See Poole and Kornblith (1973) for US results.)

The best example of this is the poor performance of the monetary variables ($R^2 = 0.18$) in the Anderson and Jordan model for 1952–60 compared to the better performance ($R^2 = 0.62$) over the 1960–8 period (Davis, 1969). The St. Louis model gained much support from its performance in the late-1960s, but since then its predictive performance has been poor. Poole and Kornblith (1973) note that the St. Louis model over-predicted GNP in the 1968–71 period, while McNees (1973) finds it inferior to the Fair model (a small Keynesian model – Fair (1971)) in the 1970–3 period. The poor performance has continued into the mid-1970s although three further points should now be noted. Firstly, the model began under-predicting GNP around 1973; secondly, recent estimations of the St. Louis model (B.M. Friedman, 1977) show that fiscal policy now plays a significant role in the determination of economic activity. A cumulative fiscal policy multiplier of 1.6 over four quarters was reported. Nevertheless, the size of this multiplier remains below that of the money multiplier which was equal to 4.6 over the same period. The validity of this result has been disputed on statistical grounds in that one of the classical assumptions of the estimation method – a constant variance of the error term – is violated when data from the 1970s is included in the sample (Carlson, 1978). This suggests a third important point. If this statistical criticism is valid, it may be due to the model being mis-specified when the latest data is included (Vrooman, 1979). If so, new concern over the simplicity of the St. Louis model must now exist.

(e) A major point of discussion has been the differences in the results obtained from reduced-form models compared to those from policy simulations of large-scale structural models. Matthews and Ormerod (1978) note that their results for the fiscal policy multiplier conflict dramatically with full model simulations of a change in government spending (Renton, 1975; Laury, Lewis and Ormerod, 1978). The results for the money multiplier in the UK cannot yet be fairly compared due to the absence of equivalent tests in the UK structural models. However, a recent collection of papers (Posner, 1978) does permit some observations on the role of monetary policy in such models. For example in a small, monetarist model for the UK economy, in which the openness of the economy is explicitly recognised, Laidler derived the prediction that under fixed exchange rates, monetary policy in the long run affected the balance of payments alone. This result was borne out by data from the 1954–70 fixed exchange rate period. However, the model performed less well in the period after 1970 due primarily to the 'middle-road' between fixed and floating rates taken by the authorities at that time. However, tentative evidence that in this era of partly floating rates, monetary policy affected income and employment provides useful evidence in favour of this model.

The chief problems in comparing simple money multiplier results for the UK with major UK structural models is the complexity of the links between monetary policy and expenditures and the limited role often afforded to monetary policy in the latter models. For example, policy simulations for certain periods are undertaken in the Cambridge Economic Policy Group (CEPG) model, the London Business School (LBS) model and the National Institute (NI) model in Posner (1978). In these simulations the contribution of monetary policy alone is not deducible given the scope of the evidence presented. In addition, the degree of complexity of the transmission mechanisms through interest rates, credit restrictions and wealth obscures the role of monetary policy, although in the LBS model, the money supply affects the exchange rate as in the monetarist model. Matthews and Ormerod (1978) do, however, present some comparisons between the prediction of their St. Louis model and the National Institute model. One notable result is that although the St. Louis model for the 1975[1]–1976[2] period does reasonably well in dynamic simulation, it is out-performed by the National Institute model. Much more evidence is needed on the comparative performances of structural and reduced form models for the UK and in the relative roles of monetary variables in such models before any firm conclusion may be drawn.

In the USA, where much of the comparison between the results of various models has occurred, the major discrepancy has been over the size of the fiscal policy multiplier (Davis, 1969). Results from model simulations in the late 1960s show the government expenditure multiplier in the FRB/MIT model to be 3.2 after twelve quarters with fiscal policy acting quickly. On the other hand, the same multiplier in the St. Louis model is insignificantly different from zero. Despite the improved performance of fiscal policy in the St. Louis model in the 1970s, there remains a considerable discrepancy in its effect in the two types of model. The results for the money multiplier are more interesting as within the group of structural models of the US economy different results are recorded. For example, for a given increase in the monetary policy variable (usually non-borrowed reserves or the monetary base) the nominal GNP multiplier after 12 quarters is 8 in the Brookings Model and 20 in the FRB/MIT model. The major difference between these results and those from the St. Louis model (Anderson and Carlson, 1970) is the much quicker response of GNP to a change in the money supply in the latter. In the St. Louis model, the effect on GNP peaks after four quarters, while for the FRB/MIT model the comparative figure is twelve quarters. Much of this discrepancy may, however, be due to the use of non-borrowed reserves by the larger models and the change in the money supply (which will have a quicker effect on GNP) by the St. Louis models as the monetary policy variable (Beare, 1978).[†]

5 UK v US results

The conclusions from UK studies that link money and economic activity are very different from those of the US economy. With US data, the role of monetary forces has been consistently significant. For the UK, with the major exception of Matthews and Ormerod, money has had a doubtful role since 1945. Money has been shown to lead income in the USA by the Sims test, while a reverse relationship, if anything, exists in the UK. In addition, as will be clear from the next section, the demand for money results for the UK suggest rather different conclusions from those obtained from reduced-form studies. This section suggests some reasons for the discrepancies in these results.

The poor results for money multipliers in the UK, and the results of Williams *et al.* (1976) that income leads money, are in large part explained by the endogeneity of the UK money supply since 1945. The UK is a small, open economy which until 1972 operated a fixed exchange rate.[†] In these circumstances, monetary theory argues that the money supply is not an independent variable but will adjust according to the demand for money both at home and abroad which will depend critically on the growth of the domestic money supply relative to monetary growth rates in the rest of the world. Both domestic prices and the money supply are endogenously determined according to the flows of funds across the foreign exchanges. Therefore changes in nominal income lead to changes in the money supply. This invalidates the reduced-form studies that use the money supply as an exogenous variable, and generates the *a priori* expected result from the study by Williams *et al*.

Exogeneity of the money supply for a small open economy can only occur in the long run in either of two situations. Firstly, as is explained in Chapter 8, a floating exchange rate will allow the authorities to operate an autonomous monetary policy (e.g., Hamburger and Wood, 1978). Secondly, if the small open economy is the reserve currency country in the world economy, exogeneity may be achieved (Putnam and Wilford, 1978). Even under fixed exchange rates, a reserve currency country can maintain control of the money supply as any deficit is financed by outflows of government securities as other countries automatically invest their surplus foreign currency in these assets. The UK is no longer a reserve currency country and so this case does not apply. Indeed, the USA alone is consistent with this category enabling the latter to retain control of its money supply even under fixed exchange rates.

A second important reason may be advanced for the endogeneity of

[†] In addition, the money supply multiplier will be smaller, *a priori*, than the non-borrowed reserves multiplier unless the non-borrowed reserves ratio at commercial banks is 100 per cent.

[†] Even since 1972, an element of exchange rate fixity has remained due to the continual intervention by the authorities to influence the value of sterling.

the UK money supply in the post-war period. Until the late 1960s, Keynesian influences dominated UK monetary policy. As argued earlier, this led the authorities to accommodate the money supply to changes in money demand in order to keep interest rates steady. The money supply was, in fact, demand determined.

Mills and Wood (1978), however, believe that the complex relationship between money and income derived by Williams *et al.* (1976) is only in part due to the endogeneity of money. They argue that while money has been endogenous at certain times in the post-war period, at other times money influenced income even in the UK. They cite the possibility that following an exchange rate adjustment or when UK monetary policy was similar to that in the rest of the world, the money supply may indeed have been exogenous with changes in the money supply leading changes in income. At still other times, money supply movements may have been reversed so quickly (due to adverse effects on the balance of payments, for example) that income was virtually unaffected, i.e.,

> Within their (Williams *et al.*) data period, on some occasions money influenced income; on some occasions income influenced money; and on other occasions monetary actions were so quickly reversed that there was not time for them to influence income. (Mills and Wood, 1978, p.23).

Clearly, a combination of these factors relating primarily to the openness of the UK economy may explain the poor money multiplier results and those of Williams *et al.*[†]

Other reasons may be advanced to explain the poor results for money multipliers in the UK. Since 1945, the path of nominal income has been fairly stable; there has been little variation in income for money to explain. In the limit, if counter-cyclical policy is perfect, so that the level of income is stabilised, monetary and other stabilisation policies would be working perfectly, but in statistical terms would be insignificant. The unsatisfactory results for money or autonomous expenditures multipliers in the early post-war period may be partly attributable to this last point. Alternatively, the poor results may also be indicative of the growing financial sophistication of the UK economy in which various alternative forms of credit and financial assets have complicated the simple money multiplier relation.

The results from the money multiplier models are also inconsistent with those from demand for money studies for the UK at least until the early 1970s. The major reason is again the endogeneity of money which, in contrast to multiplier studies, is a valid assumption in demand for money studies. However, the lack of a clear structural base to the reduced-form money multiplier models and the absence of an explicit transmission mechanism are added factors. At least, most money demand studies do include, for example, an

---

[†] To satisfy themselves that the Sims test will exhibit the expected results when the outcome should be clear-cut, Mills and Wood tried the test using data from 1870 to 1914. As expected, results from this gold standard era show money to be endogenous to income. This confirms the validity of the Sims test but in turn does cast doubt on the good money multiplier results of Walters (1966) and Barrett and Walters (1966) for this period.

interest rate variable. The results from demand for money studies are equally important as evidence of the role of money in the UK economy. The next section surveys the empirical evidence in this area.

6 Demand for money studies

The use of demand for money equations to test the role of money has been a more popular method of empirical analysis in the UK than have the tests described to date in this chapter. Around twenty studies have been published since the pioneering contribution of Brown (1939). The pattern of results obtained has been fairly consistent with stability of the function being the common conclusion until 1971 and the debate has been centred on the size of the various elasticities. Since then, while empirical analysis has become more refined, it has become increasingly suggestive that a break in the series may have occurred with the stability of the function in the 1970s being the major point of contention.

The basic equation of a typical demand for money study is:

$$M_{Dt} = a + bY_t + cr_t \qquad [20]$$

with M_D Y and r representing the demand for money, the level of nominal income and the rate of interest respectively. The maintained hypothesis that money demand is determined by income and a rate of interest is frequently augmented by other variables such as the price level, or a variable to represent the 'own rate' on money. In addition, money demand functions are often specified in real terms as an alternative to including the price level as an explicit independent variable. Equation [20] assumes that the adjustment of money holdings to their equilibrium level occurs within the time period used in the study (which may only be a quarter). To allow for lags in this adjustment process a two-equation model is frequently used:

$$M^*_{Dt} = a + bY_t + cr_t \qquad [21]$$

where M^* is the desired stock of money and

$$M_{Dt} - M_{Dt-1} = \lambda(M^*_{Dt} - M_{Dt-1}) \qquad [22]$$

with $0 < \lambda < 1$. Equation [22] assumes that only a proportion (λ) of the discrepancy between desired money holdings (M^*_{Dt}) and actual money holdings in the previous time period is eliminated during the observation period. This partial adjustment model with λ as the speed of adjustment enables the derivation of a single equation by substituting [21] into [22]:

$$M_{Dt} - M_{Dt-1} = \lambda[a + bY_t + cr_t - M_{Dt-1}] \qquad [23]$$

$$M_{Dt} = \lambda a + \lambda bY_t + \lambda cr_t + (1 - \lambda)M_{Dt-1} \qquad [24]$$

The additive functional form in eqs. [20]–[24] may be replaced by a multiplicative form:

$$M_{Dt} = a \cdot Y_t^b \cdot r_t^c \qquad [25]$$

Equation [25] is linear in logarithms:

$$\text{Log } M_{Dt} = a + b \text{ Log } Y_t + c \text{ Log } r_t \qquad [26]$$

This form has the advantage that the coefficients (b, c) are direct estimates of the elasticity of money demand with respect to the particular independent variable.[†] Transforming the partial adjustment model into logarithmic form

$$\text{Log } M_{Dt} = \lambda a + \lambda b \text{ Log } Y_t + \lambda c \text{ Log } r_t + (1 - \lambda) \text{ Log } M_{Dt-1} \qquad [27]$$

the coefficients λb, λc are the short-run or impact elasticities. Due to the lagged dependent variable (M_{Dt-1}), the long-run elasticities are $\lambda b / 1 - \lambda$ and $\lambda c / 1 - \lambda$ respectively. The advantage of the logarithmic function in providing immediately identifiable elasticity estimates is the main reason for its widespread use in this sort of empirical work.

Empirical evidence on a number of theoretical propositions will be given in this section. Firstly, the major issue is the stability of the demand for money relationship. This assumption is the most crucial part of monetarist theory as it guarantees a significant role for money in the determination of nominal income. If an equation like [20] is found to be stable over time particularly with respect to the level of income, the following simple example is valid. From a position of equilibrium in the money market $(M_S = M_D)$ any increase in the money supply must call forth appropriate adjustments in income and the rate of interest (whatever the transmission mechanisms may be) before equilibrium is restored. More specifically, a rise in the money supply must generate an increase in the level of income to remove the excess supply of money. This stability of money demand does not rule out long-term movements in the velocity of circulation. For example, since 1945 the velocity of circulation in the UK has risen with a smaller money stock being needed relative to the level of nominal income. What is rejected by monetarists is the possibility of short-term fluctuations in V which may offset any changes in the money supply. In contrast, Keynesians assume that the demand for money is unstable. In their view, a rise in the money supply may be associated with an offsetting fall in velocity (rise in money demand) to leave nominal income unchanged. This instability view is particularly associated with the Radcliffe Committee which argued that

> we cannot find any reason for supposing or any experience in monetary history indicating that there is any limit to the velocity of circulation. (Radcliffe Committee, 1959, paragraph 391).

A second set of empirical issues relates to the size of various important

---

[†] Differentiating eq. [25] with respect to Y:

$$\frac{\partial M_D}{\partial Y} = b \cdot a Y_{t-1}{}^{b-1} \cdot r_t{}^c$$

The elasticity of money demand with respect to income is:

$$\varepsilon_Y^M = \frac{\partial M_D}{\partial Y} \cdot \frac{Y}{M_D} = b \cdot \frac{a Y_t^b \cdot r_t^c}{a Y_t^b \cdot r_t^c} = b$$

elasticities. The major one is the elasticity of money demand with respect to the rate of interest. While Classical economists believed this elasticity was zero, the extreme Keynesian (liquidity-trap) version assumed it was minus infinity. Between these extremes, the key distinction is between a low interest elasticity (around -0.1) associated with the monetarists and a higher one (around -1.0) associated with the Keynesians. These alternatives reflect different assumptions on the substitutability between money and financial assets and therefore the shape of the LM curve. In addition, the Baumol (1952) model yields a prediction that this elasticity will be -0.5. For the income elasticity of the demand for money a similar range of assumed values exists. While Keynesians merely say this elasticity will be above one, monetarists and Classical economists assume a unitary elasticity. As previously, the Baumol result is between these with an elasticity of 0.5 reflecting the assumption of economies of scale in money balances. The assumption that the elasticity of money demand with respect to the price level is unity is often implicitly made (by using real balances M/P as the dependent variable). Strictly, this is a hypothesis that should be verified explicitly by including the price level as an independent variable.

Finally, a miscellaneous set of hypotheses may be tested. The issue over whether the appropriate budget constraint is measured income or wealth is an important dispute between Keynesians and monetarists. The difficulties of measuring wealth are severe (there is no data in the UK) so that permanent income is typically used instead. Again, however, the assumption that permanent income is a function of current and past *actual* income levels is only a convenient empirical simplification. The existence of a liquidity trap may be investigated while a recent development has been to analyse the role of the expected inflation rate in the demand for money.

Before the results themselves are surveyed, four major problems of empirical work in this area must be considered. Firstly, there is the identification problem. Unfortunately, the demand for money is an unobservable concept. Therefore, for these studies data on the money supply are used; this methodology assumes that the money market is always in equilibrium. While this may be valid for M1, the supply of which tends to be demand determined (Coghlan, 1978), as a general rule the assumption will be suspect at times. However, even the existence of monetary equilibrium will not guarantee the identification of the money demand function. Figure 1a shows the money market with money demand and money supply labelled as M_{D1} and M_{S1} respectively. It is assumed that the demand for money is a stable function of the interest rate. If no other variable causes movement in the demand for money, any new observations must reflect shifts in the supply of money; these observations will lie on the demand curve. Therefore, to ensure unbiased estimates, the demand function must be stably related to a particular set of variables (which will presumably include income). In addition, the supply function must have at least one determining variable that does not enter the demand function. Figure 1b depicts a situation in which the demand for money is unstable; the observations do not lie on either function. If this occurs, simultaneous estimation techniques are

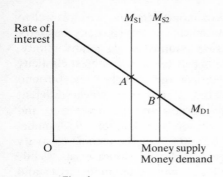

Fig. 1a.

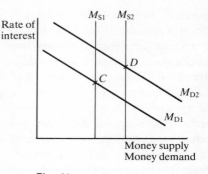

Fig. 1b.

required to provide unbiased and independent estimates of the demand and supply functions.

Such simultaneous estimation methods have not been widely used in UK studies. Confidence in the conventional estimation methods is based on two factors. Firstly, in the UK for much of the post-war period the money supply has been demand determined so that it is sensible to use money supply data to represent money demand (particularly for M1). Secondly, a separate problem, although one that requires the same solution as the identification problem, is that of simultaneity. A demand for money equation (such as eq. [20]) fitted by conventional estimation methods requires the level of income and the rate of interest to be exogenous. However, if the money supply, alternatively, is exogenous and the interest rate for example, is endogenously determined, conventional estimation of eq. [20] will yield biased results. The correct procedure would be to treat the rate of interest as the dependent variable on the lefthand side of the equation (Artis and Lewis, 1976). However, it is possible that joint dependency may exist where none of the variables in the equation are truly exogenous and all are determined simultaneously. This situation is known as the simultaneity problem, and is resolved by the use of simultaneous estimation techniques which generate unbiased estimates of the coefficients of the money demand equation.

A third problem is the need to select from the many alternative definitions of the variables included in a demand for money function. Take the money supply first. Many alternatives have been used ranging across the spectrum from narrow money to broad money with little apparent effect on the stability of the relationship until the 1970s. However, the choice is crucial as there is a clear theoretical presumption that the demand for narrow money is primarily a transactions demand and should be treated so in the specification of the function. On the other hand, broad money includes the demand for money as an asset. A general theory of money demand independent of the definition of money adopted may therefore be invalid (Coghlan, 1978). In addition, both Keynesian and monetarist theories view money demand as a demand for real balances. This assumes that the price elasticity of money demand is unity, which is a testable proposition. *Ad hoc* specification of real balances as the dependent variable is frequent but may, however, be inappropriate (Courakis, 1978).

The choice of an interest rate variable is even more complex. Many alternatives exist but the basic decision is whether to use a long-term or short-term rate. Keynes viewed the long-term rate of interest as the appropriate opportunity cost of money holding. Alternatively, close substitutability between money and other short-term financial assets may be indicative of the need to use a short-term rate. The rate of interest on government bonds is an appropriate choice of long-term rate if it is not significantly influenced by artificial smoothing operations by the authorities; the same problem frequently leads to the local authority rate being used in preference to the rate on Treasury Bills as a short-term rate. In more recent years, as the UK economy has become more 'open', foreign interest rates, particularly those on certain Eurodollar deposits, have been used (Hamburger, 1977a; Rowan and Miller, 1979; Hamburger and Wood, 1978).[†]

The major problem in the choice of the income variable is whether measured or permanent income is appropriate. For measured income, the choice between alternative definitions of 'income' is not crucial with most studies using Gross National Product. The specification of permanent income as dependent on current and past income levels, with geometrically declining weights, is familar. This issue can be considered with the final problem of these studies, that of lags. Two sorts of lag have been frequently used in this work. Firstly, a lag in the adjustment of actual to desired cash balances was introduced in eqs. [21]–[24]. Secondly, the demand for money may depend on certain expectational variables (e.g., permanent income) measured by current and lagged values of the variable in question. The model with both lags may be:

$$M^*_{Dt} = a + b Y_t^p + c r_t \qquad [28]$$

$$M_{Dt} - M_{Dt-1} = \lambda (M^*_{Dt} - M_{Dt-1}) \qquad [22]$$

and

$$Y_t^p - Y_{t-1}^p = \delta (Y_t - Y_{t-1}^p) \qquad [29]$$

with Y^p being permanent (or expected) income (Laidler and Parkin, 1970). The change in permanent income depends on a proportion (δ) of the divergence between actual income in the current period and permanent income last period. This is an adaptive expectations theory of permanent income. The estimating equation that comes from this model is complex and the interpretation of the coefficients obviously depends on the validity of the underlying assumptions.

A particular problem with a model that includes a permanent income term without partial adjustment is that the estimating equation is similar in form to one which uses actual income and a partial adjustment mechanism (Laidler, 1977a). The good results obtained from the former models may not, therefore,

---

[†] The existence of exchange control in the UK until October 1979 however, has made it theoretically unlikely that such deposits are good substitutes for the domestic money stock, particularly M1. Significant results for such interest rates should therefore be interpreted with care.

be a vindication of the use of permanent income as the budget constraint but of lags in the adjustment of money demand to changes in measured income. Tentative support for this idea comes from some evidence on the world demand for money function completed by Gray, Ward and Zis (1976). They use a model where permanent income is derived in such a way that the model is different from one that uses measured income and a partial adjustment mechanism. The inferiority of permanent income to measured income in the Gray *et al.* study suggests that the estimation of permanent income in eq. [29] erroneously attributes part of the role of the partial adjustment mechanism to permanent income.

While lags are surely appropriate in a money demand model, the danger is the specification of *ad hoc*, untested lag structures. Some studies (e.g., Price, 1972; Coghlan, 1978) have included a flexible structure in which the appropriate lags are decided by the data. In particular, the possibility that the demand for money may adjust at different speeds to changes in different explanatory variables may be appropriate.

Results

In the survey of results from demand for money analysis in this section, concentration will be placed almost entirely on UK data. The objective of the section is therefore modest and the student is referred for a full picture to the comprehensive survey of results in Laidler (1977a). In addition, the stability issue will be the focus of attention as it has become the main issue at the end of the 1970s. Full tabular surveys of other results are available in Coghlan (1978) and Fase and Kuné (1975).

That the demand for money function was a stable function of a small number of variables, in particular the level of income and the rate of interest, was a broadly acceptable conclusion for the UK at the end of the 1960s. Laidler even stated:

> This evidence seems to show that instability between the demand for money and the rate of interest has never been a factor of particular importance as far as the economic history of either the United States or Great Britain in the present century is concerned. (Laidler, 1977a, p.134).

This stability was also remarkable with respect to the level of income. This conclusion was forthcoming from the early demand for money studies published for the UK (Kavanagh and Walters, 1966; Fisher, 1968; Goodhart and Crockett, 1970; Laidler and Parkin, 1970; Laidler, 1971a) and also from more recent work using data from that period (Rowan and Miller, 1979; Laumas, 1978). However, certain doubts did exist. In particular, the dependence of the results on trends in the variables was significant so that when the models were tested in first difference form, the stability was much reduced. Therefore, the broad conclusion that a money supply policy should have stable and predictable effects on income and rates of interest was drawn; the only worry was whether this relationship was 'tight' enough to permit predictable short-term policy shifts or fine-tuning.

However, this conclusion began to be challenged as new data become available for the 1970s. The evidence of the appearance of instability in these money demand models came from the failure of equations that were fitted to the data in the 1960s to forecast the money stock at all accurately in the 1970s. In particular, Hacche (1974), Artis and Lewis (1974, 1976), Hamburger (1977a) and Hamburger and Wood (1978) all report an under-prediction of the actual money stock from the end of 1971 onwards. Rowan and Miller (1979) who have included data for later in the decade argue that the instability seemed to have been reduced and possibly removed by the beginning of 1974. The state of the demand for money function in the late 1970s remain uncertain therefore and requires new studies with more up-to-date data before a consensus is possible.

The problem with the instability noted in these equations is that it is not consistent across all studies or all definitions of variables. While Artis and Lewis report 'disastrous' results for both M1 and M3, the under-prediction noted by Hacche is very serious for M3 and MC (company holdings of money) but much less so for M1 and MP (personal holdings of money). The under-prediction noted by Hamburger and by Hamburger and Wood is also in an equation that uses M1. Three recent studies have been published that support the view that instability in the M3 relationship is almost certainly present in the 1970s, while for M1 the picture is much less clear cut.

The first of these studies by Coghlan (1978) has an even more surprising conclusion than implied above. He identified a transactions demand for money model (using M1) and fitted it to data from 1964 to 1976 including numerous sub-periods. The model incorporated a freely estimated lag structure in preference to the *a priori* distributed lags of the conventional model. Coghlan finds that his model fits the data much better than do the simpler models. The forecasts for the 1976–7 period are good, particularly as the decline in the actual money supply in 1976(4) was successfully predicted. By contrast, the predictive performance of the simple equations is significantly inferior.[†] Indeed, Coghlan concludes that using this more sophisticated model there has been no reduction at all in the stability of demand for M1 in the 1970s.[‡]

Using maximum likelihood estimation techniques, Laumas (1978) is able to conclude that there is a stable demand for money function (using both M1 and M3) in the periods from 1964–71 and from 1971–6. While the stability of the M3 equations, in particular for 1971–6, is surprising, a more important point is whether the functions shifted in 1971 before resuming a new and stable position. Certainly the estimated coefficients of the equation differ considerably in the two time periods suggesting a structural shift in 1971. This structural shift thesis is given more weight by the test of stability used by Artis and Lewis. This suggests that the null hypothesis of stability throughout the 1963–73

[†] In addition, Rowan and Miller report that their M1 equation traces the actual money stock less successfully in the 1976–7 period than does Coghlan's preferred equation.
[‡] Coghlan also argues that the conclusion that the demand for money was stable in the 1960s may be an invalid deduction from the various UK studies. He agrees that the instability postulated by the Radcliffe Committee is not present, but suggests there is a large gap between this and the conclusion that money demand is a stable function.

time period must be rejected for both M1 and M3 definitions.

In a study of different functional forms, Mills (1978) supports the conclusions of Coghlan by arguing that a stable demand for M1 function may be identified for 1963–74. These estimates are surprisingly insensitive to changes in the functional form. However, for M3 no sensible results could be obtained suggesting the existence of instability during this time period.

This collection of empirical results on the stability of money demand does not present a completely clear picture. While the demand function for M3 has definitely been subject to significant instability in the early 1970s, the same conclusion is much less certain for M1. In addition, whether the demand function shifted permanently in the early 1970s or merely exhibited temporary instability is unclear.

An attempt will be made to present a consistent explanation of these varying results. Four reasons will be identified for the instability conclusion obtained by fitting the conventional models to data from the 1970s. Firstly, the fact that Coghlan, Laumas and Mills were all able to identify a stable M1 function throughout a period from around 1963–74 indicates that the explanation may be purely statistical; the simple linear demand for money function may no longer valid with the more complex forms used by the three authors more appropriate particularly for the broad money definition M3.

Secondly, the early 1970s coincided with a major reform of the monetary system in the UK. The new 'Competition and Credit Control' system (Bank of England, 1971a) may have been the cause of a shift in the demand for money. This argument was used by both Hacche and Rowan and Miller. Although a full description of CCC must be left until Chapter 10, some points relating to the demand for money are relevant here. Through the abandonment of the clearing banks' interest rate cartel and the extension of a newly defined reserve asset ratio to non-clearing banks, the ability of the clearing banks to compete both between each other and, in particular, with other banks was increased. The clearing banks' position was also aided by the abandonment of ceiling controls on bank lending. As a result, clearing banks began to compete more actively

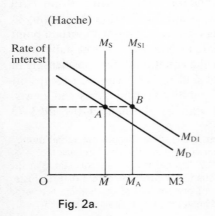

Fig. 2a.

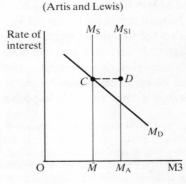

Fig. 2b.

for funds by raising interest rates on deposit accounts, issuing Certificates of Deposits (CDs) and competing for funds in parallel money markets. This process increased the demand for broad money (M3) and, according to Hacche caused a once-for-all shift in the M3 function. This argument is depicted in Fig. 2a). The increase in the demand for money to M_{D1} causes a given interest rate ($\bar{r}$) to be associated with a higher money stock (B). Monetary equilibrium ($M_D = M_S$) is being maintained.

It would seem that these developments should not affect the demand for M1. However, it can be argued that the demand for transactions balances may rise due to the increased uncertainty accompanying these changes in the monetary system (Rowan and Miller, 1979). Likewise, the demand for money of the corporate sector should rise as banks improve their competitive position, while personal money holdings should, like M1, be less affected.

These arguments are consistent with the data and results obtained by Hacche. He observed that the instability in the M1 and MP equations was very small, while that exhibited by the MC and M3 equations was much more serious. The growth rate of M3 in the 1971–3 period far outstripped that of M1 (see Ch. 1, Fig. 3), partly caused by the appearance of arbitrage opportunities. As banks began to compete for funds, their deposit rates rose, as did money market rates in this period. However, banks' loan rates rose less rapidly and so their profit margins fell. As a result, from May 1972 it became profitable for bank customers to borrow to the limit of their overdrafts and reinvest the proceeds in money market assets. Such 'round tripping' artificially inflated M3 adding to the instability of the demand function. Eventually the imposition of the 'Corset' by limiting the growth of interest-bearing deposits, and a natural movement of interest rates led to the end of these arbitrage transactions at the start of 1974. Hacche attempted to account for the instability of the M3 function by including an 'own rate' on money as an alternative opportunity-cost variable. The forecasting performance of the M3 equation over the period from 1973(1)–1974(1) was significantly improved but still left a large amount of the variation in the dependent variable unexplained.

It is therefore probable that the M3 function shifted permanently in this period. What is clear, on the contrary, is that if a certain amount of instability in the M1 function is accepted (which is doubted by Coghlan, Laumas and Mills), this was removed within three years. Rowan and Miller concluded by statistical analysis that adjustment to CCC had been completed by the end of 1973. By including a dummy variable for the 1971(4)–1973(4) period or alternatively by omitting this data completely, the M1 function was stable over the whole observation period.

A third explanation of the poor results for money demand in the 1970s, attributable to Artis and Lewis, is completely different. The basis of their argument is that the money supply increased so rapidly in the early 1970s that a disequilibrium situation ($M_S > M_D$) in the money market cannot be ruled out. The procedure of using money supply data to represent the demand for money is valid (as argued above) if the money supply is demand determined. Artis and Lewis argue, however, that in the early 1970s, the assumption of an exogenous money supply may be more acceptable. This is rationalised on the basis of increased flexibility of both bond prices and exchange rates.

Figure 2b illustrates this argument. As the independent variable, the money supply may be rising too rapidly (M_{S1}) for the demand to adjust fully to it. Therefore the observation D appears to suggest that the demand for money function has shifted whereas the correct interpretation is that the economy is 'off' from the (stable) demand curve. Support for their argument came from equations which included the money supply as an independent variable with the rate of interest as the dependent variable. These equations displayed a reasonable degree of stability in the observation period. This argument can also be made consistent with the greater stability of M1 relative to M3 during the 1970s. Clearly the exogeneity of money is more likely for M3. A stronger case may be made for M1 being demand determined so that the Artis/Lewis thesis is less valid for the narrow money supply definition.

Finally, the studies of Hamburger (1977a) and Hamburger and Wood (1978), which make use of the uncovered three-month Eurodollar rate as the opportunity-cost variable, suggest another line of argument. The inclusion of the Eurodollar rate is justified on the grounds that there is increasing integration between the world's capital markets, leading to greater substitutability between domestic and foreign assets. In addition, this rate performs better statistically, and is generally undistorted by domestic monetary policy. Instability in the equation that includes the uncovered Eurodollar rate begins in mid-1972 (Hamburger and Wood, 1978). The authors argue that the increased risk that accompanied the floating of sterling reduced the substitutability between domestic and foreign assets. Therefore, since that date, the uncovered rate on three-month Eurodollars may be an inappropriate measure of the opportunity cost of holding money. If so the instability in money demand observed in the 1970s may be due to a failure to identify a representative interest rate variable. All the proposed variables appear to suffer from a certain degree of distortion or lack of relevance.

Which of these arguments is correct and which study reflects reality most accurately is uncertain. What is clear is that developments in the 1970s have called into question one of the most stable empirical relationships in macroeconomics. Tentative conclusions may nevertheless be drawn. Firstly, the demand for M1 was probably stable in the 1970s particularly if a freely estimated lag structure is included in the model. Secondly, any instability apparent in other formulations of the M1 equation was temporary and may be accounted for by the inclusion of a dummy variable or the omission of the observations during the CCC adjustment period. Thirdly, the poor performance of the M3 equation is unlikely to have been unaffected by the rapid institutional change that followed CCC. The fact that the M3 equations predicted the 1970s so badly suggests that the excess supply argument of Artis and Lewis is relevant too. Finally, much more data and the publication of studies over a longer time period are needed before the definite effects of the 1970s on the stability of money in UK may be discovered.

It is interesting that just at the time when the stability of money demand was being questioned in the UK, similar doubts were being expressed in the USA. However, any inclination to suggest an international explanation must be resisted as the problem in the USA is that money demand functions since 1973 have *over*-predicted the actual money stock (see Goldfeld, 1976; Enzler, Johnson and Paulus, 1976; Meyer, 1976). This over-prediction has been associated primarily with the M1 definition and can be explained, as in the UK, by institutional developments; however, in this case they have facilitated economies in the holdings of transactions balances. The introduction of negotiable orders of withdrawal (NOW) accounts which are interest-bearing deposits which can be drawn on by cheque caused a movement out of current accounts and therefore checked the growth of M1. Overdraft banking whereby any cheque in excess of a customer's current account balance is cleared by the transfer of funds from that person's savings account will also reduce the demand for narrow money.

Such institutional developments would seem to provide the key to the over-prediction of M1 since 1973. Goldfeld (1976) in a wide-ranging article was unable to find a satisfactory economic explanation for the 'missing money'. However, as in the UK, opinion is not unanimous. Hamburger (1977b) reports that a more general demand for money function which includes the equity yield and the rate on long-term government bonds rather than short-term rates does not exhibit the same instability.

A brief survey will be given of other results from demand for money studies. These have become less important since the instability issue arose in the mid-1970s. Estimates of the elasticity of money demand with respect to the rate of interest vary widely. This is partly due to the different time periods and functional forms used in the various studies. In addition, this elasticity will be higher, *ceteris paribus*, when annual data are used with narrow money and a long-term rate of interest, and lower with quarterly data, broad money and a short-term rate of interest. Annual data allow a longer period for adjustment of money balances to occur following a change in an exogenous variable, while long-term interest rates fluctuate less than short-term ones generating a higher elasticity. Finally, movement between current and deposit accounts as bank interest rates change will affect the size of M1 but not M3.

Virtually all studies of the demand for money in the UK have observed a significant role for interest rates. One exception was the study by Laidler and Parkin (1970). This can be explained by their use of the Treasury Bill rate which is not independent of the monetary authorities influence. A more representative short-term market rate is that on local authority deposits. Recent attempts to explain the demand for money by using the three-month Eurodollar rate have been fairly successful (Hamburger, 1977a; Rowan and Miller, 1979; Hamburger and Wood, 1978). This confirms that the UK is a very open economy with close substitutability between domestic money and Eurodollar deposits. The interest elasticities that have been estimated are inconsistent with the extreme Keynesian and monetarist predictions. These elasticities range from around -0.15 to -0.8 with many estimates within a narrow band in the middle of this range (see Coghlan, 1978). The elasticity prediction from the Baumol model of

−0.5, however, does seem to be broadly confirmed by the data. While such a conclusion is rather untidy, it is perhaps not surprising given the extreme predictions on interest elasticity that come from the rival schools of thought.

The choice of the appropriate budget constraint in a demand for money function has been decisively concluded in favour of a permanent income or wealth variable. The inferiority of measured income is confirmed for many US studies (see, Laidler, 1977a) and Laidler and Parkin (1970) find that permanent income performs significantly better than measured income for UK data. The difficulty of measuring permanent income and the danger mentioned earlier of confusing expectations lags (on which permanent income is based) and adjustment lags do cast some doubt on this conclusion, however.

The elasticity of money demand with respect to income has tended to move downwards in the post-war period. The general conclusion at the end of the 1970s is that this elasticity is less than unity resulting in economies of scale in money holding; in other words, the velocity of circulation has risen in the post-war period particularly in respect of narrow money. As with estimates of the interest rate elasticity, wide variation exists in the results obtained. However, the notion of money as a luxury good with an income elasticity exceeding one is difficult to substantiate on the basis of post-war results. With the result that the lower is the income elasticity of money demand, the greater the impact of a given increase in the money supply on income, this downward movement in elasticity enhances the power of monetary policy.

A number of recent studies have been dissatisfied with simply assuming that the demand for money should be expressed in real terms and so have tested the implied assumption that the price elasticity of money demand is unity. While Laidler and Parkin (1970) found evidence to support this conclusion, studies using data from the 1970s have found the elasticity to be below unity (Coghlan, 1978; Rowan and Miller, 1979; Courakis, 1978). Courakis, in particular, severely criticised Hacche's work for assuming a unit price elasticity which is not borne out by the data. Part of the problem may be that the demand for money may only be homogenous of degree one with respect to the price level in the long run. Short-run homogeneity (i.e., within the observation period which may only be a quarter) may not exist. Clearly, however, this is a much neglected issue and one where accepted practice is in danger of being invalidated by empirical evidence.

There is no evidence that at low rates of interest the interest elasticity of money demand approaches minus infinity as required by the liquidity trap. Indeed, there is little support for the view that the elasticity of money demand even increases as interest rates fall. This is one part of extreme Keynesian doctrine that has been decisively rejected by empirical evidence. Finally, while a role for expected inflation in the demand for money has been observed for countries suffering high or hyper-inflation, the evidence is obscure for countries experiencing mild inflation. Rowan and Miller include the expected rate of inflation as an argument in their demand function for M1. Although the elasticity of money demand with respect to this variable is estimated at 0.7, its role in the determination of money demand is of only minor importance.

7 Conclusions

The evidence on the role of money in the determination of economic activity presented in this chapter played a vital role in the revival of interest in monetary policy. For the USA, in particular, where much of the early work was completed, a consistent picture of the importance of monetary policy was obtained, despite all the problems of the various tests. In short, the results were persuasive leading in the late 1960s to a re-assessment of the role of money.

However, some further important evidence that assisted in this process came from certain episodes in the USA during the 1960s when fiscal and monetary policy moved in opposite directions. Such a situation may be as near as economists come to a 'controlled experiment'. In 1966, US economic policy combined tight money and easy fiscal policy. With the following year bringing a recession, the conclusion was drawn that monetary policy was the more powerful. More significantly, however, the tightening of fiscal policy in mid-1968 was accompanied by rapid expansion of the money supply. The result was that most forecasting models predicted a slowdown in economic activity in 1969. In fact, aggregate demand was little affected and indeed the expansionary environment persisted for at least twelve months after the tightening of fiscal policy.

Whether the correct conclusions on the relative power of fiscal and monetary policy were drawn from these episodes is largely unimportant now. The fact is that such evidence provided a spark to set alight a revival of interest in money; it was a symbolic 'experiment'. In truth, it was the failure of fiscal policy to pull the economy out of recession in 1967 and then to reduce demand in 1968–9, rather than any belief that the money supply alone could explain the episode, that was so important. However, combined with the rapidly accumulating evidence on the role of money, these episodes were important factors in the growth of monetarism (Friedman, 1970b).

For the UK, too, periods when fiscal and monetary policy moved in opposite directions were identified for the period from 1955 to 1970 by Walters (1971). As in the USA, an easy money-tight fiscal policy combination in 1967–8[†] was followed by a boom in industrial production and an increase in the rate of inflation, although the full effects of the more rapid increase in the money supply (which continued until early 1969) were not felt until 1971 when inflation reached 10 per cent. The long lag in the effect of monetary policy is exemplified in this example.

For another time period, Laidler argued that

> this unintentionally highly expansionary fiscal policy (in 1974–5) ran against a continued tight monetary policy, and the unemployment statistics for 1974–5 are eloquent testimony as to which policy tool proved the more powerful. (Laidler, 1976a, p.497).

[†] Monetary policy was only 'easy' in the sense that the money supply was growing rapidly. Those who used interest rates as an indicator of policy would conclude that it had tightened; nominal rates rose in this period in anticipation of higher inflation following the devaluation of sterling in autumn 1967.

With the PSBR amounting to 10 per cent of GDP in 1974–5 and a monetary contraction underway in early 1974, a useful comparison of the effects of the two policies can be made. However, the rise in unemployment could be explained another way. Fane (1978) argues that a deterioration in the terms of trade occurred in 1973–4 leading to a decline in disposable income and demand. Laidler (1978) is not convinced by this view and argues that a recession would have occurred without the oil price rise in late 1973. However, it does illustrate the uncertainty which is present in the explanation of historical episodes of this type. Finally, the introduction of monetary targets with the growth of sterling M3 averaging around 12 per cent per year in the three years after 1976, accompanied by large PSBR's in the same period may provide further tests of this type. Inflation was reduced from 25 per cent in 1975 and the stability of the rate between 8 per cent and 13 per cent in the late-1970s is partly attributable to the discipline of monetary targets.

In the UK, in contrast to the USA, these episodes which may suggest that monetary policy is powerful did not have other conclusive empirical evidence to fall back upon. The single-equation studies for the UK are poor support for a monetary explanation of economic activity in the post-war period. The only sound evidence in favour of the role of money came from the stability of the demand for money. It is surely ironic that just when the British government finally became converted to the power of monetary policy by introducing monetary targets, this one clear empirical support was being called into question. The fact that little conclusive empirical justification of the role of money in the UK is yet available may, of course, be a reflection of the weaknesses of the empirical techniques. The single-equation approach is full of problems due to the absence of a structural model and any transmission mechanisms of money and the assumed simplicity of macroeconomic relationships. However, the results provided by such tests are valuable and, more importantly, have been influential in the revival of faith in monetary policy, at least, in the USA.

Chapter 7

The money supply

1 Introduction

In this chapter, the determination of the money supply in theory and in practice in the UK is examined. In the simple Keynesian IS/LM model, the determination of the money supply is usually not considered. It is assumed to be exogenous, being under the control of the monetary authorities. It is the task of this chapter to describe and compare the merits of alternative methods of amending this unrealistic exogeneity assumption. It must be remembered that in practice the authorities are unable to determine the exact value of the money supply. As shown in Chapter 2, they have available to them a series of policy instruments which impinge on the monetary base and thence onto the money supply. The actual money supply itself is the outcome of portfolio decisions made by the authorities, the banks, the non-bank public and certain overseas institutions and individuals.

The process of money supply determination is related to the existence and activities of financial intermediaries. A financial intermediary can be defined as an institution that borrows money from surplus units in the economy (those whose expenditure falls short of their income) and channels these savings to deficit units (whose expenditure exceeds income). The classic work on the role of financial intermediaries, particularly of the non-bank type, is by Gurley and Shaw (1956, 1960). More rigorously they define an intermediary as a unit which 'transmits loanable funds by issues of indirect financial assets to surplus units (lenders) and purchases of primary securities from deficit units' (borrowers).

The existence of such surplus and deficit units is a necessary condition, therefore, for the operation of financial intermediaries. To use a different terminology, in a world of balanced budgets or *internal finance* there is no role for a financial intermediary. Surplus and deficit units imply *external finance* which is therefore a necessary condition for the existence of such intermediaries. A sufficient condition for their operation is more rigorous, however. If surplus and deficit units can facilitate the borrowing and lending process directly, they will dispense with the services of financial intermediaries. Therefore, the intermediary's role occurs when it is cheaper for such surplus and deficit units to deal through a middleman – the intermediary. Therefore, the necessary and sufficient condition for the operation of financial intermediaries is the existence of a demand for external, indirect finance. The following simple scheme demonstrates the argument (Fig. 1):

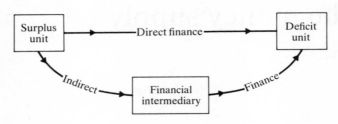

Fig. 1.

The actual activity of an intermediary involves the deposit of money with the intermediary, which the latter then lends on according to the requirements of the deficit unit. The financial intermediary issues a secondary or indirect security (i.e., claim on itself) to the lender in return for his deposit of money. Then, in the process of lending, a primary security is purchased by the intermediary from the borrower concerned in return for the loan. The secondary security is a liability of the intermediary (asset to the lender) and the primary security an asset to the intermediary (liability of the borrower). It is important to ask why the lender and borrower do not deal directly with each other. The arguments are similar to those in favour of the replacement of barter with a money commodity. In general, a lender wishes to deposit his money to earn an acceptable interest return but in a situation where the money is easily obtainable, i.e. he wants liquidity. The borrower, on the other hand, prefers a longer term loan in general (even for twenty-five years as with a building society mortgage). This provides the borrower with financial stability over a long period. Therefore, a 'middleman' who can offer attractive terms to both borrower and lender is a vital part of the process of channelling funds between surplus and deficit units. Without a financial intermediary, saving and investment would be considerably lower.

In the allocation of any funds received from surplus units, the financial intermediary itself has a complex decision to make on the issues of liquidity and profitability. An intermediary of any type needs to retain part of any money deposited with it in liquid form – either as money or a very liquid asset (e.g., a Treasury Bill or a call loan in the money markets). However, the remainder of the money deposited will be allocated to longer term assets, in particular loans to deficit units. This is explained by the general statement that the longer the term (maturity) of an asset, the greater the interest return on it. At one extreme, cash pays no explicit interest rate at all, being the ultimate liquid asset. Therefore, the need for liquidity has to be weighed against the desire for profitability. These two objectives are the horns of the dilemma facing all intermediaries.

Profitability is easy to rationalise, but why do intermediaries require liquidity? Traditionally, liquidity is required to facilitate day-to-day inflows and outflows of cash. A certain proportion of 'till money' is needed for this. However, there is more to the need for liquidity than a fear of being embarrassed by a cash shortage which is unlikely to occur in a modern financially sophisticated economy like the UK and, even if it did, may not cause 'a run' on the bank. Liquidity is needed to settle debts which accrue during dealings between the banks themselves, i.e., inter-bank clearing. It is also argued that clearing banks – the major type of financial intermediary, in the UK – are only concerned with a net loss of funds to the public or overseas sector. Any significant loss within the non-bank private sector is illusory as nearly all individuals, firms and financial institutions have clearing bank accounts. However, non-clearing banks and other intermediaries do require liquidity to cover the possibility of losing funds within the domestic financial system, to a clearing bank, for example. What is true of clearing banks cannot be so for a building society, for example.

The resolution of the liquidity v profitability dilemma is therefore crucial in the degree to which an institution can intermediate between lenders and borrowers. This problem is also linked with the general question of the ability of a financial intermediary to make the combination of short term liabilities and longer term assets viable. Solvency is ensured by the adoption of a reserve ratio which traditionally is dictated by the monetary authorities for banks alone. In addition, however, financial intermediation is made viable by the existence of economies of scale in its operation. A large intermediary by pooling its resources can spread risks so that an isolated bad debt can be handled without difficulty. Intermediaries will also reap the usual economies of large-scale operation such as administrative economies and the existence of specialised personnel. Business is also enhanced by the existence of the Bank of England as a form of 'lender of last resort'. This means that a financial intermediary of any reasonable standing would not be allowed to 'go under' due to fears for the stability of the whole system. (In fact, 'the lender of last resort' function is strictly applied to the discount market's position with the Bank of England, but the same essential principle applies to all major financial intermediaries.) Finally, of course, loan business for the intermediary is profitable as rates of return on short-term deposits will be below those on long-term assets. An adequate margin will be maintained between the two rates to ensure that the financial intermediation undertaken yields a sufficient return.

Private sector financial[†] intermediaries in the UK are usually split into three groups:

1. The clearing banks
2. The non-clearing (secondary) banks (e.g., foreign banks, accepting houses)

[†] Certain public sector institutions such as the National Giro (which became part of the banking sector in September 1978), the National Savings Bank and the Trustee Savings Bank should also be noted.

3. Non-bank institutions (e.g., building societies, hire-purchase finance companies).

As will be seen later, the deposits of the first two are part of the money stock and so their activities affect monetary policy directly. The deposits of non-bank financial intermediaries (usually termed n.b.f.i's) are not part of the money supply and so there is no *direct* influence by these institutions on the money supply. This wide variety of financial intermediaries is justified by the range of services offered by the different institutions. The assets (and often the liabilities) of each intermediary are sufficiently distinct for the existence of this range of intermediary to be viable. For example, clearing banks accept deposits which are a means of payment, make available chequing facilities and provide short-term finance for many purposes. In addition, they act as financial guardians in that they provide a range of general services (e.g., safe deposit facilities, trustee services, foreign exchange). Secondary banks do not have access to clearing facilities but offer an explicit interest return on all deposits, unlike the clearing banks, and provide mainly large, medium-term loans for business particularly of a multinational nature. Likewise, building societies provide twenty-five year mortgages and finance houses instalment credit.

The diverse range of assets offered could, of course, still be available within one intermediary. In general, however, such an enormous range and bulk of business could not be undertaken by one intermediary without the existence of severe diseconomies of scale. Hence the number of different intermediary types is the natural development in a financially sophisticated economy

The growth of financial intermediaries of all types has exhibited some interesting features since the early 1960s. Table 1 sets out the level of UK residents' bank deposits held at seven different intermediaries between 1963 and 1976, and in local authority temporary debt. Figures in brackets relate to the percentage of total deposits held at each intermediary for selected years. Many observations can be made on these figures. Firstly, significant nominal deposit growth has been experienced by all intermediaries except hire-purchase finance companies (which is wholly due to the re-definition of the category of intermediary in 1972). Secondly, in relative terms, the major gainers of deposits have been the secondary banks and the building societies. Indeed if non-resident deposits were included in the figures, the rise in the absolute and relative size of secondary banks' deposits would have been considerably more spectacular. It is the competitive situation between clearing banks and building societies which has caused most concern to the authorities and most public debate. The figures are clear. In the data period the two intermediaries together account for around 70 per cent of total deposits. However, the clearing bank position has been eroded such that at the end of 1976 only 36 per cent of total deposits were made with them compared to 50 per cent in 1963. Over the same period, the proportion of total deposits at building societies rose from 21 per cent to 38 per cent. This issue is now one of considerable interest in general and formed a central part of the debate within the Wilson Committee, which recently investigated the financial activities of the City.

Table 1 Deposits of UK residents at financial institutions in the UK

	Clearing banks	Secondary banks	Building societies	Hire-purchase finance companies	Trustee Savings Bank	National Savings Bank	Local authority Temporary debt	National Giro	Total
1963	9,398 (50.0)	656 (3.5)	4,005 (21.3)	247 (2.3)	1,702 (9.1)	1,791 (9.5)	979 (5.2)		18,778
1964	10,105	815	4,508	324	1,894	1,814	1,239		20,699
1965	10,622	1,047	5,159	412	2,030	1,822	1,315		22,407
1966	10,705 (46.1)	1,159 (5.0)	5,883 (25.4)	459 (2.0)	2,151 (9.3)	1,794 (7.7)	1,055 (4.5)		23,200
1967	11,585	1,572	6,990	424	2,272	1,783	1,135		25,760
1968	12,141	1,939	7,757	451	2,365	1,779	1,096		27,528
1969	12,124	2,103	8,677	491	2,411	1,744	1,139	28	28,717
1970	12,058 (39.4)	2,375 (7.8)	10,142 (33.4)	541 (1.8)	2,542 (8.3)	1,752 (5.7)	1,159 (3.8)	43 (0.1)	30,612
1971	12,127	2,936	12,176	548	2,797	1,830	1,300	58	33,772
1972	13,972	4,888	14,369	315	3,155	1,984	1,603	76	40,362
1973	17,683	7,274	16,531	335	3,366	2,065	2,167	92	49,533
1974	21,188	6,260	18,524	179	3,535	2,087	2,896	110	54,779
1975	22,889	7,139	22,696	215	3,849	2,141	2,641	136	61,706
1976	24,689 (35.8)	8,458 (12.2)	26,271 (38.1)	317 (0.5)	4,245 (6.2)	2,191 (3.2)	2,620 (3.8)	176 (0.3)	68,967

Source: Adapted from *Committee of the London Clearing Banks*: evidence to the Wilson Committee.

The remainder of this chapter looks at two main approaches to money supply determination. Firstly, the traditional bank credit multiplier approach is still an important, if much criticised, idea, while secondly, a more pragmatic approach has been introduced for the UK by Goodhart (1973a, 1975).

2 The endeneity of money   *because of the action of f.i's*

It is invalid for a number of reasons to assume that the money supply is exogenously determined. Firstly, as is clear from Chapter 2, the money supply cannot be directly controlled by the authorities. A move to cut back the money supply by a reduction of the monetary base, for example, could be thwarted in a number of ways. The banks could build up their reserve assets by obtaining them from elsewhere, e.g., the private sector, or they could cut back their reserve ratio. Such a general example needs substantial clarification, but the complexity of the money supply process should be seen.

Secondly, the controllability of the monetary base and therefore the money supply is particularly difficult in the UK compared to, for example, the USA. This is due to two main factors. The ratio of the National Debt to Gross Domestic Product (GDP) is higher in the UK than in most other developed countries. It fell from 84.6 per cent in 1963 to 41.6 per cent in 1976 (Downton, 1977) but has since risen again to 45.3 per cent in 1979. At these levels it is well above the National Debt/GNP ratios of 22 per cent for the USA and 4 per cent for Japan in 1973/4, for example (Greenwell & Co., 1976b). It is not the absolute size that creates the problem but the re-financing requirement of such a large debt and also the fact that the National Debt, in recent times, has increased in size year by year. For example, Table 2 shows a hypothetical example of government accounts for a year.

Table 2 Government accounts (£ m.)

	£m.
Public sector borrowing requirement	5,000
Re-financing (debt maturities)	1,000
Addition to National Debt	6,000

It is important to understand that the existence of this public sector deficit (or addition to the National Debt) will affect the money supply directly, while the financing of the deficit may do so also. In certain cases, the two effects will offset each other leaving the money supply unchanged. The addition to the National Debt of £6,000 m. will lead to an immediate impact rise in the money supply. The public sector is spending more than it is earning in revenue. This initial excess expenditure will be reflected by net payments from the public sector to the private sector. Bank deposits and therefore the money supply will rise. When these cheques are presented to the authorities for payment, the balances of the banks at the Bank of England will likewise increase. There-fore there is an 'impact' increase in the money supply equal to the public sector deficit – in this case £6,000 m. However, this is not a long-term solution. Eventually the deficit will be covered as the increase in debt is 'genuinely' financed. Some of these methods of financing will cause the money supply to return to its previous level. Four alternative financing methods may be identified :

1. The deficit is financed by sales of long-run government (gilt-edged) securities to the non-bank public. In this case, bank deposits to the value of £6,000 m. are drawn down and the money presented to the authorities in payment for these securities. The effect of this financing operation alone is a reduction in the money supply of £6,000 m.; it is the usual textbook open-market operation. However, a full picture of the impact on the money supply is only seen when the effect of the surplus expenditure of the authorities is also taken into account. In this example, the immediate money supply increase due to the surplus expenditure is removed by the open-market operation. Therefore, it is true that the open-market operation has reduced the money supply, but the overall effect of expenditure and financing on the money supply is zero. This explains the preference of the authorities for this type of financing of a government deficit.

2. The deficit is financed by sales of short-run government securities (e.g., Treasury Bills) to the non-bank public. This has the same result as Case 1.

3. The deficit is financed by sales of long-term government securities to the banks. In this case, it is assumed that these assets do not qualify as bank reserves, being of the long-run variety. The banks, in general, will finance these bond purchases by running down the very balances at the Bank of England that had increased due to the impact effect of the surplus expenditure. The initial increase in the money supply is not offset by this financing operation that causes the substitution of bonds for bankers' balances in the bank's portfolio. The advantage to the authorities of this method of expenditure and finance is that total bank assets rise, while reserve assets (including bankers balances) are un-changed. No multiple money supply increase can occur. As the net effect of these transactions on the money supply is positive, this represents monetary financing of the deficit without any increase in high-powered money. This type of financing method is a form of open-market operation. However, in this case, unlike Case 1, the combination of deficit plus financing increases the money supply. It is important to realise that this example is only possible if the banks hold excess reserves (as reserves fall while assets do not). If the reserve ratio of the banks is at the minimum level, they can only purchase bonds by running down advances to the private sector. In this case (which is unlikely to occur) the total of bank assets and the level of reserves will be unchanged. Even if the banks have some excess reserves, they may be unwilling to undertake this trans-action unless they are actually seeking to run down their short-term assets in favour of higher yielding long-term bonds.

4. The deficit is financed by the sale of Treasury Bills to the banks. This is similar to the previous example in that reserves are run down in order to purchase the Treasury Bills. The effect on the money supply of expenditure plus

compared to the prev.

financing is positive therefore. The crucial difference in this example is that high-powered money rises as the increase in bankers balances is replaced by an increase in bank holdings of Treasury Bills. The immediate rise in the money supply may as a result be augmented by a multiple expansion of deposits and eventually a further increase in the money supply.

In practice, of course, all four methods of financing may be used to some degree. However, it is important to note that methods 1 and 4 are likely to be the most important as few short-term securities are held outside the banking system (method 2) while the banks will only exchange long-term bonds for reserve assets (method 3) if they have excess reserves. Method 4 is the residual. All finance not raised through alternative channels (particularly 1 and 2 where the money supply is unaffected) is raised through the banking system by the issue of Treasury Bills which will have impact and multiple effects on the money supply. The results of this simple scenario are clear. With a large borrowing requirement year by year, the money supply is not easy to predict and is clearly not exogenous.

The second reason for the particular difficulty in controlling the monetary base in the UK originates from the considerable 'openness' of the economy. Around 25 per cent of our Gross National Expenditure is on imported goods and services. Capital flows are also very important in the UK balance of payments with London being a major banking and financial centre. In the UK, foreign exchange market intervention is undertaken by the Exchange Equalisation Account (EEA). The assets held by the EEA are foreign exchange and domestic Treasury Bills. It is assumed in the following examples that fixed exchange rates are in operation. With pure floating rates there would be no intervention by the EEA and no balance of payments disequilibrium.

Consider a current account deficit with the capital account in balance. With intervention, sterling sold by the importer is taken up by the EEA in return for foreign currency which is then paid over to the foreign exporter. The sterling gained by the EEA is invested in Treasury Bills. For a given PSBR, less of the deficit now has to be financed by Treasury Bill sales to the banks. Residual financing falls and so does the money supply therefore.

The capital account imbalance example (with a balanced current account) is rather more complex. The destination of the capital inflow is crucial to the impact on the money supply. Any inflow into the private sector will, with intervention, cause a sale of Treasury Bills by the EEA. Residual financing rises and with it the money supply. But if the inflow is into public sector debt the above transaction (which is unaltered) will be offset by the rise in debt sales abroad. The effects on residual financing cancel out and the money supply is unchanged. It is as if the sale of debt by the EEA is made to the overseas sector. Under a floating rate regime the intervention in these examples will not occur. The money supply will be unchanged except that in the last case where an inflow from overseas goes into government debt, residual financing and the money supply will fall.

A final reason for dispensing with the assumption of an exogenous money supply is a slightly different issue. So far in this chapter, reasons have

been put forward suggesting why the authorities **may not be able** to control
the money supply. A separate issue is whether the authorities **wish** to control it.
This factor is traditionally couched in terms of the simple choice between control
of the money supply (M) or the rate of interest (r).

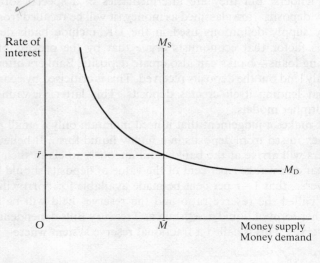

Fig. 2. The control of M or r.

Figure 2 shows the familiar equilibrium solution for an exogenous
money supply of $\bar{M}$ and $\bar{r}$. The authorities can either select the target money
supply level and let the market determine the rate of interest consistent with this,
or control the rate of interest and allow the money supply to become demand
determined. (To assume an upward sloping money supply function does not
alter the argument.) If the money supply is not easily determined by the authorities, problems clearly exist as any attempt to set the money supply and allow
market determination of the rate of interest may lead to both 'targets' being
missed. In such circumstances, to set the rate of interest at a desirable level may
be the optimal policy.

In practice, the monetary authorities in the UK were primarily concerned, until around 1968, with the control of the rate of interest (as argued in
Ch. 2). Only recently has there been a switch towards a money supply target,
which in theory is to be attained at whatever cost in terms of the rate of interest.
However, even this dichotomy may be too clear-cut. The authorities may try
to steer 'a middle way' to keep both variables within broadly acceptable ranges
as both high interest rates and monetary growth have considerable economic
and political costs.

This section has sought to demonstrate why an exogenous money supply
assumption is inappropriate – both by definition and by choice. How then is
the money supply determined?

3 Bank credit multiplier theories

[Bank credit multiplier models have been the traditional method used by economists to determine the money supply in an economy.] They are based on the fact that banks are financial intermediaries that bring together potential borrowers and lenders. But they are intermediaries of a special sort. Their liabilities – bank deposits – are classified as money (it will be recalled from Ch. 1 that the money supply definitions used in the UK include bank deposits). It is due to this factor that economists argue that by the process of credit creation – making loans – banks can also create deposits. Bankers often argue that they can only lend out the deposits received. This is criticised by economists who believe that lending itself creates deposits. This latter view underpins bank credit multiplier models.

A bank makes a judgement that it need maintain only a small proportion of the money raised from deposits in a highly liquid form. It believes that not all customers will arrive at the bank simultaneously to claim their money and establish that on average r per cent of the value of deposits should be kept liquid, or in reverse, that $1 - r$ per cent be made available for borrowing. This proportion r is called the reserve ratio and the reserves held will be kept in cash or some other form of liquid asset such as Treasury Bills dependent on the definition of reserves. This is called a fractional reserve system where

$$R = rD \qquad\qquad\qquad\qquad [1]$$

with R and D representing reserves and bank deposits respectively.]

In the early days of banking, this ratio would be self-imposed by banks at a certain minimum level which they believed was prudent. If r was too low, they may be embarrassed by some particular demands for cash from a series of customers. In addition, of course, banks would not wish to maintain r at too high a level as it is more profitable for a bank to invest in a long-term asset (e.g., make a loan) than to hold cash or buy a Treasury Bill. Nowadays, with prudential factors of less concern to the established banks, such reserve ratios are typically imposed by monetary authorities to help in the process of money supply control. This must now be investigated.

Model 1
In our first multiplier model the following assumptions are made:

1. The proportion r of deposits held in reserves is rigidly maintained in equilibrium. Assume r is 10 per cent.
2. The desired cash holdings of the public are fixed at £2,000.
3. There is only one bank in this monetary system.
4. Bank reserves are exogenous, being determined by the monetary authorities.

Table 3 considers a hypothetical sequence of events to demonstrate the operation of the multiplier. Initial equilibrium exists where, of the £3,000 of cash in the system, £2,000 is willingly held by the public and £1,000 by the bank.

Table 3 Hypothetical balance sheet of one bank with reserve ratio of 10 per cent

Assets		Liabilities	Reserve ratio (%)	Public currency holdings
1. *Equilibrium*				
Cash	1,000	Deposits 10,000	10	2,000
Loans	9,000			
	10,000			
2. *Disequilibrium* (Bank)				
Cash	2,500	Deposits 11,500	21.7	2,000
Loans	9,000			
3. *Disequilibrium* (Public)				
Cash	1,150	Deposits 11,500	10	3,350
Loans	10,350			
4. *Disequilibrium* (Bank)				
Cash	2,500	Deposits 12,850	19.5	2,000
Loans	10,350			
5. *Disequilibrium* (Public)				
Cash	1,285	Deposits 12,850	10	3,285
Loans	11,565			
n. *Equilibrium*				
Cash	2,500	Deposits 25,000	10	2,000
Loans	22,500			

Bank loans are £9,000 making total bank assets and deposits equal at £10,000. It is an equilibrium in the sense that both the bank and the public will not alter their behaviour endogenously.

Consider an open-market purchase by the authorities of £1,500 worth of government securities. If paid for in cash, the actual cash holdings of the public rise by £1,500. There is now £4,500 of cash in the system. Under assumption 2, the public will not willingly hold the cash and so it is deposited in the bank. Bank deposits and currency rise by £1,500. Under assumption 1 banks aim to hold only 10 per cent of this new deposit of currency in the form of reserves and so retain £150 as cash (reserves) and invest the remainder by, for example, making loans to the public. Loans rise by £1,350. The action of making new loans to the public puts the bank back into equilibrium with a desired reserve ratio of 10 per cent, but now the public's cash holding has risen above its optimal level. The excess cash holdings (£1,350) are re-deposited with the bank. The circle is complete and the process is repeated with deposits rising all the time.

Clearly, the problem is that neither the public nor the bank wishes to

* The effects of the public sector surplus that leads to the open-market debt purchase are assumed to have been built into the bank's balance sheet already.

hold the excess cash created by the open-market purchase. The only way for it to be demanded is for bank deposits to rise sufficiently so that the higher level of reserves (R) is at the same desired proportion (r) to deposits. There is a multiplier effect on bank deposits with

$$R = rD \text{ or} \tag{1}$$

$$D = \frac{1}{r} R \tag{2}$$

being restored in stages. Therefore [2] holds in incremental form:

$$\Delta D = \frac{1}{r} \Delta R \tag{3}$$

This enables a prediction to be made of the change in deposits following a given change in bank reserves. The bank credit multiplier is $1/r$, in this case 10. A rise in reserves of £1,500 has led ultimately to a rise in bank deposits and assets of £15,000. We have an embryonic money supply theory if we assume that:

$$M = C_p + D \tag{4}$$

where M is the money supply and C_p the currency holdings of the public. Therefore:

$$\Delta M = \Delta C_p + \frac{1}{r} \Delta R \tag{5}$$

where ΔC_p is zero, in this case.

Clearly, this is not a very realistic model. Apart from the rationale of such multiplier models – to be discussed later – the idea of having one bank only is inappropriate. Extension to a multi-bank system will not affect the final result if all banks adhere to the same reserve ratio. The new business will be distributed between the banks not necessarily evenly but the new level of bank deposits must, by definition, be the same as in the single bank case. More interestingly, if banks have different reserve ratios a more complex and less predictable outcome follows. The new level of bank deposits will be higher, the larger the proportion of the unwanted currency deposited by the public at banks with a lower reserve ratio. This is because the ability to create credit of these banks is larger. The multiplier ($1/r$) rises as the reserve ratio falls.

Model 2

A second version can answer another criticism of the basic model – that of the fixed currency holdings of the public. In this case, we assume that public currency holdings are not fixed, but bear a fixed relation (c) to the level of bank deposits:

$$C_p = cD \tag{6}$$

This assumes that desired currency holdings and deposits rise at the same rate. In addition:

$$H = C_p + R \tag{7}$$

which states that high-powered money ($\bar{H}$) or the monetary base is equal not just to actual bank reserves, but to potential reserves too, i.e., the currency holdings of the public. Dividing [4] by [7]

$$\frac{M}{H} = \frac{C_p + D}{C_p + R} \tag{8}$$

and then dividing through by D:

$$\frac{M}{H} = \frac{c+1}{c+r} \tag{9}$$

Therefore

$$M = \frac{c+1}{c+r} \cdot H \tag{10}$$

and

$$\Delta M = \frac{c+1}{c+r} \cdot \Delta H \tag{11}$$

where $(c+1)/(c+r)$ is the bank credit multiplier. Note that with M on the left-hand side eq. [11] is a more complex version of eq. [5] above. This formulation of a more flexible multiplier is a very famous one (Friedman and Schwartz, 1963a) and is much quoted (e.g., Bain, 1976). Other authors (e.g., Johnson, 1971a; Pierce and Shaw, 1974) have derived slightly different multipliers by assuming that:

$$C_p = cM = c(C_p + D) = \frac{c}{1-c} D \tag{12}$$

rather than

$$C_p = cD \tag{6}$$

Table 4 presents a hypothetical balance sheet tracing the effects of introducing the currency ratio assumption. The extra cash holding of the public (£1,500) following the open-market operation is as before placed with the banking system. In this way, the ratio of cash to deposits of 20 per cent is re-established. However, the fact that the actual deposit of money with a bank increases bank deposits by £1,500 and so causes the ratio to fall below 20 per cent is not foreseen by the public. Therefore, the ratio in Line 2 following the cash deposit is calculated on the basis of the level of deposits **before** the cash is placed in the bank. The first three lines are therefore the same as in Table 3. When the bank has re-lent 90 per cent of the new cash holding, the effect of the currency ratio is seen. The optimal cash holding of the public is not now £2,000 but

---

[*] A reserve ratio of 100 per cent has been proposed by the Chicago School (e.g., Simons, 1936) to prevent the creation of money by the private sector. In this case $r = 1$ and [10] reduces to $M = H$. The money supply is equal to the monetary base.

Table 4 Hypothetical balance sheet of one bank with reserve ratio of 10 per cent and public currency ratio of 20 per cent

Assets	Liabilities	Reserve ratio (%)	Public currency ratio
1. Equilibrium			
Cash 1,000	Deposits 10,000	10	$\dfrac{2,000}{10,000}=20\%$
Loans 9,000			
2. Disequilibrium (Banks)			
Cash 2,500	Deposits 11.500	21.7	$\dfrac{2,000}{10,000}=20\%$
Loans 9,000			
3. Disequilibrium (Public)			
Cash 1,150	Deposits 11,500	10	$\dfrac{3,350}{11,500}=29.1\%$
Loans 10,350			
4. Disequilibrium (Banks)			
Cash 2,200	Deposits 12,550	17.5	$\dfrac{2,300}{11,500}=20\%$
Loans 10,350			
5. Disequilibrium (Public)			
Cash 1,255	Deposits 12,550	10	$\dfrac{3,245}{12,550}=25.9\%$
Loans 11,295			
n. Equilibrium			
Cash 1,500	Deposits 15,000	10	$\dfrac{3,000}{15,000}=20\%$
Loans 13,500			

£2,300 (20 per cent of the new deposit level of £11,500). Less of the extra cash transferred to the public through the granting of credit – £1,050 – is redeposited with the bank. Therefore, the cash flow between the banks and the public is declining more rapidly than in Model 1, due to an 'internal cash drain' to the public. The new equilibrium position is attained with a smaller expansion of deposits. The multiplier $(c+1)(c+r)$ is four with the rise in M being:

$$\Delta M = \Delta C_p + \Delta D$$
$$= £1,000 + £5,000 \qquad\qquad [13]$$
$$= £6,000$$

Importance of cash drain on the multiplier

The effect of this cash drain is to reduce the multiplier expansion of bank deposits and the money supply when compared with Model 1.

The two basic models outlined above could be modified in a number of other ways. Firstly, the concept of a cash drain could be broadened. In Model 2, this drain was simply the result of currency being retained by the public in a fixed proportion to deposits. A cash drain could also occur for other reasons. Deposits created by the extension of bank credit could be used to purchase goods and services from abroad. Cash would therefore flow out of the economy to the overseas sector. (This is a type of external cash drain.) The public could use these deposits to purchase government securities, with cash draining to the Exchequer's accounts. It is also conceivable that deposits created could be paid over in part to individuals who do not hold a bank account of any sort, although this number has declined as a proportion of the total population, through time. Any of these factors individually or in combination will cause a cash drain from the banks so that the proportion returned to the banking system falls. This proportion is termed the re-deposit ratio (a) and is defined as:

$$a = 1 - c - x \qquad [14]$$

where c is again the currency to deposit ratio and x the ratio of all other drains to total bank deposits.

In the first round, the banks will lend out $(1-r)\,\Delta R$ and retain $r\Delta R$ in reserves. Only $a(1-r)\,\Delta R$ will, however, return to them, so that they will then lend out $a(1-r)^2\,\Delta R$ and so on. Clearly as the ratio a falls the size of the bank credit multiplier will also fall.

An important omission from this list of cash drains is one to non-bank financial intermediaries. It is very plausible that a proportion of newly created bank deposits will be placed in such intermediaries, for example a building society. However, such a deposit does not in general represent a drain of cash away from the banking system. The highest proportion of any money deposited at a society will be loaned out to the public, usually in the form of a mortgage. This money will find its way back into the banking system through the house-builder in the case of a new property or the house-seller. In addition, some of the new deposit will be retained by the society in liquid form as a bank deposit. Building societies, like the majority of the public have clearing bank accounts so that a transfer of funds from the public to a society will not alter the level of bank deposits, only their ownership. The main exception to this case of an absence of a cash drain is the extent to which such non-bank financial intermediaries invest in public sector debt. For example, 14.4 per cent of building society assets were held in public sector debt (mainly medium-term gilt-edged securities) at the end of 1977. In this situation, there is a cash drain from the financial system in the same way as occurred when the public, itself, invested in such debt.

A second modification which reflects common practice in the USA and is typically included in credit multiplier models in that country (e.g., Jordan, 1969) is to assume that the reserve ratio for time deposits (t) is different from that for demand deposits (d). In the UK there is no distinction between the two ratios. In the USA the t-ratio is usually below the d-ratio as the deposits are assumed to be less volatile and fulfil, to a lesser extent, the medium of exchange function of money. They are treated more as a store of value. The effect of this ratio on the multiplier depends on the difference between it and the demand deposit reserve ratio and on the proportion of total deposits held in the two forms. Clearly, the lower is the t-ratio relative to the d-ratio and the greater the proportion of total deposits held in time-deposit form, the higher will be this modified multiplier compared to the simple one. This is unambiguously true for the bank deposit multiplier. For the full money multiplier in eq. [11] the result depends on whether time deposits are included in the definition of money or not. If they are excluded, the bank credit multiplier for the money supply will be lower than if they are included as in the former case, part of the expansion of bank deposits will be omitted from the money supply statistics.)

The validity and internal consistency of these models is undeniable, if the assumptions hold. The mechanical result obtained from the Friedman/Schwartz model for example depends on the two ratios r and c being fixed. In addition, the exogeneity of the monetary base and therefore bank reserves is a vital element for the use of these models in such a way that the authorities can control the money supply closely. The stability of r and c are considered now with other criticisms of these models, while the controllability of the monetary base is considered in the next section.

The fundamental critique of bank credit multiplier models is that r and c will vary (e.g., Tobin, 1963). The variability of r will be considered first. In the UK the relevant ratio is the $12\frac{1}{2}$ per cent reserve asset ratio, although prior to 1971 it was the 8 per cent cash ratio and/or the 28 per cent liquid assets or liquidity ratio. When the ratio is at its minimum level, banks are said to be 'loaned up' i.e., all lending opportunities have been taken up. In practice, being 'loaned up' is rare and a cushion of excess reserves is typically maintained. The problems created by this behaviour for the predictability of money supply control are two in number. Firstly, if r is both above $12\frac{1}{2}$ per cent and unstable, any predictions of the money supply based on these models will be erratic. Secondly, and more crucially, if r is, for example, around 15 per cent, a cut in reserves engineered by the authorities in an attempt to reduce the money supply may cause the banks to reduce their reserve ratio, without reducing loans at all.)

For example, in the simple case in Table 3, if the reserve ratio was initially 15 per cent ($r = 0.15$) with a cash/loans split of 15/85, (so that cash holdings were £1,500 with deposits unchanged at £10,000) a fall in reserves of £500 could be accommodated by the bank reducing its cash holdings to £1,000. There need be no change in loans as bank deposits fall by only £500 and not by the multiple amount (£500 × 10 = £5,000) which would have occurred had the bank been 'loaned up'. It is precisely to avoid such drastic consequences that banks keep this cushion of reserves. The higher is the actual reserve ratio observed by the banks, the lower will be the multiplier. In addition, the greater the discrepancy between the minimum and the actual reserve ratio and the smaller the fall in bank reserves, the better able will banks be to cushion this fall by reducing r and so the more unstable will be the predictions based on this model.)

Another problem of these models relating to the reserve ratio (r) is that it is implicitly assumed that banks wish to lend out money to the extent determined by the model (i.e., that this business is profitable). The supply of bank loans, in fact, will depend on the expected rate of return from lending (r_L) with risk in particular taken into account. Assume that the banking system is competitive so that banks can compete for and obtain the level of reserve assets necessary to support the profit-maximising level of bank deposits. Any increase in reserves above this level will only have a multiple effect on deposits if this profit-maximising deposit level changes at the same time. Apart from this special case, the multiplier will only function if a real constraint on the banks' ability to

and depending on eco factors banks many not limit their loans

obtain reserve assets forces them to a volume of bank deposits below the profit-maximising level. In such a case, an exogenous rise in reserves will be used to create credit and will move the bank in the direction of profit maximisation. Therefore, an analysis of the supply of bank loans should consider the rate of return adjusted for risk (r_L) and the exogeneity of bank reserves and it is these arguments that will enter the money supply function.

Empirical evidence on the reserve ratio suggests that its stability has varied considerably over different time periods. Sheppard (1971) found that between 1881 and 1962, the banks' cash ratio varied between 6 per cent and 17 per cent exhibiting greatest instability in the inter-war period. The pre-1914 period saw a gradual upward trend in r, while in the 1950s and early 1960s greater stability around 8–9 per cent was noted. Crouch (1968) confirmed that this ratio has fluctuated much less since the Second World War. Once the ratio had fallen from over 10 per cent in 1945 to 8.3 per cent at the end of 1947, remarkable stability, with the ratio remaining just above 8 per cent is observed. However, since 1971 the stability of the banks' new reserve asset ratio has been rather less with the ratio fluctuating between 13.3 per cent and 16 per cent once the period of adjustment to the new system had been completed. Overall, the predictability of these multiplier models has not been greatly reduced by the fluctuations in the reserve ratio, particularly since 1945. However, a potential problem remains as the ratio has rarely been at its minimum level.

Empirical work on the currency ratio (c) has looked at the possible determinants of c and then at its level and stability. As with all consumer goods, the demand to hold currency relative to either total bank deposits or the money supply will depend on income, relative prices and other variables. As income (Y) rises, the demand for both currency and deposits will rise (unless they are inferior goods). However, the direction of change of the c-ratio (C/D) is not certain, although it is likely to fall as when income rises individuals finance a larger proportion of their transactions with bank deposits. The second set of variables relates to various yield terms. As the rate of interest on deposits (r_D) rises, currency is relatively more expensive to hold and so c will fall. By the same token, if the price level (P) is rising the yield on currency is negative. However, the positive yield on deposits will be reduced or even become negative and so the direction of change in c is ambiguous. Crouch (1968) argues that the ratio of a price index of currency transaction type goods (e.g., food and other basic items – P_1) to an index of deposit transaction type goods (e.g., durables – P_2) will influence c. As P_1/P_2 rises, c will rise. Other determinants under this heading are the tax to income ratio (T/Y) – as tax increases in proportion to income, evasion will rise and tax evaders hold more currency than deposits – and the ratio of armed servicemen to total population (s/n) – an increase in this ratio will cause c to rise. Finally c will fall through time as communications improve and financial transactions by proxy (e.g., credit card)

With some empirical studies (e.g., Cagan, 1965; Sheppard, 1971) defining the currency ratio as C/M not C/D, the multiplier is $1/r(1-c)+c$; however, the thrust of the argument over the determination of c is unaffected.

become easier. Such unquantifiable factors will be included in a catch-all term (u).

Crouch found that the currency to deposits ratio varied between 0.21 and 0.29 in the 1945–65 period. This does not represent a particularly large range of variation out in certain periods shifts in the ratio actually offset changes in the monetary base. Sheppard (1971) found that the currency to money ratio varied between 0.14 and 0.3 in the 1880–1962 period although only between 0.16 and 0.21 in the Crouch observation period.

To draw together all these arguments, the flexible bank credit multiplier is determined by the following:

Credit multiplier $= f_1(\bar{r}, \bar{c})$ [15]

where $r = f_2(\overset{+}{r}{}^*, \bar{r}_L)$ and [16]

$$c = f_3\left(\bar{Y}, \bar{r}_D, \bar{P}, \overset{+}{P}_1/P_2, \frac{\overset{+}{T}}{Y}, \frac{\overset{+}{s}}{n}, u\right)$$ [17]

where r^* is the minimum reserve ratio which is either imposed by the authorities or adhered to voluntarily by banks and the signs above each variable represent the signs of the partial derivative of the dependent variable against the relevant argument.

Combining [15]–[17]:

$$\text{Credit multiplier} = g\left(r, c, r^*, r_L, Y, r_D, P, P_1/P_2, \frac{T}{Y}, \frac{s}{n}, u\right).$$ [18]

and $$M = g\left(r, c, r^*, r_L, Y, r_D, P, P_1/P_2, \frac{T}{Y}, \frac{s}{n}, u\right) . H$$ [19]

Clearly, the simple multiplier model of eq. [2] is therefore merely a starting point.

The ability of the authorities to control the money supply depends (given H) on the stability of $g(\ )$, the multiplier. In finding evidence on c and r many researchers have also analysed the stability of the whole multiplier expression. Movements in high-powered money dominate the determination of the money supply in the USA according to the classic work of Friedman and Schwartz. Sheppard (1971) found that in the UK this was also true with 92 per cent of the changes in the money supply being determined by ΔH between 1881 and 1962. Black (1975) confirmed that for quarterly UK data from 1960 to 1970, the money supply was dominated by the monetary base with the currency ratio also being an important determinant. However, despite this apparently encouraging evidence on the stability of the multiplier, short-run fluctuations in the currency and reserve ratios have caused great instability in the $H \to M$ relationship. Analysis of these short periods has been completed for the UK by Crouch (1968). Quoting the 1946–8 period again, an increase in the money supply of 11 per cent occurred despite a 7.5 per cent fall in the monetary base. This was the simple result of a decline in the currency/deposit ratio from 0.26 to 0.21 and in the banks' reserve (cash) ratio from 0.10 to 0.08. An equally dramatic period was from 1954 to 1956, when a 9.7 per cent rise in the monetary base was accompanied by virtually an unchanged money supply, due to a rise in c from 0.24 to 0.28. Despite these short-period results, the multiplier only varied between 3.45 and 4.45 throughout the 1945–65 period.

The short-run instability of c and r had a particularly remarkable effect on the money supply during the period from 1929 to 1933 in the USA (see Ch. 5, sect. 1). The crisis in confidence in the US banking system triggered by a series of bank failures caused a rise in the reserve ratio from 7.8 per cent to 12.2 per cent between October 1929 and June 1933, and in the public's currency ratio from 9.0 per cent to 19.6 per cent over the same period (Laidler, 1971a). As a result, although the monetary base rose by 10.1 per cent, the fall in the bank credit multiplier from 6.49 to 3.76 led to a fall in the money supply of 35 per cent.

The message from these studies seems to be that while the flexible multiplier is broadly stable over a five to ten year period, short-term predictions of the money supply from data on the monetary base may be wildly inaccurate. This type of result is confirmed by a piece of work for the USA by Burger (1975). Over a period of less than six months, the multiplier is highly unstable. However, over a longer run period of one year or more, substantial offsetting of monetary base changes will not occur. For a predicted ΔM of 5 per cent, there is a 95 per cent certainty that the actual ΔM will lie between 4.2 per cent and 5.8 per cent using data over a long time period.

Evidence suggests that bank credit multiplier models should be treated with considerable caution. However, the stability of the multiplier is only part of the problem of money supply determination using this approach. The assumption of the exogeneity of high-powered money made very early in the chapter, has to be investigated. It is this that the chapter now considers.

4 The controllability of the monetary base

Much of the debate in the UK on the controllability of the money supply has centred, not on the c and r ratios discussed in the previous section, but on the monetary base. A fierce debate occurred in the period from around 1955 to the end of the 1960s, over the assets that should be included in the monetary base to maximise the authorities' prospects of controlling the money supply. This debate passed through a series of orthodox positions before being overtaken by events with the advent of Competition and Credit Control in 1971. These orthodoxy arguments will be investigated briefly. The student should consult the excellent surveys of the debate in Cramp (1971a) and Fletcher (1978), while some of the leading contributions are reprinted in Johnson (1972b).

The traditional or old orthodox view of the bank credit multiplier dates back as far as the Macmillan Committee report of 1931. It was that stability of the crucial c and r ratios could be guaranteed and that the appropriate reserve base was one that included cash alone. To put the matter another way, the cash holdings of the banks – including, of course, balances at the Bank of

England – could be controlled by the monetary authorities. Close control of these cash reserves would, combined with the stability of the ratios, ensure close control of the money supply. See, for example, Newlyn (1964).

Criticisms of this position began to appear in the mid-1950s (Sayers, 1955; Manning-Dacey, 1956), but the real debate was joined some years later by many, including Crouch (1963, 1964) and Cramp (1966, 1967). The essence of the critique was based on an example of a cash shortage engineered by the authorities to reduce the money supply that would be relieved by the banks in the discount market and by the latter, in turn, at the Bank of England, through the 'lender of last resort' function. This borrowing at the Bank of England would have to be at a penal rate to cause the multiple reduction in bank deposits essential to old orthodox theory. This sequence of events is not denied by the new orthodoxy. It however argued that the authorities at that time were concerning themselves with protecting the market for government debt (to maximise demand) and in particular stood ready to exchange Treasury Bills for cash automatically, to maintain the stability of the Treasury Bill rate. In addition, the imposition of a broad liquidity ratio on the banks widened the demand for government debt. By comparison, a narrow cash ratio (which would reduce this demand) for the benefit of money supply control (which the authorities were hardly concerned with anyway) was poor return.

On a theoretical level, Cramp (1967) argued later in the debate that no channel existed which was '*a priori*' plausible for the complete operation of the old orthodox adjustment (see Fletcher, 1978, pp.15–20). The general point was also made and is implicit in the previous paragraph that a cash shortage could be made up by the sale of other liquid assets such as Treasury Bills or money at call. Finally, the new orthodoxy believed that the money supply was essentially demand determined. An increase in income would lead, via a reduction in the reserve ratio (r) and the currency ratio (c), to a rise in the money supply even though the monetary base were unchanged.

The new orthodoxy, therefore, recommended the abandonment of reliance on the cash base as the fulcrum for monetary control and the adoption of the liquid assets ratio as the main policy weapon. In particular, the view was put forward that control of the Treasury Bill issue would lead to the control of bank liquid assets and thence by the multiplier to control of the money supply. This position itself was heavily criticised in the neo-orthodoxy theory which was a partial reversion to the old orthodox position. The critique made of new orthodoxy (e.g., Crouch, 1964) was aimed at the particular sequence of events outlined earlier in this paragraph. Firstly, a fall in the Treasury Bill issue need not lead to a fall in bank holdings of Treasury Bills. Banks can obtain more bills via the discount houses through bidding higher prices for them at the weekly Treasury Bill tender. In a sense, this is purchasing bills from the non-bank public who may have taken them up otherwise. Secondly, even if bank holdings of Treasury Bills do fall, bank liquid assets may not, as other types of asset may be taken up in greater numbers to replace them. This was particularly true of commercial bills in the 1960s. Finally, the neo-orthodoxy argued that a reduction in the liquid assets holdings of banks would not necessarily lead to a fall in the level of bank deposits. This involves an assumption that the banks will respond to a squeeze on liquidity by utilising part of their cushion of liquid assets. The reserve ratio will fall.

The neo-orthodox critique was backed up by some convincing evidence. Crouch (1964) performed a regression of Treasury Bill holdings of the public on the Treasury Bill issue in total and found that an increase in Treasury Bill issues of £100 would lead to a £79 increase in public holdings of them. This evidence suggests that as the issue of Treasury Bills fluctuates bank holdings of them remain fairly stable. Any change in issue volume is reflected in public holdings. Secondly, the dominance of Treasury Bills in banks' liquid assets in the 1950s declined in the following decade due to the growth in the volume of commercial bills. By 1968, the latter had become a larger proportion of bank asset holdings than Treasury Bills. In such a situation, the close links between the Treasury Bill holdings of the banks and their total liquid assets postulated by the new orthodoxy, were very doubtful. To combine all three strands of the argument, Crouch obtained the following result:

$$D = 11326 \quad -1.361(T_B) \qquad R^2 = 0.404$$
$$\quad (474.69) \quad\quad (0.55)$$

where D, T_B represent bank deposits and bank holdings of Treasury Bills respectively and the figures in brackets are standard deviations. This result suggests that a rise in bank holdings of Treasury Bills actually causes bank deposits to *fall*.

The neo-orthodoxy view, therefore, presented some powerful arguments and evidence against the proposal to use the liquidity ratio as the basis for monetary control. The debate raged on with the increasingly prevalent view being that close control of the money supply was impossible with either of the current ratios, particularly with interest rate stability being a major aim.

The orthodoxies debate concerning the cash and liquidity ratios was made essentially historical by the abandonment of these ratios in September 1971. Under the new Competition and Credit Control system set up at that time, they were replaced by a $12\frac{1}{2}$ per cent reserve asset ratio. In fact $12\frac{1}{2}$ per cent of all the eligible liabilities of each bank had to be held in certain eligible reserve assets. Eligible liabilities were defined as:

1. Sterling deposits of an original maturity of two years and under, from non-bank UK residents and overseas residents and all funds due to customers or third parties which are temporarily held on suspense accounts.
2. Sterling deposits from banks minus claims in sterling on such banks.
3. Sterling certificates of deposit issued, less any holdings of such certificates.
4. The bank's net deposit liability, if any, in sterling to its overseas offices.
5. The bank's net liability in non-sterling currencies
   less
6. Sixty per cent of the net value of transit items.

This is a complex list of items, but it basically includes all bank deposits except those from the public sector with a maturity of over two years. Eligible reserve assets were defined as:

1. Balances at the head office or branches of the Bank of England.
2. Treasury Bills.
3. Money at call in the London money market.
4. Government stocks with one year or less to maturity.
5. Local authority bills.
6. Commercial bills (a maximum of 2 per cent of total eligible liabilities).
7. Company Tax Reserve Certificates.

A full discussion of the new system and its implications must be left until Chapter 10. However, at this stage, some salient points need to be made about this ratio in the light of the debate over money supply control.

The immediate impression is that the new ratio is substantially more complex than the pre-1971 ratios. This is not a criticism, however, if money supply control is facilitated by the system. However, this is clearly not likely to be the case and, in fact, very soon after 1971, the money supply exploded upwards. There are a number of reasons why money supply control is difficult under this system. Firstly, there are many assets included in the definition of reserve assets. The issue of some of these is not under the control of the authorities, e.g. money at call, commercial bills. Ample scope is therefore present for banks to respond to a squeeze on, for example, Treasury Bills by substituting other assets.

Secondly, many of these assets are held by the non-bank public in considerable quantities. A cut in the supply of any assets, even those under the authorities' control, can cause the banks to react by banks bidding for these assets from the public. This is particularly true of short-term government securities (including local authority bills).

Thirdly, the 'money at call' asset is a particular problem. Morgan and Harrington (1973) and Bain (1976) argue that by lending money at call to the discount houses, reserve assets may be 'manufactured'. The process involved is simple. Banks may wish to expand credit and be unable to do so due to a shortage of reserve assets. They may issue certificates of deposit (CDs) and raise funds in that way. Part of the money raised is loaned out in advances, while part is lent at call to the discount market. The discount houses find it profitable to buy these CDs (given that the prices of reserve assets in general have risen with the increase in demand) and borrow funds from the banks to do so. Some reserve assets have been manufactured – not unrealistically as both institutions acted in a plausible way. The 50 per cent public sector debt ratio placed on the discount houses in 1971 was intended to stop such reserve asset creation. However, this could be evaded by the purchase of Treasury Bills by the discount houses at the same rate as funds were borrowed from the banks and placed in other forms of debt. As this ratio was not having the desired effect, it was replaced in July 1973 by the 'undefined assets multiple' (Bank of England, 1973). This requires a discount house to limit holdings of certain undefined assets to a maximum of twenty times its capital and reserves. The defined assets which are therefore *outside* this multiple are balances at the Bank of England, Treasury Bills, government securities with five years or less to maturity and various local authority and nationalised industry bills and bonds. This control should reduce reserve asset creation through the money at call mechanism as CDs are an undefined asset under the present arrangements.

Fourthly, banks and discount houses could distribute their holdings of government securities such that they maximised their individual holdings of reserve assets. This would involve the transfer of all securities with one year or less to run to the banks to act as reserve assets, with the discount houses being compensated by increased holdings of securities with between one and five years to run which are included in the defined assets. Such an arrangement is, however, very unlikely to occur in practice. It would involve an unusual degree of connivance between the two sets of institutions, as, in general, no rational behaviour would underpin such transactions.

The number and type of reserve assets included in the ratio does justify the view that close control of the money supply will be difficult. However, some mitigating factors exist. The limit on commercial bill holdings to 2 per cent of eligible liabilities will prevent a rapid build up of these assets, if others are in short supply. In this respect, the lessons of the 1960s have been heeded. The agreed proportion of $1\frac{1}{2}$ per cent of eligible liabilities held as balances at the Bank of England will also reduce the flexibility of action for the banks. It should also be said in fairness that close control of the money supply may not have been the primary aim of the authorities in establishing CCC. Rather, the authorities wished to use the market mechanism (rather than lending controls) through the rate of interest to influence both the money supply and credit. Therefore, the criticism that close control of the money supply is impossible under the CCC system is valid but may be irrelevant to the true aim of the monetary authorities. This point is taken up again in Chapter 10.

5 The public sector deficit and the monetary base

The simple bank credit multiplier approach has been criticised for many reasons in this chapter. The main problems have concerned the stability of the reserve and currency ratios and, in the orthodoxy debate, the ability of the private sector to offset autonomous shifts in high-powered money. Goodhart (1973a, 1975) has made use of a simple form of the government's budget constraint to add a further criticism. He concludes that the authorities themselves cannot even determine the size of the monetary base under *their* control. He argues that:

> This approach, however, abstracts from *all* the main operational problems facing the authorities. It reveals nothing about the difficulties possibly confronting the authorities in achieving any desired level for the monetary base. It suggests by itself nothing of the implications for interest rates, markets and financial institutions of the authorities' choice of targets and market procedures. It gives no idea of the underlying forces with which the authorities may have to contend in con-

trolling the money stock. Indeed, in making the initial assumption that the monetary base is under their control, all their operational problems are implicitly assumed to have been resolved. (Goodhart, 1975, p.153).

Many of the problems implicit in this statement such as the willingness of banks to lend out newly obtained reserves, the existence of suitable borrowers and whether the authorities wish to control the money supply at all have been considered earlier in this chapter. The major argument of Goodhart's analysis concerns the ability of the authorities to achieve the desired level of the monetary base given the various factors that will determine the supply of public sector reserve assets. This approach which derives ΔH (the change in high-powered money) as a residual from a simple accounting identity shows that fiscal and monetary policy are fundamentally related. The public sector deficit (PSD) plus any debt maturities (MAT) will be financed in a number of ways:

(a) External currency flows (ECF)
(b) Open-market operations with the non-bank private sector (OMO_N)
(c) Non-marketable debt sales (NMD)
(d) Sales of non-reserve asset debt to the banking system (OMO_B)
(e) Bank lending to the public sector (BL)
(f) High-powered money creation (ΔH):
  (i) Increase in notes and coins in circulation with the non-bank public (ΔNC).
  (ii) Sales of reserve asset debt to the banking system (RAD).

Therefore by definition:

$$PSD + MAT = ECF + OMO_N + NMD + OMO_B + BL + \Delta H \qquad [20]$$

A number of other definitions may be derived from [20]:

Domestic Borrowing Requirement (DBR)

$$DBR = OMO_N + NMD + OMO_B + BL + \Delta H \qquad [21]$$

Monetary Financing of the PSBR (MF)

$$MF = OMO_B + BL + \Delta H \qquad [22]$$

Public Sector Contribution to the Reserve Assets of the Banking Sector[†]
(Increase in high-powered money – ΔH)

$$\Delta H = PSD + MAT - ECF - OMO_N - NMD - OMO_B - BL \qquad [23]$$

It can be seen from these definitions that the change in the public sector contribution to high-powered money is a residual and so will, in general, be beyond the control of the authorities.[‡] The terms in eqs. [20]–[23] are evaluated

[†] As part of ΔH will be in the form of notes and coins, these only become reserve assets when transferred to the banks leading to an increase in the banking sector's balances at the Bank of England.
[‡] Note that high-powered money may also increase due to the 'creation' of private sector reserve assets such as money at call.

for the financial year 1977/8 in Table 5. In that year, the public sector borrowing requirement of £5,493 m. caused an impact increase in the money supply equal to this amount. The domestic borrowing requirement at £9,826 m. was, how-

Table 5 Statistical determination of high-powered money (1977–8 – £ m.)

1. Public sector borrowing requirement (PSD+MAT)		5,493
minus		
2. External currency flows (external financing of the public sector – ECF)	+4,333	
equals		
3. Domestic borrowing requirement (DBR)	+9,826	
minus		
4. Increase in public sector debt held by non-bank residents (OMO$_N$+NMD)	–6,601	
equals		
5. Monetary financing of the PSBR		3,225
i.e.		
(i) Sales of non-reserve asset debt to the banking sector (OMO$_B$)	+1,124	
(ii) Bank lending to the public sector (BL)	+1,165	
(iii) Increase in notes and coin in circulation with the non-bank private sector (ΔNC)	+1,165	
(iv) Sales of reserve asset debt to the banking system (RAD)	–380	
(v) Statistical adjustment[a]	+151	
		3,225
minus		
(i) Sales of non-reserve asset debt to the banking sector (OMO$_B$)	1,124	
(ii) Bank lending to the public sector (BL)	1,165	
equals		
6. Public sector contribution to the supply of reserve assets/increase in high-powered money		936

Source: *Bank of England Quarterly Bulletin*, March 1978, March 1979, Tables 2.1, 3.1, 11.1, 11.3.

[a] This adjustment, which is needed to make the data from a number of different sources consistent, is caused by two main factors. Monetary financing occurs through the banking sector (apart from ΔNC). The figures under 5 refer to the banks alone. Any net financing of the public sector through the rest of the banking sector (e.g., the discount houses) is included here. Secondly, all figures in Table 5 except those on bank assets/liabilities are built up from calendar month data; the bank's balance sheet is on the basis of banking month data. Allowance for these two factors (in Table 6 of the *Bank of England Quarterly Bulletin*) reduces this adjustment to £20 m. which can be viewed as a genuine balancing item.

ever, larger than this due to the accumulation of foreign exchange reserves by the EEA. The external financing of the public sector (ECF) was in fact negative. The rise in the money supply was, however, reduced to the extent that public sector debt to the value of £6,601 m. was sold to the non-bank private sector. The remaining methods of finance did not, however, offset the impact increase in the money supply. The sales of non-reserve and reserve debt to the banking sector do not alter bank deposits and therefore the money supply. The increase in bank lending to the public sector similarly does not affect the money supply in itself. In these three cases, therefore, the impact effect on the money supply of the deficit remains (Greenwell & Co., 1979). Monetary financing is completed by the increase of currency in circulation with the non-bank private sector. With the authorities willing to supply currency on demand, this element reflects that part of the public sector deficit financed initially, not by increasing balances at the Bank of England, but by transfers of currency to the non-bank private sector. The amount of financing completed in this way automatically increases the money supply initially and also in the long term when full financing has been completed.

While monetary financing in 1977/8 amounted to £3,225 m., the effect on high-powered money and bank holdings of reserve assets was much less than this. With part of the monetary financing leaving the reserve asset base unchanged (viz. OMO_B and BL), the increase in high-powered money due to the financing of the government deficit equalled just £936 m. In fact, the reserve asset debt of the public sector held by the banks actually fell in 1977/8 ($-£380$ m.). Therefore, it is crucial to separate the increase in high-powered money which may have a multiple effect on the money supply from the remainder of monetary financing which only has a once-for-all effect on the money supply.

Despite being part of an accounting identity, ΔH and the total monetary financing of the public sector could be at their optimal levels if the authorities were able to set the other variables in the accounting identity [20] with complete certainty. Some comments must therefore be made on each of the elements in this identity to examine this possibility.

The public sector deficit (PSD) is the major item in the overall public sector borrowing requirement. It is difficult, however, to influence quickly due to the long-term nature of many government spending projects and is determined predominantly by political and economic objectives which were unlikely (at least until 1976) to be subordinate to the need to hit a money supply target. In fact, even since the adoption of monetary targets the public sector deficit has only been altered to any significant extent when it was clear that the monetary target was going to be comprehensively missed. It is still unclear, therefore, to what extent the PSD is now considered subordinate to the money supply target. However, whatever the view on the relative importance of the two, it is still true that the PSD is very insensitive to short-run influence.

The other expenditure item, debt maturities (MAT), is also largely predetermined. Maturities are dependent on past debt sales, although the likelihood of a peak in maturities can be allowed for by funding the debt at an earlier stage. Institutional investors are willing to participate in the funding operation to keep a portfolio of balanced maturities and this helps refinancing. This is less likely to happen with the general public, however.

The sale of non-marketable debt (NMD) to the public is an important source of revenue for the authorities. This category includes all debt not sold in a market situation. Investment by the public occurs through the deposit of money in these debt forms. The major forms are National Savings and Premium Bonds. Such debt sales can be influenced by the authorities through, for example, the alteration of rates of interest offered on various categories of National Savings. However, in practice, these are examples of administered rates which are notoriously inflexible while it is unclear how sensitive such flows of savings are to interest rate changes. Goodhart argues that with sticky administered interest, flows into non-marketable debt will decline when there is a squeeze and other rates are rising. As a result, *ceteris paribus*, there will be a rise in ΔH which will partially offset the squeeze.

External currency flows (ECF) affect the financing of the PSD through the sterling counterpart mentioned in section 2 above. A current account deficit in the UK will cause, on balance, foreign exchange to be purchased by importers in return for sterling. This sterling is then invested in Treasury Bills by the EEA and helps the financing of the PSD. Conversely, a current account surplus will cause a reduction in the financing of the PSD. Clearly the balance of payments position on current account is not easily or quickly influenced in such a way as to help deficit financing. This element of ECF is therefore beyond the control of the authorities, at least in the short run. Even if these flows were capable of being influenced by specific policy action, this would involve the deliberate creation of a current account deficit in order to help to balance the public sector accounts. This is, of course, very unlikely. On the capital account, sterling inflows into the private sector will automatically raise the money supply by increasing non-resident sterling deposits. Any inflows in foreign currency will, when that currency is exchanged for sterling at the EEA, lead to a reduction in the EEA's holdings of Treasury Bills. *Ceteris paribus*, more Treasury Bills must now be sold to the banks causing ΔH to increase. If the inflows are into government debt, this will help deficit financing in this respect, but the effect is cancelled out by the sterling counterpart. An inflow of foreign exchange to purchase government securities will lead to a decline in EEA Treasury Bill holdings. On balance, the debt situation is unchanged although the average maturity of the debt will be increased. Indeed in a squeeze period, higher rates of interest at home will encourage capital inflows which will reduce financing of the PSD through these external flows.

To summarise the arguments to date, at least two elements of [20] (PSD, MAT) are beyond the short run control of the authorities. Two others (NMD, ECF) are to a lesser extent predetermined in the short run, while in addition, the latter may cause perverse effects on deficit financing when interest rates move in either direction. A final offset mentioned by Goodhart is that in a squeeze, with rates of interest rising, banks will increase their loans to the private sector and so reduce the reserve ratio. This, however, will depend on whether new and profitable business is available. In a deflationary situation, public confidence will suffer and this may reduce the demand for bank credit. Banks may be willing to increase credit flows but despite being able to raise loan rates, profitable new business may not be forthcoming. The likelihood of a declining reserve ratio when rates of interest rise will not be very high and so this offset can be ignored.

The other two elements in eq. [20] – OMO$_N$ and MF [22] – are therefore forced to act as residuals as these are the elements most easily influenced by the authorities' action. In other words, variations in all the other elements in [20] must be accommodated by open market operations with the non-bank public or monetary financing of the PSBR.

In the environment of money supply targets in the 1970s, the authorities would prefer to establish the optimal level of monetary financing and close any remaining gap in the government's accounts through open-market operations. In addition, they would like to establish the optimal level of ΔH within the total of monetary financing. This will not, however, be easy. Bank holdings of public sector non-reserve debt include government securities with more than one year before maturity, while any increase in till money held by the banking sector is included in this category. These holdings will be influenced by changes in market conditions and, in the case of till money, by the immediate needs of the banks for ready cash. In general, these two items will be beyond the control of the authorities. Bank lending to the public sector includes advances and market loans to both local authorities and public corporations, while any flow of funds to the public sector following calls for special deposits is included in this category. Although the latter is capable of close control, lending to local authorities and public corporations may not be. These organisations are part of the public sector but their expenditure is not directly controlled by Central Government. This element may work perversely as during a squeeze, bank interest rates will rise causing a decline in bank lending of this type. Residual financing, *ceteris paribus*, will increase. Therefore, the two elements of monetary financing that do not generate an increase in high-powered money are difficult to monitor closely, so that the problems of achieving the optimal ΔH are increased.

The procedure of using open-market operations to close the gap in the public sector accounts seems the most obvious method of resolving this problem. However, this is not costless, either. If the quantity of open-market sales is predetermined by given values of PSD, MAT, ECF, NMD, OMO$_B$, BL and a target ΔH, then the authorities must accept the price and interest rate on sales of government debt that the market dictates. As the required OMO$_N$ changes over time, interest rates will fluctuate wildly. To be clear about the argument, ΔH can be set as a target with OMO$_N$ as the residual but in practice the costs of doing so in terms of unstable gilt-edged prices have been considered too high.

In fact, the preference before 1968 (Ch. 2, sect. 5) for setting the desired gilt-edged price and only selling what the market would bear was underpinned by a view that the expectations of investors in the gilt-edged market were extrapolative. If the authorities tried to sell on a falling market, investors would withdraw fearing new price falls and by doing so their expectations would become self fulfilling. This view of expectations was never tested but was part of the conventional wisdom of the time. The alternative of selling on a falling market and riding out any storm was not tried until the 1970s. The ability of the authorities to control OMO_N and allow a target ΔH to be achieved was therefore dependent on the actual expectations of market investors but also the authorities' view of these expectations. The more regressive were expectations (a price fall will be followed by higher demand pushing prices back up), the more valid, in practice, it was to assume that ΔH was determined by the authorities.

In practice, the choice between achieving sales of a given quantity of securities and ensuring interest rate stability may be too stark. In practice, a compromise solution is often found with some variation in the rate of interest and some divergence from the optimal level of debt sales. The authorities may feel they have greater overall control of the market situation by adopting such a compromise. Despite this, since 1968, there has been a tendency to allow greater fluctuations in rates of interest than previously. A compromise is still being used but one that is more biased towards quantity stability than in the earlier period.

The ability of the authorities to sell the required amount of stock with little disturbance to prices will also depend on the banks' reaction to gilt sales. The effect on the private sector of increased competition from the authorities for funds will be very important. If large debt sales lead to a shortage of funds, banks may react by raising their deposit rates to attract funds from government debt. They would only do this, however, if they could lend out such funds at a profit, given the higher rates on advances they would have to charge. If the elasticity of the demand for advances with respect to the rate of interest is low, bank competition for funds will be intense. As a result, the government may have to reduce debt prices even more to sell the required amount. An interest rate spiral could be set up which may be sufficiently undesirable for the authorities that they support the market and stabilise rates. As a result, the money supply would rise as residual sales of Treasury Bills to the banks increased. The authorities have other options though. The implementation of a ceiling on bank advances or on bank deposit rates would effectively inhibit the banks from competing with the authorities in this way.

The ability of the authorities to control the monetary base and therefore the money supply will depend on many factors, the most important of which are the size of the public sector deficit, the amount of exogenous debt sales, the reaction of the non-bank public to the debt sales and the ability of the banks to compete for increasingly scarce funds. A final point is that in a fixed exchange rate world with considerable capital mobility, the domestic money supply cannot be made independent of the world's money supply. Even if the authorities succeed in controlling the monetary base from domestic sources, the external component cannot be controlled unless exchange rates are freely floating. To sterilise any external effects on the monetary base can only be a short-term policy (see Ch. 8).

6 Recent approaches to monetary base determination
(see Bank of England 1979b)

The approach of the last section demonstrated that however the reserve base is defined, if it is closely linked to the financing of the public sector deficit, it will in general be very difficult to control. In the latter part of the 1970s, therefore, the debate on the control of the money supply has come 'full circle' with arguments being presented for a return to a cash base system. The essence of these ideas is to define a monetary base for control purposes, that is independent of budgetary influences and yet directly controllable by the authorities. Two specific proposals of this type have been made (Greenwell & Co., 1977a,b, 1979; Duck and Sheppard, 1978). These approaches tackle the problem in different ways but arrive at essentially similar proposals.

The Greenwell & Co. approach criticises the current system in two respects. Firstly, as the banking sector provides residual finance for the government through the issue of Treasury Bills which are a reserve asset, the reserve base of the banking system is uncontrollable. It is the major part of ΔH in section 5 above. Secondly, the present system is eroding the traditional role of the discount market as the residual source of funds for the banks. In the past, a cash shortage experienced by the banks would have led them to seek repayment of call loans from the discount market to replenish cash stocks. But this does not generally happen under the present system. For, whatever the initial cause of the cash shortage, if the traditional channel is used a reduction in reserve assets remains. The action of replacing balances at the Bank of England by call loans described above would simply replace one reserve asset with another. Therefore, the initial loss of reserve assets (a decline in bankers' balances) has not been made good. As a result, such a loss now leads banks to recall money from the inter-bank market. These loans are *not* reserve assets and so this action causes a gain in reserve assets to alleviate the initial shortage. To facilitate this response, banks are placing increasing amounts of funds in the inter-bank market and so depriving the discount houses of their residual financing role.

The Duck and Sheppard approach is rather different. By presenting demand (the banks and the non-bank public) and supply functions for a reserve asset they focus on the private sector offset problem in monetary base control. They derive an expression for the link between bank deposits and exogenously controlled reserve assets which emphasises the slippage in the system. The demand functions for reserve assets (x) by banks (b) and the non-bank public (p) are given by:

$$x_b^d = f(r^x, \rho, r)D \tag{24}$$

$$x_p^d = g(r^x, r)D \tag{25}$$

where r^x, ρ, r, D represent the rate of return on the asset x, the reserve ratio, an expression for the rate of interest on other assets and the level of bank deposits respectively. The supply function for reserve assets is partly exogenous ($\bar{x}$) – determined by the authorities – and partly endogenous:

$$x^s = \bar{x} + h(r^x, r) \tag{26}$$

Combining [24]–[26]:

$$x^s = x_D^d + x_D^p \tag{27}$$

$$D = \frac{\bar{x} + h(r^x, r)}{f(r^x, \rho, r) + g(r^x, r)} \tag{28}$$

Assuming currency holdings of the public (C_p) are related to deposits by the function $c(\ )$:

$$C_p = c(r) \cdot D \tag{29}$$

and

$$M = C_p + D \tag{4}$$

then the full bank credit multiplier for the money supply is:

$$M = c(r) + 1 \frac{\bar{x} + h(r^x, r)}{f(r^x, \rho, r) + g(r^x, r)} \tag{30}$$

The authors then see the problems as being a lack of knowledge of the stability of the demand functions $f(\ )$ and $g(\ )$, and the fact that $h(\ )$ is likely to be erratic. Private sector behaviour on both the demand and supply side will therefore make a stable link between the exogenous element of the monetary base ($\bar{x}$) and the money supply most unlikely.

The proposals advocated in the two schemes are similar and essentially represent a return to a type of cash base control. Greenwell & Co. suggests a mandatory balance at the Bank of England ratio and Duck and Sheppard a reserve deposit (a newly-created asset) ratio. Either type of asset supply could be totally controlled by the authorities unhindered by offsetting action by the public (whose holdings of these assets would be zero) or the need to finance total government expenditure. Duck and Sheppard go further and suggest a scheme of severe penalties for non-adherence to the exact reserve deposit ratio, appreciating the slippage which may occur if banks are not fully 'loaned up'. They suggest very penal special deposits if the actual ratio falls below the agreed figure and the non-payment of interest on excess reserve deposit holdings. Such penalties would ensure that banks maintained the exact ratio whenever possible.

The primary advantage of both these schemes is the close control of the monetary base. Other advantages will be forthcoming too. With Treasury Bills and other short-term securities excluded from reserve assets, the authorities could, without fear, widen the market for government debt by selling such short-dated debt instruments to the non-bank public. (At present little such debt is held outside the banking sector.) This would assist in the financing of government deficits. In addition, a further severe cost would be reduced. With most of the National Debt held in long-term securities, large quantities of which have been sold in the 1970s when prices have been at their lowest and interest rates at their peak, the interest cost of the Debt has soared. Greater sales of short-term debt to the non-bank public would reduce the average life of the Debt and therefore the interest cost of servicing it.

However, there is a considerable weight of opinion behind the current system of control and therefore an unwillingness to change it. In general, many academics favour a change to a monetary base system while those actually working in the markets favour the *status quo*. A familiar comment is that the current system works adequately even if the interest cost of the deficit is at times excessive. The major concern over a monetary base system is its effects on interest rates (Fletcher, 1978, Bank of England, 1979b). At least in the short term, rates will become more volatile to such an extent that the authorities may have to intervene to limit such fluctuations (for example when a politically damaging rise in building society mortgage rates is imminent). Fear of this, it should be recalled, was the major reason why old orthodox methods were not permitted to work before 1971. However, such fluctuations are more acceptable now in the days of money supply targets than in the 1960s. In addition, if the scheme did monitor the growth of the monetary base sufficiently closely to reduce money supply expansion over time, the result could be lower inflation and less volatility of interest rates in the long run. The choice may simply be between short-run and long-run instability. Another problem is that while both schemes could ensure close control of the monetary base, it is the money supply that is of major importance for the economy. The stability of the public's currency ratio is essential for close control of the money supply and this is unaffected by these proposals. Finally, the artificiality of reserve deposits in the proposal of Duck and Sheppard may suggest a degree of unrealism surrounding the scheme.

Both schemes involve the satisfaction of four characteristics of a potentially successful reserve ratio. Success is measured by the ability of the authorities to determine the monetary base according to their own wishes, unhindered by fiscal considerations or offsetting actions by the private sector. These characteristics are:

1. A monetary base defined to include assets, the supply of which is under the authorities' control.
2. The inclusion of assets which are not part of residual financing of the public sector deficit.
3. The inclusion of assets which are *not* held in any quantity by the non-bank public.
4. The introduction of a given reserve ratio to be maintained at all times (subject to short-run erratic movements).

If the public's currency ratio were stable, the benefits of a monetary base scheme would be total control of bank deposits, close control of the money supply, long-run financial market stability, the independence of fiscal and monetary policy and the restoration of the discount market's traditional role. The costs would be greater fluctuations in interest rates at least in the short run, an increased feeling of interference in the affairs of the private banking system and substantial disintermediation as banks sought ways to circumvent tight control of the monetary base and therefore deposits.

7 Non-bank financial intermediaries and monetary policy

This section concerns the role of n.b.f.i.'s in the operation of monetary policy. This is separated from the treatment of banks in the money supply process considered to date in this chapter. Therefore, the money supply analysis of the previous sections encompasses intermediary types 1 and 2 defined earlier (pp. 175–6).

The traditional view of non-bank financial intermediaries (e.g., Gurley and Shaw, 1956; Clayton, 1962) is that their activities cannot affect the money supply but can influence the velocity of circulation. For a given money stock (M), if an increasing proportion of credit is provided by n.b.f.i.'s, velocity (V) will rise. This is capable of fuelling an increase in demand (PT) and will offset monetary policy (assuming this is reflected in the constant money stock).

Before the validity of this traditional view can be assessed, the issue of the basic differences between banks and non-bank financial intermediaries must be considered. Firstly, as already mentioned, the secondary securities issued by banks are a means of payment. This involves the provision of money transmission services by banks (including chequing services). In addition, bank deposits are included in official definitions of the money supply. In contrast, financial intermediary deposits have to be converted into money before they can be used for transactions. There is a 'double exchange'. However, this distinction is not an unambiguous one. For example, only clearing banks have access to the London Clearing House which is a vital part of the money transmission process.

Secondly, reserves held by banks and n.b.f.i.'s differ. Banks hold their reserves in various assets including Treasury Bills and balances at the Bank of England. The latter ultimately represent the monetary liabilities of the government. On the other hand, while a proportion of n.b.f.i. reserves is held in certain forms of public sector debt, part is also held in clearing bank deposits (including certificates of deposit). N.b.f.i.'s, in a sense represent a secondary tier of financial institution.

These are the two major differences although they do have consequences for various features of n.b.f.i. activity including credit creation and its effects on the total supply of credit and money in the economy. The comparison between the credit creation possibilities of banks and n.b.f.i.'s is interesting. Recalling the procedure for banks, these institutions can 'create' deposits by lending out money, which with the existence of a high redeposit ratio will return to the banking system. Of course, any new deposits must be 'backed' by the necessary holdings of reserve assets.

For n.b.f.i.'s the sequence is rather different. Take the case of some money being withdrawn from a bank and deposited in a building society. As around 20 per cent of building society assets are held in liquid form, the remainder will be used for new mortgage business. The liquidity ratio is a necessary behavioural constraint on the societies (although the minimum stipulated ratio is as low as $7\frac{1}{2}$ per cent) but in general the increased lending of the society can be financed without competing reserve assets away from the banks. Therefore, total credit will increase. However, that part of the societies' assets held in the form of public sector debt will reduce the supply of reserve assets to the banking system indirectly. This occurs through a decline in residual financing through the banks even if debt purchased by the society is not of the short term reserve asset type. As a result, the increased lending activity of the society may impair the ability of the banks to create new credit.

This conclusion need not always follow, however. Firstly, banks may be holding excess reserves and can accommodate the fall in reserve assets without reducing bank loans. Secondly, banks may react to a loss of reserve assets by selling long term government securities and so retain their previous level of bank advances. The ultimate effect on credit flows is made uncertain by these qualifications. However, what is clear is that if n.b.f.i.'s were subject to the same reserve asset ratio as the banks, an extension of n.b.f.i. credit would require them to compete reserve assets away from the banks. Subject to the provisos made in this paragraph, such a situation would leave total credit unchanged. A final point should be made concerning the credit creation possibilities of n.b.f.i.'s. The redeposit ratio appropriate to them will in general be much lower than that for banks as it is much less likely that funds would return to the same institution. Therefore, the second and subsequent 'rounds' of credit creation are quantitatively less significant than is the case for banks.

Leaving aside the actual credit creation process itself, the conclusions for total credit flows are also influenced by the 'sources' of the funds deposited at n.b.f.i.'s. There are a number of alternatives. Firstly, if money is transferred from idle balances held on deposit at a clearing bank, any credit expansion by n.b.f.i.'s based on such inflows will cause total credit to increase. (This is because bank lending is unaffected as reserve asset holdings of the banks are unchanged.) Secondly, the transfer may involve money which would have been used to purchase goods and services. This case will lead to an increase in saving and credit but no overall increase in final demand, as consumption has declined. Thirdly, the inflow may come from liquidated public sector debt. If so, credit provided by the n.b.f.i.'s will expand. In addition, the decline in private sector holdings of public sector debt will induce a rise in residual financing through the banks. Bank holdings of reserve assets and the money supply will also increase. Finally, the n.b.f.i. may attract a deposit from funds previously held in a private sector security. If so, total credit is unchanged, although its structure may be altered.

While the origin of new funds is therefore crucial to the ability of n.b.f.i's to offset monetary policy, an equally vital issue is the response of borrowers to the monetary squeeze. How will borrowers react if they are turned away from a bank due to a shortage of loanable funds? The differing answers to this question polarise into a familiar Keynesian v monetarist dispute. Keynesians – associated particularly with the Radcliffe Report (1959) – argue that money and near-monies (as provided by n.b.f.i's) are close substitutes. Unsatisfied demand for money is translated into an increased demand for n.b.f.i. credit which raises the velocity of circulation and circumvents monetary stringency. The situation is represented in the following Fig. 3:

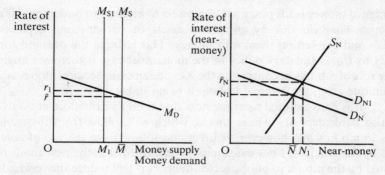

Fig. 3. Money and near-money (Substitutes case).

Both diagrams have fairly elastic demand curves reflecting the high substitutability between money and near-money. A lending ceiling at M_{S1} would lead to a decline in the demand for money if interest rates rose to r_1 (or if rates were sticky, to an unsatisfied fringe of borrowers). As a result, demand is immediately switched to near-money the supply of which rises to N_1. The tight monetary policy is offset by the rise in n.b.f.i. credit. Two points must be made. Firstly, the tight monetary policy could equally have had its origins in higher bank interest rates without the lending ceiling. The result as far as this analysis is concerned would have been the same. Secondly, the whole analysis rests crucially on the absence of official controls on n.b.f.i's, which has been a generally valid assumption in the UK. One exception was the government move to control the growth of mortgages provided by building societies in early 1978. The aim of that was more direct however – to prevent a surge in house prices similar to the one that occurred in 1972–3.

On the other hand, monetarists argue that money and near-money are not good substitutes. In fact they can be classed as complementary goods. This case is treated in Fig. 4.

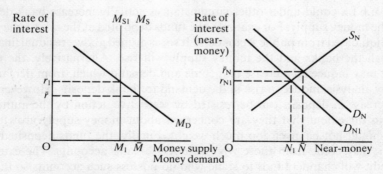

Fig. 4. Money and near-money (Complements case).

Figure 4 includes much less elastic demand curves to reflect the low substitutability assumption. In this case a lending ceiling and the resultant shortage of money leads potential borrowers to attempt to build up their money holdings. They do this by encashing assets or withdrawing deposits from n.b.f.i.'s and converting them into money. This reduces the demand for near-money to D_{N1}. Monetary policy in the monetarist case is therefore augmented by the role of n.b.f.i.'s in contrast to the Keynesian case, because money is viewed as a unique asset, the demand to hold it being stable.

It is conventional to argue now that n.b.f.i.'s can affect not only credit but also bank deposits. These effects, which will follow from the transfer of funds to n.b.f.i.'s are, however, indirect and follow from the use of new funds made by the n.b.f.i.'s. Four cases may be identified. Firstly, new funds may be invested by the n.b.f.i. in public sector debt. This will reduce the residual financing of the PSBR through the banks, leading to a decline in reserve asset holdings of the banks and therefore in bank deposits. (This may seem an unlikely case. However, while it is true that 100 per cent of a new n.b.f.i. deposit will not in general be placed in public sector debt some percentage of each new deposit – which could rise to 30 per cent dependent on the type of n.b.f.i. – will be.) Secondly, the extension of credit made possible by the increased n.b.f.i. deposits may be partly invested by borrowers in public sector debt. To the extent that this occurs, residual financing through the banks, bank reserve assets and their deposits will fall. Thirdly, the expansion in total credit induced by building society activity may lead to increased demand and inflation and cause the authorities to operate against the banks to restrict their lending and therefore deposits. Fourthly, part of the increased credit may be used by borrowers to pay off bank overdrafts. If new demand for *bank* credit is not forthcoming, the banks will be unable to replace this loan business. Bank deposits will fall. Note that in all these cases, the reduction hypothesised may simply be in the *rate of growth* of bank deposits and not in the level of deposits.

The reduction in bank deposits that follows from each of these examples will lead to a fall in the money supply. Such moves may not be unwelcome to the authorities as in some sense they are stabilising with a rise in n.b.f.i. credit being offset by a fall in the money supply. However, the same transfer of funds to an n.b.f.i. could under other circumstances actually increase bank deposits and the money supply. For example, the funds deposited at the n.b.f.i. may have been liquidated from public sector debt. If so, as argued above, residual financing through the banks and the money supply will rise. Alternatively, the rise in credit may induce an increase in income and demand which, from demand for money analysis, induces a rise in the demand for bank deposits. However, such an increase in deposits can be resisted by restrictive action by the authorities and, to the extent that they are concerned about money supply growth, this case should not be given too much weight. Finally, the funds deposited at an n.b.f.i. may come from those who do not use bank accounts. The extension of credit will channel funds to some who do possess such accounts so that, on balance, bank deposits will rise (Llewellyn, 1979).

Clearly, the final effect on the money supply of n.b.f.i. activity will depend on how each of these factors is balanced out. Empirical evidence on the role of n.b.f.i.'s in offsetting monetary policy is limited. Very simply, the mere fact that the proportion of total deposits at banks (which are controlled by policy) has declined since 1963 implies a worsening of the tightness of monetary policy. But available evidence on whether n.b.f.i's actually attempt to offset monetary policy is contrasting. The major work by Gibson (1967) is now too dated to be of current relevance although he did find that at least until 1966, there was no evidence of any offset. Two other studies have looked at this issue in very different ways. Mills and Wood (1977) found that although the elasticity of money demand has risen between 1923 and 1974, the extreme Radcliffe substitutability thesis is convincingly rejected. Finally, a general equilibrium model of the UK financial sector was constructed by Clayton, Dodds, Ford and Ghosh (1974) to investigate the offsetting role of non-bank financial inter-mediaries. Recognising the debt they owe in the method of approach to Tobin and Brainard (1963) the authors found evidence that such intermediaries can negate monetary policy operated through money supply control. In two separate experiments, they found that a fall in the money supply is accompanied by a rise in non-bank financial intermediary deposits, with the net effect being expansionary. Such clearly conflicting evidence is not helpful and much of the conflict may arise from the vastly different methodological approaches adopted.

Non-bank financial intermediaries are becoming more important in the UK in numerical terms alone. The theoretical and empirical issues of whether they actually offset monetary policy operated through the banks are still wide open. However, they do add one further complication to money supply analysis. Even if the money supply can be controlled by the authorities and some of the arguments raised in this chapter suggest this will be difficult, this may be only a part of the problem. Buoyant n.b.f.i. credit may weaken the results of the strictest money supply policies.

Chapter 8

Money in the open economy

1 Introduction

Much of the analysis in this volume so far has implicitly assumed the existence of a 'closed' economy, i.e., one where there is no trade with the rest of the world. This is clearly unrealistic as the UK, for example, is a highly 'open' economy with, at the end of the 1970s, around 25 per cent of all expenditure being on imported goods and a similar proportion of domestic output being exported. This chapter endeavours to consider some effects of an open economy analysis of monetary theory and policy. Given the considerable and growing degree of integration between the world's money and capital markets, the neglect of external influences on monetary issues is increasingly illegitimate. Some of the effects of the openness of an economy have been introduced when appropriate (e.g., Ch. 7) and most of the theory studied in Chapters 3–5 is not invalidated by the abandonment of the closed economy assumption. The task of this chapter is, formally, to modify the analysis of monetary issues to encompass a situation of openness.

2 Monetary policy in the open economy

External money flows affect the efficacy of monetary and fiscal policy under different exchange rate regimes. The theory of the effectiveness of both monetary and fiscal policy in an open economy has been developed over the last two decades with pioneering work undertaken by Fleming (1962), Mundell (1961, 1963) and latterly Swoboda (1972, 1973). Briefly, this work concludes that an independent monetary policy (i.e., different from the policy followed by the rest of the world) cannot, in the long run, be operated by a *small* country under fixed exchange rates; therefore, in this situation, monetary policy has no long-run impact on real income. For monetary policy to be independent and achieve a permanent influence on real income, floating exchange rates, where the imbalance between the supply and demand for foreign exchange is resolved by movements in the exchange rate, must be established.

These basic results may be demonstrated on an extended IS/LM

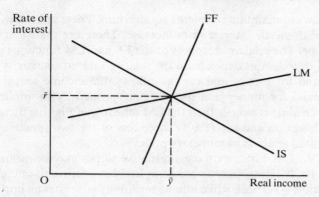

Fig. 1. Equilibrium with IS/LM and FF schedules.

diagram. Figure 1 includes an external balance schedule (FF) which is used to introduce the effects of various policies on the balance of payments.

A full derivation of the FF schedule is given by Wrightsman (1970). The schedule can be defined as the locus of points of different income and interest rate levels where the balance of payments is in equilibrium, i.e.

$$B = X + K - MP = 0 \tag{1}$$

where B, X, K, MP are the overall external balance position, exports, capital inflows (net of outflows) and imports respectively. A simple model of the FF schedule is given in eqs [2]–[5] below. For country A (with W representing the rest of the world), the functions for X, MP and K are:

$$X_A = a_0 + a_1 y_W + a_2 \frac{P_A}{P_W} \tag{2}$$

$$MP_A = b_0 + b_1 y_A \tag{3}$$

$$K_A = c_0 + c_1 r_A \tag{4}^\dagger$$

where a_1, b_1, $c_1 > 0$, $a_2 < 0$, and y, P and r represent real income, the price level and the rate of interest respectively. Substituting from [2]–[4] into [1]:

$$r_A = \frac{1}{c_1}\left[b_0 - a_0 - c_0 - a_1 y_W - a_2 \frac{P_A}{P_W} \right] + \frac{b_1}{c_1} y_A \tag{5}$$

By relating r_A and y_A, [5] is the equation for the FF schedule. The slope (b_1/c_1) is determined, *ceteris paribus*, by the marginal propensity to import (b_1) and the interest sensitivity of capital inflows (c_1). As b_1, $c_1 > 0$, the FF schedule has a positive gradient. Equation [5] postulates that a rise in the level of income in country A will lead to a rise in imports which must be matched by

---

This assumes that world interest rates (r_W) are unchanged. Alternatively, r_W could be included explicitly in eq. [4] but the above procedure is adequate to derive the slope of the FF schedule.

extra capital inflows to maintain payments equilibrium. These inflows will only be forthcoming if domestic interest rates increase. Therefore the FF schedule has a positive slope. The relative steepness of the FF and LM functions cannot be determined *a priori* as this depends on the relative interest sensitivity of the speculative demand for money and capital inflows, the income sensitivity of transactions demand for money and the marginal propensity to import. The fact that the FF schedule is steeper than the LM schedule in Fig. 1 is therefore a convenient simplification and the relative steepness of the two functions does not alter the essential analysis of monetary policy.

As with the LM curve, extreme alternative slopes may be rationalised for the FF schedule. If capital inflows are completely insensitive to interest rate changes, the schedule is vertical, while infinite sensitivity generates an horizontal function. This latter extreme implies that any other interest rate but the one ruling in the rest of the world will lead to infinite flows of capital either into or out of the domestic economy. The only sustainable interest rate is the world rate. This situation will confront a small economy which cannot influence the world rate of interest, while it also demonstrates the existence of considerable financial integration across national frontiers. Although the assumption of a perfectly elastic FF schedule (Mundell, 1963) simplifies the subsequent analysis, an upward-sloping schedule is utilised. This is because such a procedure is more general, while there is considerable evidence that despite an increase in the integration of the world's capital markets, perfect capital mobility remains an unrealistic assumption.

Monetary policy under fixed exchange rates

Figure 2 demonstrates the effects of an expansionary monetary policy in a regime of fixed exchange rates. An increase in the domestic money supply shifts the LM curve out to LM_1 causing the rate of interest to tend to fall to r_1 and income to rise to y_1. Position E_1 is, however, only a quasi-equilibrium (Swoboda 1972) as the economy moves into balance of payments deficit in a

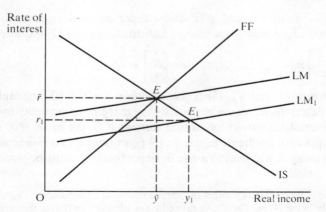

Fig. 2. Monetary policy under fixed exchange rates.

position below the FF schedule. Income has risen and the interest rate fallen from the initial equilibrium (E) which worsens both the current and capital accounts. Under fixed exchange rates this deficit must be financed by a decline in reserves. This leads, through the action of the EEA (Chs 1 and 7) in the UK, to a decline in the money supply until the deficit is removed. Final equilibrium is therefore at E again with the money supply returned to its original level.

Monetary policy has therefore failed to influence income or the rate of interest under fixed exchange rates except in short run quasi-equilibrium because the money supply is endogenously determined. However, while the aggregate money supply is beyond the control of the domestic authorities, the division between the domestic and external components of the money supply is not. In Fig. 2, although the money supply has remained constant in equilibrium, the proportion of domestic assets in the money supply has risen and that of external assets (reflected by the decline in reserves) has fallen. Domestic monetary policy therefore affects the level of foreign exchange reserves under fixed exchange rates, but not the overall stock of money.

Monetary policy under fixed exchange rates (with sterilisation)

A qualification must be made to the result of the previous section in respect of the case where a country sterilises the impact of external influences on the money supply. Sterilisation may be defined as the increase of the domestic component of the money stock to offset any fall in the external component. The objective of sterilisation is to maintain the rise in the overall money supply (LM_1) that enabled the quasi-equilibrium (E_1) to exist; in this way a more permanent increase in real income may be achieved. However, the maintenance of the money supply at LM_1 does not remove the balance of payments deficit so that the external component of the money supply (foreign exchange reserves) will continue to decline; in fact, such action simply finances the deficit. In addition, the process feeds on itself as the increase in the domestic money supply that sterilises the effects of the external deficit will reduce domestic interest rates causing new capital outflows and increasing the need for sterilisation. Eventually the stock of foreign exchange reserves will be exhausted. Such a self-defeating policy cannot succeed in the long term, permitting only a temporary independence of monetary policy and control of the level of income.

The results of this analysis will follow in the opposite case of a monetary contraction which moves the balance of payments into surplus. The constraint on sterilisation and therefore on independent monetary policy is very different, however. In the limit, sterilisation by retiring domestic money (through increased bond sales) would leave the money supply consisting of an external component alone. Again, the process is unstable as the decline in the domestic money supply causes interest rates to rise, generating new inflows of capital and the need for even greater sterilisation.

Empirical studies on sterilisation do not present a clear picture of the ability of monetary authorities to offset externally induced changes in the money supply. A problem is that negative correlation between changes in the domestic and external components of the money supply may not in fact be evidence of sterilisation (where the external component of the money supply is the independent variable) but of offsetting capital flows (where the domestic component is the independent variable). For individual countries, Herring and Marston (1976) and Neumann (1977) argue that Germany has been able to sterilise around 80 per cent of the externally induced changes in the money supply. Japan is another country that has successfully operated a sterilisation policy (Whitman, 1975). However, apart from the special case of the USA (see pages 216–17), no wholly reliable conclusion may be drawn on the incidence or future possibilities of widespread sterilisation for other countries.

Monetary policy under floating exchange rates

Figure 3 demonstrates the effects of monetary policy under floating exchange rates:

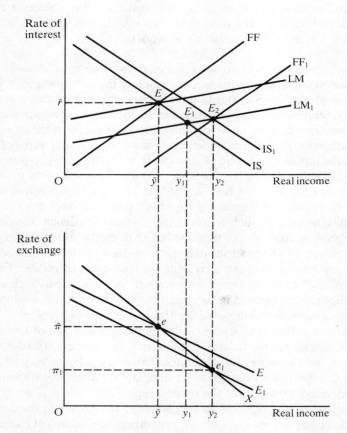

Fig. 3a and 3b. Monetary policy under floating exchange rates.

In Fig. 3a, the increase in the money supply (LM_1) which leads to a balance of payments deficit at E_1, will cause the exchange rate to depreciate. No intervention occurs in the foreign exchange market to influence the exchange rate. Reserve levels are unchanged therefore and the effect of the external situation on the money supply is zero; the external component of the money supply is therefore fixed (Mussa, 1976). The exchange rate depreciation causes a fall in export prices and a rise in import prices leading to a decline in the relative price ratio (P_A/P_W). From eq. [1] there is a once-for-all improvement in the balance of payments as exports rise $(a_2 < 0)$. The constant term in eq. [5] has declined causing the FF schedule to move downwards and to the right. Equilibrium in the balance of payments can now be restored with a lower domestic rate of interest for a given income level. The decline in the exchange rate will also affect the IS schedule. As the exchange rate declines, causing exports to fall and imports to rise, net injections into the economy will increase. This causes the IS curve to shift to the right to IS_1.[†] Equilibrium is established at E_2 with a higher income level (y_2) and lower rate of interest, with the indirect effect on the IS curve augmenting the increase in income $(y_1 - y_2)$. Monetary policy has successfully influenced the level of income at the cost of a lower exchange rate.

Figure 3a does not, however, determine the new equilibrium exchange rate. In Fig. 3b this is achieved using a diagram from Mundell (1963). The XX curve is a locus of real income and exchange rate combinations that yields internal balance. Likewise, the EE schedule represents external balance. The initial equilibrium (e) is at a common income level with Fig. 3a and at an exchange rate of $\bar{\pi}$. The increase in the money supply in Fig. 3a moves the economy away from e as income is increased at a constant exchange rate. However, the resultant depreciation of the exchange rate causes the EE schedule to shift downwards to EE_1 in line with the falling external value of domestic currency. With the internal balance schedule fixed at XX, the new equilibrium rate of exchange (π_1) is determined by its intersection with EE_1.

The conclusion of this analysis is that an independent monetary policy (i.e., one where the income level is capable of long-run influence) is only possible under floating exchange rates. However, two qualifications must be added to these results which suggest possible characteristics that an economy must possess in order to operate an independent monetary policy even under fixed exchange rates.

The first of these relates to the 'small' economy assumption made at the beginning of this chapter. While an increase in a small country's money supply will not affect the world money supply sufficiently to increase world demand (so that an independent policy is impossible under fixed exchange rates), the same is not true for a large economy. A monetary expansion in such an economy will have a noticeable impact on the world money supply, nominal income and inflation. The increase in world demand will lead to an increase in the demand for exports from the expanding country, thus making monetary policy effective

---

[†] The IS/LM model assumes a constant price level. However, it may be argued that the rise in the price of imports will increase the domestic price level and thereby reduce the real money supply. As a result, the LM curve would shift to the left. This secondary shift in the LM curve does not, however, affect the basic analysis of monetary policy in Fig. 3a and so is ignored.

in the sense of causing a permanent increase in domestic income. The effectiveness of monetary policy is, via its impact on world demand, proportional to the size of that country relative to the whole world economy (Swoboda, 1973). Figure 4 demonstrates the large economy example:

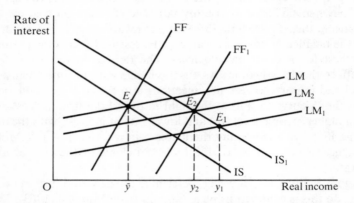

Fig. 4. Monetary policy in a large economy under fixed exchange rates.

An increase in the money supply (LM_1), by affecting world demand significantly and therefore domestic exports, shifts the IS and FF curves to the right (IS_1, FF_1). Quasi-equilibrium (E_1) is at an income level y_1. If, as in this case, a balance of payments deficit still remains, part of the increased money supply is removed by foreign exchange market intervention (LM_2). Final equilibrium (E_2) is at income level y_2.

The analysis so far in this section has defined a 'small' country as one that cannot influence its long-run income level through monetary policy under fixed exchange rates. (This is due to the insignificant effect of such a country's monetary expansion on the world money supply and therefore world demand.) In this case, both the money supply and the rate of interest are endogenous. However, in a world of perfect capital mobility (where the FF schedule is horizontal) this result also implies the inability of a small country to maintain an interest rate that is different from the world rate. Again, both the money supply and the rate of interest are endogenous but in this case, the latter is also equal to the world rate of interest. In such a world of perfect capital mobility, therefore, the 'smallness' of an economy has an added connotation. A problem may arise in identifying a 'small' economy. *A priori* it may be safe to argue that in the Western world the USA alone is a sufficiently 'large' economy to affect world demand and interest rates in a substantial way. The analysis in Fig. 2 is essentially valid for all other Western countries.

Secondly, a reserve currency country (where the currency of that country is used in world trade and is held as a foreign exchange asset by other countries) may operate an independent monetary policy under fixed exchange rates. The best example of such a country in the post-war period is the USA. A balance of payments deficit suffered by the USA will lead to an outflow of dollars to the surplus country. These dollars will be re-deposited in the USA and may eventually be converted into higher yielding US government debt. This conversion will increase the deposits of the US Treasury in the US banking system which the former may use to repurchase government debt from the private sector. The deficit itself reduces the US money supply, while the debt repurchase increases it again. Overall, the US money supply is unaffected; an independent monetary policy is therefore possible assuming the above series of transactions takes place. Therefore in the post-war period, the USA has satisfied both of the criteria for an independent monetary policy under fixed exchange rates, while it is reasonable to argue that no other developed country has fully satisfied either of them.†

Figure 5 may be used to compare the effectiveness of monetary policy for a small economy under alternative assumptions concerning exchange rate flexibility:

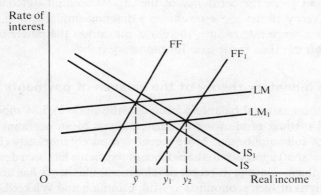

Fig. 5. A comparison of monetary policy effects.

In Fig. 5, it is clear that:

y_2 (floating rates) $> y_1$ (fixed rates with sterilisation) $>$
$\bar{y}$ (fixed rates) (e.g. Stern, 1973).

Such results enable the conclusion to be drawn that irrespective of the relative slopes of the LM and FF schedules and the degree of shift of all three schedules, monetary policy has its greatest impact on income under floating exchange rates and least impact under fixed rates. This is based on the result that any monetary expansion will lead to a balance of payments deficit so that under floating rates

† The UK case is somewhere between that of the USA and a typical small country. As the major reserve currency in the nineteenth century, sterling still retains a very minor role in this respect. Therefore, a small proportion of the external surpluses in the world economy are invested in sterling. This, combined with the large volume of government debt sold by the UK authorities abroad, permits the UK, following the analysis above, a certain independence of monetary policy even with a fixed exchange rate.

a secondary increase in income occurs due to the rise in exports (IS) as the exchange rate declines.[†]

The greater effectiveness of monetary policy under floating exchange rates compared to fixed exchange rates may be contrasted with the results for fiscal policy. Under conditions of perfect capital mobility, fiscal policy under fixed exchange rates has the full multiplier effects on income (as the rate of interest is unchanged); on the contrary, under floating rates, fiscal policy does not affect the level of income at all (e.g. Mundell, 1963). In general, if the LM schedule is steeper than the FF schedule, fiscal policy has a greater effect on income when exchange rates are fixed than when they are floating. However, if the relative slopes of the FF and LM schedules are reversed, fiscal policy is more powerful when exchange rates are floating. In the limit, should the FF schedule be vertical, capital being immobile, fiscal policy will not influence the level of income under fixed exchange rates. The economic interpretation of this last result is that the level of income must remain constant for balance of payments equilibrium given the constancy of the capital account outcome. The student should verify all the above results on a diagram similar to Fig. 5. The issue of which exchange rate regime, therefore, maximises the power of fiscal policy is less clear cut than is the case for monetary policy.

3 The monetary theory of the balance of payments

The inclusion of an external balance schedule in the static IS/LM model is a well-established method of allowing for the openness of an economy in the determination of full equilibrium. More recently, a purely monetary (but not necessarily monetarist) approach to the balance of payments has been developed to tackle this problem. Despite its recent development, the theory has historical roots in the analysis of such economists as Mill, Cantillon and Wicksell.

The fundamental basis of this monetary approach is the definition of the money supply as being equal to the domestic assets of the banking system plus the country's foreign exchange holdings (Laidler and Nobay, 1975).

$$M_S = B + R \tag{6}$$

with M_S, B, R representing the money supply, the domestic monetary base and foreign exchange reserves respectively. Equation [6] can also be expressed in terms of first differences:

$$\Delta M_S = DCE + \Delta R \tag{7}$$

where DCE is domestic credit expansion. It is ΔR that is of particular interest in this approach. This term represents one measure of a country's balance of payments position in the sense that all other items may be included 'above the line' with reserve flows being a residual. Therefore, the balance of payments as

---

[†] However, if secondary shifts in the LM curve are permitted (Footnote on p. 215), this result will not always hold. A situation may occur where a policy of fixed rates with sterilisation generates the highest level of income although only in the short run.

represented by ΔR influences the ex-post level of the money supply. (The UK concept of DCE and its relationship with the change in the money supply should be recalled at this point. The adjustments of the money supply growth for external factors will be fully explained in Section 4 below). The balance of payments in this approach is therefore seen as a monetary phenomenon. To ignore the monetary consequences of a payments disequilibria which will affect the money supply through ΔR is the basic criticism that the monetary theory has of previous balance of payments adjustment theories.[†]

Other criticisms were made of the traditional theories which in turn have become fundamental elements of the monetary theory. Firstly, traditional theories do not distinguish between full (stock) equilibrium and quasi-(flow) equilibrium. A balance of payments disequilibrium may be generated by:

> a (stock) decision to alter the composition of the community's assets by substituting other assets for domestic money, and a (flow) decision to spend currently in excess of current receipts. (Johnson, 1958).

A stock disequilibrium implies a once-for-all adjustment and so is inherently temporary. However, a flow disequilibrium is not temporary and in general will require policy changes to restore equilibrium. Analysis of external disequilibria in terms of stock/flow decisions enables their monetary implications to be noted and so is a crucial element in the monetary theory.

Secondly, in traditional theory, the exchange rate represents the price of a country's output relative to that of other countries. On the other hand, the monetary theory treats the exchange rate as being the relative price of the monetary commodity of different countries. Finally, the short-run nature of traditional theories is criticised. The monetary theory is a long-run equilibrium model and argues that it

> may be misleading to rely on the Keynesian model as a guide to policy making over a succession of short periods within each of which the Keynesian model may appear to be a reasonable approximation to reality. (Johnson, 1972a).

Having set out the background to the approach, the theory itself must be derived. Two crucial assumptions are made. Firstly, the real demand for money in an individual economy is a stable function of a few variables (e.g., real income, an interest rate). Secondly, the domestic component of the nominal money supply is exogenously controlled by the monetary authorities. Any discrepancy between the real demand for money and the nominal money supply will lead to balance of payments disequilibria which will be removed by the consequent inflows or outflows of money. In addition, the theory conventionally assumes the existence of full employment (i.e., stable output, flexible prices). However, this is not a necessary assumption in the monetary approach, which may be similarly applied to the typical Keynesian conditions of flexible output and rigid prices.

[†] The major theories are the elasticities approach, the absorption approach and finally a synthesis between the two (see for example, Stern, 1973; Johnson, 1976, 1977).

The development of the theory has been primarily associated with Mundell (1968, 1971) and Johnson (1972a), while many of the important contributions have been assembled by Frenkel and Johnson (1976). However, the historical origin of the approach goes back to David Hume's price specie flow mechanism. The essence of this mechanism is that a country's balance of payments will depend on its price level, relative to the price level of trading partners, which in turn is influenced by the degree of monetary growth at home and abroad. Therefore, a growth rate of the money supply that exceeded the 'world' average rate of monetary expansion would lead to a higher price level in the home country relative to that abroad generating a balance of payments deficit. This in turn under gold standard conditions would cause the excess money supply to flow from the deficit country to the surplus country to re-establish equilibrium. It is clear that relative prices play the crucial role in this Classical adjustment mechanism.

While the monetary approach would accept the basic outcome of this price specie flow mechanism (i.e., the role of monetary factors being crucial), the role of relative prices in the adjustment process is not accepted. In the monetary approach, the true adjustment mechanism is the disequilibrium between expenditures and incomes or between the supply and demand for money. The relative price adjustment mechanism is rejected in favour of an absorption adjustment mechanism. In this respect the monetary approach has more in common with the traditional absorption approach of Alexander (1952) than with the elasticities approach which relies on relative prices to adjust payments disequilibria.

Assuming that in the rest of the world money demand and supply are equal, a deficit situation for an individual country will occur when there is an excess money supply over money demand (expenditure over income). However, should the money supply in the rest of the world exceed the demand for money by a larger margin than is the case in the individual country, a balance of payments surplus will develop in that country. Therefore, it is the stance of domestic monetary policy relative to that in the rest of the world that will determine the balance of payments situation, according to the monetary approach. To remove a payments disequilibrium, a stock adjustment will occur. Taking the example of a deficit under fixed exchange rates, this will be financed by running down foreign exchange reserves which will lead to a decline in the money supply to restore money market equilibrium. The essence of the monetary approach is therefore that a discrepancy between absorption and income (money demand and money supply) will cause the accumulation or decumulation of certain assets to 'finance' the disequilibrium. It is this money market disequilibrium *alone* that will induce adjustment. The rejection of relative prices as being a vital part of the monetary approach therefore separates the approach from some of the Classical contributions (Frenkel and Johnson, 1976).

In the monetary approach, then, differences in monetary growth in a single country *vis-à-vis* the rest of the world cause balance of payments disequilibria with adjustment occurring through the foreign exchange market. Under fixed exchange rates, adjustment will continue until a common price level is attained in all countries. The different economies of the world become, in a sense, one economy tied by completely fixed exchange rates and having one level of prices. This equalisation of world prices is ensured by the operation of a form of international arbitrage. Markets are assumed to be sufficiently perfect so that prices of traded goods are equalised across national boundaries. If one commodity had different prices in the world economy, profit could be made by buying the commodity in the country with a low price and re-selling in another country at a higher price. Such arbitrage activity helps to equalise prices.

Problems exist for this mechanism on two counts. Firstly, perfect price equalisation cannot occur in a world of quality differences and transport costs. The second problem is more fundamental, however. The arbitrage process will be slowed by the existence of goods which are not traded (non-tradeables). The larger is the non-tradeable goods sector in an economy the more difficult will it be for the arbitrage process to function successfully. However, at least two mechanisms exist to transmit price changes from tradeables to non-tradeables. Firstly, a rise in the price of tradeable goods will reduce the demand for these goods and assuming a high elasticity of substitution between tradeables and non-tradeables, demand will be switched to the latter. Non-tradeable goods prices will rise. Secondly, a rise in the price of tradeable goods will reduce real wages in all sectors. Demands for higher wages will be made and if granted will squeeze profit margins. Therefore, firms will raise their prices. This real wage effect of import prices will clearly not be limited to the tradeable goods sector. Such mechanisms, particularly with increasing economic integration in the world economy leading to a decline in the importance of the non-tradeable goods sector, will not prevent the establishment of a world price level but will affect the speed of adjustment before it is attained (Laidler, 1976b).

The existence of the 'world' economy also implies that a common rate of interest is established. This is ensured by the international mobility of capital. Any attempt by an individual country to establish a rate of interest above (below) the world level will cause infinite inflows (outflows) of capital which will cause it to restore the world rate of interest in the long run. The world money supply is simply defined as the sum of the individual country money supplies. A more interesting issue is the distribution of the world money supply across countries. This is determined by the 'natural distribution of specie' (Gervaise, 1720, reported in Frenkel and Johnson, 1976). The money supply will be diffused over the world economy according to each country's rate of inflation and therefore balance of payments position relative to other countries. The long-run equalisation of inflation rates will stabilise the distribution of money at an equilibrium level. In long-run equilibrium where all balance of payments disequilibria are removed, the determinant of a country's money supply (assuming the income elasticity of money demand in all countries is equal) is the size of that country's output relative to world output (Duck and Zis, 1978). If the income elasticity of money demand differed between countries, two countries producing the same output would be in monetary equilibrium with the money supply equal to money demand, at different money supply levels. This proportionality rule would therefore be broken. Therefore, in equilibrium, the world money supply, and the rate of interest are uniquely determined; real output will also be given utilising the natural rate of unemployment thesis (Ch. 9) so determining the world price level. The monetary theory is therefore a long-run equilibrium model explaining the role of the money supply in the determination of balance of payments position and in equilibrium, the world price level.

Given this approach to the external sector of an economy, a balance of payments deficit will develop in the following way. Let the monetary authorities in an individual country decide to increase the domestic component of the money supply so that the average world monetary expansion rate is exceeded. The excess money balances represent a stock disequilibrium in the money market ($M_S > M_D$). The excess real balances will be run down by the purchase of domestic and foreign goods and financial assets. A payments deficit will result which under fixed exchange rates will be financed by a decline in reserves which automatically reduces the money supply. This portfolio adjustment is the essential transmission mechanism of the monetary theory. Therefore, although the substitution of domestic goods and financial assets for money will drive the domestic price level up this process is not emphasised in this approach. In particular the higher domestic prices and, as a result, the possible switch of foreign demand away from home-produced goods is not seen as the cause of the deficit. The interpretation in this paragraph is therefore consistent with the monetary approach's rejection of the pure price specie flow mechanism of Hume. Secondly, the expansion of a large country's money supply will have a significant effect on the world money supply. As a result, the world inflation rate will rise. Only in such a case will individual national monetary policies have a measure of independence which is not apparent when the small country case is examined. Restoration of payments equilibrium will be different in the large country case with the equilibrium price level being higher than the original level. In all cases, however, reserve growth and the external balance are inversely related to the growth of the domestic money supply.

A payments deficit may also develop in another way. Assume that the supply of money is equal to the demand for money in all countries and that (utilising the assumption that the income elasticity of money demand is unity) the rates of growth of the money supply are equal across all countries. Then, if the rate of growth of domestic output in one country suddenly falls, the demand for money will rise less rapidly than previously causing it to lag behind the money supply. The excess supply of money will spill over into foreign goods and securities and generate a deficit in the same way as in the previous example. To summarise, a balance of payments deficit will develop in a country if:

   (i) The country's money supply growth exceeds the growth rate of the world money supply.
  (ii) The country's price level exceeds the world's price level (which will be a result of (i)).
 (iii) The country's growth rate of output falls short of the world's growth rate (assuming that the income elasticity of money demand is unity). These results for fixed exchange-rates can finally be identified with

eq. [7]. ΔR will in general be non-zero as the balance of payments will not, except by chance, balance. As ΔR is endogenous, the change in the money supply is beyond the control of the authorities, despite the assumed exogeneity of DCE. Monetary policy, under fixed exchange rates is therefore sensitive to conditions in the rest of the world apart from any short run autonomy available through sterilisation.

The case of floating exchange rates presents very different conclusions. In this case, a deficit induced by any of the developments outlined above will cause the exchange rate to depreciate. The money supply in this case determines the exchange rate and not the payments deficit. The adjustment of the exchange rate leaves the external component of the money supply (R) fixed. As ΔR is zero, the money supply is under the control of the monetary authorities. Policy independence is achieved under floating rates so that the money supply and therefore the domestic price level can be independently determined.[†] The endogenous variable in this case is the exchange rate. A declining exchange rate is the price of inflating the domestic money supply at a faster rate than the world money supply.

Two exceptions to the rule may be identified. Firstly, if two or more economies are very closely integrated (e.g., Canada and the USA), independence may not be guaranteed as disturbances are transmitted across national boundaries (Mussa, 1976). Secondly, Laidler (1977b) has shown that independence may be lost in the short run if price expectations are influenced by prices in the world economy, and the exchange rate. If so, external prices will affect domestic output and prices causing independent control of these variables to be lost. However, in long-run equilibrium, independence will be restored.

The criticisms that have been made of the monetary approach to the balance of payments are such that it is considered more appropriate to term the approach 'monetarist'. In many ways, the critique is similar to that outlined in Chapter 5. However, it is unfair to append a monetarist label to the theory in this way. The monetary approach simply views the consequences of balance of payments disequilibria from the viewpoint of the monetary account. There is no prejudgement that monetary factors are the cause of every disequilibrium or that monetary cures are always successful. The approach analyses any disturbance in monetary terms such that a deficit by definition must mean $M_S > M_D$, even if the monetary authorities have not exogenously raised the money supply, while adjustment to equilibrium must involve the restoration of money market equilibrium.

The whole approach is criticised because of its rejection of the role of relative price changes in the adjustment process. In addition, some of the assumptions which underpin the model are considered inappropriate. The familiar view that money demand is unstable is raised against this approach. The exogeneity of the domestic component of the money supply is questioned with

[†] To assume that DCE is under the control of the authorities does not imply that they actually seek to control it in all circumstances. Exogeneity of the money supply may be sacrificed to ensure interest rate stability for example.

the real bills doctrine of demand-determined money supply being inserted as a rival hypothesis. Finally, even if exogeneity is a valid assumption, the approach is criticised for the lack of consideration that at times, particularly in the UK the authorities have chosen not to control the money supply.

4 UK monetary statistics and the external economy

This section identifies the allowances made in the monetary statistics of the UK for the effects of external transactions. As stated in Ch. 1, Sect. 5, the concept of DCE adjusts the money supply for these external effects. It will become clear, however, that this adjustment procedure is considerably more complicated in practice than in theory. In particular, the assumption that all changes in foreign exchange reserves $(\varDelta R)$ reflect transactions that affect the money supply and therefore that the only adjustment necessary to the money supply figure is through $\varDelta R$, is too simple in the UK context.

It is useful to begin this analysis by investigating the effects on the money supply (sterling M3) of various external transactions. Much of this next part draws heavily on the very concise analysis of these effects completed by the Bank of England (1975, 1978). They are of crucial importance in achieving a logical definition of DCE. The major transactions that affect the money supply are the following:

(i) *Current account deficit – Excess of imports over exports (this can be treated as a net import of goods equal to the imbalance between imports and exports)*
Sterling M3 will fall. If the imports are paid for in sterling, the currency is transferred from domestically owned bank deposits to non-resident bank deposits. The latter are not part of the money supply, which therefore falls. If the imports are paid for in foreign currency, the importer runs down his sterling bank deposits in order to purchase the necessary foreign currency from the EEA. As privately held sterling bank deposits fall so does the money supply. The increase in sterling held by the EEA is invested in Treasury Bills, which reduces residual financing through the banks, further reducing bank deposits and the money supply.

(ii) *Capital inflow – public sector borrowing from abroad*
Sale of public sector debt to the overseas sector The increase in foreign currency received in payment for the debt will increase the reserves held by the EEA. If non-bank demand for debt is unchanged, less is now sold to the banking sector (residual finance falls). The positive impact on the money supply of the reserve inflow is balanced by the decline in residual financing. Sterling M3 is unchanged. If non-bank demand for debt falls to the same extent as overseas demand rises (in effect government debt is purchased by the overseas sector from the non-bank private sector), residual financing through the banks is unchanged. Overall, the money supply rises due to the initial increase in reserves.

Foreign currency borrowing from international organisations or foreign banks Foreign currency borrowing from international organisations such as the International Monetary Fund (IMF) or the European Economic Community (EEC) will leave the money supply unchanged; domestic bank deposits remain at the same level. In addition, the effects on the money supply of the reserve inflow and the decline in the overall borrowing needs of the public sector cancel out with no effect on the Domestic Borrowing Requirement. Similarly, foreign currency borrowing from banks will increase the level of reserves, but the Domestic Borrowing Requirement and sterling M3 are both unchanged.

Foreign currency borrowing by local authorities or public corporations The effects on the money supply of foreign currency borrowing from a bank are zero as in the case above. However, if the local authority or public corporation uses these funds to repurchase debt from the non-bank private sector, domestic bank deposits and the money supply increase.

(iii) *Capital inflow – borrowing by the private sector*
The private sector may borrow by issuing shares which are purchased by the overseas sector or by direct foreign currency borrowing. Sterling deposits of the non-bank private sector rise as foreign currency is deposited by the overseas sector and switched into sterling. In addition, the rise in the EEA's holdings of foreign currency is not offset by any decline in borrowing needs leading to an increase in the Domestic Borrowing Requirement. Therefore, the money supply increases.

(iv) *Other transactions*
Non-residents may deposit sterling at banks in the UK, particularly when the currency is strong. As sterling M3 excludes non-resident deposits, it is unchanged. In addition, any foreign currency liabilities of the banks to the overseas sector may be switched into sterling and then on-lent. This rise in foreign currency liabilities which may precipitate switching does not affect the total for sterling M3. Nevertheless, in both cases, there is an increase in foreign exchange reserves (as overseas residents buy sterling in the first case and banks do in the second case in exchange for foreign currency). This leads to an increase in the Domestic Borrowing Requirement. There is, therefore, a positive secondary multiplier effect on sterling M3.[†]
The relevance of these examples of currency flows should be made clear. All the flows identified above will cause a change in the level of foreign exchange reserves. In theory, rearranging eq. [7] DCE adjusts the domestic money supply for these changes in reserves:

$$DCE = \Delta M_s - \Delta R \qquad [8]$$

[†] The above examples are the most important external transactions that affect the domestic money supply. However, the list is not exhaustive and many other cases can be found in the Bank of England's study (1978 – especially the Appendix pp. 528–9).

The rationale of this adjustment has already been stated. Any increase (decrease) in reserves should lead to an increase (decrease) in the money supply. The correction to the ex-post money supply is therefore necessary to derive the domestically created monetary expansion (DCE). It should be clear from the discussion in this section, that the actual situation in the UK is more complex than this. In particular, all flows leading to a change in reserves do *not* cause a change in the money supply. The most important quantitative flows that do not have any effect on the money supply is the group of transactions between the public and overseas sectors (i.e., debt sales and foreign currency borrowing).

This observation is important in a number of ways. Firstly, it is inappropriate to undertake a simple adjustment of the money supply (as in eq. [8]) to calculate DCE. Secondly, the theory and practical applications of DCE diverge very considerably in the UK case. Finally, it is true therefore that a particular balance of payments *equilibrium* may have a non-neutral effect on the money supply. For example, a current account deficit (flow (i)) financed by a government security sale to the overseas sector (flow (iia)) will cause the money supply to decline. These assymmetrical effects cast considerable doubt on the IS/LM/FF models which rely on the assumption that if the balance of payments is in equilibrium, the money supply does not change (Llewellyn, 1980).

DCE statistics in the UK do take account of the complex relationships between the money supply and reserve changes. However, the adjustments undertaken are confusing and at times seem difficult to justify at first impression. The balance sheet approach that will be utilised to explain these adjustments was originated by Bell and Berman (1966) although it dates from well before DCE was introduced. The approach was updated when DCE was first utilised (Economic Trends, 1969) and even more recently, the approach has been made contemporary with the publication of two official articles (Economic Progress Report, 1977; Bank of England, 1977a).

Table 1 describes a balance sheet formulation of the banking sector's assets and liabilities that is appropriate for the definition of DCE and sterling M3 at the present time. It is similar in structure to that utilised by Bell and Berman but has some modifications to accommodate the introduction of DCE and the concept of sterling M3. The figures in all the tables to follow relate to the financial year 1977–8. (Ch. 7, Table 5 includes some of the statistics used in this section.) The starting point is the PSBR (Line 1) which must be financed by a combination of the transactions in Lines 2 and 3. The external financing of the public sector (2a) does not include official debt sales to the overseas sector or foreign currency borrowing by the public sector as these leave the net borrowing requirement unchanged; the level of reserves changes but not the money supply. The transactions included are those that affect the level of reserves *and* the money supply (e.g., a current account transaction or private sector capital flow). This set of transactions is termed the 'External financing of the public sector' to reflect the fact that such reserve changes by altering the EEA portfolio of Treasury Bills affect the financing of the PSBR. (It is tempting to assume

Table 1 Balance sheet components of sterling M3 (£ m.)

		1977/8
1.	Public sector borrowing requirement	5,493
	minus	
2.	(a) External financing of the public sector	4,333
	(b) Increase in public sector debt held by the non-bank private sector	−6,601
	(c) Increase in notes and coin held by the non-bank private sector	−1,165
	equals	
3.	Banking sector financing of the public sector	2,060
	plus	
4.	(a) Increase in sterling bank lending to the non-bank private sector	3,740
	(b) Increase in sterling bank lending to non-residents	1,112
	(c) Increase in foreign currency lending	*
	equals	
5.	Increase in banking sector assets	6,912
	equals	
6.	Increase in banking sector liabilities	6,912
	minus	
7.	Increase in (net) non-deposit liabilities (+increase in (net) non-financial assets)	−414
	equals	
8.	Increase in banking sector deposits	6,498
	minus	
9.	Increase (−) in (net) foreign currency deposits of banking sector (decrease +)	+9
	equals	
10.	Increase in sterling deposits of banking sector	6,507
	minus	
11.	Increase in non-resident sterling deposits of banking sector	−1,463
	equals	
12.	Increase in resident sterling deposits of banking sector	5,044
	Sterling M3 definition	
12.	Increase in resident sterling deposits of banking sector	5,044
	plus	
2.	(c) Increase in notes and coin held by the non-bank private sector	1,165
	Increase in sterling M3	6,209

* This item is netted out in line 9.

Source: *Bank of England Quarterly Bulletin*, March 1979, Tables 11.1, 11.3.

Table 2 Alternative statistical construction of sterling M3 (£ m.)

		1977/8
A. Public sector borrowing requirement	(1)	5,493
B. External financing of the public sector	(2a)	4,333
C. Domestic borrowing requirement		9,826
financed by		
D. Increase in public sector debt held by the non-bank private sector	(2b)	−6,601
E. Monetary financing	(3)+(2c)	3,225
F. Increase in sterling bank lending to		
(i) The non-bank private sector	(4a)	3,740
(ii) Non-residents	(4b)	1,112
G. Total		8,077
Minus technical adjustments		
H. (i) Increase in non-deposit liabilities (net)	(7)	−414
(ii) Increase (−) in net foreign currency deposits of banking sector (decrease +)	(9)	+9
(iii) Increase in non-resident sterling deposits of banking sector	(11)	−1,463
J. Increase in sterling M3		6,209

Source: *Bank of England Quarterly Bulletin*, March 1979, Table 11.3.

that a term such as external financing of the public sector must reflect debt sales abroad. This must be resisted as, basically, it is only flows to and from the private sector that through ΔR will affect the financing of the PSBR.) The positive entry in Line (2a) for 1977–8 reflects the rise in reserves (due to the balance of payments surplus) which increased the domestic borrowing requirement. Any part of the PSBR not financed externally (2a), by debt sales to the non-bank public (2b) or by an increase in notes and coin held by the non-bank public (2c), must be covered through the banking system (3). Such financing includes bank lending to the public sector and sales of long-run government debt as well as residual financing through sales of Treasury Bills (Ch. 7, Table 5).

The total increase in bank assets (5) is the aggregate of the increase in public sector assets held by the banks and bank lending of various types (4). By definition, the change in assets equals the change in liabilities (6). Part of the increase in liabilities represents an increase of non-deposit liabilities net of non-financial assets (7) (the banks' own capital and reserves); this element must be deducted from the increase in liabilities to leave the increase in deposits (8). The increase in deposits total can be divided into resident sterling deposits

Table 3 Balance sheet components of DCE (£ m.)

			1977/8
A.	Public sector borrowing requirement	(1)	5,493
	financed by		
B.	Increase in public sector debt held by the non-bank private sector	(2b)	−6,601
C.	*Ex-ante* monetary financing of the public sector	(3)+(2a)+(2c)	−1,108
D.	Increase in sterling bank lending to		
	(i) The non-bank private sector	(4a)	3,740
	(ii) Non-residents	(4b)	1,112
E.	Domestic Credit Expansion		3,744
	Minus technical adjustments		
F.	(i) External financing of the public sector	(2a)	+4,333
	(ii) Increase in non-deposit liabilities (net)	(7)	−414
	(iii) Increase (−) in net foreign currency deposits of banking sector (decrease +)	(9)	+9
	(iv) Increase in non-resident sterling deposits of banking sector	(11)	−1,463
G.	Increase in sterling M3		6,209

Source: *Bank of England Quarterly Bulletin*, March 1979, Table 11.3.

(12), non-resident sterling deposits (11) and foreign currency deposits (9). The traditional definition of the increase in sterling M3 can be calculated from Table 1 above. Defined as the increase in resident sterling bank deposits (12) and in notes and coin held by the public (2c), it was equal to £6,209 m. in 1977–8.

The importance of this method of deriving the change in the money supply is its origin on the *asset* side of the balance sheet. The money supply, defined as resident sterling bank deposits plus notes and coin held by the non-bank public, is primarily a *liability* total. However, use of the balance sheet approach enables the construction of the change in sterling M3 on the assets side of the balance sheet as being equal to the banking sector financing of the PSBR (3) plus the increase in sterling bank lending (4) plus the increase in notes and coin held by the non-bank private sector (2c) – where (3)+(2c) sum to the monetary financing of the public sector – minus the various adjustments (7,9, 11). Table 2 should clarify this derivation.

Table 3 presents a similar balance sheet derivation of DCE. This table represents the statistical construction of DCE that is used by the Bank of England in its *Quarterly Bulletin* (Table 11.3). DCE is defined as an asset total representing that part of the PSBR not financed by the rise in debt held by the resident non-bank private sector (B), plus the rise in bank lending (D). A notable exclusion is the external financing of the public sector (F(i)). This will reduce the money supply (Tables 1, 2 above) and is excluded from DCE as the latter reflects the true *ex-ante* domestic expansion of the money supply before any external transactions have affected the actual *ex-post* money supply. This is the first adjustment that must be made to move from the change in sterling M3 to DCE or vice versa. The other adjustments are also listed under F in Table 3 and require some justification and discussion. It is, in fact, these adjustments some of which seem arbitrary that have caused criticism of the definition of DCE in the UK. Why should these be included in DCE and not in the change in sterling M3? Are the increases in foreign currency deposits and non-resident sterling deposits important for DCE but not for sterling M3? The inclusion of the rise in non-deposit liabilities in DCE when it is excluded from the rise in sterling M3 seems particularly arbitrary. However, a clear understanding of the balance sheet approach will clarify the reason for these adjustments although it may not rule out an alternative procedure. The real problem is that DCE is an *asset* total and the change in the money supply a *liability* figure. If the figures for DCE and the change in sterling M3 are to be consistent, and yet sterling M3 is to exclude non-deposit liabilities, foreign currency deposits and overseas sterling deposits, the balance sheet approach which cannot identify the asset equivalent of all these flows must include them in DCE. An alternative approach is to include the latter two adjustments (H(ii), (iii)) in the definition of M3 which would now be broader than sterling M3 and defined in Table 1 above as lines $8 + 2c$. The DCE figure could then include the rise in non-deposit liabilities (fall in non-financial assets) leaving the only other adjustment as being the external financing of the public sector. If this is done, the money supply figure used is a broader aggregate and not purely limited to resident sterling deposits and may be considered less appropriate to the domestic economy. The choice is clear. A broader M3 figure must be used or the adjustments to move from the change in sterling M3 to DCE accepted. The fact that the authorities use sterling M3 and DCE as policy targets suggests that they believe sterling M3 (plus adjustments) to be a better aggregate than a broader money supply definition.

The real problem with these statistics is one that is not clearly identifiable from the previous tables. It relates to the external financing of the public sector. To repeat, this line includes all external transactions that *ex post* affect the money supply. However, it is impossible to identify from the balance of payments accounts which external flows affect the money supply and which do not. The figure entered as the external financing of the public sector is therefore only an estimate which makes the final figure for DCE an inexact one. The theoretical simplicity of DCE is not borne out in practice. This is a particular problem for the UK which sells large quantities of government debt abroad (the major flow that causes the level of reserves but not the money supply to change). Therefore, any particular DCE figure must be interpreted with care.

Finally, the above balance sheet approach is *not* a theory of the determination of the money supply or DCE. It is merely a set of statistical identities representing an *ex-post* analysis of the money supply. No causality can be introduced into the analysis although the close links between fiscal policy

(PSBR) and monetary policy are obvious.

Therefore, while it is important to consider external influences on the domestic monetary situation in an open economy such as the UK, this analysis is very complex in theory and practice. The basic results of the extended IS/LM analysis are important but very simple, while in practice the identification of genuine external effects on the money supply is difficult. Not the least interesting result of this treatment is that certain external transactions have asymmetrical effects on the money supply. The theoretical assumption that a balanced external account will leave the money supply unchanged is not true when a current account deficit ($\downarrow M_S$) is financed by overseas sales of public sector debt ($\bar{M}_S$). Therefore, further work is needed to make the theoretical approaches to the analysis of external flows consistent with the real world.

Chapter 9

Inflation

1 Introduction

Inflation has become the major global economic problem of the 1970s. As such, much theoretical and empirical work has appeared on the causes of inflation. This chapter considers some of the issues surrounding inflation as a branch of monetary economics. It is not intended to be a full treatment of the subject as this is beyond the scope of this volume. The reader is referred to excellent recent surveys for further analysis of the current state of knowledge on inflation (Trevithick and Mulvey, 1975; Laidler and Parkin, 1975; Gordon, 1976; Frisch, 1977).

Inflation is most commonly defined as 'the process of continuously rising prices or equivalently of a continuously falling value of money' (Laidler and Parkin, 1975, p. 741). Many theories exist to explain the inflationary process but the oldest and most traditional view is that inflation is a purely monetary phenomenon. Such a statement has in recent years been associated most closely with the leading monetarist Milton Friedman (e.g., 1970b). However, the history of the link between an increase in the money supply and rising prices goes back at least four centuries to the work of Jean Bodin. (The link between this view and Classical economics in general should be noted by recalling the discussion in Chapter 3.) An increase in the supply of any commodity will in conditions of stable demand and flexible prices lead to an increase in the price of that commodity. The statement that inflation is a monetary phenomenon is therefore simply an application of elementary supply and demand theory.

However, the stronger statement that a rise in the money supply actually *causes* a rise in the price level is much more controversial. This is the view held by both traditional and modern quantity theorists and is most hotly disputed by those who favour explanations of inflation in terms of rising costs which may operate independent of monetary changes. However, what even the latter theorists would accept is the passive role of monetary expansion in the inflation process. Consider the case of an exogenous rise in money wages due to trade union militancy, or alternatively a rise in the price of oil. These will either be accommodated in lower profits accruing to firms using these particular factors of production or more realistically by such firms increasing the prices of the commodities they produce. This will reduce the real value of a fixed nominal supply of money. As the demand for money is couched in real terms, there is an excess of demand over supply in the money market. The result will be increasing interest rates until this discrepancy is removed. Clearly if prices continue to rise in the face of exogenous cost increases, interest rates will soon reach intolerably high levels.

The outcome of such a sequence is clear. Either interest rates will rise so much that a 'credit crunch' will occur with massive deflation or the rise in prices will be 'validated' by an increase in the money supply. The authorities will probably decide in time that the latter development is less harmful to the economy in the long term as high interest rates and deflation have substantial real and political costs attached to them. The validating increase in the money supply is not in this case the cause of inflation. However, it is clear that a *long-term* rise in the price level cannot occur without an accompanying monetary expansion. It is in this sense that inflation can, without argument, be termed a monetary phenomenon. Therefore, even if the extreme anti-monetarist view of a rise in the price level due to cost increases were advanced, this cannot be sustained without a rise in the money supply. For example, the oil price increase of autumn 1973 may have been the immediate cause of the rise in world-wide inflation in 1974. However, the fact that the inflation rate in Germany in 1974 was only 7 per cent while that in the UK was 16 per cent in that year was due to the more restrictive monetary stance adopted in the former country. This is not to say that the inflation rate in Germany did not increase in the wake of the oil price increase. Clearly it did. However, the German government decided to squeeze out part of that inflation and suffer some of the attendant unemployment by adopting a tight monetary policy. The choice between higher inflation and higher unemployment forced on governments by the oil crisis was resolved in very different ways in these two countries.

The more extreme view of monetarists that a rise in the money supply actually causes a rise in the price level in all cases is itself rather more complex than this simple statement would suggest. As argued in Chapter 5, the relationship is subject to time lags. A monetarist would argue that to study a graph of monetary expansion and inflation in any country (or even the world as a whole) would not clearly suggest this close correlation. However, much evidence (e.g., Parkin, 1975; Selden, 1976) exists of close relationships between changes in the money supply and the rate of inflation two to three years later. This lagged relationship is due to a number of factors. The major one is the argument that in the short run an increase in the money supply will lead to a rise in output. Only in the longer term will output resume its previous level and the monetary expansion be fully reflected in the price level. (Other arguments may be recalled from Ch. 5.)

With this background in mind, the current issues on inflation are very clear. The debate is not over whether inflation is a monetary phenomenon or not but over whether the role of money is active or passive. Monetary expansion is a necessary and sufficient condition for long-term increases in the price level although it may not be the ultimate cause of an initial upward impetus in prices. The role of money is all pervasive, therefore, in any analysis of inflation.

In the remainder of this chapter, various aspects of inflation will be considered with the causative role of money representing the thread that unites these arguments. The traditional cost-push v demand-pull dichotomy of inflation theory will not be utilised. In recent years, it has become more popular to classify models of inflation as being either excess demand or sociological theories. The rejection of the cost-push v demand-pull distinction can be justified with the use of Figs 1 and 2, which both demonstrate the generation of excess demand inflation.

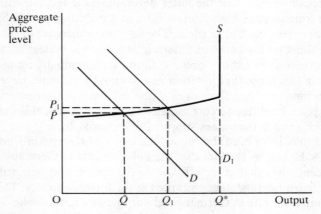

Fig. 1. Demand-pull inflation.

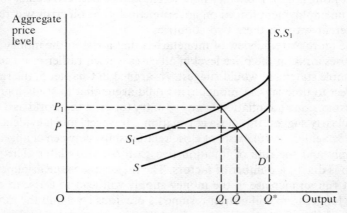

Fig. 2. Cost-push inflation.

D and S represent aggregate demand and supply curves respectively with Q^* being full employment output. In Fig. 1, demand-pull inflation is represented by an upward shift in the demand curve to D_1 (caused by an increase in the money supply, exports, etc.). The price level rises to P_1, despite the existence of unemployment due to bottlenecks in the production process as full employment is approached; output rises to Q_1. In Fig. 2 a shift in the supply curve to S_1 will cause the price level to rise to P_1; in this case, output falls. In both examples, prices rise due to the existence of aggregate excess demand at the old price level. Therefore, excess demand theories of inflation can encompass those cost-push influences which occur due to supply curve shifts as well as the more familiar demand-pull influences. The causes that cannot be accounted for within the excess demand framework are those that are independent of the state of excess demand. Models which include such factors are typically labelled 'sociological' theories and include most often trade union power which may force up wages and ultimately prices irrespective of the state of demand in the labour market. The strict cost-push v demand-pull distinction is therefore considered to be less relevant in modern inflation theory.[†] The chapter will give scant treatment to the sociological views of inflation given the subject area of this volume.

2 Traditional inflation theory – the quantity theory

As noted in the previous section, the oldest theory of inflation is the quantity theory of money. Recalling the quantity theory equation (Ch. 3, eq. [16]), this is summarised by:

$$MV_T = PT \tag{1}$$

The conditions required to convert this into a theory of the price level are a stable velocity function $(\bar{V}_T)$, full employment $(\bar{T})$ and the independence of the money supply. This ensures that a 10 per cent increase in the money supply will, in long-run equilibrium, lead to a 10 per cent increase in the price level. A stable velocity function means that the demand for money is stable and this is a necessary condition for inflation to be caused by monetary expansion. Given this, the sufficient condition is the existence of full employment. Without the latter condition a change in the money supply may simply cause a change in output and not prices.

While a monetary explanation of inflation is still favoured by many, developments of the simple quantity theory approach have occurred. Both involve the introduction of price expectations. Firstly, the Phillips curve literature was augmented by the work of Phelps (1968) and Friedman (1968) which introduced the expected rate of inflation as an argument in wage and price equations. These developments and their linkage with monetarism will be outlined in sect. 4 below. Secondly, Friedman (1956) restated the quantity theory in terms of a demand for money function and introduced the expected rate of inflation as an argument. Recalling the discussion in Ch. 5, this new demand

---

[†] The role of expectations (which may move output back in the long run to its original level through an offsetting supply shift (Fig. 1) and demand shift (Fig. 2) has been deliberately omitted to isolate the main arguments.

for money function can be simplified as

$$\frac{M}{P} = f(\dot{P}^e, X) \tag{2}$$

where $\dot{P}^e$ is the expected rate of inflation and X represents all other independent variables. The proportionality result is compromised by the presence of the expected inflation rate as an argument. A rise in the money supply will cause output to increase generating a rise in the demand for money. In addition, any increase in the price level that occurs will increase the expected rate of inflation. (This assumes that the expected inflation rate is determined by current and past actual rates of inflation.) This rise in the expected rate will reduce money demand. If the balance of these influences on money demand causes it to fall an excess money supply remains that will cause the price level to increase further. 'A self-perpetuating flight from money' will be set up. However, various studies (reported by Laidler and Parkin, 1975, the most famous of which is that by Cagan, 1956) show that the conditions for this 'flight from money' do not exist even in the severest of hyper-inflations. The lack of empirical evidence of any such 'flight' does not, however, remove the effects of the introduction of inflation expectations into demand for money theory. In the new equilibrium following monetary expansion, the actual and expected rates of inflation will again correspond and the proportionality result be achieved. However, the path to equilibrium is more complex than in the simple quantity theory example.

3 Excess demand and inflation – the Phillips curve

This section analyses the relationship between excess demand and inflation. Implicit in what follows is that monetary expansion is one of the number of causes of excess demand.

The relationship between unemployment and the rate of price inflation was first noted by Fisher (1926) and more famously Phillips (1958). Under Fisher's argument, a rise in expenditure would encourage producers to raise the prices of their products and also to increase employment and output. However, the rate of price inflation was seen as the independent variable:

$$U = U(\dot{P}) \tag{3}$$
with $U'(\ ) < 0$

where U is the unemployment rate and $\dot{P}$ the rate of price inflation.

Phillips, however, took a different approach. Firstly, he related the rate of change of money wage rates to the level of unemployment and secondly he considered unemployment to be the independent variable:

$$\dot{W} = W(U) \tag{4}$$
with $W'(\ ) < 0$

where $\dot{W}$ is the rate of change of money wage rates. Phillips plotted the observations of these two variables for the period from 1861 and 1913. These traced the now-familiar Phillips curve depicted in Fig. 3:

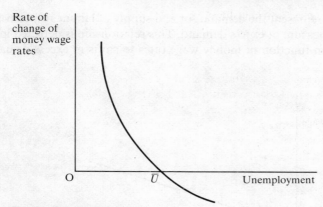

Fig. 3. The Phillips curve.

The importance of Phillips' work was two-fold. Firstly, while the relationship between the rate of change of money wage rates and unemployment in the economically disturbed days of the inter-war period did not lie along a similar function, the observations for the period between 1951 and 1957 did so almost exactly. Therefore, not only was the stability of the relationship remarkable over the pre-First World War period, but it seemed that the durability of the relationship was even more dramatic than that. Secondly and more importantly, the relationship confronted the authorities with a clear choice (Rees, 1970). A combination of low unemployment and high wage inflation could be chosen or alternatively one of high unemployment and low inflation. In particular, in the post-war period, a zero rate of wage inflation could be achieved at the cost of $5\frac{1}{2}$ per cent unemployment (Point $\bar{U}$). In addition, as argued below, if a growth rate in productivity of 2 per cent per annum is assumed, prices will rise by 2 per cent less than the increase in money wages. Therefore, with a money wage inflation rate of 2 per cent compatible with unemployment of just under $2\frac{1}{2}$ per cent, the latter is also compatible with stable prices. The failure of successive governments to achieve zero inflation and zero unemployment was very neatly explained by the Phillips curve.

However, what Phillips did not do was to rationalise this relationship in terms of any complex economic theory. He merely argued that if excess demand existed for any commodity its price should rise. This is also true for labour where the money wage rate is the price of labour, and unemployment a reflection of the state of demand in the labour market. It was left to Lipsey (1960) primarily to establish the theoretical base of the Phillips curve relationship. Firstly, in a manner reminiscent of Phillips' article itself, Lipsey argued that money wage rates (W) will rise when there is an excess demand for labour. Therefore, the rate of inflation is positively related to the excess demand for labour:

$$\dot{W} = f\left(\frac{D-S}{S}\right) \qquad [5]$$

with $f'(\ ) > 0$

where D and S represent the demand for and supply of labour respectively and $(D-S)/S$ is a measure of excess demand. This relationship is depicted in Fig. 4 and is a reaction function of money wage rates to shifts in excess demand for labour.

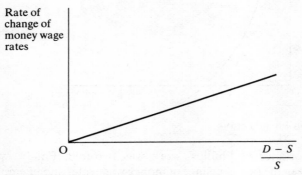

Fig. 4. Wage reaction function.

Lipsey then noted that the excess demand for labour is difficult to measure and so he used unemployment (data for which is available) as a proxy for excess demand, arguing the existence of a functional relationship between them:

$$U = g\left(\frac{D-S}{S}\right) \qquad\qquad [6]$$

with $g'(\ )<0$

This relationship is depicted in Fig. 5:

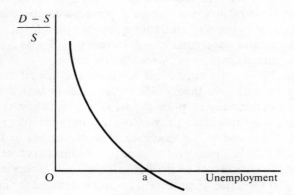

Fig. 5. Excess demand/unemployment function.

The function has a negative slope and is assumed to be non-linear. The latter is explained in terms of a limit of zero being placed on the unemployment rate so that the function approaches the vertical axis asymptotically.

To the right of 'a' the relationship is linear (Lipsey, 1960, p. 15). Point 'a' is of considerable significance. At this point there is no excess demand for labour. The demand and supply for labour can also be defined in the following ways:

$$D = E + V \tag{7}$$

$$S = E + U \tag{8}$$

where E and V represent employment and vacancies respectively. At 'a',

$$V = U > 0 \tag{9}$$

i.e., vacancies and unemployment will be equal to each other but not to zero. Therefore, Oa represents the extent of frictional unemployment in the system.

Combining the functions [5] and [6]:

$$\dot{W} = h(U) \tag{10}$$

with $h'( ) < 0$

which is the traditional Phillips curve. This is depicted in Fig. 6 and is an adjustment function of money wage rates to disequilibrium in the labour market:

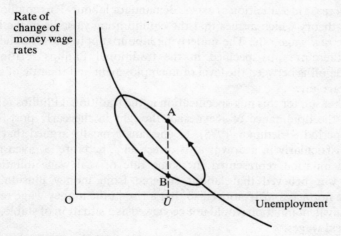

Fig. 6. The Phillips curve.

Other variables were also included in the Phillips relationship. The major one was the rate of change of unemployment. <u>Phillips had noted that if unemployment were falling, the rate of change of money wage rates for a given unemployment level was greater than if unemployment were rising.</u> These observations are reflected by points A and B respectively at unemployment level $\bar{U}$ on Fig. 6. As a result, Phillips argued for the existence of counter-clockwise loops with the actual Phillips curve being an average relationship.[†] Phillips also

---

[†] Other rationalisations of the observed loops have also been made. See Laidler and Parkin (1975).

argued that the rate of price inflation will contribute to the wage inflation, while productivity and profits are other variables that could be included. This latter group of variables will act as shift factors in the Phillips relationship which will move the whole curve to the left or to the right. For example, a rise in the rate of price inflation is predicted to cause an increase in money wage inflation for a given level of unemployment. Clearly, the Phillips curve in this case will shift to the right.

4 The expectations-augmented Phillips curve

The Phillips curve soon became an important part of macroeconomic doctrine. However, only a decade after Phillips' original contribution, the simple relationship between money wage inflation and unemployment was decisively challenged. Theoretical arguments and empirical evidence were presented which led to a substantial revision of the basic model.

The theoretical contributions came from the work of Friedman (1968) and Phelps (1967, 1968) although their arguments differed in detail. Friedman's views, which have become better known, are concentrated on here.[†] Friedman noted that the Phillips curve incorporated the hypothesis that the *money* wage rate would increase in a situation of excess demand for labour. This conflicts with neo-classical theory which argues that the equilibrating variable in the labour market is the *real* wage rate. The underlying labour supply and demand functions were therefore mis-specified in the traditional Phillips relationship. The true trade-off is between the level of unemployment and the rate of change of the real wage rate.

The reason for this mis-specification in the traditional Phillips relationship reflects the dominance of Keynesian thought in the early post-Second World War period (Friedman, 1975). Keynesians typically argued that prices were rigid, particularly in a downwards direction. Therefore, a given rate of money wage inflation represented the same rate of real wage inflation. In addition, it was believed that labour suffered from money illusion. Price changes were not necessarily noticed so that a rise in the money wage rate in a period of equivalent inflation would not be viewed as a situation of stable, but of increasing, real wages.

While this theoretical criticism was being made, empirical doubts were also being cast on the stability of the Phillips relationship in the late 1960s. A stable relationship between money wage inflation and unemployment had only ever been achieved with any consistency in the UK; in the USA, in particular, the relationship had a doubtful empirical basis (e.g., Samuelson and Solow, 1960). As these results were accumulated more direct evidence came from the suggestion that in the 1960s, the Phillips curve had shifted to the right.

[†] The work of Phelps and the contribution of the new microeconomics of inflation (e.g., Phelps *et al.*, 1970) is too lengthy and complex to be considered in this volume. Readers should consult the original work or the survey articles on this subject. See also Brinner (1977).

For a given level of unemployment, wage inflation was much higher than the trade-off predicted or alternatively higher rates of unemployment were experienced at given rates of inflation.

Before the amendments of the Phillips curve attributable to Friedman and Phelps in response to these arguments are analysed three other points must be mentioned. Firstly, with increasing frequency a typical Phillips curve is depicted as representing the trade-off between the rate of *price* inflation and the level of unemployment. The replacement of the wage inflation term is justified by the view that prices are a mark-up over costs. In particular, given a 2 per cent rate of productivity growth, stable price inflation can follow if money wages rise by 2 per cent. Secondly, while the level of unemployment is the most usual dependent variable utilised in the Phillips trade-off, it is only a proxy for excess demand. Many studies have retained excess demand as the independent variable. Excess demand is usually measured as the difference between actual and capacity output where the latter is assumed to follow a linear trend through time (Humphrey, 1978). Capacity output can also be identified as the natural rate of unemployment to be defined below. Thirdly, Phelps and Friedman introduced the concepts of anticipated and unanticipated inflation. These terms are crucial to their models in the sense that any discrepancy between anticipated and actual inflation will enable unemployment to move away from its natural rate.

Having determined that the real wage rate is the equilibrating mechanism in the labour market, the impact of this on the Phillips trade-off must be analysed. Labour bargains for real wages, and as bargains are struck at discrete intervals the appropriate inflation rate considered in the bargaining process is the expected rate. Therefore, the expected rate of inflation ($\dot{P}^e$) should be included as an explanatory variable in the wage equation:

$$\dot{W} = aU + b\dot{P}^e \qquad [11]$$

The b coefficient on the expected inflation rate is of crucial importance. Assume its value is unity. Any increase in the expected inflation rate is therefore fully reflected in a rise in money wages. It must be assumed that there is no money illusion and that workers are capable of translating expected price increases into wage rises. The simple Phillips curve assumes that b is equal to zero with price expectations playing no role at all. An intermediate value for b of between zero and one will cause partial adjustment of money wages to the expected rate of inflation. However, either some money illusion remains or workers do not have the power to secure full compensation in terms of higher money wages.

The significance of this analysis can be seen in Fig. 7. This begins with a simple Phillips curve (PC) with the economy initially stationed at U_N. Wage inflation is zero and the economy is in equilibrium. (For convenience assume that productivity growth is zero so that the rate of price inflation is also zero.) Assume the authorities stimulate demand to achieve a lower unemployment rate (U_1). Wage and price inflation have now risen to 3 per cent.

The point reached (A) is a stable equilibrium under the traditional

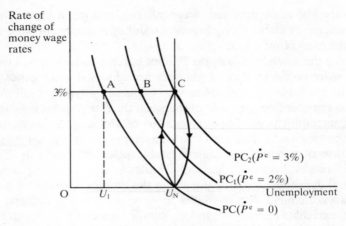

Fig. 7. The natural rate of unemployment hypothesis.

Phillips curve (eq. [10]). The authorities have willingly accepted a higher rate of inflation for a reduction in unemployment. It must be clear why unemployment has fallen. With rising *money* wages labour supply has increased causing a fall in unemployment. (*Bilhurt of R. Regression argument.*)

However, the thrust of Friedman's argument is that for this to occur, workers must be suffering from money illusion. The appropriate real wage for employees is the money wage rate deflated by the expected price level. As the actual rate of inflation increases, the expected rate will also rise on the assumption that the latter is determined by current and previous price behaviour. Once the expected rate of inflation becomes equal to the actual rate, workers will see that, in real terms, wages are unchanged. As a result, the extra labour supply will be withdrawn and U_N re-established.[†] The economy is now at point C on a new short run trade-off (PC$_2$) that corresponds to an expected inflation rate of 3 per cent. Therefore, as the expected rate of inflation rises, this short-run trade-off moves out to the right. If inflation is imperfectly anticipated (e.g., $\dot{P}^e = 2$ per cent), some money illusion remains and part of the extra labour supply is not subsequently withdrawn. The short-run trade-off moves to PC$_1$. In this case, a stable trade-off between inflation and unemployment still exists in the long run; however, if the short-run Phillips curve shifts to PC$_2$ with inflation fully anticipated, the long-run trade-off collapses.

The implications of this model are clear. Assuming that inflation is perfectly anticipated the only long-run equilibrium position is at the level of unemployment U_N. This has been labelled the natural rate of unemployment. U_N does not necessarily represent full employment but is that level of unemployment consistent with stable prices. (Friedman (1968) has a much more detailed

[†] Note that firms will willingly employ the extra labour supply when the wage rate rises as they believe the excess demand to be restricted to their individual market. Once the general increase in prices is appreciated, the employers will reassess the situation, as the employees do, and unemployment will return to U_N.

definition of the concept.) With the collapse of the long-run trade-off between the rate of inflation and unemployment, lower unemployment can only be traded for higher inflation in the short run when the actual rate of inflation exceeds the expected rate (i.e., inflation is not perfectly anticipated). Assuming $b = 1$, this can only occur through continuous stimuli to demand (to keep $U < U_N$) leading to ever-increasing inflation. In effect, this means the system will never settle down to a long-run equilibrium position. This alone keeps actual inflation ahead of its expected rate. Once the stimulus to demand is removed, expected inflation 'catches up' actual inflation and unemployment returns to U_N. Conversely, a position to the right of U_N can only be achieved at the cost of ever increasing deflation of the price level.[†]

The alternative long-run trade-offs are illustrated in Fig. 8:

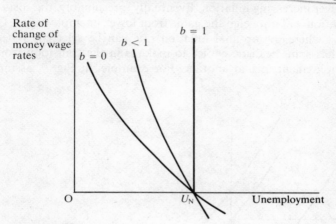

Fig. 8.

If inflationary expectations play no role in the determination of wage inflation – the traditional Phillips curve with $b = 0$ – then the short- and long-run trade-offs are equivalent. However if $(b < 1)$ a stable long-run trade-off remains but it is steeper than the traditional Phillips curve. Finally if inflation is perfectly anticipated $(b = 1)$, the long-run Phillips relationship is vertical above U_N.

The role of unanticipated inflation can be clarified using eq. [12], which represents a trade-off between the rate of price inflation and the level of unemployment assuming zero productivity growth:

$$\dot{P}_t = aU_t + b\dot{P}_t^e \qquad [12]$$

If anticipated inflation is perfectly incorporated into actual inflation $(b = 1)$ then:

$$\dot{P}_t - \dot{P}_t^e = aU_t \qquad [13]$$

If prices react rapidly to the increase in excess demand and price expectations to the rise in prices, the short-term gain in unemployment may be very small. A point such as A (Fig. 7) may never be attained with U_N and C being linked by clockwise loops (e.g., Santomero and Seater, 1978).

In this case the only trade-off is between unanticipated inflation $(\dot{P}_t - \dot{P}_t^e)$ and the level of unemployment. If actual inflation can be kept ahead of expected inflation (i.e., $\dot{P}_t - \dot{P}_t^e > 0$) then a lower level of unemployment can be *permanently* attained at the cost of ever accelerating inflation. Once actual and expected inflation converge $(\dot{P}_t - \dot{P}_t^e = 0)$ the trade-off collapses and the natural rate of unemployment is established. At U_N, the economy can operate at any inflation rate as each will be compatible with the stability of the system.

The extreme no long-run trade-off version of this theory $(b = 1)$ has been labelled the natural rate of unemployment hypothesis or alternatively the accelerationist theory.[†] The policy implications of the approach are particularly interesting. The simple choice of the optimal position on the trade-off no longer applies. If the desired unemployment rate is $U < U_N$, the cost of operating such a policy will be ever increasing inflation. Eventually, presumably, the costs of the increasing inflation will outweigh the gains from lower unemployment. Choice remains at U_N, where the optimal inflation rate can be selected. Where the policy maker has some realistic choice to make is in the transition from one inflation/unemployment mix to another. For example, in Fig. 9, assume the

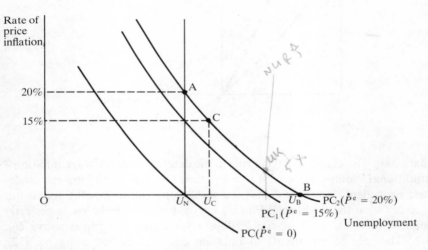

Fig. 9. Adjustment paths to U_N and zero inflation.

initial position is at point A with inflation running at 20 per cent and that zero inflation at U_N is the long-term goal. The authorities could opt for an adjustment path involving a sharp and possibly intolerable increase in unemployment to U_B with price inflation falling immediately to zero. Once price expectations have adjusted to this new inflation rate, U_N would be restored. Alternatively, the chosen adjustment period could be much longer with a gradual path chosen.

[†] Strictly, the accelerationist theory refers to the result that at $U \neq U_N$, prices accelerate in an upwards or downwards direction.

The inflation rate could be reduced to 15 per cent in the first stage with un-employment rising to U_C. As price expectations adjusted unemployment would fall again to U_N and the economy would be on PC_1. A further adjustment phase could then be started. A more gradual approach has the advantage of preventing unemployment from reaching very high levels (Laidler, 1971b).

Policy options in the influence of U_N must also be understood. It is clear from the arguments so far that demand management policies will not reduce U_N. The level of U_N depends on institutional factors such as the degree of labour mobility, job information and educational skills. To reduce this fric-tional element of unemployment and therefore U_N, labour market policies are needed. For the control of U_N demand management is dead (Laidler, 1976b).

The natural rate hypothesis has become a crucial part of the monetar-ists' tool-kit, although as will be argued below, all those who favour the hypo-thesis are not monetarists. Most of the criticisms of the natural rate hypothesis have a Keynesian flavour. Firstly, the almost blind acceptance of a b coefficient of unity has been criticised. There is no *a priori* reason why a value of unity need exist, as b may be interpreted as simply a measure of money illusion (Trevithick and Mulvey, 1975). Although in a world of increasing inflation and awareness about economic developments, money illusion is less likely to exist, its complete removal is also, argue the critics, equally implausible. Alternatively b can be viewed as reflecting the ability of workers to translate price expectations into wage rises, as well as the awareness of higher expected inflation itself. Whichever interpretation is placed on the coefficient, it is clearly the crucial empirical issue of the hypothesis.

Secondly, the concept of the natural rate of unemployment itself is difficult to capture. There is no simple and widely-accepted definition of U_N; while although various measures of it have been calculated, they seem to be implausibly low. Studies by the Manchester University Inflation Workshop have estimated U_N to be around 2 per cent in the UK (Parkin, Sumner and Ward, 1976; Laidler, 1975), while others confirm this general magnitude (e.g. Saun-ders, 1978). All these studies assumed that the natural rate hypothesis applied ($b = 1$). The measurement of U_N is hindered by the likelihood that it is not constant although, being dependent on structural factors, it may be invariant in the short run. Long-run variability of U_N does not affect the validity of this theory of inflation but it does complicate policy to deal with inflation as the position of the economy *vis-à-vis* the natural rate of unemployment may be uncertain.

Finally, a major issue is the measurement of the expected rate of inflation. For empirical analysis of this theory, this issue must be tackled. Two alternative procedures exist. Firstly, a proxy for $\dot{P}^e$ can be formed from observ-able variables. Secondly, direct estimates of $\dot{P}^e$ can be calculated. The first method has been used in most studies. The usual formulation has been to assume an error-learning process in expectations formation or, in other words an adaptive expectations hypothesis. The basic assumption involved is that price expectations for time period t are adjusted from those for the previous time period by some fraction (λ) of the difference between expected and actual inflation for that previous period. Market operators learn from the error in their previous expectations:

$$\dot{P}^e_t - \dot{P}^e_{t-1} = \lambda(\dot{P}_{t-1} - \dot{P}^e_{t-1}) \tag{14}$$

and therefore

$$\dot{P}^e_t = \lambda\dot{P}_{t-1} + (1-\lambda)\dot{P}^e_{t-1} \tag{15}$$

with $0 < \lambda < 1$

The importance of this method can be seen by lagging [15] by one period and substituting the derived equation back into [15]:

$$\dot{P}^e_t = \lambda\dot{P}_{t-1} + (1-\lambda)\lambda\dot{P}_{t-2} + (1-\lambda)^2\dot{P}^e_{t-2} \tag{16}$$

Continual substitution in this way generates the general equation for $\dot{P}^e_t$:

$$\dot{P}^e_t = \lambda\dot{P}_{t-1} + (1-\lambda)\lambda\dot{P}_{t-2} + (1-\lambda)^2\lambda\dot{P}_{t-3} + \ldots \tag{17}$$

$$= \lambda\sum_{i=1}^{\infty}(1-\lambda)^{i-1}\dot{P}_{t-i} \tag{18}$$

Therefore the adaptive expectations hypothesis states that inflationary expectations are dependent on current (as expectations for time t will be formed in period $t-1$) and past values of actual inflation. The weights given to these actual inflation rates, λ, $\lambda(1-\lambda)$, $\lambda(1-\lambda)^2$ ... decline geometrically so that the most recent rates of inflation influence expectations more than those further into the past.

This hypothesis is incorporated into empirical studies by substituting eq. [15] into an expectations-augmented Phillips curve equation such as [11]:

$$\dot{W}_t = aU_t + b\dot{P}^e_t \tag{11}$$

$$\dot{W}_t = aU_t + b\lambda\dot{P}_{t-1} + b(1-\lambda)\dot{P}^e_{t-1} \tag{19}$$

Using a Koyck transformation (Koyck, 1954) which lags eq. [11] by one period and multiplies it by $1-\lambda$:

$$(1-\lambda)\dot{W}_{t-1} = a(1-\lambda)U_{t-1} + b(1-\lambda)\dot{P}^e_{t-1} \tag{20}$$

Subtracting [20] from [19] and re-arranging:

$$\dot{W}_t = aU_t - a(1-\lambda)U_{t-1} + b\lambda\dot{P}_{t-1} + (1-\lambda)\dot{W}_{t-1} \tag{21}$$

i.e.

$$\dot{W}_t = a_0U_t + a_1U_{t-1} + a_2\dot{P}_{t-1} + a_3\dot{W}_{t-1} \tag{22}$$

where $a_0 = a$

$a_1 = -a(1-\lambda)$

$a_2 = b\lambda$

$a_3 = 1-\lambda$

Although [22] is over-identified with four independent variables and only three coefficients, it can be estimated with the appropriate constraint (i.e., $a_0 . a_3 = -a_1$).

adaptive expectations

The idea of adaptive expectations is attractively simple and as such soon became widely used in empirical work. However, it has many problems. As a proxy for price expectations, it is criticised for being inappropriate. In particular use of the adaptive expectations scheme means that the individual ignores current events (e.g., a wage freeze, devaluation) in the formation of price expectations and purely considers present and past price changes. The hypothesis is non-rational, therefore. The scheme is also inconsistent with the mechanism by which inflation is generated. In particular, if inflation is continually increasing, inflation expectations formed adaptively will always lag behind the actual inflation rate (Friedman, 1975) and to learn the mistakes in these earlier predictions is ruled out by the hypothesis.

An alternative model of expectations has recently been developed which relies on the rationality of the individual (Muth, 1961; Sargent, 1973; and Sargent and Wallace, 1976). Muth devised the hypothesis that individuals will exploit all relevant economic information and on this basis will form rational expectations of the future rate of inflation. Such expectations will be optimal. Actual and anticipated inflation rates will only deviate therefore if random shocks occur in the economy as all rational policy actions will be anticipated in advance by individuals who form expectations in this way. This has the devastating outcome that unemployment can only be altered, even in the short run, from its natural rate by random policy action, as all other action is anticipated so that actual and expected inflation do not diverge. As the use of random shocks is an inappropriate base for economic policy, the trade-off collapses in the short run also. However, the arguments against this attack on policy activism are numerous. Firstly, expectations are likely to be non-rational particularly in the short run. It is unrealistic to assume that all available information will always be utilised. Secondly, rational expectations assume that there is no information advantage accruing to the authorities, which is implausible. Thirdly, information may not be costless to accumulate. Therefore, a non-rational but cheap expectation may be formed in preference to a rational, expensive one. Fourthly, many individuals are bound by long-term contracts and so they may be unable to react to new information, even if this information were available. They would therefore act as if they were being non-rational (Laidler, 1978). Finally, rational expectations suffer from the problem of being relatively difficult to model for use in empirical studies.

The second method of measuring inflation expectations is through the use of direct survey data to generate an actual series for this concept. Turnovsky and Wachter (1972) made use of the Livingston survey data in the USA, while Carlson and Parkin (1975) have devised a method for using qualitative survey data for the same purpose. In a comparison of their series with various expectations hypotheses, Carlson and Parkin found that a more complex second order error-learning mechanism fitted the generated series best. Their method has been used to generate series for use in various empirical tests (e.g., Parkin, Sumner and Ward, 1976). An alternative method of generating an expected inflation series has been suggested by Saunders (1978). He utilised the original Phillips trade-off equation for the pre-First World War period (1861–1913) and assuming a unit coefficient on the price expectations variable derived a series for 1962–71. While this is a useful technique it makes two crucial and possibly invalid assumptions. Firstly, that the short-run trade-off is the same in the 1962–71 period as it was before the First World War, and secondly, that the natural rate hypothesis (B = 1) is valid.

Empirical evidence on the natural rate hypothesis has accumulated steadily since 1968. The crucial test of the theory is the size of the coefficient of expected inflation (b in eq. [11]). Most of the results have focussed on this coefficient. At first, the studies seemed to reject the extreme no trade-off view with some consistency. Studies that found this result included the pioneering work of Solow (1969) for both the UK and the USA, and that of Parkin (1970) for the UK.

However, theoretical criticisms of this early work plus more favourable evidence on the natural rate hypothesis accumulating in the mid-1970s have reduced the importance of the results of these early studies. For example, the Solow study includes a basic mis-specification in that real and nominal variables are combined in the equation (Lemgruber and McCallum, 1976), while, argues Friedman (1975), the equation, by relating price inflation to expected wage inflation is not even a true test of the natural rate hypothesis. In addition, it was demonstrated that if the commonly used adaptive expectations scheme is an invalid hypothesis of price expectations formation, its use will lead to a downward bias in the b coefficient. Therefore, a result that $b < 1$, may, if rational or another expectations scheme is valid, be consistent with the natural rate hypothesis, after all (Laidler and Parkin, 1975).

Evidence showing $b = 1$ has been much more common in recent years (see Parkin (1978) for a full survey of UK studies). This evidence has been accumulating in a time of increasing inflation which suggests that once a certain threshold level of inflation has been exceeded, the awareness of labour increases, and workers are more careful and perhaps more able, as well as the firms more willing, to see that wage changes fully reflect expected price movements (Gordon, 1976). UK studies which found evidence of a unit coefficient on the price expectations variable include Saunders and Nobay (1972), Parkin, Sumner and Ward (1976), Mackay and Hart (1974) and McCallum (1975). The generality of these results can be inferred from the wide range of techniques used, with McCallum, for example, using a rational expectations hypothesis and Parkin, Sumner and Ward observed price expectations. Evidence on the no trade-off hypothesis is not confined to the UK, with similar results being found for the USA, other countries (e.g., Nordhaus, 1972) and for the world economy defined as the Group of Ten Countries (Duck, Parkin, Rose and Zis, 1976).

A problem with the majority of these studies is the mis-specification of the price equation for a small, open economy under fixed exchange rates. In such a situation, inflationary expectations will be affected by international inflationary developments as well as the conventional domestic factors. Use of the latter alone implies that the economy is closed or that it is operating under conditions of floating exchange rates. Cross and Laidler (1976) have found in a multi-country study that inclusion of international influences on price expectations significantly improves the results for a number of small, open economies.

Doubt has been cast on the validity of the natural rate hypothesis by the concurrence of high inflation and unemployment above the natural level in the 1970s. If unemployment is above the natural rate, prices should fall at an accelerating rate. With estimates of U_N for the UK being around 2 per cent, the model seems to fail during this period. Three explanations are possible. Firstly, the theory is invalid after all or, secondly, the natural rate of unemployment has been wrongly estimated. Thirdly, labour market friction has increased in the 1970s so that the natural rate of unemployment is now above the level estimated using data from earlier in the post-war period.

The debate on the existence of the Phillips trade-off in the short and long runs will continue for many years on both theoretical and empirical levels. To conclude this section, it is useful to reiterate the broad conclusions of the current state of knowledge in this area:

(1) If the natural rate hypothesis is valid ($b = 1$) and expectations of price inflation are formed rationally there is no trade-off between inflation and unemployment, even in the short run, unless random unexpected price changes can be generated by the authorities.

(2) If the natural rate hypothesis is valid and expectations of price inflation are formed adaptively, then a short-run, but no long-run, trade-off exists.

(3) If the natural rate hypothesis does not hold ($0 < b < 1$) then permanent short and long run trade-offs exist, although the long run trade-off is steeper.

(4) If price expectations play no role at all in wage and price inflation ($b = 0$) then the traditional Phillips relationship is valid in both the short and long runs.

5 Complete monetary models of inflation

The degree of association between the natural rate hypothesis and monetarism has been widely misunderstood. The traditional quantity theory view that changes in the money supply cause changes in the price level (with stable velocity and full employment) forms the basis of monetarist theory. However, in the latter, the role of money in influencing the level of real income and employment at least in the short run has been given more exposure than is the case with classical theory. To recall, monetarists argue that the effect of a change in the money supply will be felt on output at first but ultimately, after a long and variable lag, on the level of prices. At this stage, output returns to its previous level.

Clearly this view is consistent with the natural rate hypothesis with the stable long-run equilibrium being at the natural level of unemployment (U_N). A monetarist, therefore, must believe in the natural rate hypothesis with a unit coefficient on the inflationary expectations variable and no long-run trade-off between unemployment and inflation. However, the excess demand that determines the rate of inflation need not be caused by excessive monetary growth.

Other factors such as fiscal expansion, autonomous increases in investment or exports may be the major determinants of excess demand. Therefore, to accept the natural rate hypothesis, one need not be a monetarist as it does not uniquely associate money with inflation (Gordon, 1976). To be a monetarist it is necessary to accept the natural rate hypothesis; however, the converse does not apply.

From the above discussion, it is clear that a monetary model of inflation, with a monetarist flavour must include a unit coefficient on the inflationary expectations variable plus a number of other features. However, a more general monetary model will be examined here. A purely Keynesian model is also eschewed as not only is a more general approach sought but the typical Keynesian macroeconomic model seeks to explain output and employment, and not the rate of inflation. In addition only in recent years has the money supply been included in such models.

The general monetary model has four separate elements. Firstly, an equation determining inflation is specified which is equivalent to the long-run Phillips curve except that it replaces unemployment with excess demand (X_t) and includes a variable reflecting other exogenous influences on inflation (Z_t):

$$\dot{P}_t = aX_t + b\dot{P}^e_t + cZ_t \qquad [23]$$

where $a, c > 0, b \geqslant 0$

Secondly, expectations of price inflation are assumed to be generated by an adaptive expectations scheme:

$$\dot{P}^e_t = \lambda\dot{P}_{t-1} + (1-\lambda)\dot{P}^e_{t-1} \qquad [15]$$

Thirdly, an equation to explain real income (y) is derived. The explanatory variables are the rate of change of the money supply relative to the rate of price inflation, and other exogenous influences on real income including fiscal influences (F_t):

$$\dot{y}_t = d(\dot{M} - \dot{P})_t + eF_t \qquad [24]$$

with $d, e > 0$

Finally, money market equilibrium is assumed:

$$M_{Dt} = M_{St} \qquad [25]$$

In eqs [23], [24], no lag structure is specified to simplify the model although a more appropriate version would incorporate the delayed influence of certain explanatory variables.

To convert this general model into a monetarist one (e.g., Laidler, 1973b), it is necessary to assume that $b = 1$, and $c, e = 0$. This establishes the no long-run trade-off hypothesis [23] and removes the impact of exogenous, non-monetary influences on real income and therefore the rate of inflation [23], [24]. Rearranging eq. [24] into a demand for money equation results in a typical monetarist model:

$$\dot{P}_t = aX_t + \dot{P}^e_t \qquad [26]$$

$$\dot{P}_t^e = \lambda \dot{P}_{t-1} + (1-\lambda)\dot{P}_{t-1}^e \qquad [15]$$

$$\dot{M}_t = \frac{1}{d}\dot{y}_t + \dot{P}_t \qquad [27]$$

$$M_{Dt} = M_{St} \qquad [25]$$

Real income (y) can be defined as full employment output (y^*) plus excess demand (X):

$$y_t = y_t^* + X_t \qquad [28]$$

In long-run equilibrium, real income will follow the long run full employment growth path so that $X = 0$. Substituting into [24]:

$$\dot{M}_t = \frac{1}{d}\dot{y}_t^* + \dot{P}_t$$

$$\therefore \quad \dot{P}_t = \dot{M}_t - \frac{1}{d}\dot{y}_t^* \qquad [29]$$

This confirms that inflation is a purely monetary phenomenon with monetary changes having no effect on long run equilibrium output. This outcome can be traced to the monetarist assumptions incorporated into the model. Firstly, the demand for money is a stable function of nominal income. Any increase in nominal income must therefore in equilibrium be accompanied by an increase in the money supply. Secondly, there is no long-run trade-off between inflation and unemployment. Unemployment returns to its natural rate in long-run equilibrium. Thirdly, expectations are endogenously determined (Frisch, 1977). Fourthly, the money supply is exogenous so that the link between the money supply and prices in the long run is uni-directional.

The operation of the model can be very briefly analysed (see Laidler and Parkin, 1975; Frisch, 1977 for fuller treatments). Monetary expansion in excess of the equilibrium growth rate of the money supply will lead to excess demand ($y > y^*$) which will cause the actual inflation rate to rise. The divergence between actual and expected inflation will only persist in the short run and once this is removed by expectations catching up, excess demand becomes zero. The equilibrium level of output (y^*) is restored at the natural level of unemployment and the inflation rate has borne the full effects of the increased growth rate of the money supply.[†]

The above model is only one variation of an extreme monetarist macroeconomic model for a closed economy. Many other variations exist (e.g., Anderson and Carlson, 1970; Vanderkamp, 1975), but the basic results of the models are consistent. The models also share a common set of problems.

[†] This assumes the new higher growth rate of the money supply is maintained, allowing the rate of inflation to stabilise at a higher level with the expected rate catching up. Should the rate of monetary growth be continuously increased, inflation will not stabilise and a gap between actual and expected inflation will remain. In the latter case, a permanent increase in excess demand is achieved.

Firstly, they utilise extreme assumptions. For example, the exclusion of fiscal policy from playing a role in the determination of excess demand and inflation is controversial, while the no long-run trade-off assumption has not been empirically proven. Secondly, the use of an adaptive expectations hypothesis can be criticised. As suggested earlier in the chapter, the doubts surrounding this hypothesis are increasing. Thirdly, the assumption of an exogenous money supply may be invalid. In the UK, for example, the authorities for part of the post-war period have maintained an interest rate target and allowed money supply to find its own level. Even if control of the money supply is sought, the existence of external influences such as large international capital flows may invalidate the exogeneity assumption.

The empirical applications of this model have been limited by its closed economy assumptions. Laidler (1973b) tested a model of this type with US data and found its performance satisfactory. The results were consistent with the natural rate hypothesis. A test by Henry, Sawyer and Smith (1976) for the UK ignored the openness of the economy and so the mixed results for the monetary model should not be taken too seriously. No attempt was made to modify the model (e.g., by incorporating foreign prices into the determination of inflation expectations) for the open economy status of the UK. The one empirically proven hypothesis within this model in the 1960s was the stability of the demand for money function. However, the uncertainty over this conclusion in many countries in the 1970s (see Ch. 6, sect. 6) raises doubts now over even this aspect of the model.

It is necessary to repeat that the basic model (eqs [15], [23]–[25]) is consistent with any excess demand theory of inflation and any non-monetary theory of excess demand. The lack of treatment afforded to sociological theories in the framework of a full macroeconomic model has been due to the limits of the subject area of this volume and to the fact that few such models have been formally derived (Laidler and Parkin, 1975).

6 Money and inflation in an international context

In recent years, inflation has increasingly been considered as an international problem. Many reasons for this development can be outlined including the dissatisfaction with 'national' theories of inflation and the increasing integration of the advanced countries of the world as external trade in goods and factors has increased. The manifestation of this integration is the decline in the dispersion of inflation rates in the post-war period (OECD, 1973; Genberg, 1975). This decline has only been reversed in the mid-1970s and as is implied in this section, this is due in part to the increased flexibility of exchange rates since 1973.

It is essential, therefore, to look at two issues on inflation in an international context. Firstly, there exist many possible alternative mechanisms by which inflation may be transmitted between countries. Secondly, it is necessary to consider the various international theories of inflation of which two, the monetary theory and the so called 'nordic' approach, dominate. The treatment of these issues will necessarily be brief as some of them were considered in Chapter 8.

The international transmission of inflation

In a full and very interesting study by the OECD (1973), the alternative transmission mechanisms of inflation were outlined. The first channel is through price effects. At its extreme this involves the assumption of one price amongst all tradeable goods, i.e., the appropriate market place and therefore price, is at the world level. This equality of tradeable goods' prices is ensured, in theory, by commodity arbitrage assisted by the appropriate exchange rate changes. However, as argued in Chapter 8, equalisation of individual country inflation rates will not occur even with the perfect operation of this mechanism due to the existence of transport costs and quality differences and unless an adequate mechanism is specified for the adjustment of non-tradeable goods' prices. Evidence in favour of the role of international price developments in the domestic inflation of small, open economies is available (OECD, 1973) but Williamson and Wood (1976) demonstrate clearly that the commodity arbitrage process works very imperfectly.

Secondly, liquidity effects may transmit inflation across national boundaries. An increase in the money supply in any country will lead individuals to spend their excess money balances partly on domestic goods which will increase prices (at full employment) and partly on imported goods. This will either cause that country's exchange rate to fall (excess supply of its currency) or the dispersal of the excess supply in the world economy if fixed rates are maintained. World inflation will be affected to the extent that the world money supply is significantly increased. This mechanism in particular is part of the monetary theory of the balance of payments.

Thirdly, the most familiar Keynesian transmission process is through demand effects. Excess demand in an individual country will again spill over into increased imports; this will stimulate demand in the exporting country leading to a multiple expansion of demand in the world economy. The effect on world prices will depend on the extent of any excess capacity. The role of these demand effects increases as the openness of an economy rises and its size falls.

Finally, a heterogenous group of other effects may exist. The OECD survey mentions the role of multinational corporations in equalising world prices. The sociological theory of inflation must depend on demonstration effects of various sorts to explain the internationalisation of inflation. It is argued that the increased militancy of workers in one country may spread to others. This may be a plausible idea but the actual transmission mechanism has not been specified, while the theory clearly fails to explain the world wide increase in inflation in the early 1970s. Finally, expectations effects must be mentioned. These may operate through expectations of price or wage rises or of the imminence of wage-price controls.

The monetarist theory of international inflation

As argued above, this theory emphasises the transmission of inflation through liquidity effects. The theory argues that the fixed exchange rate world economy should be analysed as a closed economy. Therefore, the relevant variables are the world money supply and the world price level. The study of inflation in a particular country involves the transmission of inflation and not its domestic generation.

The assumptions of the theory can be summarised:

(1) The law of one price and the existence of perfect capital mobility ensure that the price level and the interest rate are exogenous to individual countries; these variables are both set at the world level.

(2) The natural rate hypothesis ensures the stability of output in long-run equilibrium.

(3) The demand for money on a world level must be a stable function of nominal income.[†]

(4) The supply of money is equal to the demand for money in equilibrium.

The following equations (Branson, 1975) reflect these assumptions:

$$M_D = P.l(y,r) \qquad [30]$$

$$M_S = B + R \qquad [31]$$

$$M_S = M_D \qquad [25]$$

where B, and R represent the domestic monetary base and reserves respectively. Substituting into [25]:

$$B + R = P.l(y,r) \qquad [32]$$

with $\bar{P}$, $\bar{y}$ and $\bar{r}$ pegged by assumption, the domestic monetary base is in a perfectly inverse relationship with the level of reserves. The world money supply (M_{Sw}) is equal to the sum of all individual country money supplies (M_{Si}):

$$M_{Sw} = \sum_{i=1}^{n} M_{Si} \qquad [33]$$

Any increase in an individual country's money supply will only increase the world price level to the extent that the world money supply rises. For a small country, therefore, an increase in the domestic money supply will leave world prices virtually unchanged and cause a deficit in that country's balance of payments. This will reduce the money supply again. The money supply of a small country is an endogenous variable, as money demand is stable with P, y and r fixed. Hence the increase in the domestic monetary base leads to an equivalent decline in foreign exchange reserves and no change in the ex-post money supply. Any independent role for monetary policy is lost in this model. Independence for a small country can only be achieved by permitting exchange rates to alter (in which case $\bar{B}$)[†] or by the sterilisation of reserve flows which can

[†] The issue of whether and under what conditions this involves the stability of individual country demand for money functions is considered in Duck and Zis (1978).
[†] It is this factor that has caused the increased dispersion of inflation rates in the floating rate era of the 1970s.

only be successful in the short run (Laidler, 1976b).

On the other hand, of course, a significant increase in the world money supply from whatever origin must increase the world level of prices. The equilibrium distribution of the world's money supply is proportional to the country's real income weighted by the inverse of the income velocity of money (Frisch, 1977). For a given income velocity, therefore, it is the country's size that determines its equilibrium holding of the world's money supply, as argued in Ch. 8. The doubts expressed over this theory have been the familiar ones. They have centred around the unlikelihood that integration is sufficiently well advanced to prevent any deviation of individual country prices or interest rates from the world levels. Likewise, variations in the level of output do occur around that prescribed by the natural level of unemployment. The validity of assuming that the demand for money is stable has been questioned. Finally, the question of the variation in individual country price levels around the world level is a particular difficulty. The theory of the transmission mechanism of disturbances from the traded to the non-traded goods sectors is not totally convincing. To the extent that productivity differences exist in the two sectors their price levels will also differ, allowing domestic rates of inflation to diverge from the world level.

Empirical evidence on the theory suggests that it has a certain validity at the world level. Duck et al. (1976) fitted an expectations-augmented Phillips curve to the Group of Ten 'world' economy and found the relationship fitting well with a significant role for excess demand and acceptance of the no trade-off hypothesis. In addition, Gray, Ward and Zis (1976) found that the world (defined as the Group of Ten again) demand for money function was stable. Both these tests were applied to data from the virtually fixed rates regime existing before 1971. In a similar vein, considerable ad hoc and rigorous evidence links the world price level to the lagged world money supply (Heller, 1976; Keran, 1975; Selden, 1976). On the other hand, the one-to-one inverse relationship between the domestic monetary base and the level of foreign exchange reserves implied by this model is not borne out by empirical evidence (Kouri and Porter, 1974). The evidence overall is therefore persuasive but certainly not conclusive and alternative approaches to the determination of world inflation must be considered.

An eclectic theory of international inflation

Keynesians do not disagree with the concept of a world price level but rather choose to ignore it, considering it uninteresting and even irrelevant. A Keynesian model would rely for the transmission of inflation on demand effects through the operation of the familiar foreign trade multiplier. Branson (1975) developed a simple model which does not reflect extreme Keynesianism in that a Phillips curve equation is added to the familiar IS/LM framework. He argued that national price levels will converge as any reduction in the rate of inflation below the world average (so that the price *level* is also too low) will improve the trade balance, increase income and therefore the rate of inflation. A stable equilibrium is only possible where national price levels converge.

That the money supply is no part of the adjustment process is shown by its assumed exogeneity; sterilisation of monetary flows is therefore possible even in the long run. Branson argues that the convergence of inflation rates is not, therefore, proof of the monetarist theory.

Extreme Keynesian models see no convergence of national inflation rates or any role for the money supply. Inflation is assumed to be related to individual market situations. Therefore, for example, a rise in the price of oil or in labour costs, caused by shortages or any other factor, would be an important stimulus to inflation at a world level.

The Nordic model of inflation

In recent years, an approach to inflation has been developed by various Scandinavian economists (Aukrust, 1970; Edgren, Faxen and Odhner, 1973) that utilises a similar distinction as that between tradeable and non-tradeable goods. A small open economy is assumed to have an exposed sector where the country is a price taker, and a sheltered sector. Inflation in the exposed sector is equivalent to the world rate of inflation, with money wages being determined in that sector by the rate of inflation plus labour productivity. A bargaining process ensures equal wages in both sectors and with labour productivity incorporated, the inflation rate in the sheltered sector is determined. Any difference in productivity levels in the two sectors will therefore cause the national price level (which is a weighted average of the sectoral levels) to diverge from the world level.

The model which has proved fairly successful for nordic countries suffers from the complete absence of demand side factors in the determination of prices in the sheltered sector and, therefore, domestic prices.

Inflation and floating exchange rates

The discussion so far in this section has been in terms of fixed exchange rates. However, this assumption is no longer valid in the floating rate era of the 1970s. Unfortunately little work has so far been done on the generation and transmission of world inflation under floating exchange rates. What is known is that a country operating perfectly floating rates can be treated as a closed economy in that it regains the independence of monetary action (Meiselmann, 1975).[†] The money supply becomes exogenous again (see Ch. 8) with excessive monetary expansion causing an increase in inflation and a decline in the exchange rate. An independent inflation rate can now be chosen.

What is less clear is how the various transmission mechanisms of inflation operate under floating rates. Excess demand in one country would not be dispersed around the world economy while the liquidity effects would also be removed by the independence of monetary action afforded under these arrangements. While these *ad hoc* statements are useful, a full analysis of how

---

[†] The extent of independence of monetary action may be partly illusory, however, due to increasing interdependence of economies and the mobility of huge quantities of capital and 'hot' money.

floating rates can permit the transmission of inflationary impulses is clearly needed. Another issue on which work is beginning to appear (e.g., Crockett and Goldstein, 1976) is whether floating rates are inherently more inflationary than fixed rates. Various arguments exist, the most important of which is the reduced discipline of floating rates which may lead to a higher world inflation rate than under fixed rates. On balance, however, Crockett and Goldstein do not see the arguments in favour of one set of arrangements being more inflationary than another particularly conclusive.

7 Postscript

It is clear from the analysis of this chapter that money and inflation are closely linked. Inflation is truly a monetary phenomenon although whether the role of money in the determination of price changes is active or passive is a controversial issue. It is necessary to include a discussion on inflation in a volume on monetary economics, but, by concentrating on the role of money, the treatment of this chapter has been deliberately unbalanced. This lack of balance should not leave the reader with the impression that the cause and solution of every inflationary episode lies exclusively with monetary policy. Under certain conditions, particularly where inflation is combined with unemployment, a joint policy response may be appropriate, involving, for example, the combination of monetary action and direct controls on prices and incomes (e.g., Stevenson and Trevithick, 1977).

Chapter 10

Monetary policy in the UK

1 Introduction

It is appropriate that this volume should conclude with a survey of the events and development of monetary policy in the UK. The period chosen for the survey is that since 1945; events throughout this period are relevant to the conduct of monetary policy in the present day, while the period also encompasses the gradual and, as yet, incomplete succession of Keynesian orthodoxy by monetarism. The survey is essentially chronological, although not purely descriptive, and is punctuated by more detailed analysis of policy instruments or particularly important sub-periods of policy.

2 Pre-Radcliffe monetary policy (1945-59)

This fourteen year period between the end of the Second World War and the publication of the Radcliffe Report in 1959 can itself be subdivided. The so-called 'cheap money' era from 1945 to the end of 1947 was characterised by the maintenance of low interest rates; Bank Rate was held at 2 per cent from 1939 to 1951, and long-term government bond rates at $2\frac{1}{2}$ per cent. Such a policy was prompted by the fear of post-war depression (the last peace time memory was of depression) and in particular the concern over financing the National Debt, which was increasing, unusually, in peace time, and had become very liquid due to the financing methods adopted in the Second World War (Rowan, 1973). At low interest rates such financing would not be expensive. However, 'cheap money' had to be abandoned as a balance of payments crisis (partly caused by the severe winter of 1946–7) was combined with an unsuccessful attempt to make sterling convertible in August 1947. The attempt was premature, while the inflation in part generated by 'cheap money' demonstrated the futility of holding interest rates at an artificial level.

From 1948 to 1951, monetary policy was essentially in abeyance; interest-rate movements did occur, but Bank Rate remained unchanged. The crisis atmosphere generated by the 30 per cent devaluation of sterling to £1 = $2.80 in 1949 and the effects of the Korean War boom and 'cheap money' on inflation (which reached 10 per cent in 1951) and the balance of payments called for a new approach to monetary policy. The advent of a new Conservative government with *laissez-faire* attitudes and a preference for monetary policy was a further reason for the change in policy.

The 'new' monetary policy had four main elements. Firstly, an active interest rate policy was introduced to defend sterling. Bank Rate was finally altered in 1951 and in the following eight years was changed fifteen times. Secondly, the concern over debt management led to the gradual acceptance of the concept of supporting the gilt-edged markets (see Ch. 2, sect. 5). The practice of 'leaning into the wind' or the 'special buyer' developed during the 1950s. Therefore, active interest rate policy was only a feature at the short end of the market with long-term security prices being stabilised. Thirdly, the fact that both the banks and the overall maturity profile of the National Debt were very liquid caused 'funding' to be a major part of policy in this period. Most spectacularly, in 1951-2, a forced funding operation of £1,000 m. worth of Treasury Bills (with long-run stock at $1\frac{3}{4}$ per cent replacing them) with the clearing banks led to a drop in the banks' liquid assets ratio from 40 per cent to 33 per cent. This operation coincided with the final aspect of policy which was the introduction of an informal liquid assets or liquidity ratio of 30 per cent in 1952. The major aim of this ratio was not close control of bank deposits and the money supply but control of bank advances and therefore credit and also assistance in the financing of the National Debt (Nobay, 1973).

This period of policy was characterised by the use of the 'package deal'. Policy measures were not introduced individually but as a group or package. The policy weapons used in such a way were four in number (with open-market operations being a continuous element of policy and not therefore part of a package). The major instrument was a change in Bank Rate. It was seen as a clear signal of the direction of policy and because of its symbolic nature, changes had both real and psychological impacts. Secondly, ceilings on bank advances were widely used for the first time (they had been used informally in 1939, 1946 and before the defeat of the Labour government in 1951). The continued use of such qualitative advice to the banks was augmented in 1957, when the Chancellor of the Exchequer, Peter Thorneycroft, used, for the first time, a quantitative limit on bank advances. This was a very important 'watershed'.[†] Such ceilings were very successful in reducing the overall supply of credit (Pankratz, 1974), particularly as it was believed, as the Radcliffe Report later argued, that unsatisfied credit demand was not completely accommodated in other markets. However, the discriminatory effect of such ceilings on banks, the stunting of competition and the growth of other financial institutions represented the considerable costs of such ceilings.

Thirdly, hire-purchase controls were used in this period (Dow, 1970). Again, they were very effective in reducing demand and limiting credit. How-

---

[†] The call for a positive and significant reduction in bank advances in July 1955 is viewed by some as the date of the first use of quantitative lending ceilings (e.g., Radcliffe Committee, 1959, paragraph 417). However, no actual figure was mentioned at that stage.

ever, their considerable effects on certain sectors of the economy, in particular those producing consumer durables, which had the tendency to exacerbate cyclical fluctuations in demand, made them a very unsatisfactory policy weapon (Lomax, 1975). In addition, avoidance was relatively easy. Finally, controls over capital issues were used. In such periods, new issues were only allowed for certain approved undertakings (such as public utilities and exporting industries), the intention, again, being to reduce the supply of credit. However, the effect of these controls on overall investment was damaging, while it appears that they had a limited quantitative effect (Radcliffe Committee, 1959). They were finally abandoned in 1959.

Monetary policy in this period was therefore rather haphazard. A clumsy set of instruments, with many unfortunate side-effects, was imposed to alter the direction of policy with the aim being the 'jamming up of credit flows' rather than any sophisticated impact through the cost of capital channel. The credit availability transmission mechanism, central to the Radcliffe Report, was seen as the sphere of influence of monetary policy. A brief flirtation with money supply control in 1957 by Thorneycroft was speedily abandoned, with the demise of the Chancellor himself. In this environment, the Radcliffe Committee was appointed in May 1957 (by Thorneycroft) and its report was published two years later.

3 The Radcliffe Report

The Radcliffe Report enshrined a radically new approach to monetary theory, although its policy recommendations were traditional. Numerous accounts exist of Radcliffe Monetary Theory (in particular Rowan, 1961; Kaldor, 1960; Chick, 1973); a brief survey of it will be given here. The novelty of the approach was the rejection of *both* traditional Classical and Keynesian transmission mechanisms of money. The naive quantity theory link between money and expenditure was rejected for the conventional reason that the demand for money function was unstable. More familiarly, it was argued that the velocity of circulation was merely a statistical residual and according to the Committee:

> We have not made use of this concept because we cannot find any reason for supposing, or any monetary experience in history indicating, that there is any limit to the velocity of circulation. (Para. 391).

In addition, with no clear definition of the money supply available, control of *the* money supply was impossible and the velocity of circulation is whatever you want it to be dependent on the chosen money definition (Sayers, 1960).

The familiar Keynesian cost of capital transmission mechanism was rejected due to the weakness of the link between a change in the rate of interest and a change in the volume of investment (the interest-incentive effect). Such a conclusion was, as argued in Ch. 4, sect. 4, traditional at this time and it may have been more attributable to this tradition rather than to any new evidence

presented to the Committee. One writer even termed the rejection of this effect
on savings and the demand for fixed capital goods and stocks 'presumptuous'
(Gurley, 1960).

The demolition of traditional monetary theory on these grounds was
followed by the establishment of a new transmission mechanism of money:

$$\uparrow r \Rightarrow \downarrow \text{Liquidity} \Rightarrow \downarrow \text{Expenditure}$$

Although very different from the cost of capital mechanism, this Radcliffe
theory is seen as a version of Keynesianism due to its rejection of money supply
control and its emphasis on the rate of interest as the key policy variable. The
crucial and unfamiliar variable is 'liquidity'. The major problem with Radcliffe
monetary theory is that no unambiguous definition of liquidity was set out in the
Report. It was introduced by such statements as:

> spending . . . is related to the amount of money people think they can get hold of.
> (Para. 390).

and

> A decision to spend depends not simply on whether the would-be spender has
> cash or 'money in the bank'. There is the alternative of raising funds either by
> selling an asset or by borrowing. (Para. 389).

Various attempts have been made to define liquidity *ex post* as a stock
of assets to include money and certain short-term financial assets (e.g., Rowan,
1961; Harrod, 1959) rather than as a vague qualitative concept of expected
spending power. A possible problem with this concept is that an asset may not
be liquid at the aggregate level (i.e., everyone cannot encash all their assets
simultaneously). However, the ability to convert an asset into spending power is
not crucial to the transmission mechanism; rather the important fact is the
belief that this is possible. The role of money in this model is simply therefore as

> part of the wider structure of liquidity. (Para. 389).

The transmission mechanism itself was proposed by the Committee
due to their faith in the 'general liquidity effect' – that a change in the rate of
interest would affect the liquidity conditions of financial institutions and firms:

> Provided it is not confined to the short end of the market, a movement of interest-
> rates implies significant changes in the capital values of many assets held by
> financial institutions. A rise in rates makes some less willing to lend because
> capital values have fallen and others because their own interest-rate structure is
> sticky. (Para. 393).

This quotation is identifiable as a combination of the locking-in and credit
availability effects of Ch. 4, sect. 6. Figure 1 should clarify this analysis. A
rise in government bond rates by inflicting paper losses on those institutions
that hold such bonds will cause them to reduce their supply of bank loans
with $L_1 - \bar{L}$ representing the 'locking-in effect'. If bank loan rates are sticky
at $\bar{r}$, then a further 'availability effect' $L_2 - L_1$ occurs. Therefore the general
liquidity effect depends on the strength of the locking-in effect (and in the

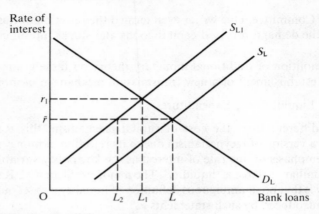

Fig. 1. Radcliffe monetary theory.

case of flexible bank loan rates on the elasticity of demand for bank loans, too). Money is therefore said to be either 'tight' or 'easy' and not 'cheap' or 'expensive' as in traditional transmission mechanisms. With the added impact of the availability effect, Radcliffe monetary theory is a disequilibrium model and relies on the inability of all frustrated borrowers to switch to other credit sources. The segmentation of credit markets or the 'diffused difficulty of borrowing' (Para. 472) is therefore essential to the analysis.

The policy recommendations follow logically from this analysis. Due to its influence on liquidity, general day-to-day policy should focus on:

> the structure of interest-rates rather than some notion of the supply of money as the centrepiece of monetary action. (Para. 395).

The role of money, itself, does however enter at this point as the money stock must be manipulated in such a way that the desired pattern of interest rates is achieved. The best that can be said about the money supply in Radcliffe theory therefore is that it is a residual. The Committee introduced the idea of interest rate gearing. Interest rates were either in high, middle (or normal) or low gear. For monetary policy to have a significant impact on the economy, a change of gear is needed. A movement within a gear will have 'some impact' but will be less significant.

Through this transmission mechanism, the focus of policy is on the banks but

> as key lenders in the system and not at the banks as creators of money. (Para. 395).

The target of policy is very clearly bank advances, or, more broadly, liquidity and not the level of bank deposits. However, the Committee rejected the use of direct controls on 'bank advances, consumer credit and capital issues' (Para. 524) except in emergency situations. The fault in this analysis lies in the Committee's inability to predict the number of emergencies that followed in the 1960s. This was partly due to unforeseen exogenous developments but was also due to an inherent contradiction in the Radcliffe analysis. While stability of long-run bond rates was needed to help National Debt financing, fluctuations in these same rates were to be used to control liquidity. The conflict between these two objectives led to the increased use of direct controls.

The Committee did not argue for the imposition of credit controls on other (non-bank) financial institutions. Linked to its dislike for credit controls on the banks alone, the Committee argued that such restraints would be:

> unwelcome . . . because the further growth of new financial institutions would allow the situation continually to slip from under the grip of the authorities. (Para. 394).

The Committee was particularly worried over the increasing loss of influence of monetary policy as direct controls caused the birth of new uncontrolled credit outlets. Therefore, the structure of interest rates was the fundamental element in Radcliffe monetary policy.

Many criticisms can be made of Radcliffe analysis and some of these have already been mentioned in this section; these particularly relate to the liquidity concept and the inconsistency between debt management and liquidity control. More generally, its analysis suffered from apparent 'woolliness' (Artis, 1961) and a particularly sharp attack on the role of money. The novelty of the theoretical approach was not immediately appreciated and was rather clouded by its failure to specify any new policy measures. This fact contributed to the view that the applied side of the Report was outdated almost before it was published. Certainly, although it is a major document in UK monetary history, it was soon pushed into the background as the developments of the 1960s unfolded (Gordon, 1972).

4 The 1960s

(a) Special deposits

A new instrument of monetary policy termed Special Deposits was introduced into the UK in 1958 and first used in 1960 (*The Banker*, 1958; Bank of England, 1960). The term refers to deposits called from certain banks and placed in a special account at the Bank of England. Such funds, which would be 'frozen' in this account for an unspecified period, were a requirement on the participating banks, in addition to reserve ratios. Until 1971, such calls were made on the clearing banks alone and were at a certain specified percentage of overall deposits. These deposits did yield a return for the banks, in normal times, at a rate close to that on Treasury Bills. However, between May 1969 and April 1970, this rate paid on Special Deposits was halved as the banks had not complied with a lending ceiling (Artis and Meadows, 1974). The scheme was heavily used during the 1960s (see Rowan, 1973).

The inequity of levying such Special Deposits on clearing banks alone led to the development of the Cash Deposits scheme (Bank of England, 1968) in 1968 which was essentially similar to the idea of Special Deposits and applied to non-clearing banks. It was never enforced, however, being overtaken by the new Competition and Credit Control system in 1971. This included a uniform Special Deposits scheme for all banks, and has been heavily used during the 1970s; however, in the late 1970s, emphasis was switched to the Supplementary Special Deposits scheme – the 'Corset' (see Ch. 10, sect. 6).

The immediate aim of the Special Deposits scheme was to reduce the liquidity of the banking system. However, the ultimate aim (control of advances or deposits) and the '*modus operandi*' of the mechanism has been the subject of considerable controversy. Such a policy instrument is peculiar to the UK. In most other countries, additional liquidity control is achieved through an increase in the appropriate reserve ratio. A Special Deposits call is equivalent to this, if such deposits are considered liquid by the banks and also receive a return similar to that on other liquid assets to eradicate any income effects of the call. If considered non-liquid, Special Deposits would lead to a further build-up of liquidity in a bank's portfolio, while a lower return than that on other liquid assets may encourage the bank to increase the proportion of higher yielding advances in its portfolio.

Three reasons can be advanced for a Special Deposits call. Firstly, the aim, at least until 1971, was to reduce the rate of growth of bank *advances* (*The Banker*, 1960). This is now widely accepted although evidence is still put forward on how Special Deposits failed to check the growth of bank *deposits*. Since 1971, the aim has been less clear, although some control over the level of interest rates has been emphasised. Indeed, a second general aim of the scheme was to restrict credit without raising interest rates. This may be contradictory, however, as a successful Special Deposits call may actually generate interest rate increases in itself. Thirdly, and rather cynically, Special Deposits may be viewed as a cheap source of funds for the government. As shown in Ch. 7, sect. 5, Special Deposits do help to finance the PSBR.

Any Special Deposits call is paid in cash. The objective, in general, was for this cash to be provided by the Bank of England through the purchase of Treasury Bills of the appropriate amount from the banks. The cash received was then deposited by the banks at the Bank of England. Assuming the banks were not holding excess reserves before the call, pressure is placed not on the bank's cash ratio but on the liquidity ratio. In theory, banks would reduce their long-term assets, in particular advances, in order to reduce the size of their balance sheets sufficiently to satisfy the liquidity ratio given the reduced holdings of Treasury Bills.

However, many more likely responses than this can be hypothesised for the banks. They may respond to the call by bidding a greater amount of Treasury Bills from the discount market. Assuming the latter's demand is unchanged, 'outside' tenderers' holdings will fall leading to an immediate increase in bank deposits. A second round of bill purchases is now needed and equilibrium is attained gradually. The important result is that the Special Deposits call has led to an *increase* in deposits. However, this increase in deposits is only possible if cash is obtainable from the Bank of England in return for Treasury Bills to satisfy the 8 per cent cash ratio, i.e., that 'the backdoor is open'. Alternatively, if the backdoor is closed, no new cash is obtained so that the deposit level must remain unchanged following the Special Deposits call.

As argued above, however, the crucial effect of Special Deposits should be on the level of advances. In the previous case, the extra Treasury Bills may be obtained at the expense of bank advances, in which case advances have fallen at an unchanged level of deposits. Again, a more likely response is that banks sell long-term bonds to finance the necessary purchase of bills to satisfy the liquidity ratio. Bond rates will rise, leading to a locking-in effect which will reduce advances (unless higher rates are charged on advances to compensate for this and an unsatisfied fringe of borrowers exists). Even if the authorities buy up the surplus bonds to keep their price stable (i.e., they accommodate the sale), advances will be reduced in response to the increased risk in the bank's portfolio following the reduction in the bonds/advances ratio (Coghlan, 1973). It is possible that this response could be offset by the income effect on the bank's portfolio causing a less sharp fall in advances, but a complete offset is unlikely.

This analysis has assumed that banks keep rigidly to their reserve ratios. If excess reserves are held and Special Deposits are considered liquid, a call for Special Deposits that is smaller than the liquidity 'cushion' will leave bank advances unchanged. However, if such Deposits are considered non-liquid, the excess reserves will be gradually built up again with advances being affected in the same way as if the liquidity ratio were strictly observed.

Evidence on the impact of Special Deposits is very sketchy. Crouch (1970) and Gibson (1964) observed that bank deposits and liquid assets increased when Special Deposits were called and it is doubtful whether liquid assets have ever been constrained by a call for Special Deposits (Goodhart, 1973b). In addition, Coghlan (1973) found that Special Deposits (in value terms) were an insignificant determinant of the level of bank deposits. While Gibson explained the behaviour of bank advances in the first period of Special Deposits (1960–2) by other factors, Coghlan using data from 1955 to 1970 obtained a significant *negative* coefficient on lagged Special Deposits in an equation explaining bank advances. The latter result suggests that Special Deposits have influenced the level of bank lending in the desired way.

Despite this, the first major doubt over the Special Deposits scheme must be its unclear rationale and uncertain results.[†] Other disadvantages exist. By forcing banks to hold a sub-optimal asset portfolio, Special Deposits impose a tax except where, due to the perceived 'liquidity' of Special Deposits and the existence of excess reserves, the balance sheet is unaffected. In addition, as a tax on banks, Special Deposits are discriminatory in effect and may encourage the growth of uncontrolled intermediaries. Finally, as a compulsory non-market control, Special Deposits are disliked by banks and so may have deleterious effects on long-term cooperation between them and the monetary authorities.

[†] What is clear is that Special Deposits calls must be very high to have a significant impact and are at best merely a reinforcing measure to add to the battery of monetary policy weapons.

(b) *Efficiency*

A major area of discussion in the UK financial system since 1960 has been the efficiency or degree of competition within the system given the existence of various historical interest rate and other conventions. This debate was partly stimulated by the Prices and Incomes Board (PIB) Report (1967) on bank charges, while the Monopolies Commission (MC) Report (1968) on the proposed merger between Barclays, Lloyds and Martins banks was also important in this respect.

Economic theory states that in a world without economies of scale and externalities, free competition will ensure an optimal allocation of resources. Such maximum efficiency involves the equality of price and marginal cost for all goods. Such ideas can be applied to banking. Banks provide four types of service (Griffiths, 1970; Johnson, 1968):

  (i) Current and deposit accounts
 (ii) Chequing services or the payments mechanism
(iii) Financial advice
 (iv) Lending.

As deposits are basically costless to produce, efficiency requires that there should be no charge for providing this service (i.e., its price should equal zero). In opportunity-cost terms, this occurs when the rate of interest on all bank deposits is equal to that on competing assets (so the opportunity-cost of holding bank deposits is zero). However, by leaving the banks without a profit margin, such a proposal would cause insolvency, while it ignores the different degrees of risk on money and other assets (Goodhart, 1975). There are real resource costs (capital, labour, etc.) in the provision of the second product, chequing services. Bank charges are levied to cover these but there is no evidence that an efficient solution, with charges exactly related to costs, exists. Thirdly, financial advice is costly but there is no charge for this service. Finally, in the case of lending, the interest charged is similar to that on alternative assets so that efficiency may be approached.

In purely theoretical terms, the UK banking system is therefore inefficient. However, correction of this for the above four products would not lead to a socially optimal monetary system as currency must also be considered. The social cost of producing currency is less than the return to the authorities in distributing it. This 'seignorage' element is reinforced by the fact that currency is legal tender and must be accepted in the settlement of a debt. To remove this seignorage element would require interest payments to be made on currency holdings which could be done explicitly or through a negative rate of inflation. However, as Goodhart (1975) argues:

> it does seem a vast and indiscriminate sledgehammer of an instrument, changing the rate of inflation, to deal with a tiny nut of an issue, efficiency within the monetary system

as the size of this seignorage is small – around £1,328 m. in 1979–80.

More practically, the main symbols of an uncompetitive monetary system in the UK during the 1960s were numerous. The non-payment of interest on current accounts leads to an 'endowment' element in bank profits. With around 50 per cent of all clearing bank deposits paying interest to their holders, while around 90 per cent of all clearing bank assets yield interest, any increase in rates of interest will automatically increase profits. Secondly, the clearing bank cartel that set interest rates on deposits and advances (Griffiths, 1973a) led to an absence of price competition, the development of service or non-price competition and the restriction of output below the optimal level. Thirdly, the monetary policy constraints on the banks impose a tax on them which encourages disintermediation and possible misallocation of credit resources. Finally, the clearing banking industry is oligopolistic with barriers to entry facing potential competitors (Griffiths, 1973b).[†]

Given this background, the PIB Report made a number of recommendations, which went far beyond its brief on bank charges. Firstly, the Report recommended the abolition of the interest rate cartel. The advantages of this cited in the Report were increased efficiency and price competition, a recapture of lost business by the clearing banks and a greater diversification of lending. These benefits were considered to exceed the costs which included a reduced role for Bank Rate, the possibility of higher and less stable interest rates and the extension of credit on more risky projects (as funds for such business became available to banks in greater amounts).[‡] The Report did not recommend the abandonment of direct controls and portfolio constraints on the clearing banks as this would be unacceptable to the authorities. In addition, they acted as a tax offset to the endowment element of profits, a change in which was not recommended either. For the sake of equity, a wider coverage of policy actions and to guarantee solvency, such direct controls were advocated for other financial institutions.[§]

The Report recommended the publication of bank charges, a closer relationship between them and costs and, finally, an increase in inter-bank competition in this respect. Other recommendations included more flexible opening hours and the publication of bank profits, while the Report made a general statement in favour of bank mergers.

Actual results following this theoretical debate on efficiency and the publication of the PIB Report occurred very rapidly. The merger of the National Provincial and Westminster banks was completed in 1968, although that between Barclays, Lloyds and Martins banks was turned down by the Monopolies Commission. The latter merger was advocated on the grounds of rationalisation (particularly of branch networks) and the possibility of increased competition (Artis, 1968). However, the majority (six votes to four) was against the merger as it would be more likely to stifle competition, would create a situation ap-

---

[†] To these may be added, the divergence between price and marginal cost in the provision of chequing services and financial advice.

[‡] The numerical cost of the cartel as a percentage of GDP was calculated by Griffiths (1972a).

[§] In theoretical terms, controls on all institutions represent a 'second-best' solution (Johnson, 1967b, 1968). However, it is more acceptable, in the real world, than a complete absence of controls.

proaching a duopoly (with Midland Bank significantly smaller than the two 'combines') and might reduce the sources of finance for small firms; despite this, a merger agreement between Barclays and Martins banks was completed by November 1968.

More dramatic developments occurred with the publication of bank profits for the first time in 1970 and the introduction of Competition and Credit Control in 1971. The new system abolished the banks' interest rate cartel and moved towards the 'second-best' solution by imposing reserve requirements on all non-clearing banks (but not n.b.f.i's) and generally drawing them under the control of the authorities. In addition, lending ceilings, which were a cause of restricted competition were abolished. On the debit side, the hours of banking remain relatively inflexible, while bank charges are not directly related to costs. In addition it could be argued that the abandonment of the cartel has not had a marked effect on interest rate competition due to the oligopolistic nature of the industry.[†] Certainly, the lack of free entry into clearing banking, remains the major stumbling block to free competition.

(c) *The Letters of Intent and new emphasis on money supply control (1967–9)*

The remaining aspect of monetary policy in the 1960s that warrants discussion is the slight shift in emphasis away from interest rate control to money supply control that occurred towards the end of the decade. In Ch. 2, sect. 5, it was argued that up to 1968, price stability in the gilt-edged market was the major objective of monetary policy. However, from November 1968 onwards, the authorities intervened less readily in a period of falling gilt-edged security prices. This presented stockholders with the possibility of capital losses as support for the market was withdrawn. The change in policy was, however, limited in scope. The prices of medium- and long-run stock alone were allowed to vary, while active support was maintained at the short end of the market. In addition, when the market became unsettled in December 1968 full support was resumed (Midland Bank, 1969), an early sign of the post-1971 commitment to withdraw market support only in 'normal' market conditions.

The new tactics had little to do with a conversion to monetarism and were only partly related to increasing scepticism over the traditional view that investor behaviour in the gilt-edged market was destabilising. The primary reason for the change in behaviour was the externally induced need to limit monetary growth. The Letter of Intent to the IMF in November 1967 (a week after the devaluation of sterling) included a non-quantitative commitment to reduce the rate of growth of the money supply. More formally, the second Letter of Intent sent in May 1969 (to request a short-term stand-by credit facility) committed the UK to a target increase of DCE in 1969–70 of £400 m. Such a tight monetary policy could only be operated with more price flexibility in the market for government debt and therefore the two developments were closely

---

[†] It has become fashionable to argue, however, that common interest rates do not demonstrate a lack of competition, but rather the opposite, i.e., the outcome of successful, keen price competition (e.g., Marks, 1973).

linked. The change in gilt-edged market tactics was permanent, however, and was formally ratified in the Competition and Credit Control system in 1971.

The late 1960s was an opportune moment to experiment with an explicit money supply policy of this sort. A period of adjustment was needed following the devaluation of sterling and the tight fiscal policy (a public sector deficit of only £450 m. in 1968–9 and a surplus of £527 m. in 1969–70) restricted the problem of financing government activity within the constraints of a DCE ceiling. However, for many government and Bank of England officials, it was a 'shotgun conversion' (Brittan, 1971) to money supply control being forced unwillingly on the country by the need to borrow from the IMF (Hodgman, 1971).

5 Competition and Credit Control (1971)

A major reform of UK monetary arrangements occurred with the establishment of the Competition and Credit Control system (CCC) in September 1971. A consultative document outlining the proposed changes was published in May 1971 (Bank of England, 1971a) and the proposals came into effect in September (although those relating to debt-management policy were implemented immediately).

The new system had a number of important features. Firstly, the clearing banks' interest rate cartel was abandoned. Secondly, the existing 8 per cent and 28 per cent reserve ratios were replaced by a $12\frac{1}{2}$ per cent reserve asset ratio to be applied to all banks (Bank of England, 1971b – details of this ratio were set out in Ch. 7, sect. 4). Thirdly, the reserve asset ratio was supplemented by a Special Deposits scheme to cover all banks. Fourthly, quantitative lending ceilings were abolished ensuring that:

> the allocation of credit is primarily determined by its cost. (Bank of England, 1971c).

Fifthly, the authorities reserved the right to offer qualitative guidance should circumstances warrant this. In addition, should the impact of the improved competitive position of banks significantly disrupt the flow of funds to both savings banks and building societies, the authorities reserved the right to blunt the competitive edge of the banks. Such a statement was, in fact, remarkably prophetic (see sect. 6 below).

As part of the reform of monetary arrangements, the authorities modified the extent of their operations in the gilt-edged market. The slight change of emphasis away from interest rate stability in 1968–9 was extended and formalised. Under the new policy, automatic support of the market would only exist for stock with under one year to run to maturity. Other stock offered on the market would be bought at the discretion of the authorities. Exchanges of stock would be possible, except those that significantly reduced the life of the debt.

A 50 per cent public sector debt ratio was imposed on the discount houses although this was altered in July 1973 (see the discussion in Ch. 7, sect. 4). A significant change for the discount houses was that although as a group they continued to cover the weekly Treasury Bill tender, this was no longer undertaken at an agreed or syndicated price. Finally, a 10 per cent reserve asset ratio was placed on finance houses.

Despite the large volume of material on the subject of CCC published in the early 1970s,[†] basic agreement existed over the reasons for the change to the new system and its major problems and points of discussion. The reasons for the establishment of CCC were a simple reflection of the problems of monetary policy in the 1960s. The major one was the lack of competition within clearing banking during this period. This was symbolised by the existence of the interest rate cartel, the proliferation of service competition, the rationing of credit by direct controls (which was almost continuous from 1965 to 1971) and the inability of the clearing banks to compete with other financial institutions. Such competitive constraints lead to a misallocation of financial resources and the encouragement of inefficiency (see sect. 4 above). The uncompetitive clearing bank structure was a major factor in the rapid growth of other financial institutions in the 1960s as was the absence of any reserve ratios or other monetary policy controls on them. This growth is easily seen in Ch. 7, Table 1, and would be even more spectacular if non-resident sterling deposits and foreign currency deposits were included in those statistics. The clearing banks did attempt to compete through the establishment and encouragement of subsidiaries which were unfettered by monetary controls and the cartel but, despite these, the clearing bank group lost ground. The wish of the authorities to increase inter-bank competition, extend the influence of monetary actions beyond the clearing banks and reduce the tiering of credit through other financial institutions which now had to compete with the banks for reserve assets (Harrington, 1974) were the major reasons for the establishment of CCC.

Other supplementary arguments did, however, exist. The previous reserve ratios and debt-management tactics did not facilitate control of the money supply. The increasing attention paid to 'monetary aggregates' due to the requirements of the IMF, the belief that the gilt-edged market was stable and the rise of monetarism all called for greater control of the money supply and less concern for interest rate stability. It is fashionable to attribute the new system to the *laissez-faire* attitudes of the new Conservative government (as occurred in 1951); however, it is likely that this was only a minor factor behind the reforms. Finally, a new approach was needed as

> economic policy may be said quite simply to have failed in that none of the major economic problems facing the U.K. in 1959 can be said to have been solved. (Bank of England, 1969b).

Most comment on the new system has centred on two aspects – the definition of the reserve asset base and whether the new system, as the authorities argued, involved a shift to controlling the money supply. The control-

[†] E.g., Artis and Parkin (1971), *The Banker* (1971), Christelow (1974), Courakis (1973), Cramp (1971b), Davis and Yeomans (1973), Dennis (1974), Gibson (1971), Gowland (1978), Griffiths (1973b), Johnson (1971b), Kern (1972), Lomax (1971, 1973), Midland Bank (1971a, 1971b), Morgan and Harrington (1973).

lability of the reserve asset base is very limited due to the wide range of assets included in the definition. It is in fact more complex than the previous liquidity ratio. Although the extension of the reserve ratio beyond the clearing banks has reduced the number of 'outside' holders, considerable scope remains, as argued in Ch. 7, sect. 4, for purchases of reserve assets from outside the banking system. In addition, the supply of certain reserve assets is beyond the control of the authorities. The reserve asset ratio is not a rigid one merely a minimum that each bank must not go below while the inclusion of Treasury Bills in the definition does not divorce fiscal policy from monetary policy. The other major potential problem is the possibility of reserve asset manufacture through transactions between the banks and the discount market.

The aim of the ratio was to treat all banks equitably. However, it is doubtful whether this has been achieved, on two counts. Firstly, till money is excluded from the definition of reserve assets. The fact that clearing banks, involved in the 'retail' side of banking, must hold larger quantities of till cash than 'wholesale' banks imposes an extra tax on them in addition to the $12\frac{1}{2}$ per cent ratio (Lomax, 1971). Johnson (1971b) points out that the US system in the 1960s moved, in fact, towards the *inclusion* of till money in reserve ratios believing this to be a more equitable arrangement. Secondly, at the inception of CCC, the London clearing banks held nearly 20 per cent of the value of eligible liabilities in reserve assets permitting an expansion of higher earning assets during the transition to the new ratio (Gibson, 1971). By contrast, most other banks suffered a loss of revenue by having to build up their reserve assets to satisfy the ratio.

It could be argued (Gibson, 1971; Johnson, 1971b) that the use of open-market operations and calls for Special Deposits, without any reserve ratio, would lead to equally efficient monetary control in a more equitable way. Given the problems of the reserve asset ratio, such a suggestion deserves serious consideration.

The issue of what is the target of monetary policy under the CCC system is a confusing one. It was argued in Ch. 2, sect. 5 that a set of potentially inconsistent statements on this point was forthcoming from the authorities. Given the 'sieve-like appearance' (Cramp, 1971b) of the reserve asset ratio, it is clear that despite certain of these statements, close control of the money supply is simply impossible. To be fair, the authorities did state that:

> it is not expected that the mechanism of the minimum asset ratio and Special Deposits can be used to achieve some precise multiple contraction or expansion of bank deposits. (Bank of England, 1971c).

However, on a different tack, it was argued that the objective was to combine:

> an effective measure of control over credit conditions with greater scope for competition and innovation. (Bank of England, 1971a).

With liquidity to be influenced through the structure of interest rates, the CCC system is, in fact, an application of the Radcliffe doctrine (Johnson, 1971b;

Rowan, 1973). The novelty of the system was to control monetary aggregates (mainly credit but where possible the money supply too) not through direct controls but by the operation of free competition in the market for funds. Transactions in reserve assets would be used to influence rates of interest to attain the desired level of credit. With control of the money supply in this environment very difficult, CCC does not, despite the pronouncements of the authorities, represent a conversion to anything approaching monetarism (Rowan, 1973; Griffiths, 1973b). Further, it could be argued that the abandonment of automatic support for the gilt-edged market is actually inconsistent with the reserve asset ratio. The absence of support should logically be combined with a cash ratio system or, alternatively, full gilt-edged market support combined with a complex government debt ratio (Courakis, 1973).

A common concern when the new arrangements were announced was the likelihood of greater fluctuations in interest rates. Should the interest elasticity of demand for bank advances be low, rates of interest would have to rise considerably, perhaps to unacceptable heights, to clear the market for credit (Davis and Yeomans, 1973). This and the possibility of excessive monetary expansion in a competitive banking system when demand is high encouraged the belief that direct controls on banks may be virtually indispensable (Nwankwo, 1972; Lomax, 1973). Indeed, by 1973, as will be discussed in sect. 6 below, direct controls, though of a different sort from those in use in the 1960s, had been re-imposed on the banking system.

Whatever the exact details and faults of CCC, the new beginning did engender a competitive spirit. This abstract objective – the 'CCC spirit' – was the subject of considerable debate in the years after 1971 as various modifications to CCC were introduced which typically were against the spirit. This will become clear in the next section.

6 Monetary policy since 1971

(a) *The floating of sterling* (Fry, 1972; Griffiths, 1972b)

A major test of the new monetary arrangements came earlier than expected – in June 1972. Selling pressure began to affect sterling in the middle of the month due to the expansionary policies of the government, and the worsening balance of payments and industrial relations situation (Stewart, 1977). The revaluation of sterling to £1 = $2.61 in December 1971 as part of the Smithsonian agreement, when the UK balance of payments was healthy, was seen by mid-1972 as being unjustified.

A capital outflow of around £1,000 m. in the week following 15 June (Griffiths, 1972b) left UK banks very short of liquidity. In January 1972, the reserve asset ratio of the clearing banks stood at 17.5 per cent and of all banks at 19.1 per cent, while the equivalent figures for 21 June, 1972, were 13.9 per cent and 14.5 per cent respectively. Sterling was floated on 23 June, but the outflow continued although as domestic interest rates moved up rapidly (the overnight inter-bank rate touched 300 per cent on 26 June) the situation gradually stabilised. However, before this occurred, the Bank of England launched controversial rescue acts for both the discount houses and the banks. The discount houses were assisted by massive Bank purchases of Treasury Bills and by the provision of short-term loans. The real controversy arose, however, over a sale and repurchase agreement (of gilts) offered to the banks on 28 June. This was outright support for the gilt-edged market and the action was viewed as being against the competitive spirit of CCC. The banks repurchased the bonds on 14 July under the second stage of the deal.

Once all the storm in the markets had subsided, the CCC system had lost credibility through the Bank's action. Other solutions to the banks' liquidity shortage could have been used. Strict application of the free-market principle would have allowed gilt-edged prices to fall until sales by the banks were possible to restore liquidity, or the banks would have been forced to borrow from the markets or the authorities at penal rates. Alternatively, the reserve asset ratio could have been temporarily reduced. Indeed, the banks were not penalised at all as they actually received the interest payable on such gilts during the support operation (Gowland, 1978). However, despite the symbolic importance of this period, the Bank of England action could alternatively be viewed as being consistent with CCC. It was only a short-term support operation and, more importantly, the authorities stated that:

> We shall not *normally* (my italics) be prepared to facilitate movements out of gilt-edged by the banks even if their sales should cause the market temporarily to weaken *quite* (my italics) sharply. (Bank of England, 1971c).

Clearly, the events of June 1972 were *not* normal and the gilt-edged market did fall *very* sharply. Despite this interpretation of CCC, the damage to the new competitive environment was considerable.

(b) The 'Corset'

In December 1973, the Bank introduced the Supplementary Special Deposits scheme (Bank of England, 1974). This new control quickly became known as the 'Corset' and was in operation until February 1975. It was also applied between November 1976 and August 1977 and was reactivated again in June 1978. Under the scheme, a maximum rate of growth of the banks interest-bearing eligible liabilities (IBELs) is specified. Should the growth rate of a bank's IBELs exceed this maximum over a particular six-month period, it must deposit funds at the Bank of England. The amount to be deposited is determined by the degree of excess growth of IBELs. When the scheme was first activated, the maximum six-month growth rate was 8 per cent, with the call rate for an excess of up to 1 per cent being equal to 5 per cent of the excess, for an excess of between 1 per cent and 3 per cent equal to 25 per cent and for over 3 per cent equal to 50 per cent. Such rates were sufficiently punitive to encourage the banks to keep within the maximum growth rate. The exact details of the maximum permissible growth of IBELs and the call rates have varied during the different periods in which the scheme has operated.

Certain features of this scheme should be noted (Midland Bank, 1974). Firstly, the Corset operated on the liabilities of the banks which is unusual in

UK monetary history but is consistent with the increased importance of money supply control in the 1970s. Secondly, IBELs alone are used as the base and not all eligible liabilities (ELs). The reason is that a bank's IBELs are essentially self-determined. It was considered unfair to base such a scheme on non-interest-bearing deposits which were in part beyond the influence of a particular bank. Thirdly, the Special Deposits, should the maximum growth rate be exceeded, are non-interest-bearing. Had such deposits borne interest, it would have become more likely that infringing the growth rate and paying the Special Deposits would have been profitable to the banks. Fourthly, retrospective base setting would be used to reduce both the possibility and the effect of banks artificially building up their IBELs in anticipation of the Corset being imposed. Finally, the scheme is flexible in that many aspects of it (the maximum growth rate of IBELs, the call rate on any excess growth and the period over which growth is calculated) may be altered to allow for changed circumstances in the economy.

The essential objective of the Corset is to:

> restrain the pace of monetary expansion, including the pace at which banks extend new facilities for bank lending, without requiring rises in short-term interest-rates and bank lending rates to unacceptable heights. (Bank of England, 1974).

A related objective was to remove the arbitrage that occurred in 1972–3 (Ch. 1, sect. 5) by altering the pattern of interest rates. Indeed, the wish to reduce this artificial stimulus to sterling M3 was the immediate reason for the establishment of the Corset.

However, in the long term, the aim of the Corset is to reduce the growth rate of IBELs and by so doing reduce the growth rate of sterling M3. It is useful to analyse the effects of the Corset by considering three types of transactions (Greenwell & Co., 1978a):

1. Those that reduce IBELS, ELs and sterling M3
2. Those that reduce IBELS, ELs but not sterling M3
3. Those that reduce IBELS, but not ELs or sterling M3.

An immediate problem with the Corset is the different definitions of, or leverage existing between, IBELs, ELs and sterling M3. For example, notes and coin held by the non-bank public, bank deposits with a maturity of over two years and the deposits of the non-bank private and public sectors with the discount houses are all included in sterling M3 but excluded from bank ELs. In reverse, non-resident sterling deposits, discount houses holdings of CDs and deposits of discount houses at banks are included in banks ELs but do not affect sterling M3. Finally, market loans to discount houses, inter-bank loans and net CD holdings by banks are counted as negative IBELs (i.e., offsets to the IBELs total) but do not affect sterling M3. It should be clear from this paragraph that a transaction which reduces IBELs may not have the desired effect on the money supply.

The objective of the authorities is for the Corset to generate transactions of Type 1 above. Many examples may be specified. If bank interest rates are held down, public sector debt becomes more attractive. Increased purchases of such debt by the non-bank public will reduce bank deposits immediately and by reducing residual financing will have a multiple effect on deposits, too. If under pressure to reduce their asset total, banks may sell public sector debt to the non-bank private sector and reduce advances. Both these responses will reduce the level of IBELs and the money supply. Finally, the fall in domestic bank interest rates may make the Eurodollar market more attractive to overseas investors, reducing the inflow of funds and therefore the level of foreign exchange reserves and sterling M3. In addition, a 'cosmetic' reduction in sterling M3 will occur (where sterling M3 falls but overall liquidity is unchanged) where disintermediation occurs, a possibility considered below.

Transactions which reduce IBELs, ELs but not M3 circumvent the purpose (but not the letter) of the Corset scheme and mainly involve transactions with the discount market. Discount houses' holdings of CDs and their deposits at the banks may fall if bank interest rates are reduced relative to those on other assets, causing IBELs to fall but leaving sterling M3 unchanged. The same outcome would follow a switch in deposits by the non-bank public from the banks to the discount market. In addition, funds could be switched by the banks from call loans (a reserve asset) to other market loans (not a reserve asset) with the discount market which would increase the offset against IBELs. A particular bank (but not the whole group of banks) may reduce IBELs by increasing net inter-bank lending and purchasing CDs from other banks (both offsets against IBELs again). Finally, a reduction in overseas sterling deposits would reduce IBELs without affecting sterling M3.

The possibilities of avoiding the desired impact of the Corset seem considerable. However, should the banks be short of reserve assets, the above transactions with the discount market will be effectively prevented. Clearly, if reserve assets are short, banks will not wish to switch funds from call loans to market loans with the discount market. A shortage of reserve assets will keep inter-bank, deposit and CD rates high, leaving no incentive for the switching of funds (above) which would reduce IBELs but not sterling M3. Reserve assets could be built up by the banks selling long-term debt to the public and through assistance from the authorities, particularly if they supported the gilt-edged market causing residual financing to rise. However, help through such official channels would be unlikely given the authorities' aim to reduce IBELs and sterling M3.

The major transaction that causes a reduction in IBELs but not ELs or sterling M3 is a switch of funds from interest-bearing to non-interest-bearing deposits. Banks may encourage this by reducing deposit rates, reducing bank charges for a customer that undertakes this switch or requesting an additional balance of non-interest-bearing deposits in return for a credit facility (Greenwell & Co., 1978b).

These transactions show clearly how a bank may control its balance sheet to alleviate 'Corset' constraints. This is a form of 'liability management'. The ability of a bank to undertake these transactions suggests that it may build up IBELs when the Corset is expected to be imposed (to create a higher base on which the maximum growth rate is levied). The possibility of establishing a retrospective base for the Corset was necessitated by such 'window-dressing'.[†]

Many other problems exist with this policy instrument. As suggested earlier, disintermediation may be encouraged, i.e., direct lending from a surplus unit to a deficit unit without any intermediary role being played by a bank. Inter-company lending may rise and with the fall in bank deposit rates, deposits may be switched to local authorities causing direct financing of the latter by the non-bank public. A bank, unwilling to see its advances and deposits increase, may encourage a company to draw a bill on the bank which is then sold to a discount house or to the non-bank public. Such commercial bills if discounted in this way are a form of disintermediation. While this phenomenon is undesirable to the authorities itself, it also disrupts the linkages between the money supply and income. As disintermediation occurs, cosmetic reductions in sterling M3 will mean a higher level of income may be 'financed' by a lower money supply (Davies, 1979). The Corset will also distort interest rate relationships in the money markets.

Finally, the authorities have been criticised for introducing an instrument that is against the spirit of CCC. The authorities argued that the scheme:

> is intended to maintain the main structural benefits to the banking system of the reforms introduced in 1971. (Bank of England, 1974).

Certainly, it is less rigid than a quantitative ceiling with the banks free to enter the 'penalty' area should profitable business be available. However, inter-bank competition is necessarily limited by its operation with the less efficient banks protected.

In conclusion, the Corset is a highly punitive control on the banks. By limiting the growth of IBELs, however, money supply control is not guaranteed. Therefore, the constraints on competition imposed by the scheme may be suffered without the attendant benefits of close control of the money supply.

(c) *Debt-management policy*[‡]

Before the developments of debt-management policy since 1971 are described, the replacement of Bank Rate by Minimum Lending Rate (MLR) in October 1972 should be noted. MLR is a market-determined rate based on the average discount rate for Treasury Bills at the tender $+\frac{1}{2}$ per cent, rounded up to the nearest $\frac{1}{4}$ per cent. The change was made following the abolition of the interest rate cartel of the banks which removed the rigid link between Bank Rate and the banks' loan and deposit rates. Now, the banks independently establish a 'base' rate in relation to MLR and fix their loan and deposit rates according to this 'base' rate. The authorities also wished to abolish the dramatic

---

[†] It is argued, however (Greenwell & Co., 1978a) that the build-up of IBELs when the imposition of the Corset was expected and their subsequent rundown in the 1976–8 period was due more to changing pressures on reserve assets than intentional 'window-dressing'.
[‡] A statement on the authorities' contemporary views concerning debt management and certain proposed reforms as well as a description of the development of policy since the 1960s is given in Bank of England (1979a).

announcement effect of a Bank Rate change and permit a more flexible determination of rates. However, the authorities reserved the right to make discretionary changes in MLR (i.e., when the formula is suspended) should they wish to signal a change in the direction of monetary policy. This waiver has been used regularly in the 1970s (below).

In the period since 1971, less systematic support has been given to the markets for government debt, carrying out the changes outlined in the CCC document. There were only two quarters when substantial net support occurred. Firstly, in the second quarter of 1972 (which included the sterling crisis) net purchases of £800 m. worth of stock occurred[†] representing purchases of short-term debt from the non-bank public and the sale/repurchase deal with the banks. Secondly, in the final quarter of 1974, persistent weakness of the market led to net stock purchases by the authorities of £403 m.

Table 1   Statistics on government debt

	1967–9 (Bear)	1970–Jan. 1972 (Bull)	Jan.–Sept. 1977 (Bull)	Oct. 1977–Dec. 1978 (Bear)
Average monthly yield fluctuations (%) of				
$3\frac{1}{2}$% War loan	0.14	0.26	0.76	0.33
20 Year stock	0.15	0.21	0.85	0.32
10 Year stock	0.16	0.21	0.80	0.35
5 Year stock	0.17	0.19	0.95	0.47
Average monthly transactions (£ m.) in				
Debt with five years or less to maturity	1,185	1,619	6,433	5,577
Other debt	717	1,736	4,456	3,851

Sources: E. V. Morgan (1973); *Bank of England Statistical Abstract*, No. 1 (1970), No. 2 (1975); *Bank of England Quarterly Bulletin*, Dec. 1978; *Financial Statistics*, March 1979.

Morgan (1973) noted that in the early history of CCC, yields did fluctuate more without reducing the volume of business in government securities. Until the 'bear' market beginning in October 1977 when MLR reached a floor level of 5 per cent, the average monthly yield fluctuation for all classes of government debt had gradually increased. Table 1 demonstrates this for four different debt types in certain 'bear' and 'bull' market periods. The greater

[†] *Bank of England Quarterly Bulletin*, December 1977, Table 8.

movement of yields is apparent although some reduction in these fluctuations did occur in the most recent period. Table 1 also shows the increase in the volume of transactions during the 1970s. It is apparent, therefore, that the greater instability of gilt-edged prices has not fundamentally weakened the market or created disorderly trading conditions.

With the greater fluctuations in debt prices during the last decade, the phenomenon known as the 'Duke of York effect' has developed. Debt sales are easier to make when prices are rising. Therefore, a policy of marching MLR up the hill to an interest rate peak and then letting rates fall gradually generating the possibility of capital gains should help debt sales. This effect was successfully exploited by the authorities in early 1975 (first quarter debt sales of £1,817 m.), late 1975 (final quarter sales of £2,157 m.) and most spectacularly of all at the end of 1976 and early in 1977. With MLR at 15 per cent in October 1976, and aided by the effects on expectations of the IMF agreement of December 1976 and the establishment of formal monetary targets, debt sales of £3,180 m. occurred in the last quarter of 1976 and a further £5,218 m. before MLR reached its low point in that cycle of 5 per cent in the autumn of 1977. (In the year following October 1976, the yield on $3\frac{1}{2}$ per cent War Loan fell from 15.37 per cent to 9.71 per cent.)

While such a pattern of rates is helpful for the authorities' funding programme, it does disrupt financial flows, particularly into building societies. With relatively sticky interest rates, the societies generally suffer a shortage of funds as market rates rise. The need to employ the 'Duke of York effect' may in fact reflect the unsatisfactory combination of fiscal ease and monetary tightness. However, the authorities have still been unable to sell stock on a falling market. To refrain from buying when prices fall is considerably easier than to make significant debt sales during such a period.

The key issue of debate in debt-management policy in the late 1970s is whether debt sales should continue to be made by a 'tap' system or whether a tender system should be adopted which is the method of selling Treasury Bills (Greenwell & Co., 1976b). Under a 'tap' system, if demand for a new issue announced at a particular price is insufficient, the unsold stock is taken up by the Bank of England and sold later as an 'unofficial tap'. Therefore 'taps' are continuously available. Under a tender system, the whole issue is sold on a particular day, with the price being the equilibrating variable.

Those in favour of the tender system argue that by using this method, a given volume of debt sales may be achieved which will facilitate close control of the money supply. (This is not strictly true, however, as the effect on the money supply will be different dependent on whether the debt is bought by the banks, the non-bank public or by overseas residents, while the final money supply figure will also be sensitive to unexpected variations in the other credit elements of the aggregate, Bank of England, 1979a.) Secondly, although short-term price instability may accompany the use of a tender system, if money supply control is possible, inflation should fall in the long term with nominal interest rates being lower. Under the tap system, accelerating inflation weakens the gilt-edged market causing monetary expansion and more inflation – this is a dangerous, vicious circle. Finally, under a tender system, the timing of debt sales is guaranteed.

The arguments in favour of the current 'tap' system and therefore against the 'tender' system, are mainly based on the long-established properties of the UK gilt-edged market. The fear is that adoption of the tender system would disrupt the long-term stability of the gilt-edged market which is a uniquely successful market for government debt in the world. More tangibly, the tap system may permit greater flexibility of debt sales. For example, should some favourable economic news be announced, the authorities may bring on to the market previously unsold 'tap' stocks to capitalise on market sentiment. In addition, sales can be partially monitored under the tap system by allowing slight price changes when there is disequilibrium in the market. Using a tap system need not therefore mean complete price fixity. Whatever the arguments, there is a considerable vested interest in the maintenance of the '*status quo*' and radical reform is probably unlikely.

Despite this, a slight movement towards the tender system did occur in early 1979. Following massive over-subscription of an under-priced tap issue in February of that year (causing a higher than necessary interest burden to be incurred by the government), a 'partial' tender issue of £800 m. was made in the next month. A minimum price was placed on the securities and bids were invited. Under such a scheme, should over-subscription occur, the stock would be allocated to the highest bidders. Under-subscription would transform the issue into a normal 'tap' stock with the unsold portion being taken up by the Bank. On this occasion, the stock was slightly under-subscribed although part of it was sold at a price above the minimum. This was not a fundamental reform, however, as no attempt was made to sell a fixed amount of debt at whatever price the market would bear.

The creation of new types of stock may also help government financing. In 1973, a convertible stock was issued for the first time. This enables investors to hold the short-dated stock until maturity or exercise the option to convert it into a long-term asset. The aim of the debt instrument is to provide the investor with the possibility of benefiting from future interest rate movements, which will increase the attractiveness of the stock. Also, in 1977 both floating rate and partly paid stock were introduced. The aim of a floating rate stock is to compensate an investor in terms of higher interest payments when stock prices are falling. This reform has not yet had outstanding success, however. Partly-paid issues spread the cost of purchase although any capital gain accrues on the full value of the stock. These have had considerable appeal to investors and they benefit the authorities by increasing the attraction of government debt and allowing a closer matching of government receipts and payments. Other suggested reforms have been an inflation-indexed government stock and a short-term stock saleable, to the non-bank private sector, that it not a reserve asset (Bank of England, 1979a). This would reduce residual financing while bank purchases of such stock from outside holders would not lead to an increase in high-powered money. Another suggestion has been the irregular use of 'tender' arrangements, dependent on the current strength of the market. Finally, it could be argued that more direct links between the authorities and the main gilt-edged investors through, for example, direct placements of government securities may help the authorities to sell the appropriate amount of stock. However, the official view of this last proposal is that it would not significantly increase debt sales as such investors would not accept private placements at times other than when they would buy on the open market anyway.

(d) *The collapse of CCC?*

It is not intended in this final section to provide a description of monetary policy events since 1971. Certain major events (including the floating of sterling and the introduction of monetary targets) have been analysed earlier in the book. This section looks at certain changes to the CCC system that have encouraged the conclusion that the new competitive environment has been abandoned. For the interested reader, excellent descriptions of post-1971 monetary events are contained in Gowland (1978) and Atkinson (1977).

Under CCC, the authorities reserved the right 'to provide the banks with such qualitative guidance as may be appropriate' (Bank of England, 1971a). The explosion of bank lending that accompanied the Barber boom (Midland Bank, 1978, p. 25) provided an immediate test for the new monetary system. Indeed, within a year of the new system being established the authorities effected this 'escape-clause' (in August 1972) and requested that the banks

> make credit less readily available to property companies and for financial transactions not associated with the maintenance and expansion of industry. (Bank of England, 1972).

Such guidance has since this first request become a familiar feature of monetary policy with another ten subsequent requests being made to the end of 1978. However, these requests do not represent actual lending ceilings as they are qualitative and are not compulsory (although the latter comment may in practice be naive as failure to comply with a request would probably lead to more stringent measures being quickly taken). Lending by property companies', particularly earlier in the period, has been the main target of such guidance (Marks, 1973), with lending to manufacturing industry being visibly encouraged. Such guidance, by restraining the banks from pursuing an independent lending policy, can be seen as an attack on the competitive environment established in 1971.

Since 1971, the authorities have intervened directly and indirectly to affect financial flows to and from the building societies. Again, such action is allowed under the CCC system although, implicitly, it was only to be used in particular circumstances (sect. 5 above). The rapid rise in interest rates in the UK economy in the latter half of 1973 made a reduction in inflows to the building societies very likely (Minimum Lending Rate rose from $7\frac{1}{2}$ per cent in July to 13 per cent in November). The building societies had already been offered a subsidy of £15 m. in May 1973 in anticipation of this and the possible result of a decline in new mortgage business and also to forestall a rise in the mortgage rate. However, a more direct effort to tackle the root cause of the inflow problem

occurred in September 1973. The authorities imposed an interest ceiling of
$9\frac{1}{2}$ per cent on bank deposits of £10,000 or less. This type of control has been
widely used in the USA, and is known there as 'Regulation Q'.

The objectives of this move were threefold.[†] Firstly, by restricting
interest payments on small deposits, it was hoped that funds would be channelled to building societies. By doing this, the second aim of preventing a
politically unpopular rise in mortgage rate would be enhanced. Thirdly, and
much less importantly, funds may be directed towards various forms of public
sector debt. Despite the ceiling, the mortgage rate did actually rise to 11 per cent
in the same month, while net inflows into building societies actually fell to only
£135 m. in the first quarter of 1974 before beginning to rise. However, significant
improvements in net inflows over 1973 levels did not occur until the beginning
of 1975. By this time, money market rates were falling anyway and the ceiling
became redundant in January 1975 when the rate on small bank deposits fell
below $9\frac{1}{2}$ per cent. The control was formally ended in the following month.
The main beneficiary of this ceiling was the public sector, with debt becoming
more attractive, while it seemed to have minor effects on building society
inflows. In fact, the building societies had to be further assisted in April 1974
with the granting of five monthly loans of £100 m. which were finally repaid in
early 1976.

The theoretical advantages of a ceiling, namely a stable mortgage rate
and lower money supply growth (due to higher gilts sales), must be balanced
against the limited effect of the policy in the UK in 1973–5 and its disadvantages.
The latter are very powerful. The control distorts competition and is a partial
return to interest rate control. More importantly, it is a blatant subsidy from
one group of society to another:

> It does however seem iniquitous by any standards to make the holders of small
> bank deposits pay for the government's desire to subsidise those buying homes
> while allowing large holders to receive the market rate. . . . It enables the authori-
> ties to keep down the whole spectrum of interest-rates available to all savers,
> again morally reprehensible on all possible criteria. (Gowland, 1978).

Finally, in 1978, the authorities sought to influence the building societies directly by imposing lending ceilings on them to curb the rate of inflation of
house prices. Although a further restraint on free competition, such controls
on non-bank financial intermediaries may become more common in the 1980s.

It can be argued that despite the replacement of the discretionary Bank
Rate by the formula-determined MLR in 1972, very little change has occurred
in the way interest rates are set. Firstly, the authorities may give signals to the
markets which will be reflected in appropriate movements in the discount rate
on Treasury Bills and therefore in MLR. Secondly, and more importantly,
the authorities have, at times, abandoned the formula and in effect reinstated
Bank Rate. This first occurred in November 1973 when MLR was raised to
13 per cent as a signal of a much tighter monetary policy. (Such a policy was

[†] The major theoretical work on such ceilings is Tobin (1970a).

needed to restrain inflation particularly of house prices and monetary growth and also to defend sterling on the foreign exchange markets.) The formula was reinstated in January 1974. Again between February and May 1977, the formula was abandoned, this time to prevent too rapid a fall in interest rates following a particularly successful 'Duke of York' operation.

Finally, in May 1978, the formula was abandoned indefinitely. This development reflected the fact that since CCC was established, interest rates had fluctuated too much and that free competition had failed, particularly when the economy was buoyant. In effect, Bank Rate was restored and it began to be used as in the 1960s with crisis increases (as in February, June and November 1979) being made to signify the direction of policy. The one major difference in the 1970s has been that changes in MLR (it has not been renamed Bank Rate) are now used in response primarily to domestic economic conditions (particularly monetary aggregates) and less to external considerations as in the 1960s.

Although certain institutional reforms such as the reserve asset ratio and Special Deposits scheme imposed on all banks remain, the free market environment of CCC had disappeared by the end of the 1970s. The exact date when CCC can be said to have ended is a source of dispute. The imposition of the Corset which replaced the formal lending ceilings of the 1960s with a 'voluntary' ceiling on IBELs in December 1973, may be said to be the end of the competitive experiment (Gowland, 1978). However, the reimposition of the Corset and the indefinite abandonment of the market-related MLR certainly represents the 'final retreat from the spirit of CCC' (Davies, 1979).

Monetary policy at the end of the 1970s was therefore being conducted in an essentially controlled environment as it was in the 1960s. The reform of certain policy instruments had occurred with the introduction of the Corset, the use of the interest rate ceiling and the formalisation of qualitative guidance. In addition, new types of debt and new methods of debt management had been introduced. However, the major development of monetary policy in the 1970s was its concentration (which became almost obsessive after 1976) on monetary targets. Further requests for IMF credit were made, with the new policy of rigorous control of the money supply being affirmed in the Letters of Intent sent to the IMF in December 1976 and 1977. Therefore, the parallel with the 1960s should not be drawn too closely despite the demise of CCC. At the end of the 1970s, it was clear that very different objectives and external factors from those in existence in the 1960s were affecting British monetary policy.

Postscript – The Green Paper on monetary control

Since delivery of the manuscript to the publisher, significant changes in monetary policy practices in the UK have been heralded through the publication by the Bank of England and the Treasury of a joint consultative document on monetary control in March 1980[†]. While a wide range of issues are discussed, the major proposals contained in the document may be summarised as:

(i) The abolition of direct quantitative controls on private sector credit growth or alternatively on the expansion of banks' balance-sheets. In particular it was announced that the Supplementary Special Deposits Scheme (the Corset) was not to have a permanent place as a money supply control technique; it was subsequently abandoned in June 1980.

(ii) The abandonment of the 12 per cent reserve asset ratio and its replacement by a cash ratio. This ratio is to apply to all banks. (Prior to this the clearing banks have been required to hold $1\frac{1}{2}$ per cent of eligible liabilities in balances at the Bank of England, see p. 195.)

(iii) The retention of the long-standing Special Deposits scheme (pp. 263–5) for use when excess liquidity builds up in the monetary system.

(iv) The maintenance of sterling M3 as the form in which monetary targets should be prescribed (pp. 35–41).

The chief reason for the abandonment of the Corset was the disintermediation encouraged by its imposition. Business moved out of the controlled sector through, in particular, the growth of acceptance credits held by the non-bank private sector, while the abolition of exchange control undermined the Corset further by introducing the possibility of disintermediation via the euro-sterling market. In addition, the impact of credit controls is greatest when they are used for short periods. The Corset had simply become too permanent and too familiar. The Green Paper recognised the fact that the tighter the credit controls, the greater is the incentive to avoid them. Finally,

[†] 'Monetary Control', a consultation paper, *Cmnd.* 7858, March 1980. As a result of the proposals discussed in this postscript, reference to certain aspects of monetary policy in the main text should now be made in the past tense. This applies in particular to the discussion of the reserve asset ratio (pp. 193–5, 269–71) and the Corset (pp. 273–6). In addition, the debate on monetary base control (pp. 202–4) is extended and brought up to date.

the absence of direct credit controls was consistent with the Conservative government's market philosophy of allowing interest-rates to equate the demand for and the supply of credit.

The reserve asset ratio was to be abolished as its retention served no useful purpose. It had never been used to control the growth of bank deposits according to the theoretical bank credit multiplier approach and was an inappropriate prudential ratio.[†] In addition, by including certain short-term assets as reserve assets, it distorted the yield relationships between these and other assets. The newly extended cash ratio is to be a broad fulcrum for the influence of short-term interest rates through the money market operations of the authorities. With the automatic lender of last resort function unimpaired, this proposal is far from the introduction of a monetary base system (see below).

The authorities resisted the temptation to introduce multiple money supply targets which may yield inconsistent signals and so call for different policy responses for particular aggregates. The retention of sterling M3 as the target money supply concept was justified on the grounds that it is well-understood by the markets and is closely linked to other policies, particularly fiscal policy.

The Green Paper also reflected the development of the monetary control debate by discussing three alternative 'monetary base' schemes. The monetary base is defined in the document as:

> 'bankers' deposits at the Central Bank and may include notes and coin held by either or both the banks and the public' (p. 8).

The three types of scheme discussed and ultimately rejected were:
   (i) Schemes without a mandatory requirement.
   (ii) Schemes with a mandatory requirement.
   (iii) Indicator systems.
   (i) Under such a scheme, control of bank deposits would be achieved through the combination of close control of the monetary base and a self-imposed reserve ratio. However it is unlikely that this ratio would be stable and as it moved a leverage effect on the money supply could occur. (For example, a fall in the ratio from 10 per cent to 9 per cent could add to the growth of the money supply up to 10 percentage points over the growth of the monetary base.) In addition, a substantial period of time would elapse before a predictable relationship between the base and the volume of deposits was established. This type of scheme was therefore rejected.
   (ii) The imposition of a mandatory reserve requirement places an upper limit on the volume of deposits for a given level of the monetary base. Whether the monetary base requirement is related to deposits in a previous period ('lagged accounting'), the current period ('current accounting') or a future period ('lead accounting'), the chief danger of such mandatory schemes is the pos-

---

[†] At the same time, the Bank of England published a consultative document: *The Measurement of Liquidity* containing proposals to tackle the problem of appropriate prudential controls.

sibility of disintermediation. Banks would be encouraged to undertake business which did not appear in their liabilities total if the monetary base were under tight control. This fear of disintermediation is sufficient, alone, for the rejection of such schemes.

(iii) Of all the schemes, a type of indicator system appeared to be most favourably considered by the authorities, although, ultimately, no decision was made to introduce one. Under such a system any deviation of the monetary base – or alternatively sterling M3 – from its desired level would *automatically* trigger changes in Minimum Lending Rate (MLR). The size of the change would be determined by the extent of the discrepancy between actual and desired levels of the aggregate. Under such an arrangement, there would be a bias against delay in adjusting MLR in comparison to the present arrangements where a change itself often has to be justified by the authorities. However, both the monetary base and the money supply move erratically for many reasons and the authorities would have to avail themselves of an 'override' power to prevent changes in MLR when transient movements in the appropriate aggregate occurred.

The debate that accompanied the publication of the Green Paper[†] recognised that a rigidly enforced monetary base scheme could attain control of some measure of bank deposits. However, how meaningful such a concept (and therefore the money supply figure) would be in the face of substantial disintermediation is limited. In addition, such a scheme would involve much greater fluctuations in key interest rates. The general conclusion appeared to be that the real focus of attention should be the credit-creating forces in the economy, the variability of debt sales to the non-bank public and the interest-inelasticity of the demand for credit (at least in the short-term) none of which were considered in detail in the Green Paper. These are the essential problems of UK monetary control at the start of the 1980s.

The results of the abandonment of the Corset in June 1980 illustrated clearly the disintermediation caused by the use of this policy instrument. Sterling M3 jumped by 5 per cent in the month to mid-July 1980 as extensive reintermediation occurred – mainly through the ending of the 'bill leak' as part of this business was reabsorbed in bank balance-sheets. The outcome was the absence of any reliable indicator of money supply growth and total ignorance of the relationship of measured sterling M3 to the contemporary money supply target (7 to 11 per cent growth at an annual rate from February 1980 to April 1981). The monetary confusion illustrated more conclusively than any academic argument is able to do the distortive and ultimately self-defeating effects of quantitative credit controls.

[†] E.g. T. Congdon (1980) 'Should Britain adopt monetary base control?', *The Banker*, February, pp. 31–7; W. Greenwell & Co. (1980) 'Monetary Base Control', *Special Monetary Bulletin*, April; B. Griffiths, R. A. Batchelor, E. Bendle & G. E. Wood (1980) 'Reforming monetary control in the UK', *The Banker*, April/May, pp. 75–80; R. Coghlan (1980) 'Abandoning monetarism for monetary control', *The Banker*, April/May, pp. 81–6; A. Davies (1980) 'Money, the base and interest-rates', *Barclays Review*, May, pp. 28–32.

References

S. Ahmad (1977) 'Transactions demand for money and the quantity theory', *Quarterly Journal of Economics* **91**, pp. 327–35.

S. S. Alexander (1952) 'The effects of devaluation on a trade balance', *International Monetary Fund Staff Papers* **2**, April, pp. 263–78.

S. Almon (1965) 'The distributed lag between capital appropriations and expenditures', *Econometrica* **33**, January, pp. 178–96.

L. C. Anderson and K. M. Carlson (1970) 'A monetarist model for economic stabilisation', *Federal Reserve Bank of St. Louis Review* **52**, April, pp. 7–25.

L. C. Anderson and J. L. Jordan (1968) 'Monetary and fiscal actions: a test of their relative importance in economic stabilisation', *Federal Reserve Bank of St. Louis Review* **50**, November, pp. 11–24.

L. C. Anderson and J. L. Jordan (1969) 'Monetary and fiscal actions: a test of their relative importance in economic stabilisation – a reply', *Federal Reserve Bank of St. Louis Review* **51**, April, pp. 12–16.

A. Ando and F. Modigliani (1965) 'The relative stability of velocity and the investment multiplier', *American Economic Review* **55**, September, pp. 693–728.

G. C. Archibald and R. G. Lipsey (1958) 'Value and monetary theory: a critique of Lange and Patinkin', *Review of Economic Studies* **25**, pp. 1–22.

P. Arestis, S. F. Frowen and E. Karakitsos (1978) 'The dynamic impacts of government expenditure and the monetary base on aggregate income: the case of four OECD countries, 1965–74', *Public Finance* **33**, (1/2), pp. 1–22.

V. Argy (1969) 'The impact of monetary policy on expenditure with particular reference to the UK', *International Monetary Fund Staff Papers* **16**, November, pp. 436–87.

V. Argy (1974) 'An evaluation of financial targets in six countries', *Banca Nazionale del Lavoro Quarterly Review* **27**, March, pp. 28–50.

M. J. Artis (1961) 'Liquidity and the attack on the quantity theory', *Bulletin of the Oxford Institute of Economics and Statistics* **23**, November, pp. 343–66.

M. J. Artis (1968) 'The Monopolies Commission Report', *Bankers Magazine* **206**, September, pp. 128–35.

M. J. Artis (1972) 'Monetary policy in the UK: the indicator problem', *Bankers Magazine* **214**, October, November, pp. 145–52, 185–91.

M. J. Artis and M. K. Lewis (1974) 'The demand for money: stable or unstable', *The* in H. G. Johnson and A. R. Nobay (eds) *Issues in Monetary Economics*, University Press, Oxford.

M. J. Artis and M. K. Lewis (1974) 'The demand for money: stable and unstable', *The Banker* **124**, March, pp. 239–47.

M. J. Artis and M. K. Lewis (1976) 'The demand for money in the U.K. 1963–73', *Manchester School* **44**, June, pp. 147–81.

M. J. Artis and P. Meadows (1974) 'Special deposits: old and new', *The Banker* **124**, May, pp. 445–8.

M. J. Artis and A. R. Nobay (1969) 'Two aspects of the monetary debate', *National Institute Economic Review* **49**, August, pp. 33–51.

M. J. Artis and J. M. Parkin (1971) 'A general appraisal', *Bankers Magazine* **212**, September, pp. 109–15.

P. Atkinson (1977) 'A monetary perspective of the U.K. economy', *Scottish Journal of Political Economy* **24**, November, pp. 207–26.

O. Aukrust (1970) 'PRIM 1: a model of the price and income distribution mechanism of an open economy', *Review of Income and Wealth* **16**, March, pp. 51–78.

A. D. Bain (1976) *The Control of the Money Supply*, Penguin, Harmondsworth.

Bank for International Settlements Annual Report, 1975.

Bank of England (1960) 'The procedure of Special Deposits', *Bank of England Quarterly Bulletin*, December, p. 18.

Bank of England (1968) 'Control of bank lending: the Cash Deposits Scheme', *Bank of England Quarterly Bulletin* **8**, June, pp. 166–70.

Bank of England (1969a) 'Domestic Credit Expansion', *Bank of England Quarterly Bulletin* **9**, September, pp. 363–82.

Bank of England (1969b) 'The operation of monetary policy since Radcliffe', *Bank of England Quarterly Bulletin* **9**, December, pp. 448–60.

Bank of England (1971a) 'Competition and Credit Control', *Bank of England Quarterly Bulletin* **11**, June, pp. 189–93.

Bank of England (1971b) 'Reserve ratios: further definitions', *Bank of England Quarterly Bulletin* **11**, December, pp. 482–9.

Bank of England (1971c) 'Key issues in monetary and credit policy'. *Bank of England Quarterly Bulletin* **11**, June, pp. 195–8.

Bank of England (1972) 'Bank lending: the governor's letter to the banking system', *Bank of England Quarterly Bulletin* **12**, September, p. 327.

Bank of England (1973) 'Competition and Credit Control: modified arrangements for the discount market', *Bank of England Quarterly Bulletin* **13**, September, pp. 306–7.

Bank of England (1974) 'Credit control: a supplementary scheme', *Bank of England Quarterly Bulletin* **14**, March, pp. 37–9.

Bank of England (1975) 'The domestic financial implications of financing a balance of payments deficit on current account', *Bank of England Quarterly Bulletin* **15**, March, pp. 41–7.

Bank of England (1977a) 'DCE and the money supply – a statistical note', *Bank of England Quarterly Bulletin* **17**, March, pp. 39–42.

Bank of England (1977b) 'The adoption of monetary targets', *Bank of England Quarterly Bulletin* **17**, June, pp. 150–5.

Bank of England (1978) 'External and foreign currency flows and the money supply', *Bank of England Quarterly Bulletin* **18**, December, pp. 523–9.

Bank of England (1979a) 'The gilt-edged market', *Bank of England Quarterly Bulletin* **19**, June, pp. 137–48.

Bank of England (1979b) 'Monetary base control', *Bank of England Quarterly Bulletin* **19**, June, pp. 149–59.

The Banker (1958) 'The new monetary weapon – full description and appraisal', **108**, August, pp. 493–506.

The Banker (1960) 'Special Deposits in practice', **110**, June, pp. 371–9.

The Banker (1971) 'The new bank controls', **121**, June, pp. 565–75.

C. R. Barrett and A. A. Walters (1966) 'The stability of Keynesian and monetary multipliers in the UK', *Review of Economics and Statistics* **48**, November, pp. 395–405.

W. J. Baumol (1952) 'The transactions demand for cash: An inventory theoretic approach', *Quarterly Journal of Economics* **66**, November, pp. 545–56.

J. B. Beare (1978) *Macroeconomics. Cycles, Growth and Policy in a Monetary Economy*, Macmillan, New York.

G. L. Bell and L. S. Berman (1966) 'Changes in the money supply in the United Kingdom, 1954 to 1964', *Economica* 33, May, pp. 146–65.

H. Black (1975) 'The relative importance of determinants of the money supply – the British case', *Journal of Monetary Economics* 1, pp. 257–64.

A. S. Blinder and R. Solow (1973) 'Does fiscal policy matter?' *Journal of Public Economics* 2, November, pp. 319–37.

A. S. Blinder and R. Solow (1976) 'Does fiscal policy still matter? A reply', *Journal of Monetary Economics* 2, pp. 501–10.

W. C. Brainard and J. Tobin (1968) 'Pitfalls in financial model building', *American Economic Review, Papers and Proceedings* 58, May, pp. 99–122.

W. H. Branson (1975) 'Monetarist and Keynesian models of the transmission of inflation', *American Economic Review, Papers and Proceedings* 65, May, pp. 115–19.

R. E. Brinner (1977) 'The death of the Phillips curve reconsidered', *Quarterly Journal of Economics* 91, August, pp. 389–418.

S. Brittan (1971) *Steering the Economy: The Role of the Treasury*, Penguin, Harmondsworth.

A. J. Brown (1939) 'Interest, prices and the demand for idle money', *Oxford Economic Papers* 2, May, pp. 46–69.

K. Brunner (1970) 'The monetarist revolution in monetary theory', *Weltwirtschaftliches Archiv* 105, (1), pp. 1–30.

K. Brunner (1976) 'Issues of post-Keynesian monetary analysis. A contribution to the discussion opened by Professor Thomas Mayer', *Kredit und Kapital* 9, (1), pp. 24–55.

K. Brunner and A. H. Meltzer (1967) 'Economies of scale in cash balances reconsidered', *Quarterly Journal of Economics* 81, August, pp. 422–36.

K. Brunner and A. H. Meltzer (1971) 'The uses of money: money in the theory of an exchange economy', *American Economic Review* 61, December, pp. 784–805.

K. Brunner and A. H. Meltzer (1972a) 'Friedman's monetary theory', *Journal of Political Economy* 80, September/October, pp. 837–51.

K. Brunner and A. H. Meltzer (1972b) 'Money, debt and economic activity', *Journal of Political Economy* 80, September/October, pp. 951–77.

A. E. Burger (1975) 'The relationship between monetary base and money: how close?', *Federal Reserve Bank of St. Louis Review* 57, October, pp. 3–8.

P. Cagan (1956) 'The monetary dynamics of hyperinflation', in M. Friedman (ed.) *Studies in the Quantity Theory of Money*, University Press, Chicago.

P. Cagan (1965) *Determinants and Effects of Changes in the Stock of Money 1875–1960*, University Press, Columbia.

J. A. Carlson and J. M. Parkin (1975) 'Inflation expectations', *Economica* 42, May, pp. 123–38.

K. M. Carlson (1978) 'Does the St. Louis equation now believe in fiscal policy?', *Federal Reserve Bank of St. Louis Review* 60, February, pp. 13–19.

K. M. Carlson and R. W. Spencer (1975) 'Crowding out and its critics', *Federal Reserve Bank of St. Louis Review* 57, December, pp. 2–17.

V. Chick (1973) *The Theory of Monetary Policy*, Gray-Mills, London.

C. F. Christ (1968) 'A simple macroeconomic model with a government budget restraint', *Journal of Political Economy* 76, January/February, pp. 53–67.

D. B. Christelow (1974) 'Britain's new monetary control system', *Federal Reserve Bank of New York Monthly Review* 56, January, pp. 12–24.

G. Clayton (1962) 'British financial intermediaries in theory and practice', *Economic Journal* 72, December, pp. 869–86.

G. Clayton, J. C. Dodds, J. L. Ford and D. Ghosh (1974) 'An econometric model of the U.K. financial sector: some preliminary findings' in H. G. Johnson and A. R. Nobay (eds) *Issues in Monetary Economics*, University Press, Oxford.

R. W. Clower (1969) 'Introduction' in Clower (ed.) *Monetary Theory*, Penguin, Harmondsworth.

R. T. Coghlan (1973) 'Special Deposits and bank advances', *Bankers Magazine* **216**, September, pp. 103–7.

R. T. Coghlan (1975) 'Bank competition and bank size', *Manchester School* **43**, June, pp. 173–97.

R. T. Coghlan (1978) 'A transactions demand for money', *Bank of England Quarterly Bulletin* **18**, March, pp. 48–60.

T. Congdon (1978) *Monetarism. An Essay in Definition*, Centre for Policy Studies.

E. G. Corrigan (1970) 'The measurement and importance of fiscal policy changes', *Federal Reserve Bank of New York Monthly Review* **52**, July, pp. 133–45.

A. S. Courakis (1973) 'Monetary policy: old wisdom behind a new façade', *Economica* **40**, February, pp. 73–86.

A. S. Courakis (1978) 'Serial correlation and a Bank of England study of the demand for money: an exercise in measurement without theory', *Economic Journal* **88**, September, pp. 537–48.

A. B. Cramp (1966) 'The control of the money supply', *Economic Journal* **76**, June, pp. 278–87.

A. B. Cramp (1967) 'The control of bank deposits', *Lloyds Bank Review* **86**, October, pp. 16–35.

A. B. Cramp (1971a) *Monetary Management*, Allen and Unwin, London.

A. B. Cramp (1971b) 'Implications for monetary policy', *Bankers Magazine* **212**, July, pp. 1–6.

A. D. Crockett (1970) 'Timing relationships between movements of monetary and national income variables', *Bank of England Quarterly Bulletin* **10**, December, pp. 459–68.

A. D. Crockett and M. Goldstein (1976) 'Inflation under fixed and flexible exchange rates', *International Monetary Fund Staff Papers* **23**, November, pp. 509–44.

R. B. Cross and D. E. W. Laidler (1976) 'Inflation, excess demand and expectations in fixed exchange rate open economies: some preliminary empirical results' in J. M. Parkin and G. Zis (eds) *Inflation in the World Economy*, University Press, Manchester.

R. L. Crouch (1963) 'A re-examination of open-market operations', *Oxford Economic Papers* **15**, June, pp. 81–94.

R. L. Crouch (1964) 'The inadequacy of 'new orthodox' methods of monetary control', *Economic Journal* **74**, December, pp. 916–34.

R. L. Crouch (1967) 'A model of the U.K.'s monetary sector', *Econometrica* **35**, July–October, pp. 398–418.

R. L. Crouch (1968) 'Money supply theory and the U.K. monetary contraction 1954–56', *Bulletin of the Oxford University Institute of Economics and Statistics* **30**, May, pp. 143–52.

R. L. Crouch (1970) 'Special deposits and the British monetary mechanism', *Economic Studies* **5**, December, pp. 3–16.

J. M. Culbertson (1960) 'The lag in the effect of monetary policy: a reply', *Journal of Political Economy* **68**, October, pp. 617–21.

P. Davidson (1972) 'A Keynesian view of Friedman's theoretical framework for monetary analysis', *Journal of Political Economy* **80**, September/October, pp. 864–81.

A. Davies (1979) 'Whatever happened to Competition and Credit Control?', *Barclays Review* **54**, February, pp. 8–11.

E. W. Davis and K. W. Yeomans (1973) 'Competition and Credit Control: the Rubicon and beyond', *Lloyds Bank Review* **107**, January, pp. 44–55.

R. G. Davis (1968) 'The role of the money supply in business cycles', *Federal Reserve Bank of New York Monthly Review* **50**, April, pp. 63–73.

R. G. Davis (1969) 'How much does money matter? A look at some recent evidence', *Federal Reserve Bank of New York Monthly Review* **51**, June, pp. 119–31.

R. G. Davis (1973) 'Implementing open-market policy with monetary aggregate objectives', *Federal Reserve Bank of New York Monthly Review* **55**, July, pp. 170–82.

R. G. Davis (1977) 'Monetary objectives and monetary policy', *Federal Reserve Bank of New York Quarterly Review* **2**, Spring, pp. 29–36.

F. De Leeuw and E. M. Gramlich (1968) 'The Federal Reserve–MIT Econometric model', *Federal Reserve Bulletin* **54**, January 1968, pp. 11–29.

F. De Leeuw and E. M. Gramlich (1969) 'The channels of monetary policy: a further report on the Federal Reserve–MIT model', *Journal of Finance* **24**, May, pp. 265–90.

F. De Leeuw and J. Kalchenbrenner (1969) 'Monetary and fiscal actions: a test of their relative importance in economic stabilisation', *Federal Reserve Bank of St. Louis Review* **51**, April, pp. 6–11.

G. E. J. Dennis (1974) 'Recent changes in the banking system and their implications', *Loughborough Paper on Recent Developments in Economic Policy and Thought*, No. 2, March.

M. De Prano and T. Mayer (1965) 'Tests of the relative importance of autonomous expenditure and money', *American Economic Review* **55**, September, pp. 729–52.

W. C. Dewald and H. G. Johnson (1963) 'An objective analysis of the objectives of American monetary policy, 1952–61' in D. Carson (ed.) *Banking and Monetary Studies*, Irwin, Homewood, Illinois.

J. C. R. Dow (1970) *The Management of the British Economy 1945–60*, University Press, Cambridge.

C. V. Downton (1977) 'The trend of the national debt in relation to national income', *Bank of England Quarterly Bulletin* **17**, September, pp. 319–24.

N. Duck, J. M. Parkin, D. Rose and G. Zis (1976) 'The determination of the rate of change of wages and prices in a fixed exchange-rate world economy, 1956–71' in J. M. Parkin and G. Zis (eds) *Inflation in the World Economy*, University Press, Manchester.

N. W. Duck and D. K. Sheppard (1978) 'A proposal for the control of the U.K. money supply', *Economic Journal* **88**, March, pp. 1–17.

N. W. Duck and G. Zis (1978) 'World inflation, the demand for money and fixed exchange-rates', *Scottish Journal of Political Economy* **25**, February, pp. 29–40.

Economic Progress Report (1977) 'Domestic credit expansion' **82**, January, p. 3.

Economic Trends (1969) 'Money supply and domestic credit', **187**, May, pp. xxi–xxv.

S. K. Edge (1967) 'The relative stability of monetary velocity and the investment multiplier', *Australian Economic Papers* **4**, December, pp. 192–207.

G. Edgren, K-O. Faxen and C. E. Odhner (1973) *Wage formation and the economy*, Allen and Unwin, London.

R. Eisner and R. Strotz (1963) 'Determinants of business investment' in Commission on Money and Credit, *Impacts of Monetary Policy*, Prentice-Hall, Englewood Cliffs.

J. W. Elliott (1975) 'The influence of monetary and fiscal actions on total spending: the St. Louis total spending equation revisited', *Journal of Money, Credit and Banking* **7**, May, pp. 181–92.

J. Enzler, L. Johnson and J. Paulus (1976) 'Some problems of money demand', *Brookings Papers on Economic Activity* **7**, (1), pp. 261–82.

R. C. Fair (1971) *A Short-Run Forecasting Model of the United States Economy*, D. C. Heath, Lexington, Mass.

G. Fane (1978) 'Inflation in Britain: A monetarist perspective: comment', *American Economic Review* **68**, September, pp. 721–9.

M. M. G. Fase and J. B. Kuné (1975) 'The demand for money in thirteen European and non-European countries', *Kredit und Kapital* **8**, (3), pp. 410–19.

E. L. Feige (1974) 'Alternative temporal cross-section specifications of the demand for demand deposits' in H. G. Johnson and A. R. Nobay (eds) *Issues in Monetary Economics*, University Press, Oxford.

D. Fisher (1968) 'The demand for money in Britain: quarterly results 1951 to 1967', *Manchester School* **36**, December, pp. 329–44.

D. Fisher (1970) 'The instruments of monetary policy and the generalised trade-off function for Britain, 1955–68', *Manchester School* **38**, September, pp. 209–22.

D. Fisher (1973) 'Targets and indicators of British monetary policy', *Bankers Magazine* **216**, September, pp. 97–103.

D. Fisher (1976) *Monetary Policy*, Macmillan, London.

I. Fisher (1911) *The Purchasing-Power of Money*, Macmillan, New York.

I. Fisher (1926) 'A statistical relation between unemployment and price changes', *International Labour Review* 13, June, pp. 785–92.

J. M. Fleming (1962) 'Domestic financial policies under fixed and under floating exchange rates', *International Monetary Fund Staff Papers* 9, November, pp. 369–79.

G. A. Fletcher (1978) 'Cash base control of bank deposits and the British banking system', *Société Universitaire Européenne de Recherches Financières* (S.U.E.R.F.).

J. A. Frenkel and H. G. Johnson (1976) *The Monetary Approach to the Balance of Payments*, Allen and Unwin, London.

B. M. Friedman (1977) 'Even the St. Louis model now believes in fiscal policy', *Journal of Money Credit and Banking* 9, May, pp. 365–7.

M. Friedman (1956) 'The quantity theory of money – a restatement' in Friedman (ed.) *Studies in the Quantity Theory of Money*, University Press, Chicago.

M. Friedman (1957) *A theory of the consumption function*, University Press, Princeton.

M. Friedman (1958) 'The supply of money and changes in prices and output' in *The Relationship of Prices to Economic Stability and Growth*.

M. Friedman (1964) 'Post-war trends in monetary theory and policy', *National Banking Review* 2, September, pp. 1–9.

M. Friedman (1968) 'The role of monetary policy', *American Economic Review* 58, March, pp. 1–17.

M. Friedman (1969) *The Optimum Quantity of Money*, Macmillan, London.

M. Friedman (1970a) 'A theoretical framework for monetary analysis', *Journal of Political Economy* 78, March/April, pp. 193–238.

M. Friedman (1970b) 'The counter-revolution in monetary theory', *Institute of Economic Affairs*, Occasional Paper, No. 33.

M. Friedman (1971) 'A monetary theory of nominal income', *Journal of Political Economy* 79, March/April, pp. 323–37.

M. Friedman (1972) 'Comments on the critics', *Journal of Political Economy* 80, September/October, pp. 906–50.

M. Friedman (1975) 'Unemployment versus inflation? An evaluation of the Phillips curve', *Institute of Economic Affairs*, London.

M. Friedman and D. I. Meiselmann (1963) 'The relative stability of monetary velocity and the investment multiplier in the United States 1897–1958' in Commission on Money and Credit, *Stabilisation Policies*, Prentice-Hall, Englewood Cliffs.

M. Friedman and D. I. Meiselmann (1964) 'Reply to Donald Hester', *Review of Economics and Statistics* 46, November, pp. 369–77.

M. Friedman and A. J. Schwartz (1963a) *The Monetary History of the U.S.A.*, National Bureau of Economic Research.

M. Friedman and A. J. Schwartz (1963b) 'Money and business cycles', *Review of Economics and Statistics* 45 (Suppl.), February, pp. 32–64.

M. Friedman and A. J. Schwartz (1969) 'The definition of money: net wealth and neutrality as criteria', *Journal of Money, Credit and Banking* 1, February, pp. 1–14.

H. Frisch (1977) 'Inflation theory 1963–1975: a "second generation" survey', *Journal of Economic Literature* 15, December, pp. 1289–1317.

G. Fromm and P. Taubman (1968) *Policy Simulations with an Econometric Model*, Brookings Institution, Washington.

R. Fry (1972) 'The midsummer credit crisis', *The Banker* 122, August, pp. 1019–22.

H. Genberg (1975) 'Aspects of the monetary approach to balance of payments theory: an empirical study of Sweden' in J. A. Frenkel and H. G. Johnson (eds) *The Monetary Theory of the Balance of Payments*, Allen and Unwin, London.

I. Gervaise (1720) 'The system or theory of the trade of the world, 1720' in *Economic Tracts*, John Hopkins University Press,

N. J. Gibson (1964) 'Special deposits as an instrument of monetary policy', *Manchester School* 32, December, pp. 239–59.

N. J. Gibson (1967) 'Financial intermediaries and monetary policy', *Institute of Economic Affairs*, Hobart Paper, No. 39.

N. J. Gibson (1971) 'Competition and innovation', *Bankers Magazine* **212**, July, pp. 6–10.

S. Goldfeld (1976) 'The case of the missing money', *Brookings Papers on Economic Activity* **7**, (3), pp. 683–739.

C. A. E. Goodhart (1973a) 'Analysis of the determinants of the stock of money' in J. M. Parkin and A. R. Nobay (eds) *Essays in Modern Economics*, Longmans, London.

C. A. E. Goodhart (1973b) 'Monetary policy in the United Kingdom' in K. Holbik (ed.) *Monetary Policy in Twelve Industrial Countries*, Federal Reserve Bank of Boston.

C. A. E. Goodhart (1975) *Money, Information and Uncertainty*, Macmillan, London.

C. A. E. Goodhart and A. D. Crockett (1970) 'The importance of money', *Bank of England Quarterly Bulletin* **10**, June, pp. 159–98.

R. J. Gordon (ed.) (1974) *Milton Friedman's Monetary Framework*, University Press, Chicago.

R. J. Gordon (1976) 'Recent developments in the theory of inflation and unemployment', *Journal of Monetary Economics* **2**, pp. 185–219.

S. Gordon (1972) 'Two monetary inquiries in Great Britain: the Macmillan Committee of 1931 and the Radcliffe Committee of 1959', *Journal of Money, Credit and Banking* **4**, November, pp. 957–77.

D. Gowland (1978) *Monetary Policy and Credit Control. The U.K. Experience*, Croom Helm, London.

S. Grace Jnr. (1975) 'Proper specification of the cost function: a comment on Baumol's and Morris' transactions demand for cash', *Quarterly Journal of Economics* **89**, November, pp. 658–59.

E. M. Gramlich (1969) 'The role of money in economic activity: complicated or simple?', *Journal of Business Economics* **4**, September, pp. 21–6.

E. M. Gramlich (1971) 'The usefulness of monetary and fiscal policy as discretionary stabilisation tools', *Journal of Money, Credit and Banking* **3**, May, pp. 506–32.

M. R. Gray, R. Ward and G. Zis (1976) 'The world demand for money function: some preliminary results' in J. M. Parkin and G. Zis (eds) *Inflation in the World Economy*, University Press, Manchester.

W. Greenwell & Co. (1976a) 'Monetary targets', *Monetary Bulletin* **55**, July.

W. Greenwell & Co. (1976b) 'Gilt-edged securities – a unique market', *Mimeo*, December.

W. Greenwell & Co. (1977a) 'A monetary base for the U.K.', *Mimeo*, January.

W. Greenwell & Co. (1977b) 'The mechanism for control of the money supply: some further thoughts', *Mimeo*, February.

W. Greenwell & Co. (1978a) 'The corset and transactions within the banking sector', *Monetary Bulletin* **81**, July/August.

W. Greenwell & Co. (1978b) 'The effect of the corset', *Monetary Bulletin* **83**, September.

W. Greenwell & Co. (1979) 'Proposed changes to the present monetary system', *Special Monetary Bulletin*, March.

B. Griffiths (1970) 'Competition in banking', *Institute of Economic Affairs*, Hobart Paper, No. 51.

B. Griffiths (1972a) 'The welfare cost of the U.K. clearing banks' cartel', *Journal of Money, Credit and Banking* **4**, May, pp. 227–44.

B. Griffiths (1972b) 'Monetary policy in the float', *The Banker* **122**, August, pp. 1023–5.

B. Griffiths (1973a) 'The development of restrictive practices in the U.K. monetary system', *Manchester School* **41**, March, pp. 3–18.

B. Griffiths (1973b) 'Resource efficiency, monetary policy and the reform of the U.K. banking system', *Journal of Money, Credit and Banking* **5**, February, pp. 61–77.

B. Griffiths (1976) *Inflation. The Price of Prosperity*, Weidenfeld and Nicholson, London.

J. G. Gurley (1960) 'The Radcliffe Report and evidence', *American Economic Review* **50**, September, pp. 672–700.

J. G. Gurley and E. S. Shaw (1956) 'Financial intermediaries and the savings–investment process', *Journal of Finance* **11**, May, pp. 257–66.

J. G. Gurley and E. S. Shaw (1960) *Money in a Theory of Finance*, Brookings Institution, Washington.

G. Hacche (1974) 'The demand for money in the U.K.: experience since 1971', *Bank of England Quarterly Bulletin* 14, September, pp. 284–306.

M. J. Hamburger (1970) 'Indicators of monetary policy: the arguments and the evidence', *American Economic Review, Papers and Proceedings* 60, May, pp. 32–9.

M. J. Hamburger (1977a) 'The demand for money in open economies: Germany and the U.K.', *Journal of Monetary Economics* 3, January, pp. 25–40.

M. J. Hamburger (1977b) 'Behaviour of the money stock – is there a puzzle?', *Journal of Monetary Economics* 3, July, pp. 265–88.

M. J. Hamburger and G. E. Wood (1978) 'Interest-rates and monetary policy in open economies', *Federal Reserve Bank of New York Working Paper*, May.

A. H. Hansen (1949) *Monetary Theory and Fiscal Policy*, McGraw-Hill, London.

R. L. Harrington (1974) 'The importance of competition for credit control' in H. G. Johnson and A. R. Nobay (eds) *Issues in Monetary Economics*, University Press, Oxford.

R. Harrod (1959) 'Is the money supply important?', *Westminster Bank Review*, November, pp. 3–7.

H. R. Heller (1976) 'International reserves and worldwide inflation', *International Monetary Fund Staff Papers* 23, March, pp. 61–87.

S. G. B. Henry, M. C. Sawyer and P. Smith (1976) 'Models of inflation in the United Kingdom: an evaluation', *National Institute Economic Review* 77, August, pp. 60–71.

R. J. Herring and R. C. Marston (1976) *National Monetary Policies and International Financial Markets*, North-Holland, Amsterdam.

D. D. Hester (1964) 'Keynes and the quantity theory. Comment on Friedman and Meiselmann's CMC paper', *Review of Economics and Statistics* 46, November, pp. 364–8.

D. R. Hodgman (1971) 'British techniques of monetary policy. A critical review', *Journal of Money, Credit and Banking* 3, November, pp. 760–79.

D. Hume (1741) 'Of money' reprinted in E. Rotwein (ed.) *Writings in Economics*, Nelson, London, 1955.

T. M. Humphrey (1978) 'Some recent developments in Phillips curve analysis', *Federal Reserve Bank of Richmond Economic Review* 64, January/February, pp. 15–23.

H. G. Johnson (1958) 'Towards a general theory of the balance of payments' in H. G. Johnson *International Trade and Economic Growth*, Allen and Unwin, London.

H. G. Johnson (1962) 'Monetary theory and policy', *American Economic Review* 52, June, pp. 335–84.

H. G. Johnson (1967a) *Essays in Monetary Economics*, Allen and Unwin, London.

H. G. Johnson (1967b) 'The report on bank charges', *Bankers Magazine* 204, August, pp. 64–8.

H. G. Johnson (1968) 'Problems of efficiency in monetary management', *Journal of Political Economy* 76, September/October, pp. 971–90.

H. G. Johnson (1969) 'Inside money, outside money, income, wealth and welfare in monetary theory', *Journal of Money, Credit and Banking* 1, February, pp. 30–45.

H. G. Johnson (1970) 'Recent developments in monetary theory; a commentary' in D. R. Croome and H. G. Johnson (eds) *Money in Britain, 1959–69*, University Press, Oxford.

H. G. Johnson (1971a) *Macroeconomics and Monetary Theory*, Gray-Mills, London.

H. G. Johnson (1971b) 'Harking back to Radcliffe', *Bankers Magazine* 212, September, pp. 115–20.

H. G. Johnson (1972a) 'The monetary approach to balance of payments theory' in H. G. Johnson *Further Essays in Monetary Economics*, Allen and Unwin, London.

H. G. Johnson (ed.) (1972b) *Readings in British Monetary Economics*, University Press, Oxford.

H. G. Johnson (1976) 'The monetary theory of balance of payments policies' in J. A. Frenkel and H. G. Johnson (eds) *The Monetary Approach to the Balance of Payments*, Allen and Unwin, London.

H. G. Johnson (1977) 'The monetary approach to balance of payments theory and policy:

explanation and policy implications', *Economica* **44**, August, pp. 217–29.

J. L. Jordan (1969) 'Elements of money stock determination', *Federal Reserve Bank of St. Louis Review* **51**, October, pp. 10–19.

D. W. Jorgenson (1963) 'Capital theory and investment behaviour', *American Economic Review, Papers and Proceedings* **53**, May, pp. 247–59.

P. N. Junankar (1972) *Investment: Theories and Evidence*, Macmillan, London.

N. Kaldor (1960) 'The Radcliffe Report', *Review of Economics and Statistics* **42**, February, pp. 14–19.

N. Kaldor (1970) 'The new monetarism', *Lloyds Bank Review* **97**, July, pp. 1–18.

J. Kareken and R. Solow (1963) 'Monetary policy. Lags versus simultaneity' in Commission on Money and Credit, *Stabilisation Policies*, Prentice-Hall, Englewood Cliffs.

N. J. Kavanagh and A. A. Walters (1966) 'The demand for money in the U.K. 1877 to 1961: some preliminary findings', *Bulletin of the Oxford University Institute of Economics and Statistics* **28**, May, pp. 93–116.

M. W. Keran (1970a) 'Monetary and fiscal influences on economic activity: the foreign experience', *Federal Reserve Bank of St. Louis Review* **52**, February, pp. 16–28.

M. W. Keran (1970b) 'Selecting a monetary indicator – evidence from the United States and other developed countries', *Federal Reserve Bank of St. Louis Review* **52**, September, pp. 8–19.

M. W. Keran (1975) 'Towards an explanation of simultaneous inflation – recession', *Federal Reserve Bank of San Francisco Business Review*, Spring, pp. 18–30.

D. Kern (1970) 'The implications of DCE', *National Westminster Bank Review* November, pp. 29–44.

D. Kern (1972) 'Monetary policy and C.C.C.', *National Westminster Bank Review* November, pp. 34–50.

D. Kern (1975) 'Monetary aspects of the current economic debate', *National Westminster Bank Review* August, pp. 6–17.

J. M. Keynes (1923) *The Tract on Monetary Reform*, Macmillan, London.

J. M. Keynes (1936) *The General Theory of Employment, Interest and Money*, Macmillan, London.

P. J. K. Kouri and M. G. Porter (1974) 'International capital flows and portfolio equilibrium', *Journal of Political Economy* **82**, May/June, pp. 443–67.

L. M. Koyck (1954) *Distributed Lags and Investment Analysis*, North-Holland, Amsterdam.

D. E. W. Laidler (1969) 'The definition of money: theoretical and empirical problems', *Journal of Money, Credit and Banking* **1**, August, pp. 509–25.

D. E. W. Laidler (1971a) 'The influence of money on economic activity: a survey of some current problems' in G. Clayton, J. C. Gilbert and R. Sedgwick (eds) *Monetary Theory and Policy in the 1970s*, University Press, Oxford.

D. E. W. Laidler (1971b) 'The Phillips curve, expectations and incomes policy' in H. G. Johnson and A. R. Nobay (eds) *The Current Inflation*, Macmillan, London.

D. E. W. Laidler (1973a) 'Monetarist policy prescriptions and their background', *Manchester School* **41**, March, pp. 59–72.

D. E. W. Laidler (1973b) 'The influence of money on real income and inflation: a simple model with some empirical tests for the United States, 1953–72', *Manchester School* **41**, December, pp. 367–95.

D. E. W. Laidler (1975) 'The end of "demand management" – how to reduce unemployment in the 1970's'. Commentary in M. Friedman 'Unemployment versus inflation?: an evaluation of the Phillips curve', *Institute of Economic Affairs*, London.

D. E. W. Laidler (1976a) 'Inflation in Britain: a monetarist perspective', *American Economic Review* **66**, September, pp. 485–500.

D. E. W. Laidler (1976b) 'Mayer on monetarism: comments from a British point of view', *Kredit und Kapital* **9**, (1), pp. 56–67.

D. E. W. Laidler (1977a) *The Demand for Money*, Dun-Donnelly, New York.

D. E. W. Laidler (1977b) 'Expectations and the behaviour of prices and output under flexible exchange-rates', *Economica* **44**, November, pp. 327–35.

D. E. W. Laidler (1978) 'Money and money income: an essay on the transmission mechanism', *Journal of Monetary Economics* **4**, April, pp. 157–91.

D. E. W. Laidler and A. R. Nobay (1975) 'Some current issues concerning the international aspects of inflation' in D. E. W. Laidler *Essays on Money and Inflation*, University Press, Manchester.

D. E. W. Laidler and J. M. Parkin (1970) 'The demand for money in the U.K., 1955–1967: some preliminary estimates', *Manchester School* **38**, September, pp. 187–208.

D. E. W. Laidler and J. M. Parkin (1975) 'Inflation – a survey', *Economic Journal* **85**, December, pp. 741–809.

O. Lange (1942) 'Say's Law: a restatement and criticism' in *Studies in Mathematical Economics and Econometrics*, University Press, Chicago.

G. S. Laumas (1978) 'A test of the stability of the demand for money', *Scottish Journal of Political Economy* **25**, November, pp. 239–51.

J. S. E. Laury, G. R. Lewis and P. A. Ormerod (1978) 'Properties of macroeconomic models of the U.K. economy. A comparative study', *National Institute Economic Review* **83**, February, pp. 52–72.

A. Leijonhufvud (1968) *On Keynesian Economics and the Economics of Keynes*, University Press, Oxford.

A. C. Lemgruber and B. T. McCallum (1976) 'A note on empirical tests of alternative versions of the natural rate hypothesis', *Manchester School* **44**, March, pp. 42–51.

R. Levacic (1976) *Macroeconomics*, Macmillan, London.

R. G. Lipsey (1960) 'The relationship between unemployment and the rate of change of money wage-rates in the U.K., 1862–1957: a further analysis', *Economica* **27**, February, pp. 1–31.

D. T. Llewellyn (1979) 'Do building societies take deposits away from banks?', *Lloyds Bank Review* **131**, January, pp. 21–34.

D. T. Llewellyn (1981) *International Financial Integration*, Macmillan, London.

D. F. Lomax (1971) 'Competition and the clearing banks', *The Banker* **121**, October, pp. 1160–5.

D. F. Lomax (1973) 'Reserve assets and Competition and Credit Control', *National Westminster Bank Review*, August, pp. 36–46.

D. F. Lomax (1975) 'Controls on personal borrowing', *The Banker* **125**, May, pp. 503–7.

D. I. Mackay and R. A. Hart (1974) 'Wage inflation and the Phillips relationship', *Manchester School* **42**, June, pp. 136–61.

G. E. Makinen (1977) *Money, Interest-Rates and the Price-Level*, Prentice-Hall, Englewood Cliffs.

W. Manning-Dacey (1956) 'The floating debt problem', *Lloyds Bank Review* **50**, April, pp. 24–38.

P. Marks (1973) 'Competition and Credit Control – the first eighteen months', *The Banker* **123**, March, pp. 265–74.

A. Marshall (1924) *Money, Credit and Commerce*, Kelley, New York – reprint (1960).

K. G. P. Matthews and P. A. Ormerod (1978) 'St. Louis models of the U.K. economy', *National Institute Economic Review* **84**, May, pp. 65–9.

T. Mayer (1967) 'The lag in the effect of monetary policy: some criticisms', *Western Economic Journal* **5**, September, pp. 324–42.

T. Mayer (1975) 'The structure of monetarism', *Kredit und Kapital* **8** (2), (3), pp. 191–215, 293–313.

B. T. McCallum (1975) 'Rational expectations and the natural rate hypothesis: some evidence for the U.K.', *Manchester School* **43**, March, pp. 55–67.

W. D. McClam (1978) 'Targets and techniques of monetary policy in Western Europe', *Banca Nazionale del Lavoro Quarterly Review* **31**, March, pp. 3–27.

S. K. McNees (1973) 'A comparison of the GNP forecasting accuracy of the Fair and St. Louis econometric models', *New England Economic Review*, September/October, pp. 29–34.

J. E. Meade and P. W. S. Andrews (1938) 'Summary of replies to questions on effects of interest-rates', *Oxford Economic Papers* **1**, October, pp. 14–31.

Y. P. Mehra (1978) 'An empirical note on some monetarist propositions', *Southern Economic Journal* **45**, July, pp. 154–67.

D. I. Meiselmann (1975) 'Worldwide inflation: a monetarist view' in D. I. Meiselmann and A. B. Laffer (eds) *The Phenomenon of Worldwide Inflation*, American Enterprise Institute for Public Policy Research, Washington.

L. H. Meyer (1976) 'Alternative definitions of the money stock and the demand for money', *Federal Reserve Bank of New York Monthly Review* **58**, October, pp. 266–74.

Midland Bank (1969) 'Managing the gilt-edged market: a temporary change of emphasis?', *Midland Bank Review*, May, pp. 3–5.

Midland Bank (1971a) 'The gilt-edged market and credit control. A new policy but an unchanged dilemma', *Midland Bank Review*, August, pp. 3–9.

Midland Bank (1971b) 'Banking regulation and competition: A resumée with commentary on the new arrangements', *Midland Bank Review*, November, pp. 3–11.

Midland Bank (1974) 'The supplementary credit control scheme', *Midland Bank Review*, August, pp. 11–18.

Midland Bank (1978) 'The banking sector and monetary policy', *Midland Bank Review*, Winter, pp. 19–25.

T. C. Mills (1978) 'The functional form of the demand for money', *Applied Statistics* **27**, February, pp. 52–7.

T. C. Mills and G. E. Wood (1977) 'Money substitutes and monetary policy in the UK, 1922–1974', *European Economic Review*, October, pp. 19–36.

T. C. Mills and G. E. Wood (1978) 'Money-income relationships and the exchange rate regime', *Federal Reserve Bank of St. Louis Review* **60**, August, pp. 22–7.

F. Modigliani and A. Ando (1976) 'Impacts of fiscal actions on aggregate income and the monetarist controversy: theory and evidence' in J. L. Stein (ed.) *Monetarism*, North-Holland, Amsterdam.

Monopolies Commission (1968) 'Report on proposed merger – Barclays, Lloyds and Martins Banks', No. 319, July, HMSO, London.

E. V. Morgan (1969) 'The essential qualities of money', *Manchester School* **37**, September, pp. 237–48.

E. V. Morgan (1973) 'The gilt-edged market under the new monetary policy', *The Banker* **123**, January, pp. 19–24.

E. V. Morgan and R. L. Harrington (1973) 'Reserve assets and the supply of money', *Manchester School* **41**, March, pp. 73–87.

J. R. Moroney and J. M. Mason (1971) 'The dynamic impacts of autonomous expenditure and the monetary base on aggregate income', *Journal of Money, Credit and Banking* **3**, November, pp. 793–814.

R. W. Morris (1971) 'A note on the transactions demand for cash', *Quarterly Journal of Economics* **85**, August, pp. 546–7.

R. A. Mundell (1961) 'Flexible exchange-rates and employment policy', *Canadian Journal of Economics and Political Science* **27**, November, pp. 509–17.

R. A. Mundell (1963) 'Capital mobility and stabilisation policy under fixed and flexible exchange-rates', *Canadian Journal of Economics and Political Science* **29**, November, pp. 475–85.

R. A. Mundell (1968) *International Economics*, Macmillan, New York.

R. A. Mundell (1971) *Monetary Theory*, Goodyear, Pacific Palisades.

M. Mussa (1976) 'The exchange rate, the balance of payments and monetary and fiscal policy under a regime of controlled floating', *Scandinavian Journal of Economics* **78**, pp. 229–48.

J. F. Muth (1961) 'Rational expectations and the theory of price movements', *Econometrica* **29**, July, pp. 315–35.

National Board for Prices and Incomes (1967) 'Bank charges', Cmnd. 3292, HMSO, London.

M. Neumann (1977) 'A theoretical and empirical analysis of the German money supply process 1958–72' in S. F. Frowen, A. S. Courakis and M. H. Miller (eds) *Monetary Policy and Economic Activity in West Germany*, University of Surrey Press, Guildford.

W. T. Newlyn (1964) 'The supply of money and its control', *Economic Journal* **74**, June, pp. 327–46.

W. T. Newlyn and R. Bootle (1978) *The Theory of Money*, Clarendon Press, Oxford.

A. R. Nobay (1973) 'The Bank of England, monetary policy and monetary theory in the U.K. 1951–1971', *Manchester School* **41**, March, pp. 43–58.

A. R. Nobay (1974) 'A model of the U.K. monetary authorities' behaviour, 1959–69' in H. G. Johnson and A. R. Nobay (eds) *Issues in Monetary Economics*, University Press, Oxford.

A. R. Nobay and H. G. Johnson (1977) 'Monetarism: a historic-theoretic perspective', *Journal of Economic Literature* **15**, June, pp. 470–85.

W. Nordhaus (1972) 'The world-wide wage explosion', *Brookings Papers on Economic Activity* **3** (2), pp. 431–64.

G. O. Nwankwo (1972) 'The new monetary regulation and the London discount market', *Bankers Magazine* **213**, June, pp. 279–83.

Organisation for Economic Co-operation and Development (OECD) (1973) 'The international transmission of inflation', *Economic Outlook*, July.

Organisation for Economic Co-operation and Development (OECD) (1977) *Towards Full-Employment and Price Stability*, OECD, Paris.

A. Pankratz (1974) 'Effects of direct lending controls: an empirical case study of the U.K.', *Journal of Economics and Business* **27**, pp. 49–59.

Y. C. Park (1972) 'Some current issues on the transmission process of monetary policy', *International Monetary Fund Staff Papers* **19**, March, pp. 1–45.

J. M. Parkin (1970) 'Incomes policy: some further results on the rate of change of money wages', *Economica* **37**, November, pp. 386–401.

J. M. Parkin (1975) 'Where is Britain's inflation going?', *Lloyds Bank Review* **117**, July, pp. 1–13.

J. M. Parkin (1978) 'Alternative explanations of United Kingdom inflation: a survey', in J. M. Parkin and M. T. Sumner (eds) *Inflation in the United Kingdom*, University Press, Manchester.

J. M. Parkin, M. T. Sumner and R. Ward (1976) 'The effects of excess demand, generalised expectations and wage-price controls on wage inflation in the U.K., 1956–71' in K. Brunner and A. H. Meltzer (eds) *The Economics of Wages and Prices Controls*, North-Holland, Amsterdam.

D. Patinkin (1956) *Money, Interest and Prices*, Harper and Row, New York.

D. Patinkin (1969) 'The Chicago tradition, the quantity theory and Friedman', *Journal of Money, Credit and Banking* **1**, February, pp. 46–70.

D. Patinkin (1972) 'Friedman on the quantity theory and Keynesian economics', *Journal of Political Economy* **80**, September/October, pp. 883–905.

D. Patinkin (1974) 'The role of the "liquidity-trap" in Keynesian economics', *Banca Nazionale del Lavoro Quarterly Review* **27**, March, pp. 3–11.

G. T. Pepper and R. L. Thomas (1978) 'Banking statistics and monetary control' in Proceedings of the *Statistics Users Conference on Financial Statistics*, Bank of England, pp. 46–50.

G. T. Pepper and G. E. Wood (1976) 'Keynesian and monetarist indicators of monetary policy' in M. L. Burstein and M. J. Allingham (eds) *Resource Allocation and Economic Policy*, Macmillan, London.

B. P. Pesek and T. R. Saving (1967) *Money, Wealth and Economic Theory*, Macmillan, New York.

E. S. Phelps (1967) 'Phillips curves, expectations of inflation and optimal unemployment over time', *Economica* **34**, August, pp. 254–81.

E. S. Phelps (1968) 'Money wage dynamics and labour market equilibrium', *Journal of Political Economy* **76**, July/August, pp. 678–711.

E. S. Phelps *et al.* (1970) *The Microeconomic Foundations of Employment and Inflation Theory*, W. W. Norton, New York.

A. W. Phillips (1958) 'The relationship between unemployment and money wage-rates in the U.K., 1861–1957', *Economica* **25**, November, pp. 283–99.

D. G. Pierce and D. M. Shaw (1974) *Monetary Economics*, Butterworths, London.

J. Pierce and T. Thomson (1973) 'Some issues in controlling the stock of money' in *Controlling Monetary Aggregates II: the Implementation*, Federal Reserve Bank of Boston.

A. C. Pigou (1917) 'The value of money', *Quarterly Journal of Economics* **32**, November, pp. 38–65.

A. C. Pigou (1943) 'The classical stationary state', *Economic Journal* **53**, December, pp. 343–51.

A. C. Pigou (1949) *The Veil of Money*, Macmillan, London.

C. A. Pissarides (1972) 'A model of British macroeconomic policy', *Manchester School* **40**, September, pp. 245–59.

W. Poole (1970) 'Optimal choice of monetary policy instruments in a simple stochastic macro-model', *Quarterly Journal of Economics* **84**, May, pp. 197–216.

W. Poole (1976) 'Interpreting the Fed.'s monetary targets', *Brookings Papers on Economic Activity* **7** (1), pp. 247–59.

W. Poole and E. B. F. Kornblith (1973) 'The Friedman-Meiselmann CMC paper: new evidence on an old controversy', *American Economic Review* **63**, December, pp. 903–17.

M. V. Posner (ed.) (1978) *Demand Management*, Heinemann, London.

L. D. D. Price (1972) 'The demand for money in the U.K.: a further investigation', *Bank of England Quarterly Bulletin* **12**, March, pp. 43–55.

R. Pringle (1977) 'New approaches to monetary policy', *The Banker* **127**, November, pp. 45–50.

B. H. Putnam and D. S. Wilford (1978) 'Money, income and causality in the United States and in the United Kingdom: A theoretical explanation of different findings', *American Economic Review* **68**, June, pp. 423–7.

Radcliffe Committee (1959) *Report on the Working of the Monetary System*, Cmnd. 827, HMSO, London.

R. A. Radford (1945) 'The economic organisation of a POW camp', *Economica* **12**, November, pp. 189–201.

A. Rees (1970) 'The Phillips Curve as a menu for policy choice', *Economica* **37**, May, pp. 227–38.

G. A. Renton (ed.) (1975) *Modelling the Economy*, Heinemann, London.

G. L. Reuber (1964) 'The objectives of Canadian monetary policy, 1949–61: empirical trade-offs and the reaction function of the authorities', *Journal of Political Economy* **72**, April, pp. 109–32.

S. Rousseas (1972) *Monetary Theory*, Knopf, New York.

D. C. Rowan (1961) 'Radcliffe monetary theory', *Economic Record* **138**, pp. 420–41.

D. C. Rowan (1973) 'The monetary system in the fifties and sixties', *Manchester School* **41**, March, pp. 19–42.

D. C. Rowan and J. Miller (1979) 'The demand for money in the U.K.: 1963–1977', *University of Southampton Discussion Paper*, No. 7902, January.

P. A. Samuelson and R. Solow (1960) 'Analytical aspects of anti-inflation policy', *American Economic Review, Papers and Proceedings* **50**, May, pp. 177–94.

A. M. Santomero and J. J. Seater (1978) 'The inflation-unemployment trade-off: a critique of the literature', *Journal of Economic Literature* **16**, June, pp. 499–544.

T. J. Sargent (1973) 'Rational expectations, the real rate of interest and the natural rate of unemployment', *Brookings Papers on Economic Activity* **4** (2), pp. 429–72.

T. J. Sargent and N. Wallace (1976) 'Rational expectations and the theory of economic policy', *Journal of Monetary Economics* **2**, April, pp. 169–83.

P. G. Saunders (1978) 'Inflation expectations and the natural rate of unemployment', *Applied Economics* **10**, September, pp. 187–93.

P. G. Saunders and A. R. Nobay (1972) 'Price expectations, the Phillips curve and incomes policy' in J. M. Parkin and M. T. Sumner (eds) *Incomes Policy and Inflation*, University Press, Manchester.

D. Savage (1978) 'The channels of monetary influence: a survey of the empirical evidence', *National Institute Economic Review* **83**, February, pp. 73–89.

T. R. Saving (1967) 'Monetary-policy targets and indicators', *Journal of Political Economy* **75**, August, pp. 446–56.

J. B. Say (1803) *Traité d'économique ou simple exposition de la manière dont se forment, se distribuent et se consomment les richesses*, Deterville, Paris.

R. S. Sayers (1955) 'The determination of the volume of bank deposits: England 1955–56', *Banca Nazionale del Lavoro Quarterly Review*, December.

R. S. Sayers (1960) 'Monetary thought and monetary policy in England', *Economic Journal* **70**, December, pp. 710–24.

R. T. Selden (1976) 'Money and inflation: some international comparisons' in M. L. Burstein and M. J. Allingham (eds) *Resource Allocation and Economic Policy*, Macmillan, London.

G. L. S. Shackle (1971) 'Discussion paper' in G. Clayton, J. C. Gilbert and R. Sedgwick (eds) *Monetary Theory and Monetary Policy in the 1970s*, University Press, Oxford.

E. Shapiro (1978) *Macroeconomic Analysis*, Harcourt Brace Jovanovich, New York.

G. K. Shaw (1977) *An Introduction to the Theory of Macroeconomic Policy*, Martin Robertson, Oxford.

D. K. Sheppard (1971) *The Growth and Role of U.K. Financial Institutions 1880–1962*, Methuen, London.

W. L. Silber (1969) 'Monetary channels and the relative importance of money supply and bank portfolios', *Journal of Finance* **24**, March, pp. 81–7.

H. C. Simons (1936) 'Rules versus authorities in monetary policy', *Journal of Political Economy* **44**, January/February, pp. 1–30.

C. A. Sims (1972) 'Money, income and causality', *American Economic Review* **62**, September, pp. 540–52.

R. Solow (1969) *Price Expectations and the Behaviour of the Price-Level*, University Press, Manchester.

R. M. Stern (1973) *The Balance of Payments. Theory and Economic Policy*, Macmillan, London.

A. A. Stevenson and J. A. Trevithick (1977) 'The complementarity of monetary and incomes policy: an examination of recent British experience', *Scottish Journal of Political Economy* **24**, February, pp. 19–31.

M. Stewart (1977) *The Jekyll and Hyde Years. Politics and Economic Policy since 1964*, J. M. Dent, London.

G. Stone (1974) 'Going broke on M1 or bust on M3?', *The Banker* **124**, March, pp. 247–51.

A. K. Swoboda (1972) 'Equilibrium, quasi-equilibrium and macro-economic policy under fixed exchange-rates', *Quarterly Journal of Economics* **86**, February, pp. 162–71.

A. K. Swoboda (1973) 'Monetary policy under fixed-exchange rates: effectiveness, the speed of adjustment and proper use', *Economica* **40**, May, pp. 136–54.

J. E. Tanner (1972) 'Indicators of monetary policy: an evaluation of five', *Banca Nazionale del Lavoro Quarterly Review* **25**, December, pp. 413–27.

R. Tarling and F. Wilkinson (1977) 'Inflation and money supply', *Economic Policy Review* **3**, March, pp. 56–60.

R. L. Teigen (1971) 'Some observations on monetarist analysis', *Kredit und Kapital* **4** (3), pp. 243–63.

H. Thornton (1802) *An Enquiry into the Nature and Effects of the Paper Credit of Great Britain*, Allen and Unwin, London – reprint (1939).

J. Tobin (1956) 'The interest-elasticity of the transactions demand for cash', *Review of Economics and Statistics* **38**, August, pp. 241–7.

J. Tobin (1958) 'Liquidity – preference as behaviour towards risk', *Review of Economic Studies* **25**, February, pp. 65–86.

J. Tobin (1963) 'Commercial banks as creators of money' in D. Carson (ed.) *Banking and Monetary Studies*, Irwin, Homewood, Illinois.

J. Tobin (1965) 'The theory of portfolio selection' in F. H. Hahn and F. P. R. Brechling (eds) *The Theory of Interest-Rates*, Macmillan, London.

J. Tobin (1970a) 'Deposit interest ceilings as a monetary control', *Journal of Money, Credit and Banking* 2, February, pp. 4–14.

J. Tobin (1970b) 'Money and income: post hoc ergo propter hoc', *Quarterly Journal of Economics* 84, May, pp. 301–17.

J. Tobin (1972) 'Friedman's theoretical framework', *Journal of Political Economy* 80, September/October, pp. 852–63.

J. Tobin and R. C. Brainard (1963) 'Financial intermediaries and the effectiveness of monetary controls', *American Economic Review, Papers and Proceedings* 53, May, pp. 383–401.

J. Tobin and W. H. Buiter (1976) 'Long-run effects of fiscal and monetary policy on aggregate demand' in J. L. Stein (ed.) *Monetarism*, North-Holland, Amsterdam.

J. A. Trevithick and C. Mulvey (1975) *The Economics of Inflation*, Martin Robertson, Oxford.

S. J. Turnovsky and M. L. Wachter (1972) 'A test of the "expectations hypothesis" using directly observed wage and price expectations', *Review of Economics and Statistics* 54, February, pp. 47–54.

J. Vanderkamp (1975) 'Inflation: a simple Friedman theory with a Phillips twist', *Journal of Monetary Economics* 1, January, pp. 117–22.

P. A. Volcker (1977) 'A broader role for monetary targets', *Federal Reserve Bank of New York Quarterly Review* 2, Spring, pp. 23–8.

J. Vrooman (1979) 'Does the St. Louis equation even believe in itself?', *Journal of Money, Credit and Banking* 11, February, pp. 111–17.

L. Walras (1954) *Elements of Pure Economics*, translated W. Jaffé, Allen and Unwin, London.

A. A. Walters (1966) 'Monetary multipliers in the U.K. 1880–1962', *Oxford Economic Papers* 18, November, pp. 270–83.

A. A. Walters (1971) 'Money in boom and slump', *Institute of Economic Affairs*, Hobart Paper No. 44.

A. J. Westaway and T. G. Weyman-Jones (1977) *Macroeconomics Theory, Evidence and Policy*, Longmans, London.

E. L. Whalen (1966) 'A rationalisation of the precautionary demand for cash', *Quarterly Journal of Economics* 80, May, pp. 314–24.

W. H. White (1956) 'Interest-inelasticity of investment demand', *American Economic Review* 46, September, pp. 565–87.

M. V. Whitman (1975) 'Global monetarism and the monetary approach to the balance of payments', *Brookings Papers on Economic Activity* 3, pp. 491–536.

K. Wicksell (1935) *Lectures on Political Economy*, volume II – *Money*, Routledge & Kegan Paul, London.

D. Williams, C. A. E. Goodhart and D. Gowland (1976) 'Money, income and causality: the U.K. experience', *American Economic Review* 66, June, pp. 417–23.

J. Williamson & G. E. Wood (1976) 'The British inflation: indigenous or imported', *American Economic Review* 66, September, pp. 520–31.

D. Wrightsman (1970) 'IS, LM and external equilibrium: a graphical analysis', *American Economic Review* 60, March, pp. 203–9.

L. B. Yeager (1968) 'Essential properties of the medium of exchange', *Kyklos* 21, pp. 45–69.

B. Zwick (1971) 'The adjustment of the economy to monetary changes', *Journal of Political Economy* 79, January–February, pp. 77–96.

Name Index

Subject Index

THE ECONOMICS OF MULTINATIONAL
ENTERPRISE
Neil Hood and Stephen Young
First published 1979

The multinational enterprise is a unique post-World War II
phenomenon. Its dramatic growth has had a major impact on
the world economy and on nation states. The text integrates
economic theory and empirical evidence to facilitate an
understanding of the role of the multinational enterprise in the
contemporary world.

The chapters cover a wide variety of topics, ranging from an
examination of the economics of multinational firms and the
role of multinational enterprises in international trade to more
policy orientated chapters concerning national and international
control of multinational enterprises. Some of the more radical
views on the subject are considered, and the final chapter is
devoted to an assessment of the future of the multinational
corporation.

The chapters are structured in such a way as to provide the
reader with a review of the economic theory underlying the
various aspects of the growth, performance, behaviour and
control of multinational enterprises. To match the relevant
theory, a comprehensive and up-to-date review of empirical
research is also included.

AN INTRODUCTION TO INTERNATIONAL
ECONOMICS
Chris Milner and David Greenaway
First published 1979

International economic relations have changed rapidly over
recent years with the emergence of new trading powers, floating
currencies and oil price rises. This book provides a thorough
grounding in a growing area of study.
The authors begin by examining the origins and consequences
of trade and growth for developed and less developed countries,
and the effects of and motives for applying general and
discriminatory tariffs. The second half of the book investigates
the monetary effects of international transactions. The nature,
causes and results of payments imbalances are established; these
form a basis for discussing the merits of alternative international
money systems. The major issues in international economics are
covered together with such topical subjects as economic
development and integration and international liquidity.

PERSPECTIVES ON INFLATION
models and policies
Edited by David Heathfield
First published 1979

This book comprises a collection of specially commissioned
essays on the topical subject of inflation, which treats the subject
in a novel way. It illuminates inflation and the diversity of views
held about it, by asking of a number of models 'what is inflation
~~~~~~~ ~~~~ ~~ ~~~thing ought to be done about it?'
~~~~~~ opens with an historical ~~~~~~ of inflation and the
~~~~~ mo~~~~ which are then dealt with include th~ : monetarist
~~~~, the ~~~~ ~~ ~~~ labour market, natur~~ resources,
~~~~~~~~ ~~ ~~~~~~~~~ inflation, and an analysis of
~~~~~~~~ of ~~~~~~~~~~ Keynes' view~ ~ on inflation
~~~ ~ ~~~~~~ a~~ ~~ ~~~~~~ gives an account of administered
~~~~~ in the U~SR and ~~land~
~~~ is an im~~~~~~~~ for the student ~~~ professional
~~~~~~~~~ who ~~~~~ ~ signi~~cant contri~~~~~ n to a crucial
~ ~~~ject~

A TEXTBOOK OF ECONOMIC THEORY
Alfred W. Stonier and Douglas C. Hague
Fifth edition published 1980

Following the major revisions of the fourth edition with its emphasis on macroeconomics, the fifth edition includes an entirely new chapter on Keynes and summarises recent developments in modern economic theory. This edition renews the emphasis on everyday economic problems, such as money supply and inflation, and updates this established student text.

The book falls into three parts. The first deals with micro-economic theory in which the pricing of goods and factors of production are considered. The second part, on macro-economics, begins with the Keynesian theory of employment and income and summarises important developments that have supplemented and amended that theory. In the final section the theory of growth is discussed examining developments in the most recent branch of economic theory.

Although primarily intended for undergraduate students, it will be of value to all who want to obtain a thorough grounding in the subject.